Power and Politics in Late Imperial China

This volume is sponsored by the
CENTER FOR CHINESE STUDIES
University of California, Berkeley

THE CENTER FOR CHINESE STUDIES
at the University of California, Berkeley, supported by the East Asian Institute (University of California, Berkeley) and the State of California, is the unifying organization for social science and interdisciplinary research on modern China.

Yuan Shi-kai (*center*) poses with two other palace officials inside the Forbidden City in 1908. From a photograph in the Morrison collection, Mitchell Library, Sydney.

Power and Politics in Late Imperial China

Yuan Shi-kai in Beijing and Tianjin, 1901-1908

Stephen R. MacKinnon

University of California Press
Berkeley · Los Angeles · London

University of California Press
Berkeley and Los Angeles, California
University of California Press, Ltd.
London, England
© 1980 The Regents of the University of California
Printed in the United States of America

1 2 3 4 5 6 7 8 9

Library of Congress Cataloging in Publication Data

MacKinnon, Stephen R.
  Power and Politics in Late Imperial China. Yuan Shi-kai in Beijing and Tianjin, 1901-1908
  "This volume is sponosred by the Center for Chinese Studies, University of California, Berkeley."
  Bibliography: p.
  Includes index.
  1. Yüan, Shih-k'ai, 1859-1916. 2. China—Presidents—Biography. I. California. University. Center for Chinese Studies. II. Title
DS777.15.683M33 951'.03 80-15779
ISBN 0-520-04025-2

For Kwang-ching Liu

Contents

Acknowledgments ix
Abbreviations Used in Notes xi
Introduction xiii

I. Yuan Shi-kai's Rise to Power 13
Early Career 14
The Influence of the Foreign Powers 23
Yuan Shi-kai's Military Power in 1901 26
Court Politics and the Empress Dowager 30

II. Stabilizing Zhili: Yuan Shi-kai's First Years as Governor-General, 1901-1903 37
Negotiating the Withdrawal of Foreign Troops 39
Military Rivalry and the Suppression of Peasant Insurgents 45
Financial Difficulties 51

III. Yuan Shi-kai's Domination of Court Politics and Foreign Affairs in Beijing, 1903-1907 62
The Triangular Relationship: Yuan Shi-kai, Empress Dowager Ci-xi, and Prince Qing 63
Yuan Shi-kai and the Powers 66
Yuan as a Central Government Official 72
Intrigue in the Grand Council and the 1907 Challenge to the Power of Yuan and Prince Qing 77

IV. Yuan Shi-kai and the Beiyang Army, 1901-1907 90
The Beiyang Army: Its Development and Organizational Structure 91
Beijing's Financial and Administrative Control of the Beiyang Army 103
Beiyang Officers and the Problem of Personal Loyalties 117

V. Reform and the Exercise of Power
in Zhili, 1901-1907 137

Educational Reform 138
Police Reform 151
Economic Reform 163

VI. Yuan Shi-kai as Grand Councillor and Foreign
Minister in Beijing, 1907-1908 180

Yuan and the Powers 182
*Yuan's Continuing Domination of Politics and the Bureaucracy
in Beijing and North China* 186
*Yuan's Continuing Influence in Military Affairs and His
Relationship to the Beiyang Army* 200

VII. Epilogue: Yuan Shi-kai's Fall from Power 205
Conclusion 213
Glossary 225
Bibliography 239
Index 255

Map of Zhili Province circa 1908 38

Acknowledgments

Interest in the enigma of Yuan Shi-kai's political power runs back to seminars at Yale University with Professors Mary Wright and Kwang-ching Liu in the mid-1960s. Under the latter I first fashioned this study as a Ph.D. dissertation at the University of California, Davis, in 1971. Drafts of material in chapters IV and V on the Beiyang Army and police reform appeared in the *Journal of Asian Studies*, vol. 32, no.3: 581-602 (May, 1973) and *Chi'ing-shih wen-t'i*, vol. 3, no.4: 82-99 (December, 1975).

Thus for more than a decade, debts to individuals and institutions have been mounting. I list just a few, beginning with institutions: History Department, University of California, Davis; Public Records Office, London; Toyo Bunko, Tokyo; National Palace Museum and Institute for Modern History, Taibei; Center for Asian Studies, University of Hong Kong; Universities Service Center, Hong Kong; Center for Chinese Studies and East Asiatic Library, University of California, Berkeley. At critical junctures, a grant from the American Council of Learned Societies and faculty grants-in-aid and sabbatical leave from Arizona State University made full-time research and writing possible. As for individuals, my parents, Cyrus and Helen MacKinnon, have been steadfast, generous supporters. The key people who read and commented on the manuscript as a whole at different stages include: Kwang-ching Liu, Ernest Young, Fred Wakeman, Edward Rhoads, Richard Smith, Roger Des Forges, and Jan MacKinnon. Charles Hayford and my colleague Hoyt Tillman offered timely advice on portions. The comments and criticisms of all the above were invaluable.

My greatest personal debt—for the will to persist and to perfect—is to Kwang-ching Liu and Jan MacKinnon. Their encouragement and support was essential. I also wish to thank Rebecca and Cyrus MacKinnon and Agnes Smedley for their patience. Finally, on the production side, Sara H. Veblen and Angela So, as well as Philip Lilienthal, John Service, and the University of California Press staff have been a pleasure to work with.

Abbreviations
USED IN NOTES

BYGD   *Beiyang gongdu leizuan* [A classified collection of public documents of the commissioner of trade for the northern ports]. *25 juan, 1907. Xubian, 24 juan,* 1910.

DFZZ   *Dongfang zazhi* [Eastern miscellany]. Monthly, Shanghai.

DHXL   Zhu Shou-peng, comp. *Guangxu chao donghua xulu* [Continuation of the Donghua records, Guangxu reign]. Shanghai, 1909.

FO   Great Britain, Foreign Office Archives. Public Records Office, London.

Guang-xu Memorials   *Gongzhongdang Guangxu chao zouzhe* [Secret palace memorials of the Guang-xu period]. 26 vols. Taibei: Palace Museum, 1973-75.

Morrison Correspondence   Lo Hui-min, ed. *The Correspondence of G. E. Morrison, 1895-1912.* Cambridge: Cambridge University Press, 1976.

NCH   *North China Herald and Supreme Court and Consular Gazette.* Weekly, Shanghai.

PTT   *Peking and Tientsin Times.* Weekly, Tianjin.

QS   *Qingshi* [History of the Qing dynasty]. 8 vols. Taibei, 1961.

Shilu   *Da Qing Dezong jing (Guangxu) huangdi shilu* [Veritable records of the Qing Guang-xu reign]. 601 *juan.* Tokyo, 1937.

YSKZZ Yuan Shi-kai. *Yuan Shi-kai zouzhe zhuanji* [The memorials of Yuan Shi-kai]. 8 vols. Taibei, 1971.

YSYZY Yuan Shi-kai. *Yangshouyuan zouyi jiyao* [Selected memorials of Yuan Shi-kai]. 44 *juan*, 1937.

Introduction

Major themes in this reassessment of the Chinese political power structure in the late Imperial period are the expansion of power at the center and the growth of imperialism as a domestic force. The focus is the political power of Yuan Shi-kai, the Chinese official who most dominated Qing court and bureaucratic politics after 1901.[1]

Twenty years after the publication of Mary Wright's pathbreaking work on the Tong-zhi restoration (1862-1874), our knowledge of formal political power structure in China during the late Imperial period, particularly at the central government level, is still fragmented and cliché-ridden.[2] This is especially true for the final decade of the Qing dynasty (1901-1911), which has been analyzed in terms of peasant uprisings, secret societies, revolutionary nationalist movements (domestic and foreign), urbanization, intellectuals, reforms (administrative, economic, and educational), foreign policy, and finally elites at provincial and local levels. Comparatively speaking, we know little about the still dominant Beijing-controlled Qing polity, the nature of external and internal pressures upon it, and how formal political power structure was changing in China at the turn of the century.

For example, imperialism, while long recognized as a major theme in modern Chinese history, is rarely analyzed systematically in terms of its impact on the domestic political power structure.[3]

---

1. By political power, I mean Yuan's influence over decisions in government regarding personnel, policy, and the use of resources. Definition derived from Harold D. Lasswell and Abraham Kaplan, *Power and Society: A Framework for Political Inquiry* (New Haven, 1950); and Leonard Krieger, "Power and Responsibility: The Historical Assumptions," in Leonard Krieger and Fritz Stern, eds., *The Responsibility of Power* (New York, 1967), pp. 3-35.

2. Mary C. Wright, *The Last Stand of Chinese Conservatism: The T'ung-chih Restoration, 1862-1874* (Stanford, 1957).

3. Two notable exceptions which deal with the early Republican period are Ernest

Scholars in the United States often argue that the destructive impact of Western and Japanese imperialism on China was more psychological and intellectual than economic. They cite the lack of evidence of significant foreign influence on the Chinese economy beyond treaty port centers, argue that foreign firms stimulated rather than hindered the development efforts of Chinese capitalists and government reformers, and emphasize the successes of the dynasty in protecting Chinese legal sovereignty over territory and economic enterprises. They conclude that Chinese nationalism is better understood as an emotional and ideological reaction to imperialism rather than as a political force precipitated by the realities of economic dependence.[4] The counterargument strongly asserts the opposite: that there was increasing foreign penetration of the Chinese economy, that it had a seriously depressive and disruptive effect generally, and that by means of financial subversion, Chinese control over the economy and territory steadily eroded.[5] The tangible and growing pressure of imperialism on late Qing polity, while noticed in passing by both sides, is rarely brought seriously into such debates. This is all the more surprising considering recent interest in the West in dependency theory (or the history of the development of underdevelopment), which in Chinese studies has led to calls for a better understanding of the impact of foreign penetration on the Chinese state in the late Imperial period.[6] In-

---

P. Young, *The Presidency of Yuan Shih-k'ai: Liberalism and Dictatorship in Early Republican China* (Ann Arbor, 1976) and Edward Friedman, *Backward Toward Revolution: The Chinese Revolutionary Party* (Berkeley and Los Angeles, 1974).

4. For a sophisticated statement of this argument in summary form, see Rhoads Murphy, *The Outsiders: The Western Experience in India and China* (Ann Arbor, 1977), as well as such representative works as Hou Chi-ming, *Foreign Investments and Economic Development in China, 1840-1937* (Cambridge, Mass., 1965); John Schrecker, *Imperialism and Chinese Nationalism: Germany in Shantung* (Cambridge, Mass., 1971); and Albert Feuerwerker, *The Foreign Establishment in China in the Early Twentieth Century* (Ann Arbor, 1976).

5. Yan Zhong-ping, *Zhongguo mian fangzhi shigao* (Beijing, 1955), is a representative work of this school; for a succinct, up-to-date statement in English of the argument, see Jean Chesneaux and Marianne Bastid, *China from the Opium Wars to the 1911 Revolution* (New York, 1976). For summaries of the debate itself, see exchanges in "Imperialism in China," *Bulletin of Concerned Asian Scholars* 4.4 (December 1972):2-16, as well as "Symposium on China's Economic History," *Modern China* 4.3 (July 1978): 251-369. A middle position of course is possible; see, for example, Edward J.M. Rhoads, in *China's Republican Revolution: The Case of Kwangtung, 1895-1913* (Cambridge, Mass., 1975).

6. Victor Lippit, "The Development of Underdevelopment in China," *Modern China* 4.3 (July 1978):280-84, and comments by Carl Riskin, *ibid.*, pp. 364-66. Two classics of

deed, there has been no systematic study of the impact of imperialism on late Imperial political power structure that I know of since the pioneering works by Chinese scholars Hu Sheng and Shao Xun-zheng.[7]

The facts of a rapidly accelerating Western and Japanese presence in China, especially after 1900, are generally acknowledged. The trade deficit was serious. Foreign control over modern transportation, heavy industry, and modern banking increased. The influx of missionaries accelerated. Foreign residents of all kinds in China increased from 10,091 in 1895 to 163,827 by 1913, and foreign enterprises were up from 603 to 3,805 over the same period. The British and their allies, the Japanese, were in the lead; from 1902 to 1914, British investments jumped from 260.3 to 607.5 million dollars (U.S.) and Japanese from near zero to 219.6 million dollars.[8]

By 1900 Western and Japanese imperialism had reached a new stage in China and generated a severe political crisis. In the 1894-95 Sino-Japanese War, the central government lost most of its navy, sovereignty over Taiwan, and suzerainty over Korea. Five years later, in response to the Boxer peasant uprising and siege of foreign legations in 1900, a joint expeditionary force (including Russians, Germans, British, Americans, and Japanese) occupied and sacked Beijing and Tianjin, driving the Court into exile. In the process most of what was left of the central government's ground forces were destroyed. Moreover, a heavy indemnity (450 million taels) was demanded by the Powers which was over four times the size of Beijing's annual budget, forcing the central government to forfeit its annual "native customs" revenues in payment. Militarily and financially, Beijing was left defenseless by the Boxer affair.

Not well understood is the profound extent to which imperialism affected late Qing political power structure during the post-Boxer decade. Besides mortgaging away the central government, the Boxer Uprising and the resulting Allied occupation of Beijing and

---

dependency theory are Charles K. Wilbur, ed., *Political Economy of Development and Underdevelopment* (New York, 1973), and Andre G. Frank, *Capitalism and Underdevelopment in Latin America* (New York, 1967).

7. Hu Sheng, *Diguozhuyi yu Zhongguo zhengzhi* (Hong Kong, 1948), translated as *Imperialism and Chinese Politics* (Beijing, 1955); and Shao Xun-zheng, "Xinhai geming qian wushi nian waiguo qinlue zhe he zhongguo maibanhua junfa guanliao shili di guanxi," *Lishi yanjiu* (August 1954):53-64.

8. Hou Chi-ming, p. 225.

environs gave the foreign powers unprecedented license to interfere in decision making in Beijing and the provinces. Foreign support became vital to the political position of leading provincial officials, like Yuan Shi-kai and Zhang Zhi-dong, a point which is pursued at length in this study.

Reforms were another aspect of imperialism's impact on the late Qing polity during the post-Boxer decade. As a condition for the return of Beijing to the Manchus in 1901, the foreign powers demanded drastic modernizing reforms, particularly of foreign relations. To fulfill this promise, the central government initiated a number of institutional reforms or "new policies" (*xinzheng*), such as the abolition of the examination system and the reorganization of the traditional six boards into eleven modern ministries, including a foreign ministry and a ministry of commerce. Outside of Beijing, the emphasis was on modernizing the military and educational system and, at the end of the decade, experimenting with local self-government and constitutional reform. The latter political reforms were so radical that they led, in the opinion of many, to the sudden and relatively bloodless downfall of the dynasty in 1911-12.[9]

From a peasant point of view, increased Western and Japanese imperialism meant greater government oppression. Direct intervention by foreign troops finally stopped the Boxers in north China. But afterward, peasant uprisings continued to occur against the new taxes accompanying the *xinzheng* reforms and foreign demands for indemnity payments. Fearing Western reprisals and using the overwhelming superiority of Western weaponry, provincial governments suppressed these uprisings swiftly and savagely.[10] Thus the paradox that, although the dynasty was militarily on its knees before the foreign powers, domestic security was reasonably good because of Western support and exclusive avail-

---

9. Esther Morrison, "The Modernization of the Confucian Bureaucracy: An Historical Study of Public Administration" (Ph.D. dissertation, Radcliffe College, 1959); Mary C. Wright, in her introduction to *China in Revolution: The First Phase, 1900-1913* (New Haven, 1968); and Rhoads, *China's Republican Revolution*.

10. *Xinhai geming wushi zhounian jinian lunwenji* (Beijing, 1962), vol. 1, pp. 115-46, 204-28; Li Wen-zhi, ed., *Zhongguo jindai nungye shi ziliao* (Beijing, 1957), vol. 1, pp. 946-68. Ernest P. Young, in *The Presidency of Yuan Shih-k'ai*, pp. 18-19, summarizes and cites the abundant Japanese scholarship on the subject; see also Jean Chesneaux, ed., *Popular Movements and Secret Societies in China, 1840-1950* (Stanford, 1972), pp. 160-70; and for a case study of the Hunan-Hubei region, Joseph W. Esherick, *Reform and Revolution in China: The 1911 Revolution in Hunan and Hubei* (Berkeley and Los Angeles, 1976), pp. 106-42.

ability of Western weaponry. Yuan Shi-kai was probably typical of officialdom in his attitude towards peasant needs and unrest. In memorials to the throne, Yuan wrote of the majority of the Chinese people as children in need of discipline and nourishment.[11] In practice, as we shall see, he dealt with them as objects of manipulation to be ruthlessly controlled and was ever vigilant to prevent the resurgence of antiforeign movements, Boxer or otherwise, in the countryside.

As Ernest Young has demonstrated for the 1911-12 revolution, there has been a tendency amongst contemporaries and historians alike to exaggerate the dimensions of Yuan Shi-kai's political power —the degree to which he succeeded in manipulating governmental policy, resources, and personnel in late Qing and early Republican periods.[12] This has led to the image of Yuan as the father of modern Chinese warlordism or militarism, whose political influence and style extended well beyond his death in 1916 and, for some, even to the present day.[13] Usually inherent in such views of Yuan as a military strong man are notions about the particularistic and regional nature of political power during the late Imperial period which require serious examination.

One purpose of this study is to challenge the argument first made by Luo Er-gang in the 1930s that the concentration of power in the hands of Yuan Shi-kai before 1911-12 was indicative of a pattern of increasing loss of power by the central government to provincial governors and governors-general after the Taiping and Nian rebellions of the 1850s and 1860s. In Yuan's case, his chief source of power is said to have been the personally-controlled and regionally-based Beiyang Army that he raised as governor-general of Zhili. But this view of Yuan's power has never been documented in detail. It grew instead out of a need to tailor an interpretation of

11. Yuan Shi-kai, *Yuan Shi-kai zuozhe zhuanji* (YSKZZ), p. 605.
12. Ernest P. Young, "Yuan Shi-k'ai's Rise to the Presidency," in Mary C. Wright, ed., *China in Revolution*, pp. 419-42.
13. See, for example, Tao Ju-yin, *Beiyang junfa tongzhi shiqi shihua* (Beijing, 1957-58); C. Martin Wilbur, "Military Separatism and the Process of Reunification Under the Nationalism Regime," in Ping-ti Ho and Tang Tsou, eds., *China in Crisis* (Chicago, 1968), vol. 1, Book 1, pp. 203-20; Andrew J. Nathan, *Peking Politics, 1918-1923: Factionalism and the Failure of Constitutionalism* (Berkeley and Los Angeles, 1976), pp. x, 8, and *passim*; Hsi-sheng Ch'i, *Warlord Politics in China, 1916-1928* (Stanford, 1976), chap. 2; Diana Lary, *Region and Nation: The Kwangsi Clique in Chinese Politics, 1925-1937* (London, 1974), pp. 1-20; and William Whitson, *The Chinese High Command: A History of Communist Military Politics, 1927-1971* (New York, 1973).

the late Qing power structure to fit a broader interpretation of nineteenth and twentieth century Chinese political history intended to explain the rise of militarism, or warlordism, and the near eclipse of central authority after Yuan's death in 1916.[14]

Over a decade ago, scholars began seriously questioning the validity of Professor Luo's argument for the immediate post-Taiping period.[15] Wang Er-min, for example, demonstrated that the Xiang and Huai Armies which were instrumental in suppressing the Taiping Rebellion of the mid-nineteenth century were not actually "regional armies." Both armies had a relatively *ad hoc*, simple organizational structure. Their regional character was by no means clearly established. The Xiang Army, founded in Hunan in 1853, was demobilized in 1864 and its units scattered about south China. Except for some units used during the campaign against the Nians in 1866-68, the Huai Army was never stationed in Anhui province, which was the home of most of its men and officers. After Li Hong-zhang, the founder and commander of the Huai Army, was appointed governor-general of Zhili in 1870, only one-third of the army accompanied him to Zhili. The remainder were beyond Li's direct control: over half in Shaanxi and the rest scattered in Jiangsu, Hubei, and Shanxi provinces. Moreover, neither the Xiang nor Huai Army was financially independent of the central government, and Beijing's administrative authority over the army was at least as important as Zeng Guo-fan's or Li Hong-zhang's. The time is ripe to reexamine Yuan Shi-kai's military base from 1901 to 1909 in these same terms.

A more recent variant of Luo Er-gang's argument has developed from the many pioneering local studies of nineteenth century political and social conditions by Japanese scholars, brilliantly synthe-

14. Luo Er-gang, "Qingji bingwei jiangyou di qiyuan," *Zhongguo shehui jingji shi jikan* 5.2 (June 1937):235-50, and *Xiangjun xinzhi* (Changsha, 1939). The most scholarly elaboration of Luo Er-gang's viewpoint is Hatano Yoshihiro, "Hokuyo gambatsu no seiritzu katei," *Nagoya daigaku bungakubu kenkyu ronshu* 6(1953):211-62, recently republished along with his other important articles in *Chūgoku kindai gumbatsu no kenkyu* (Tokyo, 1973). In English, the standard works are Ralph Powell, *The Rise of Chinese Military Power, 1895-1912* (Princeton, 1955), and Franz Michael, "Regionalism in Nineteenth-Century China," introduction to Stanley Spector, *Li Hung-chang and the Huai Army: A Study in Nineteenth-Century Regionalism* (Seattle, 1964).

15. Wang Er-min, *Huaijun zhi* (Taibei, 1967). See also Mary C. Wright's review of Stanley Spector's book *Li Hung-chang and the Huai Army*, in the *Journal of Asian Studies* 25.2 (February 1966):331-33; and Kwang-ching Liu, "The Limits of Regional Power in the Late Ch'ing Period," *Tsing Hua Journal of Chinese Studies*, n.s. 10.2 (July 1974): 176-223.

sized by Philip Kuhn.[16] In this view, the chief dividing line in late Qing power structure was not between central and provincial governments or armies, but between the entire formal apparatus of government (including the *xian* magistrate) and the informal power of local or lower gentry elites in the countryside. Defining these elites in terms of wealth and educational background is of course a crucial and complicated issue, with scholars producing almost as many definitions and categorizations of elites as studies on the subject. There is general agreement, however, that local notables of lesser degree status (*shengyuan* or lower) and/or wealth comprised the local elite. They outnumbered and were quite distinct from the national or upper elite of scholar-official families who had the necessary one or more higher degree winners—and usually the wealth and family connections as well—to be tied directly to the formal bureaucracy of government. Along the lines of Luo Er-gang's argument, local elite power is seen as rising in the nineteenth century at the expense of the authority of formal government at the *xian* level. To demonstrate his point, Kuhn shows how, with the crisis of the Taiping Rebellion acting as a catalyst, local elites assume taxation and military powers in the countryside through such *ad hoc* devices as organizing *tuanlian* or militia and exacting miscellaneous likin [*lijin*] taxes on commerce. In his concluding chapter, Kuhn strongly suggests that this accretion of political power to local elites continued well into the twentieth century. The latter suggestion has been taken up by scholars of the post-Boxer decade, like Joseph Esherick, in investigations of conditions in a particular province or region. Indeed, Esherick, following the lead of Japanese scholars like Ichiko Chūzō, takes Kuhn's argument one step further and concludes that the dominant characteristic of the 1911-12 revolution was a victory of conservative local elites over the formal centralized power of the Qing bureaucracy.[17]

An alternative view which approaches the question of local elite power more from the top down and on an empire-wide scale is now just emerging from archival research into Qing institutional history by scholars like Liu Kwang-ching [Liu Guang-jing]. In his

---

16. Philip Kuhn, *Rebellion and Its Enemies in Late Imperial China: Militarization and Social Structure, 1796-1864* (Cambridge, Mass., 1970).
17. Esherick, *Reform and Revolution*, esp. p. 116; and Ichiko Chūzō, "The Role of the Gentry: An Hypothesis," in Wright, *China in Revolution*, pp. 297-317.

view, the central government and its formal apparatus down to the *xian* magistrate was neither dormant nor declining in power during the latter half of the nineteenth century. The reverse was true. Government was vigorous and becoming more intrusive: one manifestation was the complaints of commoners and elites alike about exploitation by yamen runners and other representatives of the *xian* magistrate.[18] On the crucial issue of continuing militarization at the local level, although our knowledge of local social history in the late nineteenth century is sparse, recent studies suggest that most *tuanlian* or militia units were dissolved or at least disarmed.[19] The evidence is still clearer that even more regular troops, the regional *yongying* forces, were drastically reduced and dispersed after the suppression of the Taiping and Nian rebels.[20] Thus, by the first decade of the twentieth century, local elites *rarely* were militarized.[21] Likewise, and this is more controversial, local elite involvement in taxation seems to have been institutionalized or co-opted by government after the suppression of the Taiping and Nians. By the end of the century, *ad hoc* commercial taxes like the likin were under formal government control, and generally speaking the fiscal controls exercised by provincial governors and governors-general tightened.[22] Preliminary analysis of the official pro-

18. Kwang-ching Liu, "Li Hung-chang in Chihli: The Emergence of a Policy, 1870-1875," in Albert Feuerwerker, Rhoads Murphy, and Mary C. Wright, eds., *Approaches to Modern Chinese History* (Berkeley and Los Angeles, 1967), pp. 68-104; "Limits of Regional Power in the Late Ch'ing Period"; and "The Ch'ing Restoration," in John K. Fairbank, ed., *The Cambridge History of China*, vol. 10. *Late Ch'ing, 1800-1911* (Cambridge, 1978), pp. 609-90.

19. Kwang-ching Liu, "The Ch'ing Restoration"; Mary B. Rankin, "Local Reform Currents in Chekiang Before 1900," in Paul Cohen and John Schrecker, eds., *Reform in Nineteenth Century China* (Cambridge, Mass., 1976), p. 223; and David D. Buck, "The Provincial Elite in Shantung During the Republican Period: Their Successes and Failures," *Modern China* 1.4 (October 1975):428.

20. Wang Er-min, *Huaijun zhi*; Kwang-ching Liu, "Limits of Regional Power"; and Luo Er-gang, *Xiangjun xinzhi*.

21. Studies cited in the notes and bibliography by Rhoads on Guangdong, Esherick on Hunan and Hubei, Buck on Shandong, Rankin on Zhejiang, and my own study of Zhili in Chapter 5 show little evidence of continuing militarization of local elites into *tuanlian* or other *ad hoc* militia units.

22. Luo Yu-dong, "Guangxu chao bujiu caizheng zhi fangce," *Zhongguo jindai jingji shi yanjiu jikan*, 1.2 (May 1933):189-270, and *Zhongguo lijin shi* (Shanghai, 1936); Kwang-ching Liu, "Li Hung-chang in Chihli"; Daniel H. Bays, "The Nature of Provincial Authority in Late Ch'ing Times: Chang Chih-tung in Canton, 1884-1889," *Modern Asian Studies* 4.4 (October 1970):325-47; S.A.M. Adshead, "Viceregal Government in Szechwan in the Kuang-hsu Period (1875-1909)," *Papers on Far Eastern History* 4 (September 1971):41-52; and Li Guo-qi, "Tongzhi zhongxing shiqi Liu Kun-

INTRODUCTION

vincial correspondence in the Palace Museum (Taibei) shows the close attention Beijing paid to reports on provincial and local finances, as well as to the appointment and transfer of *xian* magistrates. The percentage of reports on these matters increased during the course of the nineteenth century, even for elite strongholds like Hunan.[23] Finally, few question the increased activity and intrusiveness of Qing government after the Boxer affair of 1900-01. Led by the central government, the formal government apparatus took the initiative, reasserting fiscal and military controls down to the *xian* level through a series of educational, military, economic and police reforms. By the end of the post-Boxer decade, government at the local level had responsibility for population census, economic surveys of many kinds (often for tax and development purposes), self-government associations, chambers of commerce, agricultural associations, land taxes, currency control, and sweeping fiscal reorganization. Looking at the empire as a whole (in chapter V we shall look at Zhili province in detail), initiative for nearly all of these reforms lay with *xian* magistrates, with the provincial/central government in the background.[24]

This is not to say that the power of local elites did not expand after the Taiping Rebellion. The evidence is overwhelming that it did, but not necessarily at the expense of formal government. As Ernest Young has cogently argued, Qing elites became less particularistic and more politicized in a modern sense during the last decade or two of the dynasty. Nationalism galvanized them into a new force along provincial lines—Young calls this "provincialism" —that was not necessarily antithetical to the centripetal influence

---

yi zai Jiangxi xunfu rennei di biaoxian," *Guoli Taiwan shifan daxue lishi xuebao* 1 (1973): 241-70. On the continuing struggle in the late nineteenth century between magistrates and local elites over land taxes, see David Faure, "Land Tax Collection in Kiangsu Province in the Late Ch'ing Period," *Ch'ing-shih wen-t'i* 3.7 (December 1976), esp. pp. 65-73.

23. Robert Weiss, "Archival Material for the Study of Provincial Government: The Case of Hunan in the Nineteenth Century," paper read at International Ch'ing Archives Symposium, July 2-6, 1978, in Taibei, Taiwan.

24. Daniel H. Bays, *China Enters the Twentieth Century: Chang Chih-tung and the Issues of a New Age, 1895-1909* (Ann Arbor, 1978); David D. Buck, *Urban Change in China: Politics and Development in Tsinan, Shantung, 1890-1949* (Madison, 1978), chap. 3; Rhoads, *China's Republican Revolution*; Robert H.G. Lee, *The Manchurian Frontier in Ch'ing History* (Cambridge, Mass., 1970), chap. 7; and Roger Des Forges, *Hsi-liang and the Chinese National Revolution* (New Haven, 1973). For a dissenting view emphasizing local elite initiative, see Esherick, *Reform and Revolution*, chaps. 3 and 4.

of government. The new movement was motivated in part by self-interest and in part by nationalism, with contradictory consequences for formal government, depending on how it was perceived as serving national and elite interests.[25]

The latter argument has convinced me that the differing scholarly notions about basic power structure in late Imperial China from Luo Er-gang to Philip Kuhn to Kwang-ching Liu are not incompatible. In part it is a question of emphasis which can be explained by the different source materials used and regions studied (North-South differences being particularly important and in need of much more exploration). A useful model or paradigm of political power structure in the later Imperial period is one of three simultaneously expanding and overlapping nodes of power: the central government in Beijing; provincial governments and armies at the regional level; and local elites at the sub-*xian* level. Included in the paradigm is the idea that there was less competition and more cooperation between power centers than is usually acknowledged. There was a good reason for this: the need to stick together in face of accelerating pressure from a common enemy—Western and Japanese imperialism. Moreover, if this triple-leveled expansion of power was at the expense of anyone, it was the peasantry, who, despite their restlessness, seemed as firmly bound by a combination of government and elite controls as at any time during middle or early Qing dynasty.[26]

Finally, the focus in this study is on the two chief determinants of the political power structure in the late Imperial period: (1) the domestic influence of imperialism, and (2) the relationship between expanding nodes of power at the central/provincial government and local elite levels. It is not on the main and well-studied ideological issue dividing bureaucracy and local elites at the time: reform or modernization along Western lines and how far and fast it should proceed.[27] My vehicle is an analysis of Yuan Shi-kai's political

25. Ernest P. Young, *The Presidency of Yuan*, chap. 1.
26. On this last point, see Jing Su and Luo Lun, *Qingdai Shandong jingying dizhu de shehui xingzhi* (Jinan, 1959) and Yuji Muramatsu, "A Documentary Study of Chinese Landlordism in Late Ch'ing and Early Republican Kiangnan," *Bulletin of the School of Oriental and African Studies* 29.3 (1966):566-99.
27. For a summary of the state of the field in reform studies and an indication of the degree of interest in the subject, see Paul Cohen and John Schrecker, eds., *Reform in Nineteenth-Century China* (Cambridge, Mass., 1976). A fine study of the reform issue in the early twentieth century is Bays, *China Enters the Twentieth Century*.

power as a late Qing official, paying special attention to his career as governor-general of Zhili province and a high official in Beijing from 1901 to 1909. Unlike the great self-strengthening statesmen of an earlier generation such as Li Hong-zhang and Zhang Zhi-dong, Yuan Shi-kai was not much interested in, nor sensitive to, issues of formal political ideology—a weakness which proved fatal by the end of his career. Although probably the most effective reform administrator of his generation, Yuan's explanations were consistently brief and trite. As a man of action and few words, Yuan Shi-kai was first and foremost concerned with the levers of power.

CHAPTER I

Yuan Shi-kai's Rise to Power

Historically, the governor-generalship of Zhili province (*Zhili zongdu*) and the commissionership of trade for the northern ports (*Beiyang dachen*) were the most important and prestigious provincial appointments in the Empire. Appointment to these posts usually crowned a long illustrious career of a scholar-official. Yuan Shi-kai was unique in the history of the Qing dynasty to receive these appointments at the young age of 42.[1] Moreover, Yuan's rise to high office was meteoric and all the more remarkable if one considers that he held no civil service examination degree. His rapid promotion had little to do with a regional military power base or local elite support in north China. In part, the extraordinary times and series of crises that shook Beijing during the decade before 1901 discredited or eliminated senior officials who might otherwise have been appointed. But the key to Yuan's success was his extraordinary political instinct—his skill in mollifying foreigners and his ability to maneuver and intrigue in court and bureaucratic politics. Yuan was helped too by his ideological insensitivity, his willingness to play all sides of the complicated conservative/moderate/radical reform spectrum which divided political life in Beijing after 1895. In 1895 and again in 1898, Yuan skillfully switched from one set of patrons to another just when the latter were gaining ascendancy at Court. In the process he made permanent enemies of former pa-

1. For Yuan's predecessors, see tables in Xiao Yi-shan, *Qingdai tongshi* (Taibei, 1953), vol. 5, pp. 214-16, 229-31. In the nineteenth century, the Zhili governor-general closest in age to Yuan was Li Hong-zhang, who was first appointed in 1870 at age 47.

trons, like Li Hong-zhang in 1895 and the Guang-xu emperor in 1898. In 1900-01, when the fortunes of the dynasty reached a nadir with the flight of the Court to Xi'an, Yuan cultivated close relations with the foreign powers who had taken over in Beijing (and Tianjin). All the while Yuan's personal stock rose gradually at Court, first with the senior Manchu court politician, Rong-lu, and then with the Empress Dowager herself. In short, the story of Yuan's rise to power in Beijing and Tianjin not only demonstrates Yuan's touch as a Machiavellian politician, it also reveals much about the forces that shaped late Qing political power structure at the turn of the century.

Early Career

Yuan Shi-kai was born in 1859 into an important landlord official family of Henan province. Yuan's great-uncle, Yuan Jia-san, had been nationally known as a censor and military figure in the suppression of the Taipings in the Henan and Anhui area during the 1850s and 1860s. An uncle, Yuan Bao-ling, and Yuan's father, Yuan Bao-zhong, lived as prominent local gentry near the family seat of Xiangzheng, Henan. The Yuans were one of the biggest landlord families in Henan, holding 4,000-5,000 *mu* of cultivated land at the time of Shi-kai's birth. As happened frequently in such wealthy extended upper or national elite families, Yuan Shi-kai was adopted while an infant by a childless uncle, Yuan Bao-qing, who was a civil degree holder and a *xian* magistrate. In 1873, when Yuan Shi-kai was 14, Yuan Bao-qing died in Nanjing where he was serving as acting salt intendant. The young Yuan Shi-kai then lived with various uncles and cousins, including Yuan Bao-heng, who was senior vice-president of the Board of Revenue (in Beijing) between 1875 and 1877. In 1876, at the age of 17, Yuan competed unsuccessfully for the prefectural *shengyuan* degree. Between 1876 and 1880, Yuan remained around Xiangzheng, married for the first time (during his life he fathered 16 sons and 14 daughters by an unknown number of wives), and lived as the scion of a leading landlord-official family. Yuan was active in literary societies and fraternized frequently with local prefects and their secretaries. When Yuan failed the prefectural examination for the second time in 1879, he lost patience with literary studies, reportedly burning his student essays and papers and announcing that he intended to pursue a military career. His first move was to purchase a title as

Secretary of the Imperial Patent Office (*zhongshu ke zhongshu*). Then in 1880, using family connections, Yuan joined the staff of Wu Chang-qing, commander of Huai Army forces in Shandong province.[2]

Within Wu Chang-qing's *mufu* or secretariat, Yuan was put in charge of troop training and discipline. Yuan proved an efficient and tough administrator, ordering execution of peasant conscripts for serious breaches of discipline such as plundering. Yuan also studied military modernization techniques intensively and got along well with associates, particularly the most learned and ambitious among them, like the promising young Jiangsu scholar, Zhang Jian. Indeed Yuan's failure in the examination system seemed to have bred little in the way of inferiority or resentment in him toward contemporaries who were working up the bureaucratic ladder via the conventional examination route. If John Schrecker is correct, the reverse was in fact true: literati often resented the success of men like Yuan in rising by irregular (non-examination) means. Regardless, the social prominence of the Yuan family as national elite was evidently sufficient to give Yuan the confidence to work well with, and befriend, many degree-winning scholar-officials. Later, as we shall see, when Yuan organized his own yamen in Zhili, his preference was for able men with civil service examination degrees in their portfolio.[3]

In 1882, Yuan and Zhang Jian accompanied Wu Chang-qing and 3,000 troops to Korea to stop an impending *coup d'état* against Chinese interests at the Korean court. After distinguishing himself in the crisis (which was resolved satisfactorily from the Chinese point of view by the removal to Tianjin of the chief trouble-maker, the Taewongun), Yuan was put in charge of training five hundred Korean soldiers in modern warfare. The highly volatile political situation in Korea provided good opportunities for self-advancement: Yuan soon rose above the rest of the field in Wu Chang-qing's *mufu*, and drew the attention of officialdom at the highest levels in Beijing. By 1883, Yuan was in charge of the small Korean

---

2. *Rongan dizi ji* (1919), *juan* 1:1-4; Li Wen-zhi, ed., *Zhongguo jindai nungye shi ziliao*, pp. 187-89.

3. Jerome Ch'en, *Yuan Shih-k'ai*, 2nd ed. (Stanford, 1972), pp. 2-3, 6; Liu Hou-sheng (Liu Yuan), *Zhang Jian zhuanji* (Shanghai, 1958), p. 64; and John Schrecker, "The Reform Movement of 1898 and the Ch'ing-i: Reform as Opposition," in Cohen and Schrecker, *Reform in Nineteenth-Century China*, pp. 289-305.

army of 5,000 men and was a favorite at the Korean court. The next year, by a combination of luck, ingenuity, and boldness, Yuan personally foiled a Japanese-inspired *coup d'etát* against the Korean king, Yi Hui, who was considered an ally of China. This brought Yuan, who was only 25 years old at the time, the patronage of Li Hong-zhang, the most powerful Chinese official in the Empire and principal architect of the dynasty's Korean policy.[4]

In 1885 Li Hong-zhang arranged to have Yuan appointed Chinese "Resident" (*zongli*) in Korea.[5] Over the next nine years, from 1885 to 1894, Yuan rather rigidly pursued Li Hong-zhang's policy of preserving Chinese strategic interests and outmaneuvering the Japanese at the Korean court by any means possible. Yuan succeeded by backing highly corrupt and conservative elements at court who opposed reform and the Japanese, in that order. In the process, Yuan eschewed and eventually alienated pro-Chinese moderate reform leaders like the classically educated scholar, Kim Yun-sik. As if in anticipation of his later alliance in Beijing with the Empress Dowager Ci-xi, Yuan much preferred to work in Seoul with the notoriously corrupt and conservative Queen Min. Thus Yuan's commitment to reform in Korea—even to Kim Yun-sik's self-strengthening or *yangwu* variety of reform—was incomplete and overshadowed by his pragmatic instincts as a politician.[6]

By the early 1890s Yuan Shi-kai was a young man of considerable reputation in Beijing, Tokyo, and Seoul. The Korean court erected stone tablets honoring him; the Japanese and most Western diplomats cursed him as a "smuggler, conspirator, and diplomatic outlaw;" and in Beijing he was praised by Li Hong-zhang and promoted to the rank of customs *daotai* in 1892.[7] Personally Yuan projected an image of maturity and solemnity beyond his years. A short, heavyset man who wobbled when he walked, Yuan was physically unimpressive. It was his prematurely grey hair and penetrating eyes of almost demonic intensity and intelligence which

4. Li Hong-zhang, *Li Wenzhonggong quanji* (Nanjing, 1905), *zougao, juan* 45:6-12, 16-21, 29; *Rongan dizi ji, juan* 1:7; Liu Feng-han, *Xinjian lujun* (Taibei, 1967), pp. 5-14; Lin Ming-de, *Yuan Shi-kai yu Chaoxian* (Taibei, 1970), pp. 13-67.

5. Li Hong-zhang, *zougao, juan* 55:7.

6. The most perceptive and thorough exploration of Yuan's activities in Korea to date is Lin Ming-de, *Yuan Shi-kai yu Chaoxian*. I have also benefited from conversations with Professor K.H. Kim.

7. Ch'en, *Yuan Shih-k'ai* (1972), p. 17; O.N. Denny, *China and Korea* (Shanghai, 1888), p. 38; Li Hong-zhang, *zougao, juan* 67:4, 74:46, 76:30.

commanded one's attention.⁸ Yuan's rise had been fast and a bit frightening—even to friends like Zhang Jian who confided prophetically in a letter to a member of Yuan's family that:

> Shi-kai (Yen-ding) has both courage and tenacity, but when the situation becomes complicated he is also capable of old-fashioned bureaucratic deceit, and so his actions do not always meet expectations. In spite of this, when the country is in trouble, he is fit to be a minister.⁹

When the Sino-Japanese conflict over Korea finally broke out in 1894, Li Hong-zhang, not Yuan Shi-kai, was blamed for the disastrous war. This was at least partly because, just before its outbreak, Yuan deftly sought out new allies and patrons in Beijing. Yuan cultivated both the literati-dominated and reform-minded *qingliu pai* opposition and the more conservative court opposition to Li Hong-zhang's allegedly conciliatory policies toward Japan. Specifically, with the help of Zhang Jian, by then a scholar of great prestige as top *jinshi* degree winner for 1894 and a leader of the *qingliu pai* war faction, Yuan cultivated relations with Li Hong-zhang's most important critics at Court, namely Li Hong-cao and Weng Tong-he of the *qingliu pai* and so-called conservatives Wang Wen-shao and Rong-lu.¹⁰ Among these men, the patronage of Rong-lu was the most important to Yuan's subsequent career.

Rong-lu (1836-1903) was born into a family of Manchu generals and had himself pursued a military career. He won the Empress Dowager's trust as early as 1861, when he led the troops escorting her back to Beijing from Chengde. Thereafter, he held a variety of military posts but wielded little direct political influence at Court until 1895, when he was appointed president of the Board of War and concurrently a grand secretary in 1896 in order to help fill the vacuum left by the discredited Li Hong-zhang.¹¹ Rong-lu's ascen-

---

8. *Rongan dizi ji, juan* 1:13a; Wu Xiang-xiang, *Minguo renheshi* (Taibei, 1971), pp. 42-44; Ernest P. Young, *The Presidency of Yuan Shih-k'ai*, p. 57. For a vivid contemporary description of Yuan's appearance, see Fernand Farjenel, *A travers la révolution chinoise* (Paris, 1914), pp. 293-94.

9. Zhang Jian, *Zhang jizi jiulu* (Shanghai, 1930), *zhengwen lu, juan* 1:7.

10. Liu Feng-han, *Xinjian lujun*, pp. 34-47; Liu Hou-sheng, pp. 64-70; and Schrecker, "Reform Movement of 1898."

11. Liu Feng-han's thorough and sympathetic portrait of Rong-lu in *Wuwei jun* (Taibei, 1978), esp. pp. 21-47, supersedes biographies in Arthur W. Hummel, ed., *Eminent Chinese of the Ch'ing Period, 1644-1912* (Washington, 1944), pp. 405-09, and *Qingshi* (hereafter QS), pp. 4903-04. Rumors persist to this day that Rong-lu and the Empress Dowager were once lovers; see, for example, Liu Hou-sheng, p. 69.

sion was in opposition to and at the expense of the *qingliu pai* group of literati reformers who also opposed Li Hong-zhang in 1894-95.[12]

Yuan probably met Rong-lu for the first time in August, 1894, in Beijing. Rong-lu had just returned from Xi'an, where he was Tartar General (*jiangjun*), in order to help with preparations for the Empress Dowager's sixtieth birthday celebrations. Yuan was in Beijing maneuvering to disassociate himself from Li Hong-zhang and the Sino-Japanese war.[13] By the next year, 1895, Rong-lu was actively supporting Yuan Shi-kai's career. During the summer of that year, at Rong-lu's suggestion, Yuan compiled and presented to the Court a report on how to use foreign methods in training troops. This report led directly to Yuan's appointment on December 8, 1895, to train and command the foreign-style Newly Created Army (*Xinjian lujun*) of 7,000 men. Rong-lu was one of the "princes and high officials" (*wang dachen*) on the War Council (*Junwu ju*) which formally recommended Yuan's appointment to the Empress Dowager.[14] In May, 1896, a censor, Hu Jing-gui, accused Yuan of embezzling military revenues and murdering a vegetable seller outside the gates of his camp at Xiaozhan (about 20 miles east of Tianjin).[15] Rong-lu was ordered to go to Xiaozhan and investigate the charges. Rong-lu's secretary at the time, Chen Kui-long, later recalled how very impressed Rong-lu was with Yuan's achievements at Xiaozhan. In his report to the Empress Dowager on June 24, 1896, Rong-lu completely exonerated Yuan and the Newly Created Army.[16] On May 7, 1897, Yuan went to Beijing to report to Rong-lu and the War Council on the progress of the Newly Created Army.[17] Shortly thereafter Yuan was promoted to judicial commissioner of Zhili province. Moreover, Rong-lu informally promised Yuan 3,000 additional troops, which were authorized officially a

12. Schrecker, "Reform Movement of 1898."
13. Liu Feng-han, *Xinjian lujun*, pp. 34-37; Liu Hou-sheng, p. 70. Hatano Yoshihiro, in "Hokuyō gumbatsu no seiritsu katei," p. 241, has made an inadequately documented assertion that Yuan bribed Rong-lu heavily at about this time.
14. Yuan Shi-kai, *Xinjian lujun binglie luzun* (Xiaozhan, 1898), juan 1:19.
15. *Da Qing Dezong jing huangdi shilu* (hereafter cited as *Shilu*), juan 389:1a; *Rongan dizi ji*, juan 2:7b-8a.
16. Liu Feng-han, *Xinjian lujun*, pp. 292-95; Chen Kui-long, *Mengjiao ting zaji* (1925), juan 2:2-3a. Li Hong-cao apparently was behind Hu Jing-gui's attack upon Yuan. Possible reasons for Li's suddenly turning against Yuan might have been pressure from Zhili gentry, of whom Li was one (Gaoyang *xian*), and Zhang Pei-lun's (a close associate of Li Hong-zhang) denunciations of Yuan to Li; see Liu Feng-han, *Xinjian lujun*, and Ch'en, *Yuan Shih-k'ai* (1972), p. 33.
17. Yuan Shi-kai, *Yangzhou yuan diangao*, p. 274.

few months later, suggesting again the growing intimacy of their relationship.[18]

Understandably, Li Hong-zhang had never forgiven Yuan for his betrayal on the eve of the Sino-Japanese war. Li's sometime secretary, Wu Yong, recorded two incidents which well illustrate Li's continuing enmity toward Yuan. Wu's vivid recollections, as told to Liu Zhi-xiang and translated by Ida Pruitt, are worth quoting at length:

> When Li Hung-chang was viceroy of Chihli province, his career was blocked by Weng of Chang-shu whom he hated. He also disliked Yüan Shih-k'ai. One day when he was living at the Hsien-liang temple, Yüan came to see him, and I went into another room. Yüan said to him:
>
> "You are the most famous of those who have recreated the country and won much merit, but now the government is treating you rather coldly. You have been given the title of premier but you are treated more or less like a hotel guest. It is not good enough for you. You had better retire for the time being and let your reputation grow at home. There may well be occasions when the government is in difficulty and will think of you. Then they will depend upon you and will send for you, and you can come back in an official cart and show that you are valuable."
>
> . . . .
>
> Yüan Shih-k'ai hung his head and apologized and went away. Li Hung-chang called me to his room and said:
>
> "Yüan Shih-k'ai came a moment ago. Do you know him?"
>
> "I recognized him but do not know him well."
>
> "Don't you know Shih-k'ai? He is a small minded man! He flattered Weng Shu-p'ing and came to speak for him. He talked shrewdly and asked me to resign so that Weng might be promoted to my vacancy as assistant grand secretary. I certainly will not resign. Let him die of longing! Now is the time for me to make use of the straight rule of my teacher. I will hold fast, according to the principles of my teacher, and see what they can do. Face to face, I exhorted and reviled him so that he will not come to trouble me a second time. I have worked many decades and experienced everything. How could his generation deceive me?"
>
> . . . .

18. Liu Feng-han, *Xinjian lujun*, p. 302, and *Shilu*, juan 413:16b.

On another occasion Yüan was still more embarrassed. When Li Hung-chang returned from abroad, he stayed in Tientsin before he reported to the Court. I went to see him with other candidates for official positions in Chihli province. At that time, Yüan had been promoted to be judge of Chihli, but had not yet assumed office because he had concentrated his energy in training soldiers. Being qualified as a taotai, he was a leader of our group. We were all seated and, after a few sentences of welcome, Yüan began to report on his work in training soldiers:

"Now the arrangements are almost completed. German officers have been appointed and their contracts are to be signed in a day or two." Li Hung-chang changed colour and, pounding the ground with his stick, interrupted Yüan:

"Ha! You boy! How much do you know about training soldiers? What contract are you going to sign? I have directed soldiers for several decades, yet I dare not to say that I am confident of myself. So it is easy to train soldiers! Do you consider your troops a modern army after hiring a few foreigners, putting foreign guns on the men's shoulders and shouting a few military commands?"

Yüan's face became red and he said nothing. All bent their heads and dared not to look at each other. Yüan was at that time beginning to lift his head above the crowd. Li's purpose seemed to be to dampen his ardour. As Li Hung-chang became older, like ginger he became hotter.[19]

Li Hong-zhang underestimated the Newly Created Army which Yuan organized and trained at Xiaozhan between 1896 and 1899. It was an important achievement and is still considered a milestone in modern Chinese military history because of the improved quality of officers and men Yuan recruited as well as the modern discipline and training given to the troops.[20] As noted earlier, by 1897, Yuan's success with the army brought immediate recognition in the form of promotions, a reputation as the empire's foremost military reformer, and direct involvement in Beijing's court politics. It is also said that the loss of the Sino-Japanese War and its devastating impact on Li Hong-zhang's career had a profound effect on Yuan. Throughout the remainder of his career Yuan would never con-

19. Wu Yong, *Gengzi xishou congtan* (1918), pp. 163-65, translated by Ida Pruitt in *The Flight of an Empress* (London, 1937), pp. 256-59.
20. Liu Feng-han, *Xinjian lujun*; Ralph Powell, *The Rise of Chinese Military Power, 1895-1912*, chap. 2.

sider pitting soldiers under his command against foreign troops.[21]

In 1897-98, while receiving political support mostly from the so-called conservative court politicians around the Empress Dowager like Rong-lu and Wang Wen-shao, Yuan remained on good terms with the *qingyi* reformers around the young Guang-xu emperor like Weng Tong-he and even Liang Qi-chao and Kang You-wei. As is well known, Yuan was a central figure in the intrigues at Court which surrounded the 1898 reform movement led by Kang You-wei and Liang Qi-chao. At first, Yuan professed loyalty to the Guang-xu emperor and the reformers. Then, at the critical juncture on September 20, 1898, Yuan withdrew this support by refusing to commit the Newly Created Army as a defending force against the *coup d'état* launched by the Empress Dowager using troops led by Rong-lu.[22]

Needless to say, the impact on Yuan's career of the successful *coup* and his tacit support of it was favorable. For a few weeks he replaced Rong-lu as acting governor-general of Zhili and commissioner of trade for the northern ports.[23] Yuan returned to Xiaozhan to resume training troops. Rong-lu became commander of all Beiyang forces on October 11 and shortly thereafter promised Yuan money to train more troops. On December 7, at Rong-lu's request, the Empress Dowager Ci-xi approved the reorganization of the Beiyang armies into what was called four months later the Military Guards Army (*Wuwei jun*) of five divisions, each of which was to be modeled after Yuan's Newly Created Army. On March 31, 1899, Rong-lu formally praised to the throne Yuan's efforts in troop training over the last three years.[24]

Yuan Shi-kai was now a personal favorite of the Empress Dowager Ci-xi. On September 26 and 29, 1898, she sent cash awards to Yuan and his Newly Created Army.[25] Doubtless it was because of her encouragement that at this time Yuan began memorializing on subjects other than troop training: distribution of troops, unified

21. Ch'en, *Yuan Shih-k'ai* (1961), p. 249.
22. YSKZZ, p. 1. Yuan's role in the 1898 reform movement and *coup d'état* is a complex and controversial subject. The best single work is Liu Feng-han, *Yuan Shi-kai yu Wuxu zhengbian* (Taibei, 1964).
23. *Shilu*, juan 426:14a.
24. *Yuzhe huicun*, Guang-xu 25/2/20; *Shilu*, juan 439:19; YSKZZ, pp. 11-13, 15. On Rong-lu and the origins of the Military Guards Army, see Liu Feng-han, *Wuwei jun*, pp. 57-72.
25. *Guangxu chao donghua xulu* (DHXL), p. 4184. *Shilu*, juan 427:7; YSKZZ, pp. 6-7.

military reform, arsenals, salt taxes, currency reform, stamp tax, and preservation of national sovereignty. By spring, 1899, she made him a junior vice-president of the Board of Works with privileges to ride on barges on palace lakes and on horseback in the Imperial City.[26]

On December 6, 1899, the Empress Dowager appointed Yuan governor of Shandong province. Yuan's predecessor, Yu-xian, had refused to suppress the initially antidynastic and increasingly antiforeign uprisings of the Boxers and it was hoped that with the Newly Created Army Yuan could control the troublesome insurgents. But Yuan suppressed the Boxer movement too vigorously, driving the Boxers out of Shandong and into neighboring Zhili toward Beijing. Moreover, by protecting missionaries and mollifying the German and British diplomats in Shandong, Yuan cultivated good relations with foreigners at a time when xenophobia was gripping the Court. During the early summer of 1900, Yuan resisted making military commitments in defense of Beijing and Tianjin against the impending invasion by an allied expeditionary force. Censorial attacks upon him for his conduct in Shandong were an indication that Yuan's suppression of the Boxers and his forcing them into Zhili, his attentiveness to foreign interests, and his reluctance to answer a call to arms were displeasing conservative officials in Beijing.[27]

During 1900 and 1901 Yuan also instituted a wide range of reforms in Shandong. They included reorganization of local Braves (*xiangyong*) into the Vanguard Division (*Xianfeng dui*) fashioned after the Newly Created Army; introduction of a Western-style school system; establishment of a college and military academies; reorganization of the salt monopoly; new taxes on salt, medicine, tobacco, wine, brokers, and pawnshops; and establishment of a mint and an Office of Commerce (*Shangwu ju*). The rhetoric of Yuan's reform memorials was brief and derivative of the thinking of more senior statesmen such as Zhang Zhi-dong, Li Hong-zhang, and Liu Kun-yi. Institutional reform, Yuan argued, was necessary to bring

26. *Shilu, juan* 434:12b, 444:11, 454:3a; YSKZZ, pp. 17-21; Yuan Shi-kai, *Yang-shouyuan zouyi jiyao* (YSYZY), *juan* 1:2-5, 9-11.

27. Chester Tan, *The Boxer Catastrophe* (New York, 1955), pp. 45-52; Liu Feng-han, *Wuwei jun*, pp. 578-602 and 786-87, and *Xinjian lujun*, pp. 330-46; Edmund S. Wehrle, *Britain, China, and the Anti-missionary Riots, 1891-1900* (Minneapolis, 1966), pp. 146-49; John Schrecker, *Imperialism and Chinese Nationalism*, pp. 130-39; *Yihetuan yundong shi lun cong* (Beijing, 1956), pp. 1-9.

wealth and power to the empire. Foreign loans and expertise should be utilized to the fullest, as long as China's sovereign rights were not compromised from the point of view of international law. These were themes to which Yuan would return repeatedly throughout the rest of his career. In retrospect, little was new or distinctive about Yuan's reform rhetoric nor was there much that was original about the content of his reform program *per se*. What impressed the Empress Dowager and contemporaries alike was Yuan's genius for getting results. He achieved more in the way of institutional reform in Shandong in two years than any other governor of that province in the history of the dynasty.[28]

In 1900 the Boxer Uprising, the siege of the legations, and the allied expedition against Tianjin and Beijing changed the political climate rapidly and dramatically. For a while in late summer, 1900, after the Court was driven into exile to the northwest (Xi'an) and before Li Hong-zhang returned as Zhili governor-general and commissioner for the northern ports, Yuan Shi-kai's yamen in Jinan, the capital of Shandong, served as a communications center for the central government in North China.[29] By 1901, with the allied powers still occupying Beijing and Tianjin, the Empress Dowager and her Court had a forced conversion to institutional reform along the lines of what Yuan was implementing in Shandong. In the fall of 1901, after a treaty had been signed with the Allied Powers in September, Li Hong-zhang became fatally ill. According to rumor, Yuan was the favorite to replace Li in Zhili.[30] The factors which made Yuan seem the obvious choice are worth examining in detail.

The Influence of the Foreign Powers

Historians in China have emphasized the connection between the imperialist powers' backing of Yuan and his appointment to the Zhili posts. The late Shao Xun-zheng of Beijing University argued that the support which Yuan received from the Germans, English,

---

28. YSKZZ, pp. 35-37, 43-46, 66-68, 302-04, 307-09, 311-14; YSYZY, *juan* 9:20b-27b; *Shilu, juan* 485:19b; David D. Buck, *Urban Change in China*, chap. 3. See also Arthur J. Brown, *New Forces in Old China* (New York, 1904), pp. 338-46 (Mr. Brown toured Shandong and visited Yuan Shi-kai during the spring of 1901). For Yuan Shi-kai's concept of sovereign rights, see Schrecker, *Imperialism and Chinese Nationalism*.

29. Tan, chaps. 6 and 7.

30. *Peking and Tientsin Times* (PTT), Oct. 12 and Nov. 9, 1901; and *North China Herald* (NCH), July 3, Aug. 21, and Oct. 16, 1901.

and Americans determined his appointment. In Shandong, Yuan's suppression of the Boxers and his protection of foreigners in 1900, as well as his later reluctance to cooperate with pro-Boxer officials in Beijing, had earned him the backing of these powers. Moreover, Yuan was closely tied to the Germans, who were already in Shandong at Jiaozhou and seeking further concessions. A day before Li Hong-zhang died, the German ambassador in Beijing recommended to the Court that Yuan should succeed Li. Shao interpreted this German endorsement of Yuan as having determined the Empress Dowager's choice.[31]

Indeed, after 1900, the Empress Dowager was careful not to choose men for important provincial posts who were objectionable to the Powers. This was especially true just after the Boxer affair, when foreign ministers in Beijing protested successfully the appointment to high provincial posts of most Manchus and certain Chinese officials whom they considered to be Boxer sympathizers. In March, 1901, for example, the governor of Shanxi province, the Mongol bannerman Xi-liang, was removed from office because of foreign pressure. Likewise, the influence of the British was the critical factor in the selection of a new governor of Hubei province.[32] Thus the military presence of the foreign powers in Zhili certainly intimidated the Empress Dowager enough to assure that Li Hong-zhang's successor be a Chinese with diplomatic experience who had the confidence of one or more major powers. Rong-lu, for example, who was the Empress Dowager's closest Manchu advisor and might have been considered a candidate, was *persona non grata* with the Powers because he had commanded the troops that had surrounded the foreign legations in 1900.[33]

31. Hu Sheng, *Diguozhuyi yu Zhongguo zhengzi*, p. 186; Shao Xun-zheng, "Xinhai geming qian wushi . . . ," pp. 53-54; Zhang Zhi-dong, *Zhang Wenxianggong quanji* (Shucheng, 1928), *diangao, juan* 47:35, 48:6.
32. Roger Des Forges, *Hsi-liang and the Chinese National Revolution*, pp. 17-24; Daniel H. Bays, *China Enters the Twentieth Century*, p. 106. Des Forges demonstrates quite clearly that foreign opposition to Xi-liang (Hsi-liang) consistently thwarted his career after 1900.
33. Whether or not Rong-lu tried to restrain the Empress Dowager and in other ways protected the legations during the Boxer crisis are questions that will probably never be resolved. The Powers, and later historians, adopted a more generous view toward Rong-lu after his death, perhaps because of Yuan Shi-kai's persistent defense of him, which included the circulation of false diaries and other materials; see, for example, Tan, *The Boxer Catastrophe*, pp. 112-15, 135-36, and the influential but spurious J.O.P. Bland and Edmund Backhouse, *China Under the Empress Dowager*

The Powers, however, were not unified in their endorsement of Yuan. They were deeply divided into two camps: the Germans, British, Americans, and Japanese against the Russians, French, and Belgians. In October, 1900, the Germans and British signed a formal alliance. The British and Japanese were cooperating closely in anticipation of the Anglo-Japanese Alliance of 1902. And the Americans at this point were still following the British lead in their "open-door" China policy. On the other side, the Russians, French, and Belgians worked together as they were doing in Europe. Their partnership in China was eventually formalized in the Franco-Russian declaration of March 16, 1902.[34] Hostility in China between these two camps increased after 1900 as the Russians angled for greater control over Manchuria at the expense of the British and the Japanese. Reflecting this tension, fighting between the British and the Russians nearly broke out during a railway dispute in Tianjin in March, 1901.[35] It was not surprising, therefore, that there was considerable disagreement among the Powers about Yuan Shi-kai. The Russians and their allies thought well of Li Hong-zhang and his close associates. They were hostile to Yuan, preferring instead for the Zhili posts a protégé of Li Hong-zhang such as Zhou Fu.[36] On the other hand, the British and their allies considered Li too partisan toward the Russians. Yuan, with whom they enjoyed much better relations, was their choice to succeed Li in Zhili.[37] In his first interview after being appointed, Yuan was quick to acknowledge to the British minister, Sir Ernest Satow, his debt to the British and their allies:

> His Excellency Yuan Shih-kai thought that his appointment to the Viceroyalty of Chili—a post usually entrusted to senior Statesmen of higher standing—should be taken as an earnest of the Court's intentions. The Emperor was aware of his success in Shantung, the seed-bed of last year's troubles, and

---

(London, 1910). For extraordinary insights into the making of the latter, see Hugh Trevor-Roper, *Hermit of Peking* (London, 1977).

34. Lung Chang, *La Chine à l'aube de XXe siècle* (Paris, 1962), pp. 273-303; A. W. Griswold, *The Far Eastern Policy of the United States* (New Haven, 1938), chap. 2; Andrew Malezemoff, *Russian Far Eastern Policy, 1881-1904* (Berkeley and Los Angeles, 1958), p. 174; and L. K. Young, *British Policy in China, 1895-1902* (Oxford, 1970), pp. 193-318.

35. Lung Chang, p. 300; *British Parliamentary Papers*, vol. 91 (1901), China nos. 2 and 4.

36. B. A. Romanov (trans. Susan W. Jones), *Russia in Manchuria, 1892-1906* (Ann Arbor, 1952), pp. 232, 246.

37. *Times* (London), Nov. 9, 1901, p. 7.

that foreign nations placed some confidence in his powers and will. That was, no doubt, the special reason why he had been selected, and he thought that it ought to have some effect in removing foreign distrust. . . .[38]

With Beijing and Tianjin under occupation in 1901, the Empress Dowager and her government were at the mercy of the Powers. Still the Powers' preoccupation with outmaneuvering one another, and the resulting split over candidates for the Zhili posts, could have given the Empress Dowager some leeway in her decision. Yet at this point, in trying to play one "barbarian" against another, the Empress Dowager was leaning diplomatically toward the British and Germans, in hopes of frustrating Russian ambitions in Manchuria.[39] Thus one must conclude that the will of certain foreign powers, in particular the British and the Germans, was a very important factor influencing the Empress Dowager's choice. But there are two other important factors to also consider, namely, Yuan's military influence and his personal popularity at court and with the Empress Dowager.

Yuan Shi-kai's Military Power in 1901

It has been argued that the Empress Dowager had little choice but to appoint Yuan to succeed Li Hong-zhang in Zhili because Yuan's military control over Beijing and Zhili was a *fait accompli*.[40] By the end of 1900, three out of five divisions of the new Military Guards Army—those commanded by Nie Shi-cheng, Song Qing, and Rong-lu—had been defeated and dispersed by the allied expeditionary forces. A fourth division, commanded by Dong Fu-xiang, had accompanied the Empress Dowager and her Court to Xi'an where, due to pressure from the Powers, it was ordered to disband. Thus, the argument holds, by 1901 the only division intact was Yuan Shi-kai's Fifth or Right Division, which was in Shandong and had doubled in size. If true, this meant that in 1901 Yuan commanded the only force in north China capable of resisting Boxers, brigands, and foreigners who might threaten Beijing and its envi-

38. FO 405/118 (confidential prints), item no. 54, memorandum of interview between Sir E. Satow and Yuan Shih-k'ai, Acting Viceroy of Chihli (Zhili), Dec. 5, 1901, pp. 24 ff.
39. Bays, *China Enters the Twentieth Century*, pp. 105-06.
40. The clearest presentation of this thesis has been by Hatano Yoshihiro, "Hokuyō gumbatsu no seiritsu katei," pp. 238-39; see also Powell, *The Rise of Chinese Military Power*, pp. 125-26, 138.

rons. Moreover, this seemed to be a function which Yuan's troops were already performing; before his appointment in 1901, one of Yuan's commanders, Jiang Gui-ti, was policing Beijing with 3,000 of Yuan's Shandong troops. But the actual military situation in north China during 1901, and especially in Zhili province, was much more complicated than the above suggests.

In the spring of 1901, as the Powers began to withdraw troops, there were serious problems in Zhili with Boxers, wandering bands of brigands, and sporadic uprisings in various villages.[41] In order to establish order and to convince the foreigners that they should continue to withdraw troops, Li Hong-zhang raised and armed troops from remnants of his old Huai Army and other units from the south. In charge of the army and of restoring order in the province were Lu Ben-yuan and Mei Dong-yi, Huai Army commanders whose loyalties to Li dated back to the 1860s.[42] Plundering more than policing, Lu and Mei's force of 10,000 to 15,000 men failed to restore order in Zhili.[43] It became necessary for Li to call in additional troops from neighboring provinces. Available were three large, well-armed, and relatively well-disciplined armies commanded by Dong Fu-xiang, Ma Yu-kun, and Yuan Shi-kai respectively.

In 1900 at the insistence of the foreign powers, Dong Fu-xiang had been nominally stripped of his command and his army disbanded. But, in fact, Dong had proceeded to Ningxia on the Gansu-Mongolia border with most of his former troops (perhaps 20,000 in number). The foreign community in north China considered the continued existence of Dong and his army in Gansu to threaten a revival of a Boxer-like antiforeign movement. Therefore for Li Hong-zhang to call Dong and his men back to Zhili risked foreign intervention, another war, and the probable reoccupation of the province by the Powers.[44] Ma Yu-kun's and Yuan Shi-kai's armies were more realistic possibilities.

Since the 1860s Ma Yu-kun had served under Song Qing as

---

41. YSKZZ, pp. 718-19; Li Hong-zhang, *zougao, juan* 80:30; PTT, Feb. 16 and 23, March 2, April 20, and June 29, 1901.

42. Li Hong-zhang, *zougao, juan* 80:8a; Wang Er-ming, *Huai junzhi*, pp. 159-60, 364-65; Fei Xing-jian, *Jindai mingren xiaochuan* (Shanghai, 1920), p. 351; QS, p. 355; PTT, Sept. 4 and Dec. 1, 1900; NCH, Nov. 14, 1900, and Nov. 13, 1901.

43. *Yihetuan dangan shiliao* (Beijing, 1959), vol. 2, pp. 1136, 1141; PTT, July 16 and 27, 1901.

44. Liu Feng-han, *Wuwei jun*, pp. 760-62; PTT, March 23, 1901; Hosea B. Morse, *The International Relations of the Chinese Empire* (London, 1918), vol. 3, pp. 341, 348.

deputy commander of the *Yijun*, which had been a division, numbering about 15,000 men, of the Military Guards Army between 1898 and 1900. After the battle of Tianjin in August, 1900, Ma reassembled a force of more than 10,000 men from remnants of the *Yijun* and Nie Shi-cheng's and Rong-lu's defeated units. Song Qing was still nominally commander of this new *Yijun*, but Song was 80 years old and in bad health; actual command lay with Ma. Ma and his army accompanied the Empress Dowager in flight from Beijing as far as Shanxi province. Ma then remained in Shanxi as commander-in-chief (*tidu*) of the province, almost colliding in March, 1901, with a German expedition at the Zhili-Shanxi border.[45]

As governor of Shandong between 1899 and 1901, Yuan Shi-kai had doubled the number of troops under his command. As noted earlier, at Jinan he retrained about 10,000 local braves to become the Vanguard Division of the army. This new division was similar to Yuan's Newly Created Army in terms of pay scale, organization, armament, and discipline. However, there were important differences: officers and men were of lower quality, being recruits from existing traditional local units; financing was from local provincial revenues, not from Beijing; and the Vanguard's appearance was more ragged because of irregularities in equipment, particularly uniforms.[46] In addition, in 1901 Yuan managed to have 3,000 men from Liu Kun-yi's Western-style Self-Strengthening Army (*Ziqiang jun*) transferred north to his control.[47] Thus by the eve of Yuan's appointment to the Zhili posts, he commanded a force of approximately 20,000 well-trained men which was generally regarded as the best army in the Empire.[48]

In the spring of 1901, recognizing the need for a substantial number of troops to reestablish order in Zhili, Li Hong-zhang requested that Ma Yu-kun's entire army and a few units of Yuan Shi-kai's force be sent to Zhili. Li's request, first suggested by him in February but not formally made until May 28, 1901, was couched in terms of the need to insure order in the capital and its environs as the foreign troops withdrew.[49] Ma Yu-kun's troops were to

45. Liu Feng-han, *Wuwei jun*, pp. 409-36, 479, 737-41, 769-76; Wang Yan-wei and Wang Liang, eds., *Xixun da shiji* (Beijing, 1933), juan 5:36-38; PTT, March 30, 1901.
46. Liu Feng-han, *Xinjian lujun*, pp. 317-29.
47. *Shilu*, juan 484:1b-2a and 485:10a; Liu Feng-han, *Wuwei jun*, pp. 787-88; PTT, Aug. 24, 1901; NCH, Oct. 9 and Sept. 25, 1901.
48. See, for example, Brown, *New Forces*, pp. 84-98.
49. Wang Yan-wei and Wang Liang, juan 5:39-40; Li Hong-zhang, *zougao*, juan 80:32-33a.

protect the approaches to the city, most of them to be stationed along the railway line from Tianjin to Beijing. Yuan Shi-kai was instructed to send Jiang Gui-ti, who once had been associated with Li and his Huai Army, with 3,000 men to Beijing.[50] Jiang's troops were to serve in Beijing as a special police force under the general direction of Hu Yu-fen, an elder statesman with whom Yuan was on good terms.[51] Ma and Jiang led their troops into Zhili in June, 1901, and thereafter appeared to have carried the main burden of pacifying the entire province. But it was not until mid-September, when order appeared to have been restored to the countryside, that Ma and Jiang's troops actually took up positions in Beijing.[52]

We should note that Li Hong-zhang received most of the necessary outside help from Ma Yu-kun and the *Yijun*, not from Yuan Shi-kai, whom Li never forgave for his betrayal in 1894. Ma Yu-kun's troops in Zhili outnumbered Jiang Gui-ti's by at least four to one. Moreover, Ma was higher in the chain of command than Jiang and in October, 1901, replaced Lu Ben-yuan as commander-in-chief of Zhili province.[53]

Thus military necessity, like diplomatic necessity, did not absolutely dictate that Yuan Shi-kai succeed Li Hong-zhang in Zhili. Yuan Shi-kai's troops were not already occupying Zhili province and theirs was only a token presence in Beijing. Nor did Yuan command the only force in north China of any strength. Besides the incompetent Huai Army units in Zhili, there was the reconstituted *Yijun* commanded by Ma Yu-kun and, in Gansu, Dong Fu-xiang's army in exile. Ma Yu-kun's and Dong Fu-xiang's troops, if combined, would have outnumbered Yuan's forces in Shandong by about two to one. On the other hand, Yuan commanded the largest—and by far the best—single army in the empire. Its utility was well understood by the Empress Dowager, who had learned from her *coup d'état* of 1898 the importance of having at hand a major force whose commander she could trust.

50. Liu Feng-han, *Wuwei jun*, pp. 461-62.
51. QS, p. 4928; *Times* (London), May 29, 1901, p. 3. Yuan replaced Hu in 1896 as commander of the Newly Created Army, and after 1901 Yuan cooperated with Hu in the administration of the Peking-Mukden (Beijing-Shenyang) Railway.
52. Li Hong-zhang, *zougao*, juan 80:84; *diangao*, juan 39:8a, 10a, 22; Wang Yan-wei and Wang Liang, *juan* 9:13b-14; PTT, July 27, Aug. 17 and 24, and Sept. 7, 14, 21, and 23, 1901; NCH, July 24, Oct. 9 and 23, and Nov. 13, 1901.
53. Li Hong-zhang, *zougao*, juan 80:84; PTT, Oct. 19, 1901.

Court Politics and the Empress Dowager

It was the Empress Dowager's personal trust which assured Yuan Shi-kai his appointment to the Zhili posts, and this in turn hinged on the strength of Yuan's position at her Court in exile. The key to both was Yuan's alliance with the Manchu court politician Rong-lu, a grand councillor since the *coup* of 1898 and the most important single figure around the Empress Dowager until his death in 1903. Rong-lu's power at Court between 1898 and 1903 has been compared to that of Yi-xin and Yi-huan (Prince Gong and Prince Chun) during the reign of the Tong-zhi emperor.[54]

The events of 1900, including the Boxer disturbances in north China, the occupation and sacking of Beijing and Tianjin by the powers, and forced exile to Xi'an, were an even greater trauma for the Empress Dowager than the threat posed by the Guang-xu Emperor and the reformers in 1898. She and Rong-lu had at least tacitly sided with the Boxers. Yet the dynasty and her regency survived. By the fall of 1901 the Empress Dowager was once again in control of her Court and Empire. This she accomplished by accommodating the foreign powers' demands for repentance and reform and by shifting the blame for what had happened to a pro-Boxer faction at court.

Compared to the last decade of the Qing, court and bureaucratic politics in Beijing during the Empress Dowager's reign in the late nineteenth century have been relatively well studied. In the process a consensus has emerged that the Empress Dowager ruled by balancing two or more contending factions at Court, each of which consisted of a mixture of Manchu and high Chinese officials.[55] Between 1898 and 1900, Manchus Zai-yi and Gang-yi combined with such high Chinese officials as Xu Tong and Zhao Shu-giao as the faction sympathetic to the Boxer movement. In opposition were two factions: one of Rong-lu and his Chinese allies like Yuan Shi-kai, and the other led by Prince Qing and Li Hong-zhang. A strategically timed shift of support during the summer of 1900 from the former faction to the latter two enabled the Empress

---

54. See, for example, Fang Chao-ying's biography of Rong-lu in Hummel, pp. 405-09.

55. Wu Xiang-xiang, *Wan Qing gongding shiji* (Taibei, 1952); Lloyd Eastman, *Throne and Mandarins* (Cambridge, Mass., 1967); Cohen and Schrecker, *Reform in Nineteenth-Century China*, esp. Kwang-Ching Liu, "Politics, Intellectual Outlook, and Reform: The T'ung-wen kuan Controversy of 1867," pp. 87-100, and Schrecker, "The Reform Movement of 1898 and the Ch'ing-i."

Dowager to control her Court and to deflect responsibility for the Boxer rampage and the foreign occupation away from herself and onto Zai-yi's losing faction, which she subsequently purged altogether.[56]

By 1901 the makeup of the Empress Dowager's Court in exile had drastically changed. The Boxer sympathizers (Zai-yi, his brother Zai-lan, Ying-nian, Zhao Shu-jiao, Yu-xian, Zai-xun, Xu Tong, and Gang-yi) were retired or dead. New grand councillors Qu Hong-ji and Li Hong-zhang, her plenipotentiaries in Beijing negotiating the Empress Dowager's most important advisory body on matters of state. She was also in daily contact by telegraph with Prince Qing and Li Hong-zhang, her plenipotentiaries in Beijing negotiating the Boxer Protocol with the Allied Powers. Now the two major opposing factions were under the leadership of Rong-lu and Prince Qing respectively. Added to this was the direct participation of the Powers for the first time in Beijing factional politics. The Germans, British, and their allies sided with Rong-lu and his faction against Prince Qing and Li Hong-zhang, who were supported by the Russians and their allies. In striking contrast to the 1890s, ideological differences between these two major factions seemed to have been minimal.[57]

The question of who should succeed Li Hong-zhang in Zhili was one of the issues dividing the two factions and their foreign supporters. Besides Rong-lu, traveling with the Empress Dowager and supporting Yuan's appointment to the Zhili posts were grand councillors Lu Chuan-lin, Wang Wen-shao, and Qu Hong-ji. Lu Chuan-lin (1836-1910) was an able senior official who had risen gradually up the bureaucratic ladder to governor-general of Liang-jiang in September, 1900, when at Rong-lu's suggestion, the Em-

56. For detailed accounts of the shift, see Tan, *passim*; Hummel, pp. 393-94, 405-09; and Xiao Yi-shan, pp. 2242-46, 2249-53.

57. Also traveling with the Empress Dowager was her chief eunuch, Li Lian-ying, who was rumored to have played an advisory role in matters of state, especially during the Court exile in Xi'an. See, for example, the numerous references to him in the works of Wu Yong and of Bland and Backhouse. There is no concrete evidence, however, that Li Lian-ying's opinion was as important as that of the grand councillors in such matters as the appointment of Li Hong-zhang's successor in Zhili. Regardless, Li Lian-ying was known to favor openly those who regularly bribed him with presents, and for this reason his relations with Rong-lu were good. Later on, he became good friends also with Yuan Shi-kai, who was not averse to bribing when necessary. On bribing Li Lian-ying in this period, see Des Forges, *Hsi-liang and the Chinese National Revolution*, p. 26, and Rosemary Quested, *The Russo-Chinese Bank* (Birmingham, 1977), p. 59.

press Dowager appointed him to the Grand Council. His brother-in-law and close confidant was Zhang Zhi-dong, who likewise seemed tacitly to support Yuan's appointment.[58] Wang Wen-shao (1829-1908) had been of direct assistance to Yuan's career in Beijing in 1894-95 and had continued to help him as governor-general of Zhili from 1895 to 1898, when Yuan was training the Newly Created Army at Xiaozhan. A grand councillor since 1898, Wang was now old and in poor health. He had consistently sided with Rong-lu in court politics since 1895. Thus, although Wang was less obligated to Rong-lu than Lu Chuan-lin, he probably was just as willing to accept Rong-lu's choice of Yuan to succeed Li Hong-zhang.[59]

Qu Hong-ji (1850-1918) had a stronger personality and might have opposed Yuan's appointment had he dared to cross Rong-lu. Qu was a brilliant scholar, receiving a *jinshi* degree in 1870 at the age of twenty. But for the next twenty-five years his bureaucratic career was relatively undistinguished (perhaps because of his age) until 1897 when Li Hong-cao recommended his appointment as provincial director of education (*xuezheng*) of Jiangsu. The latter's support and Qu's apparent friendship with Wang Kang-nian suggests association with *qingyi* reformers of a less radical bent than Kang You-wei and Liang Qi-chao. Qu served in Jiangsu until late in 1900 when he was ordered to report to the Empress Dowager's court in Xi'an. Because of Rong-lu's endorsement, Qu was appointed in rapid succession (and sometimes concurrently): vice-president of the Board of Rites, president of the Censorate (*zuo du yushi*), president of the Board of Works, and then in May, 1901, grand councillor and one of four members on a new Bureau of Government Affairs (*zhengwu chu*), created to coordinate the administration of reforms. Later, as spokesman for the "Hunan faction" at Court, Qu became one of the three or four most influential officials in the Empire and, as we shall see in Chapter 3, a leading opponent of Yuan Shi-kai. Qu may have opposed Yuan as early as November, 1901, but he was not willing to do so publicly and anger Rong-lu, to whom he owed his central government appointments and position on the Grand Council.[60]

58. Chen Kui-long, *Mengjiao*, juan 2:22b; QS, pp. 4909-10; Bays, *China Enters the Twentieth Century*, pp. 105-07, 112.

59. QS, pp. 4904-05; Liu Hou-sheng, *Zhang Jian zhuanji*, p. 130.

60. Xu Yi-shi, "Qu Hong-ji yu Zhang Bai-xi," *Yishi danhui*, pp. 112-27; QS, p. 4905; Wu Yong, pp. 123-24. Both *chu* and *ju* can mean bureau or office. In the following, *chu* is translated as bureau and *ju* as office.

The opposition to Yuan's appointment was led by Prince Qing and Li Hong-zhang in Beijing. Yi-kuang or Prince Qing (1836-1916) was a grandson of the original Prince Qing (Yong-lin). He held his first important office in 1884 when he inherited the family title and replaced Prince Gong (or Yi-xin) as the head of the Zongli Yamen. Prince Qing continued thereafter to hold high posts in Beijing but never seemed to wield significant political power until after 1898, when he emerged at court as a leader in opposition to Rong-lu. In 1899, for example, Rong-lu and Prince Qing clashed over the former's opposition to the appointment of Li Hong-zhang as Zhili governor-general. Thus, in 1901 it was Prince Qing's rivalry with Rong-lu and his alliance with the Russians through Li Hong-zhang which dictated his opposition to Yuan's appointment to the Zhili posts.[61]

As for Li Hong-zhang, his opposition to Yuan was more personal, involving the grudge which ran back to the Sino-Japanese War of 1894-95. It is alleged that on the day he died, Li dictated to You Shi-mei, his secretary, a memorial recommending that Yuan Shi-kai succeed him as Zhili governor-general. Li is supposed to have said: "Looking around the whole Empire, I see Yuan Shi-kai standing head and shoulders above the rest."[62] However, considering Li's deeply-felt enmity for Yuan, and the fact that they apparently had been rivals a year earlier (late summer of 1900) for the Zhili appointments, this seems unlikely.[63] In 1900-01, as governor-general and governor of neighboring provinces, Li and Yuan rarely cooperated or corresponded. Neither among Li's published papers nor among court records is there any trace of a memorial in which Li recommended Yuan for the Zhili posts. Moreover, Rong-lu was opposed to Li in court politics, making it doubly unlikely that Li

---

61. Hummel, pp. 964-65; Shen Yun-long, "Zhangwo wanqing zhangbing zhi Yi-kuang," *Xiandai zhengzhi renwu shuping* (Taibei, 1966), 2:70; Morse, *International Relations*, vol. 3, pp. 173, 181, 191, 200; NCH, Nov. 13, 1901; Bays, *China Enters the Twentieth Century*, p. 111.

62. Ch'en, *Yuan Shih-k'ai* (1961), p. 73; and Li Chien-nung, *The Political History of China, 1840-1928* (Princeton, 1956), pp. 186-87. A more contemporary source is Luo Dun-yong, "Gengzi guobian ji" in Zuo Shun-sheng, comp., *Zhongguo jinbai nian shi ziliao* (Shanghai, 1926), pp. 533-34. Quite possibly the source of the story was Yuan Shi-kai himself; see his authorized biography, *Rongan dizi ji*, juan 3:1a, and Xiao Yi-shan, p. 2249. Ironically, in the pose of inheriting Li Hong-zhang's legacy, Yuan praised Li's memory on a number of occasions and supported the erection of a monument to Li in Tianjin in 1903; YSKZZ, pp. 345, 713, 966-67.

63. Sheng Xuan-huai, *Yuzhai cungao* (Wujin, 1939), juan 37:17a; Ch'en, *Yuan Shih-k'ai* (1972), p. 50.

would support Yuan, who was clearly Rong-lu's candidate.[64]

In October, 1901, the Empress Dowager left Xi'an for Beijing, returning from exile by permission of the Powers. The influence of Rong-lu at the time—and of the Germans and British—was definitely on the ascendancy. The two other senior officials with influence at her Court, Liu Kun-yi and Zhang Zhi-dong, had no objections to Yuan's appointment to the Zhili posts.[65] Thus isolated in Beijing, Prince Qing and Li Hong-zhang were a minority of two, with their ability to persuade seriously hampered by the distance between them and the Empress Dowager on the road between Xi'an and Beijing.

Finally, the Empress Dowager had good reasons of her own for appointing Yuan Shi-kai to the Zhili posts. In 1901 she held Yuan in even higher personal esteem than she had after her *coup d'etat* of 1898. In part this was because Yuan made timely contributions to the Empress Dowager's treasury in 1900 and 1901. On August 29, 1900, while she was in flight to Xi'an, Yuan forwarded to her 100,000 taels of Shandong tax revenues and 160,000 taels of revenues being sent to Beijing from Anhui and Jiangsu provinces which Yuan intercepted and diverted to Xi'an.[66] A few weeks later Yuan sent 100,000 taels more from Shandong's coffers and 37,000 taels collected from local gentry.[67] Yuan's contributions were apparently the largest made by any single official.[68] A year later, the relatively poor province of Shandong contributed the second largest share to the Boxer indemnity fund for 1901, the payment of which helped to reestablish the Empress Dowager's credibility with the foreign powers.[69] But more important than monetary contributions were Yuan's proven talents and influence as a diplomat and military commander.

Basically, like Yuan Shi-kai, the Empress Dowager was a realist, a pragmatic political tactician with an instinct for survival and intrigue. As Sue Fawn has rightly pointed out, traditional political histories of this period which emphasize the influence of personal

64. Xu Yi-shi, "Rong-lu yu Yuan Shi-kai," pp. 110-11.
65. Bays, *China Enters the Twentieth Century*, pp. 105-06, 110-12; Zhang Zhi-dong, *diangao, juan* 47:35, 48:6.
66. YSYZY, *juan* 6:8.
67. *Rongan dizi ji, juan* 2:19b-20a; *Shilu, juan* 470:5b.
68. Liu Hou-sheng, p. 113.
69. Luo Yu-dong, "Guangxu chao bujiu caizheng zhi fangce," p. 246; Ch'en, *Yuan Shih-k'ai* (1972), p. 51.

flattery, sex, and bribery upon her state decisions are misleading.[70] To remain in power for almost fifty years, as she did, required political sophistication which was superior to that of most Manchu nobles around her. Witness the fact that soon after the Empress Dowager's death in 1908, petty squabbles and jealousies amongst Manchus and splits over substantive issues between Manchus and Chinese engulfed the Court and bureaucracy in Beijing, leading directly to the collapse of the dynasty in 1911-12.[71] As a female ruler, the Empress Dowager's monarchical power was not legitimate in the eyes of many, if not most, of the male officials around her and of course she understood this very well.[72] To survive as an usurper, she had to balance factions at Court, never going too far in favoring one faction over another for fear of losing control and —ultimately—being removed from power. After the Boxer debacle of 1900, she was acutely aware as well of the foreign powers' potential for removing her. Therefore, especially after 1900, consistency on such issues as institutional reform mattered much less to her than the realities of political power; survival was her chief concern.

In order to continue her domination of the national power structure, the Empress Dowager wanted Yuan Shi-kai, with his considerable diplomatic skills and his army, near her in Zhili. Men like Xi-liang, Cen Chun-xuan, Duan-fang, Zhou Fu, Liu Kun-yi, and Qu Hong-ji were equally as energetic and reform minded. But they lacked experience in foreign affairs and/or were unacceptable to the British and the Germans. Moreover, the Powers insisted that the next Zhili governor-general be Chinese. The only other Chinese official with strong foreign backing was Zhang Zhi-dong. However Zhang did not command an army of comparable strength to Yuan's nor by statute could he serve in Zhili, the province of his birth. In the final analysis, it was a combination of Yuan's leadership of the largest modern army in the empire, his popularity with the British, Germans, and their allies, and the support his candidacy received from Rong-lu's dominant faction at Court which lifted Yuan above other possible candidates and made him the obvious choice.

70. Sue Fawn, "The Image of the Empress Dowager Tz'u-hsi," in Cohen and Schrecker, pp. 101-10.
71. See Chapter 6.
72. See, for example, Schrecker, "Reform Movement of 1898."

The appointment itself was made while the Empress Dowager was en route from Xi'an to Beijing. Arriving at Sishui in the mountains of northern Henan province, midway between Luoyang and Kaifeng, on November 6, 1901, she received a telegram from Li Hong-zhang stating that he was too seriously ill to perform his duties and that he had already ordered his judicial commissioner, Zhou Fu, to take over for him. On the next day, November 7, the Empress Dowager and her entourage stopped for the night in the small mountain village of Rongyang and received there a telegram from Zhou Fu reporting Li Hong-zhang's death. On that same day (November 7) she decreed that Yuan Shi-kai replace Li as Zhili governor-general and commissioner of trade for the northern ports.[73]

73. Xu Yi-shi, "Rong-lu yu Yuan Shi-kai," *Yishi danhui* (1945), pp. 110-11; Wang Yan-wei and Wang Liang, *juan* 10:46; Wu Yong, pp. 176-79.

CHAPTER II

Stabilizing Zhili: Yuan Shi-kai's First Years as Governor-General, 1901-1903

Yuan Shi-kai faced three very serious problems when he became governor-general of Zhili and commissioner of trade for the northern ports in November, 1901. Foreign troops occupied and governed the province's major city and provincial capital, Tianjin. Popular unrest was still widespread in the countryside. And thirdly, the provincial treasury he took over from Li Hong-zhang was bankrupt.

To further complicate the picture, Yuan had to spend the first month in office working in conjunction with General Ma Yu-kun on the costly and time-consuming effort of escorting the Empress Dowager and her traveling Court through troubled Zhili from the Henan border to Beijing. Early in December, the Empress Dowager and her entourage crossed into Zhili at Cizhou. Yuan preceded her, arranging each step of the Court's journey north.[1] At enormous expense, he prepared the 150-mile first leg by palanquin to Zhengding:

> Throughout its entire distance the road over which the Imperial palanquins were borne had been covered into a smooth,

1. YSKZZ, pp. 363-65; PTT, Dec. 21 (supplement) and 28 (supp.), 1901.

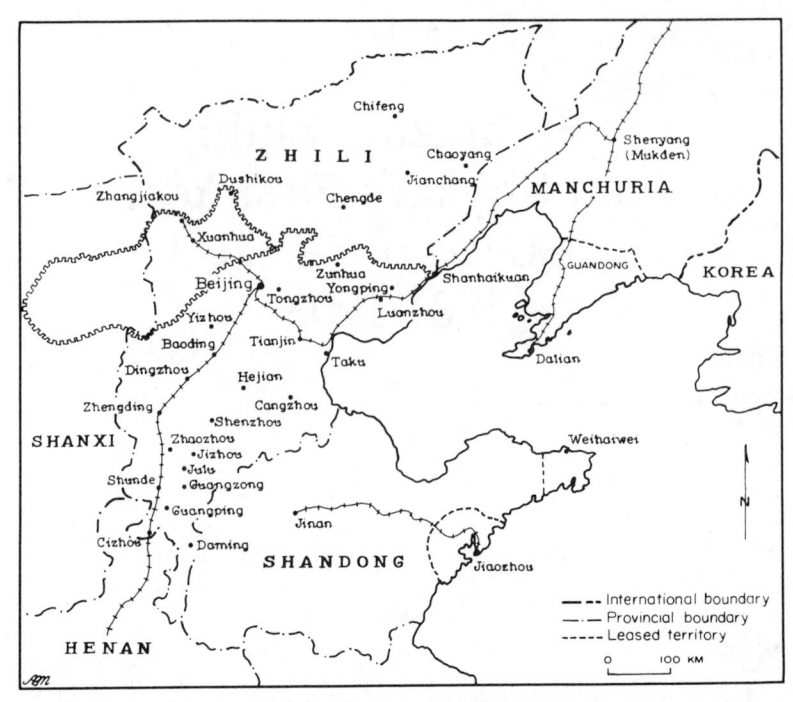

Zhili Province circa 1908

even surface of shining clay, soft and noiseless under foot; not only had every stone been removed, but as the procession approached gangs of men were employed in brushing the surface with feather brooms. At intervals of about ten miles well appointed resthouses had been built, where all manner of food was prepared. The cost of this King's highway, quite useless, of course, for ordinary traffic of the country, was stated by the native contractor to amount roughly to fifty Mexican dollars for every eight yards—say 1,000 English pounds a mile—the clay having to be carried in some places from a great distance.[2]

It was General Ma Yu-kun's responsibility to screen the Empress Dowager and her Court from the human misery and unrest so pervasive at the time in southern Zhili and, as we shall soon see, so near the exploding point. Units of General Ma's *Yijun* had been engaged in "bandit suppression" along the Henan-Zhili border since October. The Empress Dowager and her party finally arrived at

2. *Times* (London), March 13, 1902, p. 8.

Zhengding on January 3, 1902, and boarded a special train (of the new Beijing-Hankou Railway, then completed only as far as Zhengding) for Baoding, the temporary provincial capital. In Baoding, a city still in shambles from the ravages of a year before by foreign troops, Yuan and General Ma entertained the Empress Dowager and her Court lavishly. It must have been with considerable relief that Yuan left with the Empress Dowager by train for Beijing on January 7.[3]

Seemingly untroubled by foreigners or peasant disturbances, the Empress Dowager was pleased by the comfort, pomp, and incident-free quality of her trip north through Zhili. In Beijing she awarded Yuan a yellow jacket and reconfirmed his right to ride horseback in the Forbidden City as a Junior Guardian of the Heir Apparent (*Taizi shaobao*). In doing so, she allegedly told Yuan: "The lives of myself and my son have been saved by you alone."[4] However, for Yuan the real test lay ahead, with his political future dependent upon his ability as Zhili's chief administrator to solve the province's serious security and financial problems.

Yuan Shi-kai succeeded spectacularly, performing what seemed a miracle at the time. He restored Chinese government in Tianjin and stability to the province. But in the process, Yuan became frustrated by the military and financial limits which he was encountering in Zhili to the use and expansion of his political power. Moreover, for the quick recovery of Tianjin, he paid a political price which would color the rest of his career. Yuan made a pact with the British "foreign devils."

Negotiating the Withdrawal of Foreign Troops

Yuan Shi-kai's most celebrated achievement during his initial year in Zhili was negotiating the rapid evacuation by the powers of Tianjin and the Beijing-Shenyang Railway (Jing-Feng Tielu). Ironically, the story behind it is indicative of the reasons today Yuan is condemned as a *maiguo zei*—a "country-selling bandit." Tianjin was the administrative and economic capital of Zhili; the Beijing to Shenyang [Mukden] Railway, the only completed trunk line in north China, was of enormous economic and military value. Yuan

---

3. Sheng Xuan-huai, *Yuzhai cungao, juan* 56:30-1, 33; PTT, Jan. 11, 1902 (supp.); *Shilu, juan* 486:14, 487:4.

4. YSKZZ, p. 391; *Shilu, juan* 490:14b; Yuan Ke-wen, comp., *Danshang sicheng* (Taibei, 1966), p. 4.

recovered both quickly by striking a bargain with the British, whose influence dominated the forces occupying Tianjin and the railway.

Early in December 1901, during his first visit to Beijing as Zhili governor-general, Yuan asked the Powers to return Tianjin to Chinese control. The representatives of the Powers refused to consider the matter until the Empress Dowager and her Court returned to Beijing.[5] Once the Empress Dowager arrived on January 7, 1902, serious negotiations about Tianjin began. During the rest of January, Yuan concentrated on the subject in talks with the Powers' representatives in Beijing.[6] Their favorable response made a quick return of Tianjin seem possible. By the end of January there was general agreement among the Powers' diplomatic representatives for a speedy withdrawal. However, some Allied military commanders in north China, especially the German, feared a Boxer revival and were more reluctant to withdraw their troops. Only after heavy civilian pressure was applied did the Allied commanders agree on April 12, 1902, to the restoration of Tianjin, and then only after insisting on a list of twenty-eight conditions and two recommendations. These conditions were pared down by Western diplomats, and Yuan Shi-kai accepted them in July, 1902. On August 15, 1902, the Powers' Tianjin Provisional Government formally handed the city over to Yuan Shi-kai.[7]

Yuan was personally persuasive and impressive in his talks with the Powers, giving special attention to the British minister in Beijing, Sir Ernest Satow. In talks with Sir Ernest, using the American-educated customs *daotai* of Tianjin, Tang Shao-yi, as his interpreter, Yuan argued that only he himself "would be able to keep order in Tianjin, foster trade, and maintain the best relations with foreign nations." The commercial health of Tianjin was vitally important to the Powers because its customs revenues serviced foreign indemnities. Tianjin was important to Britain in particular because her trading interests there were the largest of the Powers. Civil disorder and economic depression in the area around the city were destroying confidence in Tianjin as a trading center. Yuan "was very much afraid that, unless confidence was quickly re-

    5. FO 405/118 (confidential print), February 1902, no. 54.
    6. FO 405/117 (conf. print), January 1902, nos. 47, 63, 64, 82; *Papers Relating to the Foreign Relations of the United States: 1902* (FRUS) (Washington, 1903), p. 184.
    7. YSKZZ, pp. 646-48; *The International Relations of the Chinese Empire*, vol. 3, pp. 364-65; FRUS, pp. 184-200; FO 228/1464, Consul-general Hopkins, no. 43.

stored, the port of Tianjin would suffer permanent injury." Yuan warned that much of Tianjin's old trade might be lost to the Yangzi ports. Only a governor-general with control over all Zhili and hence with greater resources at hand could restore Tianjin. Yuan "was anxious to be in a position to discharge his functions as Viceroy, and restore tranquility and confidence to the principal city in his jurisdiction."[8]

The foreign community in Tianjin was also impressed by the responsible image that Yuan's new administration projected. The *Peking and Tientsin Times*, published in English in Tianjin, reflected the interests of the foreign community there. Initially, the paper opposed rapid return of Chinese administration to Tianjin, arguing that even the Chinese residents of the city agreed that a Chinese government would be incapable of maintaining order and public works (such as the dredging of Taku Bar and paved roads) sufficiently for the reestablishment of Tianjin as the thriving commerical capital of north China.[9] However, esteem for Yuan's administration grew; by the summer of 1902 the paper was optimistic about the prospect of having a Chinese administration in Tianjin run by Yuan Shi-kai.[10]

In addition, there was a trade-off between regaining Tianjin and letting the British have their way with the Beijing-Shenyang Railway. Having loaned the capital for construction, a British corporation had controlled the Beijing-Shenyang Railway under cover of a nominally Chinese administration since 1898. From 1900 to 1902 British and Russian military forces occupied sections of the railway southwest and northeast respectively of Shanhaiguan. During the spring of 1902 the British sought to negotiate their withdrawal from the section of the railway they occupied, and obtain a new administrative agreement for the railway which would insure British control over the railway more clearly than the 1898 agreement.[11]

Yuan and Hu Yu-fen had been associated, directly or indirectly, with the Beijing-Shenyang Railway since 1898. Hu Yu-fen had been the principal Chinese administrator of the railway between 1898 and 1900. One of Yuan's closest associates, Tang Shao-yi, had

8. FO 405/118 (conf. print), February 1902, no. 54; memorandum of an interview between Sir E. Satow and Yuan Shi-Kai, Dec. 2, 1901, nos. 24 ff.
9. PTT, April 12 and June 15, 1901, and Jan. 4, 1902.
10. PTT, April 26, May 17, July 26, and Aug. 2, 1902.
11. Arthur Rosenbaum, "Imperialism and Chinese Railway Policy: The Peking-Mukden Railway, 1895-1911," *Ch'ing-shih wen-t'i* 2.1 (October 1969):38-70.

been chief of Hu's foreign-language secretariat (*Yangwen zongban*). One source indicates that Yuan himself had also been active in the administration of the railway after 1898.[12] At any rate, early in January, 1902, the British insisted that Hu again be made one of the Chinese administrators of the railway. On January 10, 1902, the Court appointed Hu and Yuan to be administrators-general of the railway, empowered to negotiate a new agreement with the British.[13]

The agreement that Yuan and Hu signed on April 29, 1902, gave the British what they wanted and angered the Russians, for in addition to getting clearer administrative control over the existing railway, the British seemed to gain control over all new branch lines. The Russians had just agreed on April 8, 1902, to withdraw from their section of the railway within the next six months, and they were angry because they had been led to believe that they could construct and hence control at least one of the railway's proposed branches (preferably the Beijing-Zhangjiakou line).[14]

As a result, the Russians did not wish to hand over their section of the Beijing-Shenyang Railway to Yuan, whose partiality for the British they believed had been demonstrated in the April 29 agreement. They delayed the railway's return on the pretext of the seriousness of the bandit problems between Shanhaiguan and Shenyang. Then suddenly, in late September, 1902, the Russians decided to hand over the railway at Shanhaiguan to Zeng-qi, the Tartar General of Fengtian (then Shengjing) province. Yuan immediately protested to the Ministry of Foreign Affairs and sent his own representative, Yang Shih-qi, to Shanhaiguan. On September 29, 1902, Zeng-qi, who was worried about incurring Yuan's wrath, received the formal transfer of the railway from the Russians and handed it to Yang Shi-qi. On the same day at Shanhaiguan, the British transferred their section of the railway to Yang Shi-qi.[15] Later, in what was apparently an effort to improve relations with the Russians, Yuan travelled to Shanhaiguan and returned with Russian officials to Tianjin where he entertained them at a series of banquets.[16]

12. Jiaotong Bu, *Jiaotong shi* (Nanjing, 1930); *Luzheng bian*, 7:145, 171.
13. FO 405/118 (conf. print), February 1902, nos. 71, 113; DHXL, *juan* 171:1b.
14. FO 405/122 (conf. print), June 1902, nos. 14, 16, 98; 405/123 (conf. print), July 1902, nos. 20, 23, 24; DHXL, *juan* 173:3-4a.
15. YSKZZ, pp. 704-07; FO 405/127 (conf. print), November 1902, nos. 76, 78; 405/128 (conf. print), December 1902, nos. 24, 55.
16. PTT, Oct. 11 and 18, 1902. It is also possible that Yuan may have accepted

In the process of recovering Tianjin and accommodating the British over the Beijing-Shenyang Railway, Yuan became, in the words of London *Times* correspondent G. E. Morrison, "in closer touch with us than any official has been for many years."[17] Formal and informal contact was frequent, with each willing, as we shall see, to do the other favors, small and large. To the British, Yuan was their man; they now cared enough about him to intervene directly at Court in his defense if necessary.

The battle between the Powers over the Beijing-Shenyang Railway caused Yuan to be attacked at Court. After the Russians lodged a strong protest with the Ministry of Foreign Affairs over the April 29 agreement with the British, Prince Qing and Grand Councillor Qu Hong-ji drew up a memorial which denounced Yuan and Hu for conceding too much control over branch lines of the railway to the British. An edict was said to have been drafted secretly that reprimanded Yuan and Hu and demoted them in rank.[18]

In response, Satow, the British minister in Beijing, met personally with Prince Qing, stating that any attack on Yuan was an attack on him. Prince Qing assured Satow that Yuan and Hu would not be given any kind of official reprimand or punishment.[19] Working in Yuan's favor, in conjunction with British pressure on Prince Qing, was the factional struggle at Court. Prince Qing and Qu Hong-ji now openly opposed Yuan; but Yuan's staunch defender and patron, Rong-lu, rallied the other three members of the Grand Council—Lu Chuan-lin, Wang Wen-shao, and Na-tong.[20] In the end, Yuan and Hu emerged unscathed.

Ironically, the Russian protest and the denunciations by Prince Qing and Qu Hong-ji had the effect of turning the Beijing-Shenyang Railway situation into a personal triumph for Yuan. During the summer of 1902 when negotiations over the railway's new

---

bribes from the Russians at about this time; see Rosemary Quested, *The Russo-Chinese Bank*, pp. 59-60.

17. Lo Hui-min, ed., *The Correspondence of G. E. Morrison, 1895-1912* (hereafter cited as *Morrison Correspondence*) (Cambridge, 1976), p. 177 (Morrison to Bland, Feb. 1, 1902).

18. FO 405/123 (conf. print), July 1902, nos. 23, 24.

19. FO 405/123 (conf. print), July 1902, no. 20.

20. DHXL, *juan* 174:2b. It is indicative of the strength of the alliance between Yuan and Rong-lu that when Rong-lu was attacked for alleged pro-Boxer sympathies, Yuan vigorously defended him; YSYZY, *juan* 12:1-3; FO 405/119 (conf. print), March 1902, no. 10.

branches were reopened because of Russian pressure, the British relinquished control over the projected branch line from Beijing to Zhangjiakou on the condition that it be built solely with Chinese capital.[21] Thus by September, 1902, when the railway was formally returned, Yuan could take credit for its safe return, as well as the plan for a Chinese-owned and operated Beijing-Zhangjiakou branch.

But Yuan also paid a price for British support and cooperation. He now had to tolerate British interference in the internal affairs of Zhili province. For example, during the summer of 1902, Yuan tried to remove a corrupt and incompetent old crony of Li Hongzhang, Mei Dong-yi, who still commanded a small force at Cangzhou. At the instigation of local salt merchants and gentry in the Cangzhou area, the British minister in Beijing applied friendly pressure on Yuan, citing Mei's protection of missionary lives and property in 1900-01. Yuan was forced to retain Mei and to recommend his reward for meritorious conduct during the Boxer period.[22]

Regardless of such costs and the long-term political consequences, Yuan's pact with the British brought immediate political dividends. In Beijing the Empress Dowager was delighted with Yuan's success in negotiating the withdrawal of foreign troops from Tianjin and the Beijing-Shenyang Railway. Late in 1902 she allegedly made the following comment about Yuan and another favorite, Cen Chunxuan:

> Who would have thought that with the events of the year of 1900 which swept me up in disaster would be the opportunity for me to find two such loyal officials, one being Cen Chunxuan, the other being Yuan Shi-kai. Both were brave, courageous, and young. In the south, Cen pacified the disturbances in Guangdong and Guangxi for me; *in the north, Yuan dealt with the foreigners for me, recovering Beijing and Tianjin.* Although their years are very few, they are really able to accomplish things; for the next twenty years, I can rest easily without worrying.[23]

---

21. FO 405/124 (conf. print), August 1902, nos. 43, 75; also Rosenbaum, "Imperialism and Chinese Railway Policy."

22. PTT, Aug. 2, 1902; FO 405/118 (conf. print), February 1902, no. 59; YSKZZ, pp. 718, 721, 2181-83. For background on Mei Dong-yi, see Liu Feng-han, *Wuwei jun*, pp. 305-06.

23. Liu Hou-sheng, *Zhang Jian zhuanji*, p. 121, emphasis added.

In Zhili, the recovery of Tianjin and the railway put Yuan in a much better position to deal with the province's financial crisis. His attention was now drawn to other impediments to the exercise of full military control over the province.

Military Rivalry and the Suppression of Peasant Insurgents

Concurrently with negotiating with the Powers over Tianjin and the Beijing-Shenyang Railway, Yuan Shi-kai tried to quiet local unrest which was continuing in Zhili. Yuan considered "bandit suppression" an urgent matter, if only to convince the Powers that there was no longer any danger of Boxer-type insurrections getting out of control, and thus that withdrawal of their troops was justified. In southern Zhili, Yuan was eventually successful in quelling unrest by the ruthless application of scorched earth tactics by units of his Newly Created Army. But in northeast Zhili, where equally serious banditry and religious sect uprisings had been endemic since the 1890s, he could do little. Authority for "bandit suppression" in this region remained in the hands of General Ma Yu-kun and the *Yijun*. With the recovery of Tianjin and the Beijing-Shenyang Railway, Ma Yu-kun's and Yuan Shi-kai's rivalry for military control of the province became open.

In southern Zhili, the "allied villagers" (*lianzhuang hui*) insurrections that had troubled Li Hong-zhang's administration in 1901 continued to occur in 1902, presenting Yuan with much the same kind of problem that Li had faced. These insurrections originated as local protests against the levy of additional taxes said to be needed to meet the province's quotas for Boxer indemnity payments.[24] The first outbreak of this sort during Yuan's administration occurred in April, 1902, when an uprising of villagers at Jingding on the Beijing-Hankou Railway line was swiftly suppressed.[25] In the next month, May, an uprising in southwestern Zhili developed into the most serious disturbance faced by Yuan while governor-general.

24. YSKZZ, pp. 539, 718-19; PTT, June 29 and July 27 (supp.), 1901. Southwest Zhili had long been a hotbed of peasant organization and insurrection; see Susan Nacquin, *Millenarian Rebellion in China: Eight Trigrams Uprisings in 1813* (New Haven, 1976), and Dai Xuan-zhi, *Yihetuan yanjiu* (Taibei, 1963). On similar uprisings at about the same time in neighboring Henan province, see Roger Des Forges, *Hsi-liang and the Chinese National Revolution*, pp. 28-30; and on *lianzhuang hui* in general, see references in Jean Chesneaux, ed., *Popular Movements and Secret Societies in China, 1840-1950*.
25. PTT, May 3, 1902 (supp.).

The Empress Dowager had passed through southwestern Zhili on her way back to Beijing at about the time that signs of serious unrest in Julu, Wei, and Guangzong *xian* were first noticed. The area (east and southeast of Shunde, near the Shandong-Zhili border) was one of the poorest in the province and recently had been suffering from poor harvests.[26] In contrast to such poverty, the opulence of the Empress Dowager's passage through the area was outrageous. Indeed, a connection may have existed between the spectacle presented by the Empress Dowager and her entourage and the rebellion that erupted in these three districts a few months later.

The immediate causes of the rebellion, however, were oppressive taxes and Yuan's military conscription campaign. Guangzong, Wei, and Julu *xian* had been almost completely free of Boxer activity in 1900. Yet, in 1901 and 1902 opium, sugar, and tea taxes were raised and new cigarette, liquor, stamp, and special assessment taxes were added, allegedly to meet Zhili's quota of Boxer indemnity payments.[27] In Guangzong the *xian* magistrate also levied a heavy extra tax on each *mou* of land.[28] As early as the fall of 1901 in the Guangzong, Wei, and Julu area, there was considerable local indignation about the new taxes.[29] By the spring of 1902, when a severe drought seemed to portend another poor harvest, the situation became serious. Hostility was directed mainly against the government; but foreigners, too, became targets because of the indemnity issue. Moreover, Yuan had announced his intention to enlist 100-140 men from each *xian* in Zhili for a new division of his army. Clearly the threat and fact of forced conscription was also a cause of the rebellion.[30] One of the first incidents was the massacre of a local recruiter and his men.

The rebellion itself developed out of incidents which occurred in late April, 1902. On April 21 a Lieutenant Bao, who was in Wei *xian* recruiting troops for a new division, unwittingly entered the small village of Shatusi which a small band of determined insurrectionists led by Jing Ting-bin had just succeeded in capturing. Bao and sixty of his recruits were killed. Three days later, 1,500 of the old-

26. YSKZZ, pp. 539, 553; FRUS, pp. 167-69; PTT, May 10, 1902.
27. *Yihetuan yundong shi luncong*, p. 52.
28. *Guangzong xianzhi* (1933), *juan* 1:11a.
29. YSKZZ, pp. 414-16, 474, 623-24.
30. YSKZZ, p. 629; PTT, May 10, 1902. For more on the army and conscription, see Chapter 4.

style Huai and Green Standard Army soldiers marched from Nangong, a nearby prefecture capital, to avenge Bao; but they too were badly beaten. Then, on April 26, a French Catholic priest and some converts were killed; his head hung on the south gate of Jinian, a small village not far from Shatusi. By May, insurrection swept the area, with its center the district capital of Julu. Quite possibly, as many as 20,000 men took up arms against the government.[31]

It was Jing Ting-bin's leadership which gave the insurrection cohesion and force enough to become a full-blown rebellion. A native of Guangzong district, by then in his mid-50s, Jing had a military *juren* degree. He was deadly earnest and a fatalist about the rebellion. Anticipating defeat even before raising the cry of revolt —"Sweep out the Qing and destroy the foreigner" (*sao-Qing mie-yang*)—Jing killed all members of his family to spare them torture and execution by the state. Little wonder that in radical student circles of the time, Jing was admired as a revolutionary hero.[32]

Today Jing Ting-bin is depicted as a social as well as political revolutionary, suggesting that his rebellion involved class warfare.[33] Jing was a local elite or gentry member himself. Together with other local gentry, he initially met with the local magistrate to complain about oppressive taxation. Only later, toward the end of 1901, did Jing break with his gentry associates and call for rebellion, leading a growing number of peasant insurrectionists through the incidents narrated above.[34] No information has been found as yet on how the rebels treated local gentry in areas that they controlled. Thus the class character of the rebellion is not clear and requires further investigation.

Unquestionably the rebellion led by Jing Ting-bin alarmed the Court in Beijing. During May, 1902, apprehensive grand councillors repeatedly assured representatives of the Powers that the situation in southwestern Zhili was under control. The man responsible for controlling the situation, of course, was Yuan Shi-kai.[35]

Yuan reacted quickly and decisively. On May 7 he dispatched a trusted deputy, Duan Qi-rui, to the area with about 4,000 of his best Western-drilled and armed troops. Duan won a large battle at

31. YSKZZ, p. 533; FRUS, pp. 167-69; PTT, May 10 and 17 (supp.), 1902.
32. YSKZZ, pp. 604-09; *Yihetuan yundong shi luncong*, pp. 56-58.
33. *Yihetuan yundong shi luncong*, pp. 56-58.
34. YSKZZ, p. 623.

Julu and by the end of May, through scorched earth tactics, had suppressed the rebellion completely.[36] Late in July Jing Ting-bin was captured in northern Henan, executed, and his head displayed in the *xian* capital of Guangzong.[37]

Yuan and the foreign press applauded the behavior of Duan's troops in the disturbed areas because they refrained from pillaging.[38] However, the basic situation did not improve; it grew worse. By applying scorched earth tactics against the rebels, Duan had devastated much of Guangzong, Wei, and Julu *xians*.[39] By October, 1902, the area was in desperate economic condition, plagued by marauding gangs of disbanded soldiers, and neglected by Yuan's administration.[40]

On July 13, 1902, the Grand Council commented to the throne that they had received complaints about Yuan's severity in handling of the Jing Ting-bin rebellion.[41] The substance of the complaints was that oppressive taxation was the chief cause of the rebellion; hence, blame lay with local officials. More leniency, it was argued, should have been shown toward the people upon whom unjust exactions had been forced. The grand councillors asked that the offending officials be punished severely. Although indirect, these complaints constituted an attack upon Yuan's policies toward the rebellion and may well have been initiated by his enemies at Court, Prince Qing and Qu Hong-ji.

Yuan Shi-kai answered the charges in a long memorial to the throne.[42] Comparing the Jing Ting-bin rebels with the Boxers and the Taipings, he argued that in the past it had been necessary to deal severely with rebellions. Yuan's models were Zeng Guo-fan and Hu Lin-yi. He quoted Hu Lin-yi as saying: "If military resolve is not firm, then good people become contentious; how much more is it true for unruly people [*luan-min*]!" In this case, Yuan continued, punishment of local officials for their oppression of the people would be ludicrous. The problem was that local officials had been

---

35. FRUS, pp. 168-70; PTT, May 10, 1902; DHXL, *juan* 172:20b.
36. YSKZZ, pp. 533-37, 538-40; Wu Ting-xie, *Hefei zhizheng nianpu* (1938), *juan* 1:5b; PTT, May 17 (supp.), 1902.
37. PTT, Aug. 2, 1902.
38. YSKZZ, p. 625; PTT, June 21, 1902 (supp.).
39. FO 228/1464, Consul-general Hopkins to Satow, telegram no. 5, May 26, 1902.
40. PTT, Aug. 2 and Oct. 11, 1902.
41. DHXL, *juan* 174:2b.   42. YSKZZ, pp. 604-09.

too lenient with the rebels, who were irreconcilable, unsavory types (here Yuan cites the rebel slogan: "Sweep out the Qing and destroy the foreigner"). Yuan criticized local gentry for at first representing the rebels' grievances to the local officials. Yuan further insisted that the taxes local officials were asking the people to pay were not onerous. In Guangzong, for example, a significant portion of the amount required was raised from sources such as existing surpluses of educational and salt monopoly funds. Yuan related how at the time of the Empress Dowager's trip through southwestern Zhili he had gone to the disturbed area and dismissed incompetent officials. But local officials and gentry again proved weak, permitting Jing Ting-bin and his gang to prosper. Finally, when the old Huai and Green Standard Army units stationed in the area had completely failed to cope with the situation, Yuan had to send Duan Qi-rui with his troops. Duan quickly defeated the rebels and executed their principal leaders. Yuan ended the memorial by stating that now, with the rebellion thoroughly suppressed, he was ready to request tax exemptions and relief funds for the stricken area.[43]

The brutal suppression of Jing Ting-bin's rebellion ended the string of popular uprisings that had occurred in southern Zhili since the summer of 1900. Simultaneously a series of campaigns were launched to bring order to northeast Zhili. But this task the Empress Dowager entrusted to Ma Yu-kun, not to Yuan Shi-kai.

During the first year of Yuan's administration in Zhili, the military power of Ma Yu-kun and the *Yijun* was nearly equal to Yuan's. Li Hong-zhang had relied heavily upon Ma for military aid and had given him considerable military power in the province before Yuan was in office. Although nominally a subordinate of Yuan as Zhili's commander-in-chief, Ma was independent because of the personal favor he enjoyed with the Empress Dowager. Ma had accompanied the Empress Dowager on her flight from Beijing, and Ma and Yuan had shared responsibilities as protectors on her return trip through Zhili. In January, 1902, the Empress Dowager awarded Ma the title of Junior Guardian of the Heir Apparent, the same title she had bestowed on Yuan a month earlier. In February, Song Qing died and the Empress Dowager made Ma formally head of the *Yijun*, about 8,000 to 10,000 men stationed at Tongzhou (some fifteen miles east of Beijing). In addition, the *Yijun* was not dependent

43. See also later memorials, YSKZZ, pp. 622-25.

financially on Yuan; like Yuan's Newly Created Army, it was financed directly from Beijing.[44]

Banditry and religious sect uprisings had been rife in the area west and north of Shanhaiguan since the 1890s. Wanton killing and pillaging by large groups of bandits was an especially serious problem. Occasionally the insurgents overran large towns—causing concern in Beijing and Tianjin. An additional worry was that Russian troops might intervene from Manchuria to restore order, or that the unrest might be used by the Russians as an excuse to retain control of Russian-occupied sections of the Beijing-Shenyang Railway.[45]

In March, 1902, Ma Yu-kun opened an offensive against the traditional bandit and religious sect base at Zhaoyang in Jehol (about 100 miles north of Shanhaiguan), later also sending units to pursue bandits to the southwest of Shanhaiguan at Yongping. Not until the end of the year could Ma report that the situation was well under control and return to Tongzhou.[46]

Yuan Shi-kai and his troops played only a secondary role in the northeast. Their most important engagement was in March, 1902, against bandits whose raids in an area just east of Tongzhou had become serious enough to force the Empress Dowager to cancel a trip to the eastern ancestral tombs. By April, a contingent from the Newly Created Army had restored order to the area, and the Court made the trip to and from the tombs without incident.[47] In 1903 and afterwards, Yuan sent troops to help Ma Yu-kun in northeastern Zhili; but until his death in 1907 Ma remained in overall command of operations there.[48]

The Empress Dowager rewarded both Yuan Shi-kai and Ma Yu-kun for restoring order in Zhili. In June, 1902, after Yuan's sup-

44. See note 3, above, and *Shilu, juan* 490:18a, 510:7, 521:5; Liu Feng-han, *Wuwei jun*, pp. 432-36, 573-74, 769-77; FO 405/128 (conf. print), December 1902, no. 25.

45. *Rongan dizi ji, juan* 3:8a; YSKZZ, pp. 577, 605-06; DHXL, *juan* 171:22b; PTT, March 29 (supp.), May 24 (supp.), July 26, Aug. 2 and 16, and Sept. 6, 1902. For background, see Richard Shek's paper on the *Zaili* millenarian sect uprisings of 1891 in the Zhaoyang area, read at the Association of Asian Studies meeting, Washington, D.C., March 1978, and the International Ch'ing Archives Symposium, Taibei, July 1978. On the bandit problem in northeast Zhili and Manchuria generally, see Mark Mancall and Georges Jidkoff, "The Hung Hu-tsu of Northeast China," in Chesneaux, *Popular Movements*, pp. 125-34; and Des Forges, pp. 36-38.

46. *Shilu, juan* 497:15, 505:5, 510:7; Liu Feng-han, *Wuwei jun*, pp. 777-78; PTT, March 29, May 24 (supp.) and 31, June 21, Aug. 30, and Oct. 4 and 18, 1902.

47. PTT, March 15 (supp.) and 29 (supp.) and April 26, 1902.

48. YSKZZ, pp. 576, 644-46, 652-54; Liu Feng-han, *Wuwei jun*, pp. 778-80.

pression of the Jing Ting-bin rebellion and after the first phase of Ma's campaign against bandits in the northeast, the Empress Dowager regularized Yuan's appointment as Zhili governor-general and commissioner of trade for the northern ports and held a special audience honoring Ma Yu-kun for his bandit suppression activities.[49] Her actions signified again that Yuan and Ma shared military power in Zhili, as well as the role of protector of the Empress Dowager and her Court in Beijing.

The restoration of order in Zhili thus demonstrated Yuan Shi-kai's lack of military control over the province. Since he could not remove General Ma, Yuan's strategy was to isolate him as much as possible, using his influence in Beijing to keep Ma in the northeast, away from Tongzhou and from proximity to Beijing and the Empress Dowager. From the latter half of 1903 until his death in 1907, General Ma remained in the northeast, rarely returning to his headquarters at Tongzhou.[50] Within his sphere of influence in southern Zhili, Yuan was exceedingly ruthless in the suppression of peasant insurgencies. Reigns of terror like that which Yuan's lieutenant Duan Qi-rui unleashed against the Jing Ting-bin rebellion probably explain the paucity in Zhili of anti-reform tax rebellions like those prevalent elsewhere throughout the empire during the last decade of the dynasty.

Financial Difficulties

The bankrupt condition of the provincial treasury which Yuan Shi-kai inherited from Li Hong-zhang was as serious a problem for Yuan as the restoration of order and ending the occupation of Tianjin and the Beijing-Shenyang Railway by foreign troops. During his initial months in office, Yuan's administration was saved by the astronomical sum of 13.08 million taels that was raised in 1901 through the sale of offices. Although this money was earmarked for Beijing, Yuan was successful in getting permission to retain most of it to cover the province's enormous debt and meet immediate military expenses. But this was a temporary expedient; for Yuan's administration sale of offices was never fiscally significant again—netting only 74,000 taels in 1905 for example. By summer, 1902, his administration was destitute as expenses mounted. The Empress Dowager's return trip through southern Zhili alone cost 1.5 million taels, half of

49. DHXL, *juan* 173:10b; PTT, May 31 and June 21, 1902.
50. Liu Feng-han, *Wuwei jun*, pp. 573-74, 778-80.

which was defrayed by provincial funds.[51] Yuan may have hoped for a substantial windfall of surplus funds in August with the return of Tianjin by the Powers. Indeed, a small surplus was handed over by the British-dominated Temporary Provisional Government of Tianjin, but within a month it was consumed by the needs of the city itself.[52] By October, 1902, the emptiness of the Zhili treasury reached crisis proportions. Two hundred thousand taels were borrowed from the Shandong provincial treasury and the remaining deficit for the year had to be met, with special permission, from Zhili land taxes.[53] In such financial straits it was difficult for Yuan's administration to perform normal functions, let alone initiate the major military, economic, and educational reforms which are discussed in detail in chapters 4 and 5. Somehow Yuan had to find additional revenues. Trying first in Zhili in 1902-03, he had only limited success.

From any standpoint, Zhili's economy in the spring of 1902 was still prostrate from the disruptions of the Boxer era. Merchant hoarding and poor harvests had driven up grain and rice prices.[54] The volume of foreign trade reported at Tianjin was unusually small, and the surplus of imports over exports unusually large.[55] The currency market at Tianjin was in chaos; and local currencies were debased, accelerating further the rise in prices.[56] Many of the salt merchants at Changlu (or Cangzhou)—the center of salt trade in north China—were bankrupt.[57] There were serious problems with pauperism in such towns as Tongzhou.[58] Moreover, managerial control over important railway and mining enterprises such

51. YSKZZ, pp. 425-27, 601, 2319-20.
52. PTT, Sept. 13, 1902.
53. YSKZZ, pp. 512-15, 576-79, 591-92, 683-85; *Rongan dizi ji, juan* 3:2b-3a; PTT, Oct. 18, 1902.
54. PTT, March 29 (supp.), May 31, and June 21, 1902.
55. Imperial Maritime Customs, *Tientsin Decennial Report, 1892-1901* (Tianjin, 1905), p. 541; this report, delayed because of the Boxer disturbances, actually covers up to 1905. There is reason to doubt the accuracy of customs figures as a measure of foreign trade, since a part of the amounts shown represents intraport trade; see Rhoads Murphy, *The Treaty Ports and China's Modernization: What Went Wrong?* (Ann Arbor, 1970), pp. 44-46.
56. Jian Bo-zan et al., eds., *Yihetuan* (Shanghai, 1951), vol. 2, pp. 132-33; *Zhongguo jindai huobi shi ziliao* (Beijing, 1964), vol. 1, p. 913; PTT, April 26, May 10 and 24, Aug. 9, and Sept. 13, 1902; YSKZZ, pp. 744-46, 884-86.
57. FO 371/1092, Ambassador Jordan, no. 320 of Aug. 14, 1911.
58. PTT, Jan. 25 (supp.) and March 1 (supp.), 1902.

as the Kaiping mines and the Beijing-Shenyang Railway had fallen into the hands of foreigners.[59]

Rhoads Murphey and others argue that the commercial economy of treaty ports like Tianjin, which was hardest hit by the Boxer disruptions, was only loosely tied to economic life of the agricultural hinterland. The fact that the agricultural sector of Zhili's economy was the first to recover in the post-Boxer period supports this thesis. Although reliable figures on agricultural production are not available, we know that the value of agricultural land and wages in Zhili began rising again in 1902, an indication that the agricultural sector was returning to normal.[60] Grain prices also dropped during the year because of good weather and harvests, another good sign.[61] Beyond the restoration of order, did actions by Yuan's administration contribute significantly to the recovery of agriculture? Probably not. Throughout 1902, Yuan memorialized and was granted requests for general exemptions in the payment of land taxes (in Zhili such taxes were mostly in the form of *diding*) for much of the war-torn province. But in practice the effects of these exemptions seemed negligible. Ding *zhou* in south central Zhili is the only district for which we have good statistics on changing land tax burden. These show that, after an upward jump in 1900, land tax burden in Ding *zhou* remained about the same from 1901 through 1903.[62] In southwest Zhili we know that the land tax burden also increased dramatically in 1900-01, leading to the Jing Ting-bin rebellion in 1902.

There were few signs of revival in Zhili's commercial economy, of which Tianjin was the heart, until 1903. Soon after recovery of the city from the foreign powers in 1902, customs *daotai* Tang

59. Ellsworth Carlson, *The Kaiping Mines, 1877-1912* (Cambridge, Mass., 1957); Wang Xi, *Zhong Ying Kaiping Kuangquan jiaoshe* (Taibei, 1962); Rosenbaum, pp. 38-70.

60. Ramon Myers, *The Chinese Peasant Economy: Agricultural Development in Hopei and Shantung* (Cambridge, Mass., 1970), pp. 142-48. *Morrison Correspondence*, p. 267, notes an especially good harvest in Zhili in 1904, and available information on prices of goods also suggests that Zhili's agricultural economy had recovered by 1904; see Charles Gary Watson, "Economic Change and Development in Chihli: Preconditions and Early Growth of Handicraft Weaving in the Kaoyang Area, 1870-1914" (M.A. thesis, Arizona State University, 1976). For Rhoads Murphy's argument, see *The Outsiders*, chap. 11.

61. PTT, June 28 and Oct. 11, 1902.

62. YSKZZ, pp. 394-96, 509, 553, 593, 760-61, 787-88; *Shilu, juan* 492:15b, 504: 17b, 505:4a; PTT, Oct. 11 and 18, 1902; DHXL, *juan* 171:13a. On Ding *zhou*, see Wang Yeh-chien, *Land Taxation in Imperial China* (Cambridge, Mass., 1973), p. 126.

Shao-yi attempted to regulate native banking practices by limiting the premiums charged on loans, and tried to bolster the strength of local currency by negotiating currency loans from foreign banks, importing sound coin from other provinces, replacing spurious cash, and forbidding the export of silver.[63] But in general, trade conditions in Tianjin were reported to have been poor throughout 1902.[64] With the exception of rice, commodity prices continued to soar. Native bankers ignored Tang Shao-yi's limitations on the premiums to be charged on loans. Silver was being hoarded. In October, one-half million taels were imported into Tianjin as an emergency measure to strengthen the currency market.[65] Then, rather suddenly at the very end of the year, Tang's measures began to take hold and the commercial economy of Tianjin and the province began to move forward. The next year, 1903, turned out to be a more prosperous year than any in the immediate pre-Boxer era, despite the fact that inflation remained a serious problem and the local currency situation continued to be chaotic.[66]

Zhili's return to relative economic stability by 1903, however, did not produce significant increases in tax revenues for Yuan's administration. The reasons for this are complex, relating to tax structure and Yuan's lack of control over most of the revenues that taxes generated.

In the first place, whether prosperous or not, Zhili was poor in commercial revenues, compared to the wealthier Yangzi provinces to the south. Likin, an internal transit tax which had become the major source of provincial revenue in the south since the Taiping rebellion, produced comparatively meager revenues in Zhili. In 1903, for example, Zhili was reported to have collected about 182,295 taels in likin revenues. At the same time about 3.5 million taels were being collected in Jiangsu province. Of nineteen provinces for which 1903 figures are known, Zhili ranked sixteenth in likin collection.[67]

A potentially richer source of income for Yuan's administration might have been customs revenues. Tianjin was one of the four

63. PTT, Aug. 30, Sept. 6 and 13, and Oct. 11, 1902; YSKZZ, pp. 744-46, 884-86.
64. PTT, Sept. 13, 1902.
65. PTT, Sept. 6 and Oct. 11, 1902.
66. *Tientsin Decennial Report, 1892-1901*, pp. 530, 545-49; FO 228/1621, "Report on the Trade of Tientsin for the Years 1904 and 1905"; *Zhongguo jindai huobi shi ziliao*, vol. 1, pp. 864-67; YSKZZ, pp. 938-41.
67. Luo Yu-dong, *Zhongguo lijin shi* (Shanghai, 1936), pp. 140-41, 468.

most important ports in China (the others being Shanghai, Hankou, and Guangzhou) and the most important center of foreign trade in north China.[68] Moreover, customs revenues were efficiently collected by the foreign-managed Imperial Maritime Customs service, headed by Sir Robert Hart. The problem was that Sir Robert collected customs revenues on behalf of the central government in Beijing, which owed most of these revenues to foreign powers as interest on foreign loans and the enormous Boxer indemnity.

Nearly all of Zhili's customs revenues, as well as increasing amounts of likin, salt levies, native customs revenues, and even land taxes went to paying interest to foreigners. After 1901 the amount that Zhili sent annually to Beijing to meet financial obligations to the Powers was large, about 2 million taels on the average. In 1902 the amount forwarded as Zhili's quota for Boxer indemnity payments alone was 800,000 taels.[69]

For governors and governors-general throughout the Empire, land taxes were also a poor source of revenue because of competition from Beijing and local tax collecting interests. Most of the amount that was officially reported as collected was forwarded to Beijing for the Beijing Fund (*Jingxiang*). But actual land tax collections throughout the Empire exceeded the amount reported in official figures by two to three times on the average. We know that during the last half of the nineteenth century extralegal levies in land taxes as well as in likin were accelerating in all provinces of the empire and that little of these unofficial surpluses reached provincial treasuries, let alone Beijing. The men who were close to the actual collection of land taxes—tax farmers, yamen runners, and local magistrates—absorbed most of the surpluses.[70]

68. Murphy, *Treaty Ports*, pp. 49-51; Hosea B. Morse, *The Trade and Administration of the Chinese Empire* (London, 1908), pp. 211-14.

69. Tang Xiang-long, "Minguo yiqian guanshui danbao zhi waizhai," *Zhongguo jindai jingji shi yanjiu jikan* 3.1 (May 1935):1-49 (esp. pp. 47-49); DHXL, *juan* 175:11; Luo Yu-dong, "Guangxu chao bujiu caizheng zhi fangce," p. 247. The situation in general is summarized by Albert Feuerwerker, *The Chinese Economy, ca. 1870-1911* (Ann Arbor, 1969), pp. 69-72.

70. The classic technical work is Wang Yeh-chien, *Land Taxation in Imperial China*. In addition to the numerous works by Kwang-ching Liu discussed in the introduction, see David Pong, "The Income and Military Expenditures of Kiangsi Province in the Last Years (1860-1864) of the Taiping Rebellion," *Journal of Asian Studies* 26.1 (November 1966):49-66; James Polachek, "Gentry Hegemony: Soochow in the T'ungchih Restoration," in Frederick Wakeman and Carolyn Grant, eds., *Conflict and Control in Late Imperial China* (Berkeley and Los Angeles, 1975), pp. 211-56; Yuji Muramatsu,

There seems no reason to doubt that in Zhili too most of the land taxes either remained with the tax collectors themselves or ended up in Beijing. Yuan's administration officially reported in 1902 the collection of 2.7 million taels in land taxes, most of which was sent to Beijing for the Beijing Fund.[71] In fact, probably over 4 million taels were collected at the *xian* level in 1902. But there is little evidence that much of the surplus (over the 2.7 million official quota) reached the provincial treasury. One indication of the hopelessness of trying to change the situation was that Yuan never attempted to increase or tighten control over collection of land taxes for the purpose of raising additional provincial revenues. Later, when there were significant increases of nearly 50 percent in local land taxes, the provincial treasury was not a beneficiary. The new taxes came in the form of special surcharges (*tankuan*) at the *xian* level which were used to finance local education and police reforms (see chapter 5). In Ding *zhou*, for example, the land tax burden jumped 50 percent in 1906, but the new revenues were absorbed by Ding *zhou* itself.[72] Earlier, such surcharges (for the Boxer indemnity fund in Beijing) had been the principal cause of the Jing Ting-bin rebellion in southwest Zhili. Thus, the contention that Yuan and other leading provincial officials of the period achieved fiscal and political independence from Beijing by increasing their control over land taxation is not supported by the facts.[73]

Like likin, foreign customs, and land taxes, the so-called native customs (or "regular customs," *changguan*) was an established source

---

"A Documentary Study of Chinese Landlordism"; and Wang Yu-quan, "Qingmo dianfu yu nongmin," in *Zhongguo jindai luncong* (Taibei, 1958), 2.5:63-84. On the Beijing Fund, see Peng Yu-xin, "Qingmo zhongyang yu gesheng caizheng guanxi," *Shehui kexue zazhi* 9.1 (June 1947):83-84. On the land tax problem in 1900-11, from the point of view of provincial treasuries other than Zhili, see Des Forges, pp. 29, 31; and Esherick, pp. 113-17.

71. *Zhili qingli caizheng shuoming shu* (1911), *bian* 1:2-7; Morse, *Trade and Administration*, pp. 292-93; YSKZZ, pp. 733, 1032, 1037.

72. I have scaled down Wang Yeh-chien's estimate for 1908 (p. 75) of 6.7 million taels because of the known increases, on the order of 50 percent, which occurred in the province between 1902 and 1908. In 1903 there were rumors that Yuan might double land taxes, and Yuan's administration also investigated land tax problems; *Subao*, April 3, 1903, p. 2, and BYGD, *juan* 14:24b-26. For tax burden in Ding *zhou*, see Wang Yeh-chien, p. 126, and Li Wen-zhi, *Zhongguo jindai nungye shi ziliao*, p. 310. On surcharges on land tax in general, see Wang Yeh-chien, *passim*, and Peng Yu-xin, pp. 90-100. For a description of the land tax collection system in Zhili, see Myers, pp. 63-64, 86-87, 102-04, 120-22, 268-71.

73. Ralph Powell, *The Rise of Chinese Military Power*, p. 170.

of revenue. It too was difficult for Yuan to exploit effectively. By 1902 most of the annual amount collected officially in Zhili was forwarded to Beijing and used for repaying foreign loans and the Boxer indemnity. Yuan's administration tried to restructure native customs collection by reducing or ending anachronistic exactions and by establishing a series of more modern levies—such as certificate fees, flag fees, port entry fees, a ship tax, and tax violations fees. But its financial importance to Yuan's administration remained negligible.[74]

Thus, with traditional sources of revenue—likin, customs, and land tax—outside of Yuan's control, his administration needed desperately to find new sources of revenue, no matter how small. During the spring and summer of 1902, he haphazardly tried such devices as lotteries and raising liquor taxes.[75] Then in August, Yuan established a Fund Raising Office (*Choukuan zongju*) headed by Lu Jia-gu to centralize, coordinate, and innovate in the collection of revenue.[76] This was the first step in a more systematic and successful effort to find additional revenues and to avert recurrence of the fiscal crises that were besetting Yuan. By the spring of 1903, Yuan's administration had increased its revenues from Zhili's salt monopoly; levied new taxes on tobacco, liquor, and stamps on official documents; begun profitably minting currency; and established an official provincial bank to handle all revenues.

Yuan's administration initially exercised little control over Zhili's Changlu salt monopoly. As indicated earlier, the Boxer conflict curtailed operation of the monopoly between July, 1900, and October, 1902. Loss of business and destruction of property had bankrupted many of the merchants of Cangzhou who ran the monopoly. The salt commissioner, Yang Zong-lian, arranged a few loans for Chinese merchants from foreign banks, especially French, but did little else to remedy the depressed conditions of the salt monopoly. Yang was an old Huai Army commander and had been Li Hong-zhang's appointee as salt commissioner. Yang's prestige was such that until his death late in 1902 Yuan was obligated to retain him and to permit the salt monopoly and its merchants a great deal of autonomy.[77]

74. Wang Yeh-chien, pp. 77-78; YSKZZ, pp. 1155-56; *Zhili qingli caizheng* . . . , *bian* 3:23-28; Morse, *Trade and Administration*, pp. 98-100.
75. PTT, June 7, Sept. 13, and Oct. 18, 1902.
76. YSKZZ, p. 627.
77. FO 371/1092, Ambassador Jordan, no. 320, Aug. 14, 1911. On Yang Zong-lian, see Liu Feng-han, *Wuwei jun*, pp. 316, 640, 652, 671, 792.

In the next year, 1903, Yuan obtained the appointment of his own man, Wang Rui-gao, as salt commissioner and began moving to put the salt merchants financially back on their feet and to restructure the monopoly so as to maximize its contribution to his provincial treasury. In January 1903, Yuan petitioned the Empress Dowager to excuse the Changlu monopoly merchants from paying levies owed since July, 1900.[78] By mid-1902, Tang Shao-yi had negotiated a loan of 400,000 taels from a Japanese bank which helped to reestablish bankrupt salt merchants.[79] But Yuan also cracked down, using the merchants of the Yongping area northeast of Beijing as an example to the rest of the salt merchant community. Commissioner Wang assumed full control of the Yongping operations, turning it into a government enterprise (*guan yingye*), ostensibly because the merchants there had embezzled tax revenues in 1900. Yuan's administration also objected to the fact that the Yongping merchants were paying only 11,000 taels annually to the government while pocketing about 16,000 taels in profits for themselves.[80] As soon as Yuan's administration began running operations in the Yongping area, the price per catty (*jin*) of salt rose from about 2 to 4 cash (*wen*) to 14 cash.[81] At that rate, by 1905 the Yongping operation was contributing at least 150,000 taels annually to the provincial treasury.[82] Moreover, Yuan placed the salt monopoly for the Zhangjiakou and Xuanhua area to the northwest of Beijing under "official supervision and merchant operation [*guandu shangban*]." As in the Yongping area, restructuring operations to exercise more direct control proved successful, increasing the annual salt revenues from the Zhangjiakou-Xuanhua area from 30,000 taels to 50,000 taels in 1904, and to 80,000 taels by 1906.[83] Finally, Yuan's administration increased salt tariffs generally by levying an additional 4 cash tax on every catty of salt, and initiated a series of complicated reforms of the administration of the Changlu system at Cangzhou which were intended to increase revenues through greater efficiency.[84]

The Changlu salt monopoly was the only major traditional source of revenue from which the Yuan Shi-kai administration

78. Yuan Shi-kai, YSYZY, *juan* 21:2b-5.
79. DHXL, *juan* 183:9b; *Dongfang zazhi* (DFZZ) 1.5 (1904): *shangwu* 80.
80. YSKZZ, pp. 810-12; *Zhili qingli caizheng* . . . , *bian* 7:7.
81. *Subao*, March 8, 1903, p. 2.   82. *Zhili qingli caizheng* . . . , *bian* 7:7, 13.
83. *Zhili qingli caizheng* . . . , *bian* 2:13; BYGD, *juan* 15:19b-20.
84. *Zhili qingli caizheng* . . . , *bian* 2:8, 12-13; DFZZ 1.6 (1904), *caizheng* 160; 1.8: *caizheng* 212; 1.11 (1904): *neiwu* 131-33.

managed to obtain significant increases in revenues for provincial coffers. The administration's other successes were with new taxes on such items as tobacco, liquor, and stamps on official documents.

Beginning in 1902, Yuan met Zhili's annual Boxer indemnity quota of 800,000 taels with increases in existing opium, tea, sugar, tobacco, and liquor taxes.[85] To achieve this, tea and sugar taxes were raised 50 percent; liquor and cigarette taxes increased 130 percent.[86] Then late in 1902, Yuan announced new taxes on tobacco and liquor which were intended to raise another 800,000 taels annually for new divisions of Yuan's New Army. At the same time, Yuan announced a stamp tax (*yinhua shui*) on all official documents used by the public. Merchant opposition to the new taxes (especially the stamp tax) was so great, however, that in May, 1903, the Empress Dowager ordered them discontinued as "unwarranted miscellaneous exactions." Yuan memorialized an appeal, winning continuance only of the new tobacco and liquor levies.[87] The rates of these new taxes were indeed high—18 cash per catty of tobacco —and stringently enforced; so that the required 800,000 taels was raised in 1903 and subsequent years.[88]

Yuan also raised extra revenues by minting new currency. In October, 1902, Yuan's administration established the Beiyang mint (*Beiyang tongyuan ju*) just north of Tianjin which immediately began minting coins of small denominations. The mint was run as a government enterprise by Zhou Xue-xi, whose father, Zhou Fu, was formerly Li Hong-zhang's right-hand man in Zhili and now governor of neighboring Shandong. Zhou Xue-xi's able leadership, and the influence of his family name and connections in Zhili, enabled the new mint to achieve modest success.[89] At first cash shops in Tianjin seemed reluctant to accept the supplementary cash

85. Luo Yu-dong, "Guangxu chao . . . ," p. 247.
86. *Zhili qingli caizheng* . . . , bian 5:1-2.
87. *Zhili qingli caizheng* . . . , bian 7:5; YSKZZ, pp. 654, 757-58, 888-91; *Beiyang gondu leizuan* (BYGD), *juan* 14:20; *Subao*, April 9 and 12, 1903; FO 228/1507, Consul-general Hopkins, no. 14, April 10, 1903; *Guangxu zhengyao* (Shanghai, 1909), *juan* 29:10; Luo Yu-dong, "Guangxu chao . . . ," p. 251; *Times* (London), April 14, 1903, p. 3. The stamp tax idea lay fallow only until early in 1904, when at the Court's request Yuan instituted a modified version in the form of a deed tax (*shuiqi*) on property transactions, as part of an effort to raise 300,000 taels more for the standing army; Luo Yu-dong, "Guangxu chao . . . ," p. 250; *Zhili qingli caizheng* . . . , bian 6:1; BYGD, *juan* 14:29b-32a.
88. *Zhili qingli caizheng* . . . , bian 6:5; *Subao*, April 15, 1903; Luo Yu-dong, "Guangxu chao . . . ," p. 249.
89. *Zhou Zhi-an (Xue-xi) xiansheng biezhuan* (Beijing, 1948), pp. 11-13; FO 228/1594, Consul-general Hopkins, no. 424, Nov. 27, 1905; YSKZZ, pp. 372, 771.

being produced at the new mint.[90] However the mint soon proved profitable enough so that in 1904 its funds financed the establishment of an industrial (*gongyi*) primary and middle school, and in 1905 supplied Yuan with 500,000 taels for military purposes.[91]

In addition to the Beiyang mint, Yuan also tried to establish at Tianjin a modern national bank under the auspices of the Board of Revenue (*Hu Bu*) which would supersede Sheng Xuan-huai's privately-operated Imperial Bank of China (*Zhongguo tongshang yinhang*). In December, 1902, Yuan proposed to the throne the establishment of such a bank, the Hu Pu Bank (*Hu Bu yinhang*), in Tianjin. Yuan suggested that Mao Qing-fan, a former director of the Jiangnan arsenal, supervise the establishment of the bank, with a British banker, a Mr. Whitehead, as financial advisor and general manager. However, for want of capital and support from the Board of Revenue, Yuan's plan failed.[92]

Yuan Shi-kai succeeded instead in establishing the more modest Bank of Tianjin (*Tianjin yinhao*) through which he could channel and control the financial transactions of his administration and thereby avoid use of foreign banks. With local merchant and gentry support, Yuan established the bank late in 1902. Tang Shao-yi, acting for Yuan's administration, pledged one million taels in provincial revenues, or one-half the amount needed, as seed capital. Thereafter, Yuan's administration conducted most of its business transactions through the Bank of Tianjin and no doubt saved revenue by doing so.[93]

To summarize, comprehensive figures on Zhili revenues during Yuan's governor-generalship are not available; but from the pre-

90. PTT, Oct. 18, 1902; *Subao*, April 2 and 24, 1903.

91. DFZZ 1.9 (1904): *caizheng* 232; *Zhili qingli caizheng* . . . , *bian* 7:9; FO 228-1507, Consul-general Hopkins, no. 63, Dec. 21, 1902; FO 17/1688, intelligence report for June 5, 1905, p. 487. For a financial report on the mint up to 1907, see *Zhongguo jindai huobi shi ziliao* vol. 1, pp. 904-07. Also see Chapter 5, below.

92. YSKZZ, pp. 744-45; FO 17/1603, Townley telegrams nos. 35, 38, and 57 of Feb. 10 and 14 and March 13, 1903; 17/1617, Whitehead to Campbell, March 19, 1903. The Hu Pu Bank eventually materialized in 1904-05, but with its head office in Beijing under the purview of the Board of Revenue; see Ray O. Hall, *Chapters and Documents on Chinese National Banking* (Shanghai, 1920), pp. 8-17, and DFZZ 1.6 (1904): *caizheng* 145-47. On Sheng Xuan-huai's Imperial Bank of China, see Albert Feuerwerker, *China's Early Industrialization: Sheng Hsuan-huai (1844-1916) and Mandarin Enterprise* (Cambridge, Mass., 1958), pp. 225-41.

93. *Zhili qingli caizheng* . . . , *bian* 7:3-4; BYGD, *juan* 21:15b-16; FO 17/1603, Townley telegram no. 35, Feb. 10, 1903. For a parallel bank of the same type which Yuan started in Jinan, see David D. Buck, *Urban Change in China*, p. 69.

ceding discussion some educated guesses are possible. In 1903 Yuan Shi-kai probably raised about 8 to 9 million taels in Zhili from new and old sources. Out of this it appears that roughly 5 million taels were forwarded to Beijing. This left Yuan with precious little—3 to 4 million taels—to run a province and lead the Empire in military, educational, and economic reform. In a 1903 memorial Yuan appealed to Beijing for help, stating that he needed at least 5 million taels annually for reforms, but at most could provide 1.7 million from Zhili sources. Would Beijing (the Board of Revenue) make up the difference?[94] Yuan's financial predicament in Zhili was actually not much different from that which afflicted his contemporary governors and governor-generals elsewhere in the Empire.[95] Thus there are little or no grounds for the assertion that as governor-general Yuan built up an independent satrapy in Zhili on the basis of his control over local revenues. For the economic basis of Yuan's power, one must look elsewhere—to Beijing.

For Yuan Shi-kai, frustrations balanced achievements during his first two years in office as Zhili governor-general and commissioner of trade for the northern ports. By allying with the British, Yuan had coaxed the foreign powers into withdrawing troops and was subsequently able to restore order and economic stability to the province. But he also learned the limits to the regional power of a governor-general. His powers to raise and keep tax revenues, to exercise military control province-wide, and to institute sweeping reforms, all were circumscribed by controls emanating from Beijing. Thus it was not surprising that after 1903 Yuan increasingly concentrated his energies on the political and bureaucratic struggle in Beijing, both to strengthen his reform administration in Zhili and to build a national power base. It was in Beijing, not Tianjin, that Yuan became more powerful politically than any Qing governor-general before or after him.

94. YSKZZ, pp. 929-32.
95. See S. A. M. Adshead, "Viceregal Government in Szechwan in the Kuang-hsu period (1875-1909)"; Des Forges, pp. 2, 29, 31, 56, 63-64, 94-95, 99, 107-08, 162, 177, 190; and Joseph W. Esherick, *Reform and Revolution in China*, pp. 113-17, for comparable situations in Szechwan, Hunan-Hubei, and areas where Xi-liang officiated.

CHAPTER III

Yuan Shi-kai's Domination of Court Politics and Foreign Affairs in Beijing, 1903-1907

Just as Yuan Shi-kai was turning to Beijing to overcome difficulties in Zhili and to expand his political influence, he lost his major ally at Court, Chief Grand Councillor Rong-lu. On April 11, 1903, Rong-lu who had been seriously ill for weeks, died in Beijing. The Empress Dowager Ci-xi at the time was visiting Yuan Shi-kai in Baoding after a trip to the Western Tombs. She immediately issued the usual posthumous titles and euologies appropriate to the death of a chief grand councillor.[1] But she did not interrupt her visit to Baoding to mourn Rong-lu further, choosing instead to vacation with Yuan for four more days before returning to Beijing.[2] The rumor, in the words of one foreign observer, was that she "does not regret [the loss of] the Councillor [Rong-lu] whose great power and influence had become irksome to her." The Empress Dowager, it seems, had become resentful of her dependency upon Rong-lu and his accumulation of power since 1900. It was said that when the Empress Dowager first heard the news of Rong-lu's death, she was being entertained by a troupe of comedians supplied

1. *Shilu, juan* 513:9.
2. J.O.P. Bland and Edmund Backhouse, *China Under the Empress Dowager*, p. 415.

by Yuan. Undisturbed by the news, she ordered the comedians to continue the evening as planned.³

On the day after Rong-lu died, the Empress Dowager appointed Rong-lu's arch rival, Prince Qing, her new chief grand councillor.⁴ Thus, overnight Prince Qing became the most powerful official in Beijing. To Yuan Shi-kai, and others like him who had sided in court politics with Rong-lu's faction, Prince Qing's appointment must have seemed ominous.

Indeed, Rong-lu's death and the rise of Prince Qing did seriously jeopardize Yuan Shi-kai's career. Yuan was soon criticized in memorials to the throne, with at least one demanding his impeachment.⁵ Moreover, there were rumors that Yuan was to lose his Zhili post and be transferred to Guangzhou [Canton]. These were followed by rumors that Yuan would stage a *coup d'état* against the Empress Dowager and Prince Qing.⁶ A British diplomat reported back to London that "he [Yuan] has made many enemies and few friends among either Chinese or foreigners. . . . The danger seems to me that Yuan may go too far and come down with a [crash]. . . ."⁷

In this chapter we look at how Yuan weathered this crisis and went on to dominate court and bureaucratic politics in Beijing until 1909. In the process much about the dynamics of court politics at the time is revealed, in particular their nonideological character and the important influence of foreign powers on direction.

The Triangular Relationship: Yuan Shi-kai, Empress Dowager Ci-xi, and Prince Qing

In part, Yuan Shi-kai politically survived Rong-lu's death because of his success in retaining the personal trust of the Empress Dowager and in cultivating an alliance with Prince Qing. Yuan used a number of stratagems, including simple flattery and bribery.

3. FO 17/1597, memorandum on Rong-lu by Mayers, no. 146, April 16, 1903.
4. DHXL, *juan* 179:4b.
5. Yuan was criticized on separate occasions for maladministration in Zhili, for favoring the abolition of the examination system, and for excessive taxation; see *Subao*, April 4 and May 10 and 18, 1903; *Shilu, juan* 512:16b-17 and 514:10a; also FO 405/134 (conf. print), April-June 1903, nos. 255, 299; 405/135 (conf. print), July-September 1903, no. 15. Zhang Zhi-dong likewise felt threatened by Prince Qing and was attacked with Yuan over the abolition of the examination system issue; Daniel Bays, *China Enters the Twentieth Century*, pp. 117-18.
6. FO 405/134 (conf. print), April-June 1903, nos. 78, 125, 166.
7. FO 17/1597, Townley to Campbell, March 26, 1903.

While governor-general of Zhili, Yuan showered the Empress Dowager with gifts. At the lunar New Year, 1904, according to Princess Der Ling, Yuan presented Ci-xi with a

> yellow satin robe, embroidered with different colored precious stones and pearls designed to represent the peony flowers; the leaves were green jade. . . . It was truly a magnificent thing, and must have cost a fortune. The only drawback was its weight; it was too heavy to wear comfortably. Her Majesty appeared delighted with this gown, and wore it the first day. . . .[8]

Over the next few years, excluding birthdays, Yuan gave the Empress Dowager a troupe of dancers from India, lent her his Western-style marching band, and sent her an elaborate tricycle, which was such a hit that he sent her an automobile.[9] Birthdays were special. Probably her seventy-third in 1907 was typical. On that occasion Yuan presented her with "two fox fur gowns, a large piece of calambac inlaid with precious stones, a pair of filigree and pearl phoenixes and a branch of coral as tall as a man."[10]

Yuan also made a practice of showering the Empress Dowager with personal attention. Just before Rong-lu's death, for example, he did all that was possible to insure the success of her tour of the Western Tombs. Built expressly for the trip was a 25-mile-long railway line running west from the Beijing-Baoding Railway to Yizhou, near the tombs. This was the first railway in China built with Chinese capital and by a Chinese engineer, Zhan Tian-you.[11] Yuan supervised its construction and, a few weeks before the Empress Dowager left Beijing, he personally inspected the railway and all other facilities for the tour.[12] Yuan then accompanied the Empress Dowager and her entourage to the tombs, leading them on the way back to Baoding, where they were housed in the new Baoding Provincial School buildings and entertained lavishly for a week.[13] The Empress Dowager was delighted with the whole trip

---

8. Princess Der Ling, *Two Years in the Forbidden City* (New York, 1911), p. 332.
9. Yu Rong-ling, *Qinggong suoji* (Beijing, 1957), pp. 75, 77, 79.
10. Yu Rong-ling, pp. 84-85; translation in Jerome Ch'en, *Yuan Shih-k'ai* (1961), p. 98.
11. On Zhan Tian-you and the Xinyi Railway, see Xu Ying, Li Xi-mi, and Xu Qi-heng, eds., *Zhan Tian-you* (Beijing, 1956), pp. 27-40; Xu Qi-heng and Li Xi-mi, eds., *Zhan Tian-you he Zhongguo tielu* (Shanghai, 1957), pp. 40-41; Ling Hong-xun, *Zhan Tian-you xiansheng nianpu* (Taibei, 1961), pp. 1-40.
12. YSKZZ, p. 742; and *Subao*, March 2, 13, 19, and 21 and April 9, 1903.
13. *Rongan dizi ji, juan* 3:13b.

and later formally complimented Yuan's judicial commissioner, Yang Shi-xiang, and his salt commissioner, Wang Rui-gao, who had helped with the arrangements.[14]

Yuan demonstrated concern for the Empress Dowager's well-being by serving her personally in ways which normally would have been performed by a more minor official. He accepted responsibility for the expensive construction of Beijing's south gate (*zhengyang men*), a project of great personal concern to the Empress Dowager. In 1905, when a bomb was thrown at the Imperial Constitutional Commission made up of leading Beijing officials as it left the Beijing railway station for a trip abroad, the Empress Dowager asked Yuan to lead a contingent of a thousand men to the Summer Palace to guard her and to investigate personally the entire affair.[15]

Besides carefully cultivating the Empress Dowager after Rong-lu's death in 1903, Yuan sought an alliance with his erstwhile enemy, Prince Qing. The speed with which this alliance was effected was remarkable, reflecting again the unprincipled and non-ideological quality of factionalism in Beijing at the time. It was Prince Qing of course who led the attack at Court upon Yuan during the spring of 1903. Yet by the fall, Yuan and Prince Qing were working in harmony on the problem of Russian challenges to Chinese sovereignty in Manchuria, and on new military and financial reorganization schemes for the Empire.

The Yuan-Prince Qing alliance was quite obviously a marriage of convenience. Both men had come to the Machiavellian conclusion that they needed one another to stay in power. For Yuan, the support of the chief grand councillor and highest official in the Empire nullified any immediate threat to his career. As the Empire's most dynamic and ambitious Chinese official who had the support of the Empress Dowager, Yuan likewise posed a potentially dangerous threat to Prince Qing, whose personal power was never as great as that of Rong-lu. Thus for both men an alliance was insurance against the future.

The liaison men who cemented the alliance were the Yang brothers, Yang Shi-qi and Yang Shi-xiang. They had assisted Prince Qing and Li Hong-zhang in the negotiations in Beijing with representatives of the Powers which resulted in the Boxer Protocol of

14. DHXL, *juan* 17:4b-5a.
15. DHXL, *juan* 182:3b-4; DFZZ 1.6 (1904): *shiping* 29, and (1905): *zazu* 75; YSKZZ, pp. 941, 961, 1073, 2021. This incident touched off police reform in Beijing and the creation of a Ministry of Police, which Yuan and his associates dominated.

1901. Afterwards, they stayed in Zhili, serving Yuan in a variety of capacities as indicated in Chapter 2 (the elder, Yang Shi-xiang, was Zhili's judicial commissioner by 1903). At the same time they remained in close contact with their former boss, Prince Qing.[16]

The alliance was allegedly helped by bribes that the Yang brothers passed from Yuan to Prince Qing. At about the time of Rong-lu's death, Yang Shi-qi reportedly handed Prince Qing 100,000 taels. Later Yuan paid for celebrations of the birthdays of the Prince and his wife, the marriage of their son, Zai-zhen, and the birth of a grandson.[17]

Prince Qing and his family were notoriously corrupt, so the likelihood that Yuan bribed Prince Qing is strong.[18] However, such bribes probably only lubricated relations between Prince Qing and Yuan. Prince Qing became preeminent at Court not through administrative achievement but by being a willing instrument of the Empress Dowager. The Empire was racked by crisis, domestic and foreign. Thus it is understandable that Prince Qing would ally with an effective administrator and friend of the foreign powers like Yuan in the interest of self-protection, with or without Yuan's bribes.

Yuan Shi-kai and the Powers

Cultivating the Empress Dowager and an alliance with Prince Qing may account for Yuan's survival in court politics, but it does not explain Yuan's expanding influence in Beijing after Rong-lu's death. For this one must move the analysis to another level. The Empress Dowager and Prince Qing, after all, were realists. The Boxer affair had made them painfully aware of foreign military threats to her reign and to the Qing dynasty itself. In 1903 and 1904, with storm clouds of war forming over Manchuria, the Empress Dowager relied increasingly upon Yuan, in whose personal loyalty and ability to handle foreign affairs she most believed.

Manchuria was the chief issue for Chinese foreign policy between 1903 and 1907. Manchuria was also within Yuan's official sphere of responsibility as governor-general of Zhili and commis-

16. Liu Hou-sheng, pp. 128-29.
17. Liu Hou-sheng, p. 128; DFZZ 3.10 (1906): *zazu* 43.
18. Shen Yun-long, "Zhangwo wanqing zhan bing zhi Yi-kuang," pp. 70-80; Hosea B. Morse, *The International Relations of the Chinese Empire*, vol. 3, pp. 443-44. FO 405/134 (conf. print), April-June 1903, no. 295; Li Chien-nung, *The Political History of China, 1840-1928*, p. 197.

sioner of trade for the northern ports. Moreover, the Empress Dowager used Yuan's permanent appointment as imperial commissioner for negotiation of commercial treaties as a pretext for consulting regularly with Yuan about foreign affairs. The net effect was that, although Prince Qing was nominally in charge of foreign affairs, Yuan increasingly acted as *de facto* foreign minister. In 1903 he was instrumental in the negotiation of commercial treaty agreements with Japan and the United States, in which the dynasty agreed for the first time to voluntarily create (self-open, *zikai*) treaty ports. Yuan then advised the Empress Dowager during the negotiations with the Powers over Manchuria which preceded the Russo-Japanese War of 1904-05. And after the war, in December, 1905, Yuan led the Chinese delegation which negotiated a new agreement for Manchuria with Japan.

There were also negotiations of a more regional nature, such as those concerning the recovery of control of the Beijing-Shenyang Railway and the Kaiping mines, in which Yuan played the leading role. Moreover, through protégés like Tang Shao-yi, Yuan had a hand in nearly all negotiations conducted by the Ministry of Foreign Affairs, of which Prince Qing remained titular head.[19]

Tang Shao-yi, vice-president of the Ministry of Foreign Affairs in 1906, is viewed by many historians today as the most able diplomat of the period. Tang was from a wealthy Cantonese merchant family of Xiangshan *xian* near Macao. His father, Tang Mao-zhi, had been the comprador of a large British trading firm, Jardine, Matheson and Company. Tang Ting-shu (Tong King-sing), who managed the China Merchants Steam Navigation Company and the Kaiping mines in the 1870s and 1880s, was Tang Shao-yi's uncle. It was Tang Ting-shu who recommended young Tang Shao-yi to Yong Wing (Rong-hong), the leader of China's first overseas educational mission to the United States in 1872. As a protégé of Yong Wing, Tang studied in Hartford, Connecticut, and at Columbia University. By 1882, Tang was in Korea, where he met and worked with Yuan Shi-kai until Yuan's departure in 1894. Tang remained in Korea to 1898, then served with the Chinese administration of the Beijing-Shenyang Railway as head of its liaison with the British. In 1900, Tang joined Yuan Shi-kai in Shandong as head

---

19. The best account of Yuan's role in the complex diplomatic history of this period is in Michael H. Hunt, *Frontier Defense and the Open Door: Manchuria in Chinese-American Relations, 1895-1911* (New Haven, 1973), pp. 70-76, 85-87, 100-37.

of Yuan's Bureau of Foreign Affairs (*Yangwu chu*). In his first memorial as Zhili governor-general, Yuan requested Tang's transfer to Zhili. The Court agreed and Tang became customs *daotai* of Tianjin, probably the most sensitive and important position in Yuan's administration. In 1904, despite Yuan's protests that Tang was indispensable to his administration in Zhili, Tang led an emergency mission to India to negotiate with the British about the threat to Chinese suzerainty over Tibet posed by the recent Younghusband expedition to Lhasa. Negotiations in Calcutta soon stalemated, and Tang returned to Beijing in 1905 in time to play a leading role as Yuan's deputy in negotiations with the Japanese over Manchuria. In 1906, as a vice-president of the Ministry of Foreign Affairs, Tang negotiated an Anglo-Chinese settlement concerning Tibet and handled negotiations with the Russians over Manchuria. As a newly created customs commissioner (*shuiwu dachen*), he also began in 1906 to monitor Sir Robert Hart's Imperial Maritime Customs Service. Tang was considered the leader of the "Cantonese" clique of modernizing officials like Liang Ru-hao, Shi Zhao-ji, Liang Tun-yan, and Liang Shi-yi, who were allied politically with Yuan Shi-kai and active in foreign affairs. For his time, Tang was outspokenly nationalistic for a Qing diplomat. Western and Japanese diplomats in Beijing liked him for his forthrightness and appreciation of foreign ways, although they also considered him a bit emotional and reckless.[20]

The record indicates that from 1903 through 1905 Yuan continued to cooperate with Britain and her ally, Japan, in Manchuria against the Russians. In order to challenge the Russians in Manchuria, the British and Japanese wanted the Chinese government to open treaty ports there. Yuan was reluctant at first to commit the dynasty to a definite open door policy in Manchuria. He feared Russian reprisals, and opposed further encroachment by the Powers on Chinese sovereignty. The delay until late in 1903 in the ratification of the commercial treaties with Japan and the United States was due in part to Yuan's objections to the opening of treaty

20. Howard Boorman, ed., *Biographical Dictionary of Republican China* (New York, 1967-71), vol. 3, pp. 232-36; *Times* (London), Jan. 18, 1907; YSKZZ, pp. 341, 369, 383, 396, 1536. Hao Yen-p'ing, *The Comprador in Nineteenth-Century China: Bridge Between East and West* (Cambridge, Mass., 1970), pp. 32, 170, 173, 188-89. For recent assessments of Tang's importance, see Hunt, *Frontier Defense*; Louis T. Sigel, "T'ang Shao-yi (1860-1938): The Diplomacy of Chinese Nationalism" (Ph.D. dissertation, Harvard University, 1972); and Li En-han, "Tang Shao-yi yu wanqing waijiao," *Jindai shi yanjiusuo jikan* 4 (May 1973):53-126.

ports in Manchuria. In the end, Yuan's views prevailed, and the dynasty agreed only on the basis that cities became self-opened (*zikai*) ports, which it was hoped would give the dynasty more control.[21] Still, Yuan was consistently pro-British and pro-Japanese in his opposition to Russian expansion in Manchuria. After the Russo-Japanese War broke out in the fall of 1904, Yuan consulted with the British and then advocated a formal declaration of strict neutrality toward Russia and Japan, though cooperating with the Japanese by providing them with military intelligence. This was the position that the British and the Japanese wanted the Chinese government to take, and the policy which was eventually adopted. It was unpopular with students and many officials, like Cen Chunxuan and Ma Yu-kun who advocated a stronger, interventionist, and anti-Russian policy.[22]

In return for his cooperation, the British continued to support Yuan politically at Court. At the time of Rong-lu's death in April, 1903, for example, Yuan expressed fears about his own future to the British minister in Beijing, Sir Ernest Satow, and asked for British help. The British were alarmed about the attacks on Yuan. In a note to Prince Qing and the Ministry of Foreign Affairs, Satow indicated Britain's concern about Yuan's future. Among themselves, British army officers and diplomats discussed the need for reinforcements, and even the possibility of reoccupying Tianjin and Beijing should Yuan lose the Zhili governor-generalship. It will be remembered that in 1902 Satow had intervened directly and successfully on Yuan's behalf when it appeared that Yuan might be censured for his handling of the Beijing-Shenyang Railway negotiations. In 1903, as in 1902, the British considered Yuan indispensable if only because Yuan seemed to support their aims in Manchuria.[23]

21. YSKZZ, pp. 1351-53, 1741-43; Masataka Kosaka, "Ch'ing Policy Over Manchuria (1900-1903)," *Papers on China* 16 (1962):126-53; John A. White, *The Diplomacy of the Russo-Japanese War* (Princeton, 1964), pp. 95-111; Hunt, pp. 70-76; and David D. Buck, *Urban Change in China*, pp. 50-53.

22. YSKZZ, pp. 1205-07; White, pp. 115-16; Hunt, pp. 85-87. Yuan asked the British for advice on China's policy toward the war; FO 228/1563, Consul-general Hopkins, telegram no. 4 and dispatch no. 6. On Yuan's providing the Japanese with military intelligence, see Chapter 4, note 106. On the unpopularity of Yuan's position, see Hunt, pp. 130-31; and Akira Iriye, "Public Opinion and Foreign Policy: The Case of Late Ch'ing China," in Albert Feuerwerker et al., eds., *Approaches to Modern Chinese History* (Berkeley and Los Angeles, 1967), pp. 216-38.

23. FO 405/134 (conf. print), April-June 1903, nos. 125, 255, 298, 299; 405/135 (conf. print), July-September 1903, nos. 15, 97; 17/1597, Townley to Campbell,

After 1905, with the Russians more or less out of the picture as a result of the Russo-Japanese War, Yuan drastically altered his position vis-à-vis Britain's ally, Japan, and her interests in Manchuria. Perhaps because of growing elite pressure and the influence of associates like Tang Shao-yi, Yuan moved toward a more vigorous defense of Chinese sovereignty in Manchuria. At first Yuan's relations with the Japanese continued to be amicable in the negotiations following the Russo-Japanese War. Although Yuan and Tang Shao-yi were tough enough to win a few concessions in the agreements of December, 1905 (namely, control over mines in Fengtian and over a new railway from Jilin to Changchun, the right to purchase the Shenyang-Xinmintun Railway, and autonomous control over the opening of certain Manchurian towns to foreign trade), the Japanese returned to Tokyo reasonably satisfied.[24] It was Yuan's build-up over the next three years, 1906 through 1908, of a tough reform administration in Manchuria (led by his protégés Zhao Er-sun and Xu Shi-chang) which angered the Japanese.[25] Yuan and Tang Shao-yi's attempt in 1907 and 1908 to effect massive American investment in Manchuria to further offset Japanese and Russian influence there was the last straw.[26] By 1909, the Japanese were thoroughly disillusioned with Yuan.[27]

Yuan was careful, however, not to alienate the British. He probably was relatively unconcerned about the problem of Britain's alliance with Japan, knowing that many of the Englishmen with whom he had the most contact, like G.E. Morrison of the London *Times*, were applauding in private his stand against the Japanese in Manchuria.[28] Moreover, when Yuan challenged British interests,

---

March 26, 1903; 17/1617, Hopkins, dispatches dated March 21 and 25, 1903.

24. *Qingji waijiao shiliao* (Beijing, 1932-35), *juan* 193 and 194; White, pp. 330-41; Hunt, pp. 159-61; Cao Ru-lin, *Yisheng zhi huiyi* (Hong Kong, 1966), pp. 45-49. Cao, who was present at the negotiations, thought that Yuan and Tang had taken too hard a line with the Japanese. Manchurian students and merchants, on the other hand, thought that too much was being sacrificed to the Japanese; see Hunt, p. 131.

25. Yuan supported Zhao and Xu from Beijing and Tianjin. Xu Shi-chang's administration especially was made up of personnel from Yuan's Zhili administration. On the Manchurian reforms in general, see Merebeth Cameron, *Reform and Revolution in China, 1898-1912* (Stanford, 1931), pp. 197-98; Shu-hsi Hsu, *China and Her Political Entity* (London, 1926), pp. 282-346; Robert H.G. Lee, *Manchurian Frontier in Ch'ing History* (Cambridge, Mass., 1970), chap. 7; and Hunt, pp. 119-37.

26. Hunt, *passim*.

27. White, p. 344. In 1909 when Yuan was forced into retirement from public office, the Japanese were obviously pleased; see Chapter 7.

28. *Morrison Correspondence*, pp. 413-15, 431-32, 437-38, 440-43.

he did so over issues for which the British minister in Beijing considered the dynasty's claims to be just, and thus not meriting intervention on behalf of the British business interests concerned.

The recovery of the Beijing-Shenyang Railway during Yuan's tenure as its director from 1902 to 1906 is a case in point. The turning point came in 1905 when profits shot up to 8.1 million taels per annum. These enormous profits repaid the construction loan which had been the basis of British control, and freed surplus profits for reinvestment by the Chinese management in other railways and projects. Thus the British lost veto power over the railway's finances in 1905, and then the right to supervise and appoint foreign staff. Needless to say, the railway became an important new source of revenue for Yuan and the central government. Moreover, Chinese control served to curtail Japanese and Russian influence in Manchuria east of the Liao River. Perhaps because recovery of the railway threatened the territorial interests of other powers more than her own, but also because of Britain's generally more restrained railway policy after 1901, the British minister in Beijing offered no real resistance to the Chinese takeover of the railway.[29]

Yuan also combatted British interests in his efforts to recover the Kaiping mines in northeast Zhili from a British firm. The mines had been founded by Li Hong-zhang in 1877 as a joint government-sponsored, privately-owned enterprise. In 1900, however, the company's director, Zhang Yi (or Zhang Yan-mou) sold the company to a British firm in order to protect it from confiscation by the Russians or Japanese during the Boxer affair. The central government did not discover that the mines were no longer Chinese-owned until November, 1902, when there was a flag hoisting dispute between British and Chinese staff. For the next two years, Yuan tried to get Zhang Yi to clarify the question of who owned the mines. Finally in 1904 Zhang Yi was dismissed on Yuan's request, and in 1905 the British firm was taken to court in London by the Qing government. But the Kaiping mines remained in British hands. Yuan then made plans for the founding of a rival mine at Luanzhou, about 30 miles east of the Kaiping mines. Under Zhou Xue-xi's able direction, the Luanzhou company was successfully established in 1907, with Yuan's provincial government providing one-fourth of the necessary seed capital and the promise of government

29. Arthur Rosenbaum, "Imperialism and Chinese Railway Policy," pp. 56-59.

and railway business. The British owners of the Kaiping mines of course objected vehemently, but the new minister in Beijing, Sir John Jordan, while defending British ownership of the Kaiping mines, refused to challenge Yuan's right to open the Luanzhou mines.[30]

Yuan as a Central Government Official

A leading role in foreign affairs, coupled with the continuing support of the Empress Dowager and his alliance with Prince Qing, put Yuan in a position to expand his bureaucratic power in Beijing. Crucial to this process were the concurrent appointments he held in Beijing while serving in Tianjin as governor-general. In contrast to the days of Li Hong-zhang and earlier governors-general, Beijing was now only three or four hours by railway from Tianjin. Thus during most of his term as governor-general, Yuan served actively in Beijing as a member of the powerful Government Affairs Bureau (*Zhengwu chu*) and of the Military Reorganization Bureau (*Lianbing chu*); as head of both the Beijing-Shenyang and Beijing-Hankou Railway administrations and of the Imperial Telegraph Administration; and as imperial commissioner for the negotiation of commercial treaties.

After 1901, the Government Affairs Bureau, an auxiliary of the Grand Council created in 1901 to coordinate administrative reforms, was probably the most dynamic high-level agency in the central government. Channeled through it were most of the major reform measures that Beijing initiated during the decade from 1901 to 1911. Most of its members, eight to eleven in number, were grand councillors and presidents of boards. Yuan was a member from 1901 until his retirement early in 1909. The only other provincial governor-general who was a member was Zhang Zhi-dong; but the great distance separating Wuchang from Beijing precluded Zhang's active participation on the bureau.[31]

---

30. YSKZZ, pp. 830, 1141, 1157, 1314, 1818; YSYZY, *juan* 35:1b-2; *Morrison Correspondence*, pp. 374-75; FO 405/174 (conf. prints), April-June 1903, no. 105; 405/175 (conf. prints), July-December 1907, nos. 6, 8, 25, 56, 69, 70. See also Ellsworth Carlson, *The Kaiping Mines, 1877-1912*; Wang Xi, *Zhong Ying Kaiping Kuangquan jiaoshe*; and Watanabe Atsushi, "En Seigai seiken no keizaiteki kiban-hokuyō-ha no kigyō katsudō," in *Chūgoku kindaika no shakai kōzō* (Tokyo, 1960), pp. 135-71.

31. Qian Shi-fu, comp., *Qingli xinshe zhiguan nianbiao* (Beijing, 1961), pp. 53-55. On the role of the Government Affairs Bureau in the central government, see Esther Morrison, "The Modernization of the Confucian Bureaucracy," esp. chap. 5.

The Military Reorganization Bureau, established in December, 1903, to direct centralization and modernization of the Empire's armed forces, was initially proposed by Yuan, who himself became its associate director (*huiban dachen*). Modeled after Yuan's military organization in Zhili, the bureau was divided into three departments, under the general supervision of Xu Shi-chang and each headed by leading figures from Yuan's Zhili military administration—Liu Yong-qing, Duan Qi-rui, and Wang Shi-zhen. The bureau soon ordered recruitment of new troops and the retraining of selected old troops for a modern national army on the model of Yuan's divisions in Zhili. The crucial importance of the bureau to the development of the Beiyang Army in Zhili will be discussed in Chapter 4.[32]

Yuan's official positions as head of the Beijing-Shenyang Railway, Beijing-Hankou Railway, and the Imperial Telegraph Administration—the head offices of which were all in Beijing—made Yuan a key figure in the central government's effort to control the development of modern means of communication as well as the modern sector of the economy. The Beijing-Shenyang and Beijing-Hankou railways (the latter completed in 1905) were the longest existing trunk-lines in the empire before 1911. Their strategic and financial value to Beijing was enormous.[33]

Yuan had taken over leadership of the Imperial Telegraph Administration (*Dianbao zongju*) as part of an effort to dismantle the business empire of steamship, railway, telegraph, banking, ironworks, and mining enterprises that Sheng Xuan-huai had built up in the 1880s and 1890s under Li Hong-zhang's patronage. After the death of Li Hong-zhang and Liu Kun-yi, Sheng lacked supporters at Court. In December, 1902, Yuan requested and received the Empress Dowager's sanction to reorganize the Imperial Telegraph Administration and the China Merchants' Steam Navigation Company (*Lunchuan Zhaoshang ju*), which had been the heart of Sheng's empire. Yuan delegated the task of reorganizing and administering these two companies to Yang Shi-qi, one of his top assistants. Both the telegraph and steamship companies had strategic as well as

32. Ralph Powell, *The Rise of Chinese Military Power, 1895-1912*, pp. 166-67; *Guangxu zhengyao*, juan 29:37b; DHXL, juan 184:4b.
33. For further discussion of these railways and Yuan's railway power in general, see MacKinnon, "Liang Shih-i and the Communications Clique," *Journal of Asian Studies* 29.3 (May 1970):584-88.

commercial importance in terms of communications and the shipment of tribute rice north to the capital.[34]

Needless to say, gaining managerial control of railways and other modern means of communication increased Yuan's bureaucratic influence over the modern sector of the economy. However, although on occasion Yuan drew on revenues from these railway, steamship, and telegraph enterprises, there is no evidence to support the contention that they became his major source for financing military and other reforms in Zhili.[35] Like Li Hong-zhang before him, control of these enterprises was primarily of political importance to Yuan as sources of patronage, prestige, and control over economic policy.[36]

Another expression of Yuan's bureaucratic influence in Beijing was the positions attained by his protégés and allies. Yuan's influence over the Ministry of Foreign Affairs, through men like Tang Shao-yi, has already been noted. Two other examples of protégés who became influential figures in Beijing are Yang Shi-qi and Xu Shi-chang.

Yang Shi-qi and his elder brother, Yang Shi-xiang, were instrumental in cementing Yuan's alliance with Prince Qing. The Yang brothers were scions of a well-to-do Anhui family with the traditional educational background and degrees (*jinshi, juren*) appropriate for high office. By 1903 Yang Shi-qi was shuttling back and forth between Beijing and Tianjin as one of Yuan's top personal aides, especially in economic matters, and Yang Shi-xiang was Zhili's judicial commissioner. Yang Shi-qi's role in construction of the Xin-yi Railway in 1903, in the recovery of the Beijing-Shenyang Railway in 1905, and in management for Yuan of the Imperial Telegraph Administration, the China Merchants Steam Navigation Company and the Beijing-Zhangjiakou Railway project has been noted. In addition, when a Ministry of Commerce (*Shangbu*) under Prince Qing's son, Zai-zhen, was established in 1903 to regulate

---

34. On Sheng's empire, the classic work is Albert Feuerwerker, *China's Early Industrialization: Sheng Hsuan-huai (1844-1916) and Mandarin Enterprise*. See also YSKZZ, pp. 741, 1188; YSYZY, *juan* 24:1-2, 25:1; Liu Hou-sheng, *Zhang Jian zhuanji*, p. 118; and *Subao*, March 18, 24, and 27, 1903.

35. Jerome Ch'en, *Yuan Shih-k'ai* (1972), pp. 64-70. The largest single amount which Yuan drew was 700,000 taels from the Beijing-Shenyang Railway for the Beiyang Army in 1906; see Table 6, and also YSKZZ, pp. 1732 and 1827, and Rosemary Quested, *The Russo-Chinese Bank*, pp. 59-60, for other instances. On the financing of reform in Zhili, see Chapters 4 and 5.

36. Feuerwerker, *China's Early Industrialization*, pp. 157-59, 161, 197-98, 250.

and modernize commerce throughout the empire, Yang became a councillor (*cheng*), a position just below a vice-president, of the new ministry. These positions made Yang Shi-qi a major figure in Beijing in the fields of communications, commerce, and industry. At the same time, his personal ties to Yuan Shi-kai remained strong. Yang joined Yuan in the Sino-Japanese negotiations over Manchuria in 1905, helped Yuan in efforts to recover the Kaiping mines, and insured the general cooperation of the Ministry of Commerce with Yuan's administration in Zhili.[37]

Xu Shi-chang (1855-1939) was probably Yuan's oldest friend and closest associate. Xu was from a poor but respectable Tianjin scholar-official family. In the late 1870s, Xu met and befriended Yuan in Henan, where Xu was born and raised. Yuan helped to subsidize Xu's studies, which eventually led to the metropolitan *jinshi* degree in 1886. During the 1880s and early 1890s, Xu was a compiler (*bianxiu*) of the Hanlin Academy in Beijing while Yuan was busy in Korea. A fine scholar, calligrapher, and poet in his own right, Xu intellectually fell under the influence of the famous Tongcheng scholar, Wu Ru-lun. Wu's advocacy of modified reform along Western lines, especially in education, impressed Xu. In 1896, Yuan recruited Xu as his commander-in-chief for training and equipping the Newly Created Army at Xiaozhan. Xu remained at Xiaozhan with Yuan at least until the summer of 1898, when Xu acted as liaison between Yuan and the radical reformers Kang You-wei and Liang Qi-chao, with whom Xu was genuinely sympathetic. Xu never joined Yuan in Shandong, remaining in Beijing throughout the Boxer affair. On May 27, 1901, Yuan recommended Xu to the Court as a man of unusual talent. A few months later when Yuan returned to Zhili as governor-general, he appointed Xu head of his Military Secretariat (*yingwu chu*). More important, he assigned to Xu the delicate task of acting as his liaison with the administrative boards in Beijing. Xu was especially helpful in facilitating the trans-

---

37. Chen Xi-zhang, *Beiyang cangsang shihua* (Tainan, 1967), p. 339; Liu Hou-sheng, p. 112; Feuerwerker, *China's Early Industrialization*, p. 120; Cao Ru-lin, pp. 36, 45; *Jiaotong shi, Luzheng bian*, vol. 7, p. 171; Ch'en, *Yuan Shi-kai* (1972), p. 70; Wang Xi, pp. 114-15; Watanabe Atsushi, "En Seigai"; YSKZZ, pp. 992, 1188; YSYZY, *juan* 25:1. On the Ministry of Commerce, see the recent work of Wellington Chan, *Merchants, Mandarins, and Modern Enterprise in Late Ch'ing China* (Cambridge, Mass., 1977), pp. 157-69. However, Professor Chan's contention (p. 169) that there was rivalry between the Ministry of Commerce and Yuan's provincial network of power seems baseless. From its inception, the ministry was sprinkled with Yuan's protégés and allies, including its head, Prince Qing's son, Zai-zhen.

fer of one million taels of "relief funds" from the Board of Revenue for use in training and equipping new troops in Zhili. In 1903 Xu became first a councillor of the Ministry of Commerce, and then a grand secretary and member of the Military Reorganization Bureau. In 1905 Xu was appointed grand councillor, a post which he held concurrently with an associate directorship of the Military Reorganization Bureau, membership on the Government Affairs Bureau, and the vice-presidency of the Board of War (switching later in the year to the presidency of a new Ministry of Police). Yuan and Xu remained in constant contact, working closely for example on a reform administration in Manchuria (which Xu was to head in 1907). Xu has been characterized by contemporaries and historians alike as Yuan's alter-ego in Beijing from 1901 to 1907.[38]

The extent to which Yuan's influence in the central government grew while he was governor-general of Zhili is revealed in the following excerpt from a memorial by censor Wang Nai-zheng in early 1904:

> The governor-general, just over forty years of age, has no outstanding service, but has received favors far greater than those conferred upon Zeng Guo-fan and Li Hong-zhang. . . . It is a long standing tradition that the Imperial Guards in the Forbidden City must be Bannerman. Yet now the governor-general's troops are everywhere in the Palaces. . . . Yang Shi-qi is made a counsellor and Xu Shi-chang a member of the Grand Secretariat, so the governor-general's henchmen are in the Inner Court as well. . . . For through Prince Qing's recommendations the governor-general has extended his power into vitally important offices. Why does the Prince trust and rely on him ten times more than Rong-lu ever did?[39]

Wang's memorial had no effect and Yuan's power continued to grow. But Wang's attack was not the last. In 1907 Yuan had to enlist all the bureaucratic strength, support from the foreign community, and influence with the Empress Dowager that he could muster to beat back an attack on him and Prince Qing led by grand councillor Qu Hong-ji.

---

38. Shen Yun-long, "Xu Shi-chang pingzhuan (1-3)," *Zhuanji wenxue* 13.1-3 (July, August, and September 1968):6-11, 25-29, and 32-38, respectively; Liu Feng-han, *Xinjian lujun*, p. 112; YSKZZ, pp. 421, 1913; *Rongan dizi ji, juan* 3:2b-3; Qian Shi-fu, p. 82.

39. Ch'en, *Yuan Shih-k'ai* (1972), p. 59; DHXL, *juan*, 185:9a.

Intrigue in the Grand Council and the 1907 Challenge to the Power of Yuan and Prince Qing

The Grand Council was the highest organ advising the Empress Dowager, and its members were usually Beijing's most influential officials; but functionally, as an administrative body, the Grand Council was in decline. Between 1901 and 1907 most of the administrative reform measures that characterized the period were proposed by four auxiliary bureaus of the Grand Council and not by the Grand Council itself. Most important was the coordinating body, the Government Affairs Bureau. Beneath it, in the three areas in which reforms were concentrated, were the Finance Bureau (*Caizheng chu*), Education Bureau (*Xuewu chu*), and the Military Reorganization Bureau. With these new bureaus in direct contact with the Empress Dowager, the formal, institutional role of the Grand Council in the decision-making process declined.[40]

The grand councillors as individuals, however, still controlled decision making because they held concurrent appointments on the Government Affairs Bureau and as heads of one or more of the new bureaus or ministries concerned with reform. In 1903, for example, Prince Qing was chief grand councillor, head of the Government Affairs, Finance, and Military Reorganization bureaus, and Commissioner of Foreign Affairs. Moreover, as was apparently the practice during most of the Empress Dowager's reign, individual grand councillors often drafted rescripts and edicts on her behalf.[41] Thus the Grand Council can still be said to have dominated court and bureaucratic politics in Beijing because membership on it defined the elite of high officials who wielded the most decision-making power.

In 1903 and 1904 the other grand councillors besides Prince Qing

---

40. Samuel C. Chu, in "The Grand Council in the T'ung-chih Kuang-hsu Periods (1860-1900): A Preliminary Study," *Jindai shi yanjiusuo jikan* 4.2 (December 1974): 825-42, argued that by the 1880s the Grand Council had lost its importance. Chu failed to make a distinction between the institutional and the political functions of the Grand Council. Institutionally, the Grand Council had deteriorated, but politically it remained preeminent.

The monumental work on the central government reform measures of the late Qing period, including the role of the Government Affairs Bureau and the other three bureaus, is Morrison, "The Modernization of the Confucian Bureaucracy," esp. chap. 5.

41. Evidence abounds in the Grand Council archives in Taibei's Palace Museum—for example: *Shangyu dang, fangben, zoubian* for Guang-xu 10/3/1 (00001ff.); I am indebted to Beatrice Bartlett for this reference and insight.

were Lu Chuan-lin, Rong-qing, Wang Wen-shao, and Qu Hong-ji. Lu Chuan-lin was also a member of the Government Affairs Bureau and president of the Board of Revenue. He was a Rong-lu appointee to the Grand Council and the brother-in-law and alter-ego of Zhang Zhi-dong, with whom Yuan was working well on educational and railway matters during these years. Lu never interfered with the policies of Yuan or Prince Qing.[42] The new man on the Grand Council, appointed late in 1903, was Rong-qing, an incompetent, corrupt, and ineffectual Manchu who was allegedly the choice of Yuan and Prince Qing. Rong-qing was at the same time a member of the Government Affairs Bureau, president of the Board of Revenue, and joint supervisor of Beijing Normal University.[43]

Wang Wen-shao we have met before. He had been governor-general of Zhili and Yuan's patron before becoming a grand councillor in 1898. By 1903 he was also a member of the Government Affairs Bureau, manager of the General Office of Railways and Mines, and a grand secretary. However, being old (he was seventy-three in 1903) and sickly, Wang was uninterested in the reform issues that were the focus of attention at Court after 1901 and he eagerly awaited retirement. Wang withdrew from controversies and, except for his opposition to the abolition of the civil service examination system, he rarely interfered with the activities of Yuan and Prince Qing. Finally, in the summer of 1905, Wang was allowed to retire from the Grand Council. He was replaced by two men: Xu Shi-chang and Yuan's erstwhile protégé, Tie-liang.[44]

The young Manchu Tie-liang owed his meteoric rise to the Grand Council in part to Yuan Shi-kai. In 1900 Tie-liang (b. 1863) had been with the first group of Chinese students who went to Japan for military schooling. In 1902, at Yuan's suggestion, the Empress Dowager appointed Tie-liang, then only a *daotai* candidate, to codirect with Yuan the training of 3,000 Manchu recruits as the nucleus for a division of modern-trained Manchu troops. In 1903, Tie-liang became vice-president of the Board of Revenue and led a military delegation to observe war games in Japan. After returning

42. QS, pp. 4909-10; Xiao Yi-shan, *Qingdai tongshi*, p. 2738; Liu Hou-sheng, p. 130; and Bays, *China Enters the Twentieth Century*, pp. 106-07, 117-23.
43. QS, p. 4915; Liu Hou-sheng, p. 134; Jin Liang, *Guang Xuan xiaoji* (1934), p. 38.
44. QS, pp. 4904-05; Liu Hou-sheng, p. 130; Jin Liang, *Jinshi renwu zhi* (Tianjin, 1934), p. 236, and *Guang Xuan xiaoji*, p. 37; Bays, *China Enters the Twentieth Century*, p. 118.

late that year, he worked with Yuan on the creation of the Military Reorganization Bureau, of which both he and Yuan became directors. In the fall of 1904, Tie-liang visited the southern Yangzi provinces to inspect the conditions of arsenals there, and to enforce collection of funds overdue from these provinces for Yuan's Beiyang Army in Zhili. Upon his return to Beijing, Tie-liang endorsed Yuan's plan for the dissolution of the Jiangnan arsenal at Shanghai and creation of a new arsenal in north China. In 1905 when Tie-liang was appointed to the Grand Council, he was also president of the Board of War (transferring to president of the Board of Revenue by the end of the year), a member of the Government Affairs Bureau, and still in charge with Yuan of training a special division of Manchu troops at Baoding.[45]

Thus, through their own positions or those of protégés and allies, the influence of Yuan and Prince Qing permeated the Grand Council and its auxiliaries—the Government Affairs, Military Reorganization, Finance, and Education bureaus. Not until the winter of 1906-1907 was there a serious attempt, led by grand councillor Qu Hong-ji, to break the grip of Prince Qing, and indirectly of Yuan, on court politics in Beijing.

Qu Hong-ji was the only grand councillor who was sufficiently trusted by the Empress Dowager and had the strength of character to challenge Yuan and Prince Qing. Qu's concurrent appointments to important posts numbered almost as many as Prince Qing's. Between 1903 and 1905, besides being a grand councillor, Qu was president of the Ministry of Foreign Affairs, a member of the Government Affairs Bureau, manager of the Beijing-Tianjin Railway, joint director with Wang Wen-shao of the General Office of Railways and Mines, and codirector with Prince Qing of the Finance Bureau. Qu had attacked Yuan once, in the spring of 1902, regarding Yuan's handling of the Beijing-Shenyang Railway. Later, after the Yuan and Prince Qing alliance of 1903, Qu was independent of but not openly opposed to Yuan and Prince Qing.[46]

Grand councillor Qu's struggle for power with Prince Qing and

45. Chen Xi-zhang, pp. 261-62; YSYZY, *juan* 21:4b-5; YSKZZ, p. 922; BYGD, *juan* 12:10-12.
46. Xiao Yi-shan, p. 2378; QS, p. 4905. In 1905, Qu sided with Yuan and Prince Qing in their effort to curtail Sheng Xuan-huai's influence in railway affairs; see FO 405/157 (conf. print), October-December 1905, no. 132. On the other hand, Cao Ru-lin, pp. 45-49, noted tension between Qu and Yuan at the Sino-Japanese negotiations in Beijing during December 1905.

Yuan began in the fall of 1906 in a clash over one of the most controversial issues aired at Court during the last decade of the Qing dynasty. This was the question of whether or not to abolish the Grand Council and the Grand Secretariat in favor of a modern cabinet system of executive government as part of the overall effort to modernize central government along constitutional lines. A special review committee had been created on September 1, 1906, to make the final proposals for the restructuring of the central government. Its membership was essentially the same as the Government Affairs Bureau, which we have already described as being dominated by Prince Qing and Yuan, and their allies and protégés. Not surprisingly, the special reviewing committee adopted the views of Yuan and Prince Qing and was in favor of a cabinet led by a prime minister.[47]

Being outnumbered on the special review committee, Qu Hong-ji did not publicly dissent from its recommendations to the Empress Dowager. Instead, Qu expressed his strong objections to the committee's recommendations in private audiences with the Empress Dowager.[48] During October, 1906, before the committee had made its recommendations, censors also voiced opposition in memorials to adoption of a cabinet system and abolition of the Grand Council and Grand Secretariat. Qu and the censors argued that a cabinet system, and especially the creation of a prime minister, would diminish the power of the throne, the role of which was being ignored in the committee's recommendations. Moreover, a cabinet system would enhance the power of Yuan and Prince Qing, who could be expected to dominate the cabinet by controlling the premiership. Qu and the censors argued that the essentials of the old system for decision making in the central government, especially the Grand Council as the throne's highest advisory body, should be retained.[49]

The issue between Qu and Yuan was power—and who should hold it. On the basic question of the need for constitutional monarchy and representative government, they apparently agreed, though probably for different reasons. More so than Zhang Zhi-

47. Morrison, pp. 971-86; Cameron, pp. 103-04; Guo Ding-yi, *Jindai Zhongguo shizhi erzhi* (Taibei, 1963), p. 1258; for recommendations of the special review committee, see *Guangxu zhengyao, juan* 32:39-41.
48. Liu Hou-sheng, p. 137.
49. Zhao Bing-lin, *Zhao Boyan ji* (Quanzhou, 1922-24), *Zhoushi, juan* 1:1-18; *Guangxu dashi, juan* 12:3b-8; Guo Ding-yi, pp. 1260-61.

dong, and at the urging of his old friend Zhang Jian, Yuan took a consistent stand in favor of a constitution and some form of representative government as necessary to the formation of a strong centralized modern state. Qu Hong-ji identified with elite interests in his native Hunan; his support of constitutional government presumably resembled that of propagandists like Wang Kang-nian, with whom Qu was associated.[50]

The special review committee's recommendations did seem to slight the role of the throne in its proposal of a cabinet system, and this proved politically to be a serious mistake for Yuan and Prince Qing. On November 6, 1906, four days after the review committee made its recommendations, the Empress Dowager issued an edict that probably was written by Qu Hong-ji. It rejected the cabinet proposal and retained the Grand Council and Grand Secretariat. The traditional six boards, as well as the recently added ministries of foreign affairs, commerce, and education, were reorganized into eleven modern ministries. Excepting the Ministry of Foreign Affairs, presidents of the new ministries could not hold concurrent appointments.[51] The new appointments to the Grand Council and to the presidencies of the new ministries altered the balance of power at Court. Lu Chuan-lin, Rong-qing, Tie-liang, and Xu Shi-chang were removed from the Grand Council to become ministry presidents. Remaining on the Grand Council was Prince Qing and Qu Hong-ji, who also continued as president of the Ministry of Foreign Affairs.[52] Lin Shao-nian and Shi-xu, men who lacked ties to either Yuan or Prince Qing, became new grand councillors.[53] Thus, the influence of Yuan and Prince Qing on the Grand Council had been seriously undercut, an indication of the extent to which Qu's views seemed to be prevailing upon the Empress Dowager.

It was also at this time that significant Manchu opposition to Yuan began to develop at Court. At the center of the Manchu movement against Yuan was Tie-liang, the Manchu bannerman who, as noted earlier, had risen with Yuan's help to a grand councillorship and presidency of the Board of War. On September 30,

50. Zhang Yu-fa, *Qingji de lixian tuanti* (Taibei, 1971), pp. 307-12; and Bays, *China Enters the Twentieth Century*, pp. 127-28, 199-201. On Qu and Wang Kang-nian, see note 61 below.
51. Liu Hou-sheng, p. 138; the edict is translated in full in H. T. Bell and H. G. W. Woodhead, eds., *China Yearbook, 1912* (London, 1912), pp. 354-55.
52. *Shilu*, juan 564:14b-15a.
53. QS, pp. 4910-11, 5082; Liu Hou-sheng, pp. 137, 142-46.

1906, at a meeting of the special review commission Yuan and Tie-liang were reported to have argued violently. The argument was apparently about Yuan's advocacy of a cabinet system and Tie-liang's insistence that all governor-generalships be abolished. Thereafter Tie-liang sided against Yuan and with his enemy, Qu Hong-ji.[54]

In the attacks led by grand councillor Qu and the censors, Yuan was slandered personally. Censor Chen Tian implicated him in a bribery scandal involving both Prince Qing and Yang Shi-xiang. In order to be appointed governor of Shandong, Yang Shi-xiang was alleged to have given Prince Qing a 100,000 tael bribe, with Yuan acting as the go-between.[55] Rumors were rampant that Yuan might be divested of his governor-generalship and "kicked upstairs" to an appointment in Beijing.[56] On October 20, while the special review committee was still meeting, Yuan left Beijing ostensibly to supervise war games in Zhangde, Henan, but actually, many thought, to escape further harassment in Court and embarrassment before the Empress Dowager.[57] Yuan returned to Tianjin in mid-November and promptly offered in a memorial to relinquish control over four out of six Beiyang Army divisions to the new Ministry of War (*Lujun bu*), of which Tie-liang was head. Moreover, in another memorial Yuan resigned eight posts (the six named on page 72), plus the directorships of the Manchu division at Baoding and the proposed Tianjin-Jinjiang Railway) that he held concurrently with the Zhili governor-generalship.[58] Yuan acted in a penitent fashion, hoping to impress and reconcile the Empress Dowager, but initially, she seemed slow in responding.

Having won the first round in his struggle with Yuan and Prince Qing, Qu Hong-ji pressed his advantage. Using his influence with the Empress Dowager, Qu made sure that the Third, Fifth, and Sixth divisions of Yuan's Beiyang Army were transferred to Tie-liang's Ministry of War. Qu was behind the attack by censors in

54. DFZZ 3.10 (1906): *zazu* 44-45; and Li Chien-nung, pp. 211, 213-16. Zhang Zhi-dong also vigorously opposed efforts to narrow the powers of governors and governors-general; Bays, *China Enters the Twentieth Century*, pp. 201-03. Manchu attacks, led by Tie-liang, on Yuan's military power are discussed more fully in Chapter 4.

55. DFZZ 3.10 (1906): *zazu* 43. Apparently Yang's appointment also received the prior approval of the Germans; *Morrison Correspondence*, p. 288.

56. NCH, Aug. 3 and Oct. 5, 1906.

57. Zhao Bing-lin, *Zoushi*, juan 1:18; *Guangxu dashi*, juan 12:8; Guo Ding-yi, p. 1259.

58. YSYZY, *juan* 42:1-3.

January, 1907, on Tang Shao-yi and his eventual removal as vice-president of the new Ministry of Posts and Communications (*You-chuan bu*).[59] Allegedly at Qu's instigation during the spring of 1907, censors memorialized further attacks upon Yuan, Prince Qing, and their protégés and allies. On May 4, Censor Zhao Qi-lin called for the impeachment of Duan Zhi-gui, who had been an important figure in Yuan's military administration in Zhili and just appointed governor of the newly created province of Heilongjiang in Manchuria. To secure this post, Duan was said to have bribed Prince Qing with 100,000 taels and purchased for the latter's son, Zai-zhen, the services of a famous Tianjin prostitute. These accusations were investigated by Zai-feng and Sun Jia-nai, but their report was inconclusive. More censors, including Zhao Bing-lin, defended the validity of Zhao Qi-lin's charges. By the end of May, Duan Zhi-gui had lost his governorship and Zai-zhen had resigned his posts in Beijing.[60]

At the same time slanderous attacks upon Yuan, Prince Qing, Zai-zhen, and others were appearing daily in a Beijing newspaper, the *Jingbao*. These attacks provided censors with much of the material used in impeaching Duan Zhi-gui. The editor of the newspaper and author of most of the controversial articles was Wang Kang-nian, who had been a radical reformer in Hunan and Shanghai in the 1890s and now was an associate of Qu Hong-ji. Qu gave the newspaper substantive support, providing it with funds and necessary political protection.[61]

Qu Hong-ji's principal political ally in his struggle against Yuan and Prince Qing was Cen Chun-xuan, the governor-general of the Guangdong-Guangxi region. Since at least 1900 Cen and Yuan probably had been on poor personal terms and since 1902, as governor-general of Liangguang, Cen had rivaled Yuan for the Empress Dowager's attention.[62] Early in 1907 Cen was transferred

59. Liu Hou-sheng, p. 139; FO 405/173 (conf. print), January-March 1907, nos. 86 and 107.
60. Xu Yi-shi, "Qing Guangxu dingwei zhengchao zhi zhongyao shiliao," *Guowen zhoubao*, 14.5 (January 1937):71-76; *ibid.*, 14.6 (February 1937):73-76; Liu Hou-sheng, pp. 140-41; Shen Yun-long, "Zhangwo wanqing zhengbing zhi Yi-kuang," pp. 73-74; Zhao Bing-lin, *Zoushi*, *juan* 3:4-6.
61. Xu Yi-shi, "Qing Guangxu dingwei zhengchao zhi zhongyao shiliao"; Wang Yi-nian, ed., *Wang Rang-qing (Kang-nian) xiansheng chuan ji* (1937), *juan* 4:2-6; Shen Yun-long, "Liang Qi-chao yu Wang Kang-nian," *Xiandai zhengzhi renwu shuping* 1 (1968):20-21. On Wang Kang-nian's earlier career, see Bays, *China Enters the Twentieth Century*, pp. 28, 34-36, 39, 55, 65-66, 68, 80-83, 89, 93, 97, 170.
62. Wu Yong, pp. 83, 102-03, 127-30, 137, 156-58. For an illustration of rivalry

from Liangguang to the Yunan-Guizhou governor-generalship, a move which he regarded as a demotion. Cen proceeded to Shanghai, where he feigned illness and entered a hospital, waiting and hoping for a change in assignment. On March 3, 1907, Cen was appointed to the governor-generalship of Sichuan, a post that he was willing to accept. Then early in May, 1907, while en route to Sichuan, Cen suddenly memorialized the throne, requesting an audience. Without waiting for a reply, Cen travelled to Beijing on the newly completed Beijing-Hankou Railway. In audience with the Empress Dowager he requested permission to stay in Beijing because of poor health. On the next day, May 3, 1907, the Empress Dowager appointed Cen to the presidency of the Ministry of Posts and Communications.

Cen blamed Yuan and prince Qing for his transfer to the Yunan-Guizhou post. The Sichuan appointment convinced him that his political position vis-à-vis the Empress Dowager was still intact; so Cen came to Beijing for revenge. In a second audience with the Empress Dowager on May 3, 1907, Cen accused Prince Qing of corruption and incompetence. Two days later, as president of the Ministry of Posts and Communications, Cen impeached the ministry's vice-president, Zhu Bao-kui, who was considered a protégé of both Prince Qing and Yuan. Cen's sudden appearance in Beijing, his appointment by the throne, and his attacks upon Yuan and Prince Qing coincided with the offensive led by Qu Hong-ji. However, there is little evidence of an explicit conspiracy between Qu and Cen.[63]

Faced by the wave of attacks from Cen and Qu, Yuan and Prince Qing retaliated. On May 27, Prince Qing talked the Empress Dowager into sending Cen Chun-xuan back to Liangguang as governor-

---

between Yuan and Cen for the Empress Dowager's favor, see Chapter 2, note 23, above. For a portrait of Cen in Guangdong, see Edward J.M. Rhoads, *China's Republican Revolution*, pp. 51-58, 72-73, 78, 86-92.

63. Cen Chun-xuan, *Lezhai manbi* (Taibei, 1962), pp. 14-17; Liu Hou-sheng, pp. 139-57; Shen Yun-long, "Qingmou minchu zhi Cen Chun-xuan," *Xiandai zhengzhi renwu shuping* 1:133-38; Xu Yi-shi, "Qing Guangxu dingwei zhengchao zhi zhongyao shiliao." That cooperation between Qu and Cen was superficial is indicated by the fact that Cen chose to impeach Chu Bao-gui. No doubt Cen acted at the urging of Sheng Xuan-huai, with whom he was associated and who was an arch-enemy of Chu Bao-gui. Qu Hong-ji, however, disliked Sheng Xuan-huai and thus disassociated himself from the Chu Bao-gui affair; see Liu Hou-sheng, pp. 146-47. And for Qu's attitudes toward Sheng Xuan-huai, FO 405/157 (conf. print), October-December 1905, no. 132.

general because of the alleged seriousness of renewed disturbances there. Chen Bi, an old associate of Yuan's from Zhili, replaced Cen as president of the Ministry of Posts and Communications. Prince Qing also maneuvered the transfer of Lin Shao-nian, who had been siding with Qu and Cen, from the Grand Council to the presidency of the new Ministry of Finance (*Duzhi bu*). However, the day after the transfer of Lin was announced, the order was rescinded, due undoubtedly to Qu Hong-ji's success in persuading the Empress Dowager to reconsider the transfer.[64]

Still, by the end of May, 1907, the tide of battle with Qu Hong-ji and Cen Chun-xuan had turned in favor of Yuan and Prince Qing. Yuan Shi-kai in a remarkable letter from Tianjin on May 30 explained the situation to Duan-fang, a Manchu friend and governor-general of Huguang:

> Cen Chun-xuan came suddenly to Beijing and conspired with Qu Hong-ji. Before Cen came, Qu had been stirring up the censors. When Cen arrived, he attacked Prince Qing in an audience with the Empress Dowager. The censors, taking advantage of the opportunity, then continued to memorialize. Some attacked Prince Qing; some attacked Zai-zhen. Prince Qing was surrounded by enemies on all sides, making the situation very dangerous. Fortunately . . . with the help of men such as Grand Councillor Shi-xu and governor-general of Manchuria, Xu Shi-chang, the Empress Dowager's anger was dissipated. . . . On May 27 Prince Qing had an audience alone with the Empress Dowager and they settled on what should be done. The Empress Dowager agreed to transfer Cen [out of Beijing] and the next day [May 28] she announced it. Cen did not want to go, but it had already been arranged by Prince Qing and the Empress Dowager on May 27. . . . In short, the influence of these fellows is already waning, there is nothing they can do—it would have been better for him [Cen] if he had not come to Beijing at all. . . . The Empress Dowager had heard that this [plot] to overthrow Prince Qing and Yuan Shi-kai represented an attempt to restore the reformers [of 1898 and the Guang-xu Emperor]. . . . Still, the Empress Dowager is dissatisfied with Zai-zhen and he has lost all posts—entirely due to the machinations of Qu Hong-ji. Now the Empress Dowager is more relaxed. Reflecting on the situation, the Prince [Qing] at the moment can not make a

64. Liu Hou-sheng, pp. 142-45; Guo Ding-yi, p. 1276.

move, but the future of his colleague, Qu, does not look bright. . . .⁶⁵

Yuan proved to be correct. By the end of May, Qu and Cen were in serious trouble. In his May 27 audience with the Empress Dowager, Prince Qing apparently convinced her that Qu and Cen were linked to Kang You-wei and Liang Qi-chao and a plot to return them to power in Beijing. Prince Qing's proof was a faked photograph of Cen and Kang together in Shanghai, and documentary evidence of the support Qu and Cen had given the reformers in and before 1898. In the middle of June, 1907, Cen left Beijing for Canton. On June 17, Hanlin graduate and reader of the Grand Secretariat (*shidu xueshi*), Yun Yu-ding, memorialized a request for the impeachment of Qu. Reportedly, Yang Shi-qi had written the impeachment memorial for Yun and bribed him with 20,000 taels. Qu was accused of divulging the Empress Dowager's confidential remark that she was displeased with Prince Qing to Wang Kang-nian for publication in the *Jingbao* and to a foreign correspondent, namely, G. E. Morrison of the London *Times*. The impeachment was successful and Qu was dismissed from all offices.⁶⁶

Although censorial attack upon Yuan, Prince Qing, and their allies continued sporadically, by the summer of 1907 it appeared that Yuan and Prince Qing had recovered their former influence with the Empress Dowager and their grip on court politics. Qu had been dismissed. The final blow to Cen came on August 12, when he was summarily dismissed from Liangguang governor-generalship. On the same day, Lin Shao-nian, Qu's ally on the Grand Council, lost his grand councillorship and was sent to Henan as its new governor. Moreover, also in August, Wang Kang-nian's *Jingbao* was closed.⁶⁷ This left only the young Manchu Tie-liang as a significant court figure in opposition to Yuan and Prince Qing. But Tie-liang was no longer a grand councillor and, as we shall see in Chapters 4 and 6, he was eventually isolated by Yuan and Prince Qing, even within the Ministry of War of which he was head, where he was

65. In the original text, Yuan used code names and abbreviated language. It was reproduced for the first time in Xu Yi-shi, "Qing Guangxu dingwei . . . ." The best annotated explanations of the text are by Liu Hou-sheng, pp. 142-46. My translation owes much to Liu Hou-sheng and is necessarily not literal.
66. Xu Yi-shi, "Qing Guangxu dingwei . . ."; Liu Hou-sheng, pp. 143, 150-53; *Wang Rang-qing (Kang-nian) xiansheng zhuanji*, juan 4:9; and Li Chien-nung, p. 213.
67. Guo Ding-yi, pp. 1278-85.

surrounded by Yuan's men and exercised little direct authority over troops.

The prolonged struggle between grand councillors Qu and Prince Qing and their respective allies, governors-general Cen and Yuan, turned in favor of Prince Qing and Yuan rather suddenly in late May, 1907. Why? The standard explanation for their triumph is that the Empress Dowager was frightened into moving against Qu and Cen by Prince Qing's trumped-up charges of collusion with the exiled radical reformers Kang You-wei and Liang Qi-chao. Thus, emphasizing ideological differences and the Empress Dowager's gullibility, historians have tended to see Qu as progressive and nationalistic and Yuan Shi-kai and Prince Qing as the reverse.[68] Yet contemporary foreign opinion considered Yuan and his Cantonese associates as more progressive and Western-minded.[69] Differences over foreign policy do not seem to have been relevant to the struggle, although Qu and Cen were thought to advocate a tougher line on Manchuria and greater limits on foreign investment.[70] The one issue that divided them was the question of establishing a cabinet vis-à-vis the role of the throne. Here Yuan and Prince Qing took the more liberal position in favor of a cabinet, but Qu was equally committed to constitutional monarchy. Given the Empress Dowager's profound understanding of the politics of intrigue, and the contradictory claims of each side to represent progressive reform against their opponents' corrupt conservatism, I submit that ideological and policy differences were secondary. No doubt the Empress Dowager permitted the power struggle to continue so long because of her usual strategy of balancing factions. In her mind, Yuan and Prince Qing had acquired too great a monopoly of political and bureaucratic power and needed trimming. But the outcome—the destruction of the Qu-Cen clique altogether—was probably unexpected. A major factor producing this result was concern of the foreign powers, particularly the British, about Yuan and about the administrative paralysis and confusion that accompanied the struggle.

By spring, 1907, the rise of grand councillor Qu and governor-

68. Xu Yi-shi, "Qing Guangxu dingwei . . ."; Shen Yun-long, "Zhangwo wanqing zhangbing zhi Yi-kuang"; Li Chien-nung, p. 213.
69. FO 405/174 (conf. print), April-June 1907, no. 98; 405/175 (conf. print), July-December 1907, no. 45; 405/178 (conf. print), Annual Report for 1907, pp. 2-6.
70. Hunt, pp. 124-26.

general Cen and the apparent disenfranchisement of Yuan and Prince Qing had seriously disrupted the conduct of foreign policy as well as other affairs of state. Foreign representatives in Beijing were dismayed by the more-than-usual confusion, stalling, and apparent refusal to make decisions which characterized the Foreign Ministry at the time.[71] Caught in the middle of the power struggle was the Ministry of Posts and Communications. Its chief business, railway management and recovery, seemed stymied.[72] Likewise, there were serious problems with resignations, insubordination, and corruption in the Ministry of War.[73] It seems reasonable to assume that by May, 1907, these problems must have come to the Empress Dowager's attention.

Not surprisingly, the new British minister in Beijing, Sir John Jordan, was worried about what was happening to his ally, Yuan Shi-kai. In despatches to London, Jordan characterized Qu Hong-ji as "a narrow-minded pedant." Still Yuan's position as Zhili governor-general was not under direct attack and so no formal British message of concern was communicated to the Court (nor did Yuan request it), as had been done earlier in 1902 and 1903 when Yuan seemed threatened with impeachment. But the British minister followed the situation very closely.[74] Qu and his allies appeared to have no defenders among the major Powers generally. The Empress Dowager must have been aware of this—as well as British concern for Yuan—in her final decision to remove both Qu and Cen from office.

To conclude, Beijing politics in the 1900s was determined much less by the ideological spectrum of conservative/moderate/radical reform and more by foreign influence than the politics of the 1890s. From 1903 to 1905, Yuan Shi-kai's political position at

71. FO 405/174 (conf. print), April-June 1907, nos. 48, 98; 405/175 (conf. print), July-December 1907, nos. 21, 85; Hunt, p. 164.

72. FO 228/2482, Jordan telegrams nos. 58, 69, and 70 of April 7 and May 3 and 5, 1907. A good example of disruption is the delay caused in negotiations to recover the Beijing-Hankou Railway from a Belgian-French Syndicate; see MacKinnon, "Liang Shih-i and the Communications Clique."

73. FO 405/174 (conf. prints), April-June 1907, nos. 12, 95; 371/231, Jordan letter no. 332, July 10, 1907; *Morrison Correspondence*, p. 411. Also see Chapter 4.

74. Lau Kit-ching, "Sir John Jordan and Affairs of China, 1906-1916, with Special Reference to the 1911 Revolution and Yuan Shih-k'ai" (Ph.D. dissertation, University of London, 1968), p. 25. FO 405/173 (conf. print), January-March 1907, nos. 86, 197; 405/174 (conf. print), April-June 1907, nos. 20, 48, 70, 98; 405/175 (conf. print), July-December 1907, nos. 45, 85; 228/2482, Jordan telegram no. 73, May 7, 1907; Jordan letter no. 227, May 14, 1907.

Court seemed unassailable because of the personal favor of the Empress Dowager, his effectiveness as an official in Tianjin and Beijing, the intervention of the British, and the strength of his new alliance with Prince Qing—whose influence dominated the Grand Council and its auxiliary bureaus. Then suddenly, during the winter of 1906-07, significant opposition to Prince Qing and Yuan developed in the Grand Council. The ensuing struggle between Yuan and Prince Qing on the one hand, and Qu Hong-ji, Cen Chun-xuan, and Tie-liang on the other, was over power. Ideological and policy differences were secondary. In the end, with the backing of the British and other Powers, Yuan and Prince Qing prevailed. We shall see, in Chapters 4 and 6, how in 1907-08 they reasserted control over the central government's new reform bureaucracies in Beijing, and over the Beijing Army that Yuan had been raising and training in Zhili since 1903.

CHAPTER IV

Yuan Shi-kai and the Beiyang Army, 1901-1907

The Beiyang Army was the most significant military development in China between the Xiang and Huai Armies which suppressed the Taiping and Nian rebellions in the 1860s and the army that Chiang Kai-shek raised and employed in the Northern Expedition of 1926-27. Compared to its nineteenth century predecessors, the Beiyang was well disciplined and trained in the use of Western arms. Formed for the most part by Yuan Shi-kai while he was governor-general of Zhili, by 1906 the Beiyang Army grew to six divisions of about 10,000 men each. Size alone gave the army a major role in politics during the last decade of the Qing and the early years of the Republic. There is no doubt that the Beiyang Army was both a manifestation and a major source of Yuan's political power as a Qing official. What remain to be settled are questions about the nature of Yuan's control of the Beiyang Army and of the political power derived therefrom.

The prevailing view is that the Beiyang Army originated as a regionally-based, private army of Yuan Shi-kai. Accordingly, the Beiyang Army is grouped with the Huai and Xiang Armies of the mid-nineteenth century as precursors of the warlord armies of the 1920s. Although the Beiyang Army is viewed as more modernized in a strictly military sense, all three are said to have been regionally-based private armies and, as such, semiindependent financially and administratively from the central government in Beijing.[1]

Yuan's control of the Beiyang Army was derived from his influence in Beijing. After the Russo-Japanese War over Manchuria the Empress Dowager was persuaded that the creation of a new army under Yuan Shi-kai in north China was vital to her security and that of the dynasty. The resulting Beiyang Army was organized much more along the lines of a centralized, modern professional army than its predecessors, the Huai and Xiang Armies. It was clearly not Yuan's personal, regional force, as is shown by Beijing's financial and administrative control of the army and the tenuous loyalties to Yuan of the majority of Beiyang Army officers.

The Beiyang Army:
Its Development and Organizational Structure

In contrast to the Xiang and Huai Armies, the origins of which lay in local responses to the Taiping Rebellion, the Beiyang Army grew systematically according to plans formulated in Tianjin and Beijing. In its training, discipline, and organizational structure, contemporary Japanese military models were followed. The resulting army itself became a model, impressing foreigners and Chinese alike with its efficiency, discipline, and polish.

Yuan Shi-kai actively pursued military reorganization and reform from the beginning of his Zhili governor-generalship. On February 20, 1902, he informed the Court of plans to recruit and train 6,000 Zhili men for a "New Army" (*xinjun*).[2] Yuan was responding to the Court's action, made a few weeks earlier, freeing one million taels of relief funds for use in expanding the number of foreign-trained troops in Zhili.[3] In June, Yuan reorganized Zhili's military administrative system by establishing a Department of Military Administration (*Junzheng si*) as the new administrative body through which all military matters were to be channeled. The Department of Military Administration was divided into three bureaus: military supplies (*Bingbei chu*), planning (*Canmou chu*), and training (*Jiaolian chu*).[4] At the same time Yuan proposed a new military system for the entire Empire. He recommended that a "Regular Army" (*Changbei jun*) be gradually built up and organized

---

1. See works by Hatano Yoshihiro, Ralph Powell, Franz Michael, Luo Er-gang, and Diana Lary cited in the Introduction.
2. YSKZZ, pp. 448-50.   3. YSKZZ, p. 427.   4. YSKZZ, pp. 566-68.

along modern Western lines, with the men serving three years on active duty and then retiring into reserve units. Yuan added that in Zhili he would begin by training two new divisions, or roughly 20,000 men, in 1902.[5] Yuan's proposal for a national system was accepted in principle, but he was instructed to confer with Liu Kun-yi and Zhang Zhi-dong, who had made similar proposals, and agree upon a uniform system.[6]

Principally for financial reasons, Yuan failed to train two new divisions in 1902 as planned. Because of the desperate fiscal plight of his administration (described in Chapter 2), Yuan had to rely on Beijing for the funds with which to expand the army. The Empress Dowager did allocate one million taels for troop training in Zhili, but this was only two-thirds of the minimum required to support a new division for a year.[7] In a military intelligence survey dated October 7, 1902, Lieutenant-Colonel Ducat, the British military attaché in Beijing, indicated that financial difficulties were preventing Yuan from recruiting and training any sizeable number of troops. Ducat reported that 1,000 men were at Baoding comprising the Regular Army, the name for the new division being raised; his figures also indicated that there were approximately 3,000-4,000 cadets receiving training at Baoding. Hence, Yuan's troop training program progressed slowly during 1902, processing at most 5,000 men.[8]

In his report, Lieutenant-Colonel Ducat also indicated the absence of a centralized military command in Zhili. As indicated in Chapter 2, Ma Yu-kun rivaled Yuan for military control of the province. In October, 1902, of the roughly 30,000 troops spread about Zhili, Yuan directly controlled about 15,000. These included the Newly Created Army of 7,000 men, brought from Shandong by Yuan and now stationed around Beijing and Tianjin, where they saw action against the Jing Ting-bin rebels during the spring of 1902. At his old training camp of Xiaozhan near Tianjin, Yuan put the small "Self-Strengthening Army" (*Ziqiang jun*) of about 2,000 men which had been originally raised by Zhang Zhi-dong and transferred to Yuan in 1900.[9] Also under Yuan were the 5,000-

5. YSKZZ, pp. 562-65; and Powell, pp. 142-43.   6. *Shilu, juan* 499:14a.
7. YSKZZ, pp. 448, 565; and Powell, p. 143.
8. FO 405/128 (conf. print), December 1902, no. 25. Wen Gong-zhi, in *Zuijin sanshinian Zhongguo junshi shi* (Shanghai, 1932), vol. 1, p. 40, and Powell, pp. 143-44, have both asserted inaccurately that Yuan trained two new divisions in 1902.
9. See Chapter 1, note 23, above.

6,000 trainees at Baoding for the new Regular Army mentioned above. Yuan's rival and Zhili commander-in-chief, Ma Yu-kun, commanded 7,000-8,000 men at Tongzhou, the area around which he was said to rule as a personal satrapy.[10] As we have seen, Ma was not Yuan's man, although he was officially subordinate to him. Scattered elsewhere were miscellaneous troops, mostly Green Standard and Huai Army units, most of which Yuan wished to disband. But in 1902, although these troops had been consistently useless in the suppression of insurgencies during Li Hong-zhang's last term as Zhili governor-general, they formed a vocal vested interest which Yuan was reluctant to disturb.[11] In any case, the point is that Yuan's creation by fiat of a centralized military command in the Department of Military Administration did not immediately give him control over all troops in the province.

Yuan did succeed, however, in taking a few steps in 1902 that helped to centralize military command in his hands. Whereas Yuan could not unseat Ma Yu-kun, who was a favorite of the Empress Dowager, he was able to occupy Ma with bandit suppression activities in northeast Zhili and thereby isolate him (a process described in Chapter 2). Moreover, Yuan maneuvered the transfer or retirement of other local commanders over whom he had difficulty exercising authority. Prime targets were old Huai army commanders like Lu Ben-yuan and Mei Dong-yi. Lu was Zhili's commander-in-chief in February, 1902, when Yuan had him transferred to Zhejiang.[12] Yuan was also successful in dissolving the remaining Zhili units of Rong-lu's old Center Division of the Military Guards Army commanded by Sun Wan-lin.[13] But when Yuan initiated impeachment proceedings against Mei Dong-yi, commander of a garrison at Cangzhou, Yuan ran into trouble. As noted earlier, chiefly because of protests by the British minister, Sir Earnest Satow, who felt indebted to Mei for good works during the Boxer crisis of 1900, Mei was permitted to remain at Cangzhou, but with a smaller force.[14]

Yuan also laid the foundations for an effective officers training and recruiting program in 1902. At Baoding he established a Beiyang Officers Academy (*Beiyang jiangbian xuetang*) for retraining of-

10. PTT, Oct. 18, 1902.   11. *Shilu, juan* 488:11b, 489:5b, 492:15a.
12. PTT, Feb. 15 (supp.) and May 17 (supp.), 1902.
13. *Shilu, juan* 492:14a; DHXL, *juan* 171:12b.
14. See Chapter 2, note 22, above.

ficers and sub-officers.[15] In addition, he subsidized the sending of fifty-five students to Japan for higher military education and brought fourteen Japanese instructors to teach at Baoding.[16] A well-trained, disciplined officer corps was to become the hallmark of the Beiyang Army.

During 1903 Yuan Shi-kai trained about 5,000 more men at Baoding, so that by the end of the year he commanded about 22,000 comparatively modern troops. This included one division of about 10,000 newly trained troops, his old Newly Created Army division, now about 9,000 men, and about 3,000 Manchu bannermen which he and Tie-liang were training at Baoding. Besides these troops, as *Beiyang dachen* Yuan wielded authority over Shandong's Vanguard Army of about 10,000 men that he had organized when governor in 1899-1901. Personal influence in Shandong was exercised through a friendly governor (Zhou Fu), an old associate (Xia Xin-you) as commander, and protégés as high ranking officers (including Yuan's brother, Yuan Shi-xun, as commandant of the officers' academy, and his son, Yuan Ke-ding).[17]

The coming of the Russo-Japanese War in 1904 provided Yuan with the opportunity to double the size of his force and turn the troops under his command into an army which was national in scope. As the deteriorating situation in Manchuria reached crisis proportions in January, 1904, the Empress Dowager considered what precautionary military measures to take in case China was drawn into the conflict. Yuan persuaded the Empress Dowager and her advisers to finance the creation of a unified, 60,000-man-strong Beiyang Army by doubling the number of modern troops under Yuan's command in north China. Organizationally the Beiyang was to be a national army, along lines established five years earlier by Rong-lu for the five-division Military Guards Army (*Wuwei jun*).[18]

The creation of the Beiyang Army had been only one of several possibilities. The quickest way to strengthen the northeastern

15. YSKZZ, pp. 561-62; *Shilu, juan* 499:13b-14a; PTT, May 31 and Oct. 18, 1902; and FO 405/128 (conf. print), December 1902, no. 25.

16. YSKZZ, p. 514; PTT, March 1, 1902 (supp.).

17. FO 405/143 (conf. print), April-June 1904, no. 2; PTT, Oct. 11, 1902; FO 17/1654, Intelligence Diary for the period ending Feb. 2, 1904; 371/41, enclosure no. 4 in Jordan no. 420 of Oct. 15, 1906; 405/156 (conf. print), July-September 1905, no. 103; David Buck, *Urban Change*, chap. 3.

18. YSKZZ, pp. 1205-07; Guo Ding-yi, p. 1195. On the *Wuwei jun* as the institutional parent of the Beiyang Army, see Liu Feng-han, *Wuwei jun*, esp. pp. 1-3.

frontier would have been to supplement the troops already there with troops from the southern Yangzi provinces. Yuan, not surprisingly, was opposed to the idea, calling instead for the enlargement of his forces in Zhili. Nevertheless, a few units from southern provinces did arrive in Zhili early in 1904. Eight battalions, or about 4,000 men, of Zhang Zhi-dong's troops in Hubei were sent to Tongzhou, Zhili. At Tongzhou trouble erupted between local residents and the Hubei troops, and Yuan used this as a pretext to restrict severely their movement in the area.[19]

Another possibility would have been to build up the troops of Yuan's rival, Zhili's commander-in-chief, Ma Yu-kun, along with those of Yuan Shi-kai. In 1903 Ma enjoyed enough favor at Court to be called to Beijing for audiences with the Empress Dowager.[20] His troops, stationed normally at Tongzhou, numbered about 8,200 and had more battle experience than Beiyang Army units. Moreover, Ma was eager to fight the Russians. Early in 1904 he led his army outside the Great Wall into the Jehol area, ostensibly to deal with banditry problems.[21] To counter Ma, Yuan moved a division from Baoding to Shanhaiguan and the Yongping area inside the Great Wall, keeping them separate from Ma's troops.[22] Yuan also tried to undercut Ma's position in Jehol by helping to build up the local troops of Jehol's Tarter General Song-shou.[23] Then Yuan delivered the decisive blow, by persuading the Empress Dowager to support the doubling of troops under his command. General Ma's forces increased at most by 1,500 men, so that by 1905 the Beiyang Army had the old general hopelessly outmanned and outgunned.[24]

As we shall see, the Empress Dowager's decision in February, 1904, to help finance Yuan's plans for doubling the size of the modern forces in north China was crucial to the creation of what is

19. FO 17/1654, telegram from Tianjin dated March 18, 1904; 17/655, Intelligence Diaries for the periods ending March 1 and 29 and April 12, 1904; Duan-fang, *Duan Zhong-min gong zougao* (1918), juan 3:49b-50; Powell, p. 219.
20. FO 405/134 (conf. print), April-June 1903, nos. 78, 166; *Subao*, April 2, 1903.
21. Liu Feng-han, *Wuwei jun*, pp. 573-75, 779-80; FO 17/1654, telegram from Tianjin dated March 18, 1904, and Intelligence Diary for the period ending Jan. 19, 1904; 17/1655, Intelligence Diaries for periods ending Feb. 16 and March 1 and 15, 1904.
22. FO 17/1654, Intelligence Diary for the period ending Jan. 19, 1904; 17/1655, Intelligence Diaries for periods ending Feb. 16, March 1, 15, and 29, and April 12, 1904; 17/1657, Intelligence Diaries for periods ending Sept. 13 and 27, 1904.
23. FO 17/1655, Intelligence Diary for the period ending March 29, 1904.
24. Liu Feng-han, *Wuwei jun*, pp. 779-80; FO 17/1655, Intelligence Diary for the period ending April 12, 1904.

known today as the Beiyang Army. The title "Beiyang Army" (*Beiyang jun*) designated the six northern divisions, stationed in Zhili and Shandong, of a new national army (*Lujun*).[25] Yuan wasted little time in hammering the army into shape. By the end of 1904 he had filled out two new divisions (3rd and 4th) of his Zhili forces and expanded the number of retrained Manchu bannermen to full division strength of 10,000 men. Early in 1905 Shandong's Vanguard Army was formally incorporated into the Beiyang Army as its 5th division and the 6th division was completed. The resulting six Beiyang divisions, five of which were stationed in Zhili, are identified and their growth reviewed in Table 1.

TABLE 1. *Growth of the Beiyang Army*
(completed division = 10,000 men)

First Division	Predominantly Manchu, established 1902-05
Second Division ..	Established 1902-03
Third Division	Established 1904
Fourth Division ...	Formerly Newly Created Army, established 1896-98
Fifth Division	Formerly Vanguard Army, established 1899-1901
Sixth Division	Established 1904-05

SOURCE: FO 17/1656, Intelligence Diary for the period ending Aug. 16, 1904; 17/1657, Intelligence Diary for the period ending Nov. 8, 1904; 17/1688, Intelligence Diary for the period ending March 28, 1905; 405/154, (Confidential Print), Jan.-March, 1905, no. 71, "Review of military affairs in China during the year 1904 by Lieutenant-Colonel C.M. Ducat." YSKZZ, pp. 1935-36, 2183, 2319; Liu Feng-han, *Wuwei jun*, pp. 794-98.

Formal education was the keystone in the training of the rapidly expanding Beiyang Army. During Yuan's governor-generalship over Zhili, the number of academies, schools, and special courses established for the Beiyang Army personnel was large and increased each year. By the end of 1903 there were six military schools in Baoding: a one-year staff college (*Junguan xuetang*), a new Beiyang Military Academy (*Wubei xuetang*), a three-year accelerated training center for non-commissioned officers (*Sucheng xuetang*), a school devoted to topography (*Cehui xuetang*), an eight-month cram course in trigonometry and ballistics for officers, and a school for retraining old officers from other provinces (*Fenjian xuetang*).[26] In addition, by 1907 Yuan had opened in Baoding and elsewhere three

25. YSKZZ, pp. 1205-07, 1239; see also Rong Meng-yuan, "Beiyang junfa di laili," in *Jin ershi nian Zhongguo shixue lunzhu huibian* (Hong Kong, 1971), vol. 1, pp. 336-38 (originally in *Lishi jiaoxue*, April 1956).
26. Powell, p. 145; BYGD, *juan* 12:22-31.

military primary schools (*Xiao xuetang*), in-service divisional schools (*Suiying xuetang*), a new model staff college (*Jiang wutang*), a veterinary school specializing in horses (*Mayi xuetang*), schools of administration (*Jingli*) and ordnance (*Junxue*), and two medical schools (*Junyi xuetang* and *Beiyang yiyuan*).[27] Combined enrollment in all these schools was over 4,100 by 1907 (see Table 13).

Through Yuan's military education program, Japanese influence on the development of the Beiyang Army was profound. Much of the instruction at Yuan's military schools was given by foreign instructors, the majority of whom were Japanese.[28] Moreover, high Beiyang officers traveled frequently to Japan to view exercises there and, as we shall see, many newly recruited junior officers in the Beiyang Army were graduates of Japanese military schools. It was no surprise that the Beiyang Army increasingly resembled Japanese armies in training and organization.

Beiyang infantry units, for example, were drilled rigorously to conform with contemporary Japanese standards. A British officer described the drill of units of the Third Division in 1906:

> The men looked to be young and I was struck by their smartness and the cleanliness of their uniforms. . . . At first one company was sent out, and they ran very fast, extending to about 3 paces with 3 men flanking guard, echeloned out on either flank. The attack was carried out across the parade ground, the first halt was given as 800 metres from the position. The distance was clearly given by the company commander, but beyond its being repeated by section leaders, there was no noise. The men fired standing. The right section made a rush of about 50 [paces] and was then reinforced by the other two sections. At 600 metres the men began to kneel, a company in extended order following about 100 [paces] behind and soon reinforcing in the gaps of the firing line. The other companies reinforced in a similar manner. When 300 metres from the position, the men lay down and started rapid independent fire, after which bayonets were fixed and the final charge was made, the distance really not being 100 [paces]. As the men charged they gave three distinct and unanimous roars or cheers. The things that impressed me

27. YSKZZ, p. 1805; BYGD, *juan* 12:19-21; FO 371/41, enclosure no. 1 in Jordan no. 420 of Oct. 15, 1906; 271/435, enclosure in Jordan no. 506 of Nov. 8, 1908; Powell, pp. 182-83, 202-03, 236-37. Apparently in 1904 the *Junguan xuetang* was renamed the *Jiangbian xuetang*.

28. Powell, pp. 161-62.

were the absence of noise, the giving of the distances and the rapidity with which the men moved, *a fair copy of the Japanese* [emphasis added].[29]

As portrayed in regulations, the Beiyang Army soldier compared favorably to his predecessor in the Huai and Xiang Armies. Recruits were required to be between 20 and 25 years of age, over 5′ 6½″ in height, able to lift 133 pounds, in good health, from a respectable family, and not smoke opium. In addition, the army's leadership hoped that one-fifth of the new recruits would be literate and thus trainable as non-commissioned officers. By regulation, the army was not to obtain men by forced conscription, but was to accept volunteers recommended by village headmen. The pay scale for a private first class (*zhengbing*) was 4½ taels a month, or about the same (actually less because of inflation) as that received in the Huai Army (see Table 5). Part of this pay was to be forwarded to the soldier's family, which was entitled to a tax reduction and was to be guaranteed protection by local authorities. An elaborate system of retirement into reserve units (*Xubei jun*) after three years of active duty was also devised as an added inducement to join the Beiyang Army.[30]

Probably what most impressed contemporary Chinese and foreign observers about the Beiyang Army was its discipline. Discipline was maintained by the threat of severe punishment for infractions of the soldier's code. There were eighteen offenses for which a man could be beheaded, including such crimes as feigning illness, vagrancy, opium smoking, disobeying orders, carelessness on guard duty, losing weapons, firing indiscriminately in combat, and desertion.[31] Moreover, in-service examinations were the chief means by which the promotion of officers and men was decided. These tests were based on training manuals which condensed Western and Japanese materials, often in the form of catechisms. The following example deals with the importance of obeying directions from an officer:

29. FO 371/41, enclosure no. 1 in Jordan no. 420 of Oct. 15, 1906.
30. *Da Qing Guangxu xinfaling* (Shanghai, 1909), *ce* 14:58-59; Wen Gong-zhi, vol. 1, pp. 46-47; H.S. Brunnert and V.V. Hagelstrom, *Present-Day Political Organization in China* (Shanghai, 1912), pp. 285-86. One tael was worth about $1.40 (U.S.) in the 1860s, and about $0.60 (U.S.) in the 1900s.
31. *Xunbing yaoyan* (1908), p. 7. This code was initially promulgated for the Newly Created Army; see Duan Qi-rui et al., *Xunlian caofa yangxiang tushuo* (Xiaozhan, 1899), *cuo* 21:5b-6; and Liu Feng-han, *Xinjian lujun*, pp. 139-55. See also Powell, p. 227.

Q. When the infantry attacks the enemy, what is most important?
A. Firing guns.
Q. Who gives directions about firing guns?
A. The officer leading the troops.
Q. What kind of directions [are given]?
A. (1) Estimated distance; (2) What size gun to use; (3) What is to be attacked; (4) What method(s) of firing to use; (5) Where to fire; (6) Check on whether or not each soldier is on target; (7) Check on whether or not bullets are firing; and, (8) When to stop firing.
Q. What is wrong with having no directions?
A. [There will be] no estimate of distance, confusion about gun size, aiming at nothing [in particular], no knowledge of firing method, [so that] all will miss the target; without checking the bullets it is difficult to calculate [effect]; by not co-ordinating the stopping of firing, bullets will be wasted; all the worse are all of these evils together; all of this ought to be directed.[32]

The Beiyang Army's organizational structure was in sharp contrast to that of the Hsiang and Huai Armies, which had a simply structured, highly personalized chain of command centering on the battalion (*ying*). As illustrated in Tables 2 and 3, the Beiyang Army's command structure was centralized and functionally divided, again following closely Japanese (which in turn followed German) models. Within the personalized command structure of the Huai and Xiang Armies, considerable power went to the battalion officers (*yingguan*) whose troops were primarily loyal to him. The commander (*tongling*) supervised and directed the battalion officers, acting as their personal link to the governor-general or governor. The Beiyang Army, on the other hand, was more impersonal in organization. Its basic unit, the division, was quite large and, as we shall soon see, its division commanders (*tongzhi guan*) were transferred frequently and therefore did not have fixed ties with a particular set of subordinate officers. The chain of command of the various units formed a many-tiered bureaucracy, rising in pyramid fashion, with the governor-general of Zhili at the apex.

32. *Xunbing yaoyan*, pp. 8-9; see also Feng Yu-xiang, *Wodi dushu shenghuo* (Shanghai, 1947), pp. 83-84, and James E. Sheridan, *Chinese Warlord: The Career of Feng Yu-hsiang* (Stanford, 1966), p. 40, for a different translation of the first part of the "catechism" quoted above.

TABLE 2. *Organizational Chart of the Beiyang Army*

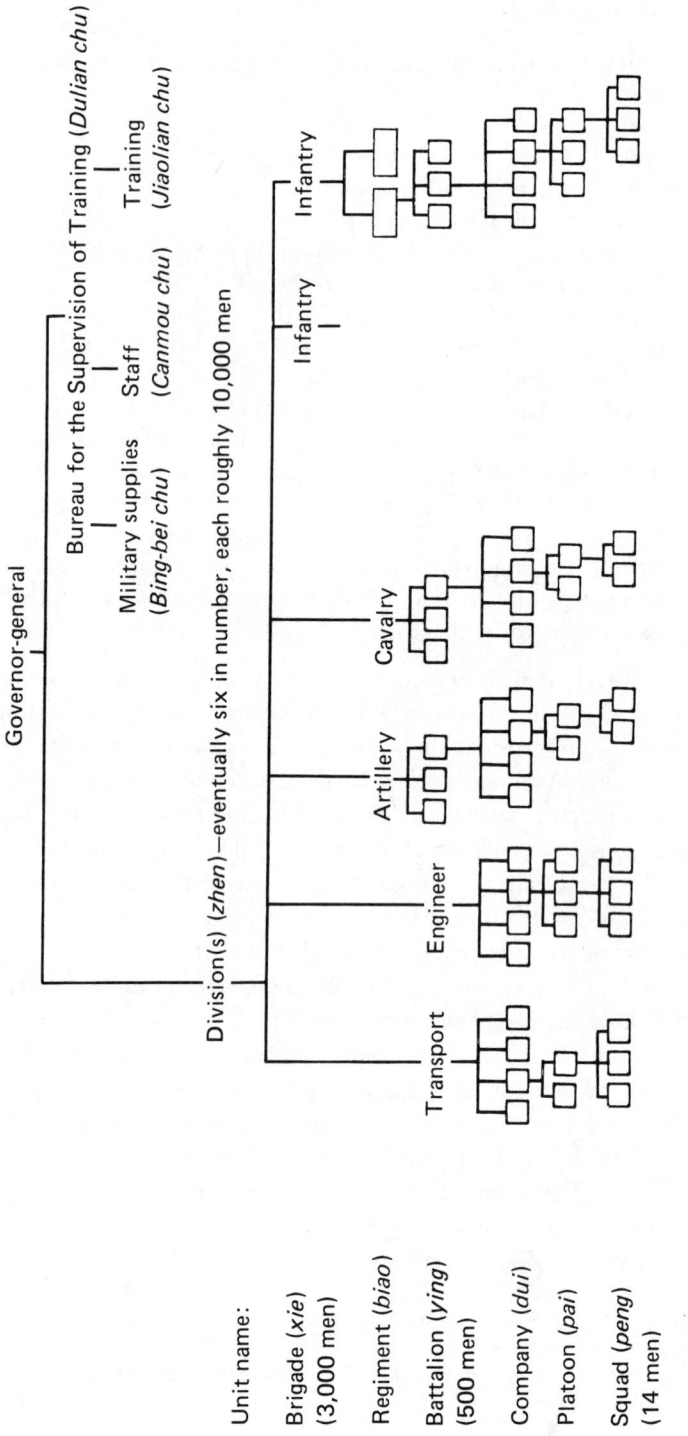

```
                        Governor-general
                              |
        ┌─────────────────────┼─────────────────────┐
        |                     |                     |
Bureau for the Supervision of Training (Dulian chu)
        |                     |                     |
Military supplies        Staff              Training
(Bing-bei chu)         (Canmou chu)       (Jiaolian chu)

Division(s) (zhen) — eventually six in number, each roughly 10,000 men
        |
  ┌─────┬─────────┬──────────┬──────────┬──────────┐
Transport  Engineer  Artillery  Cavalry  Infantry  Infantry
```

Unit name:

Brigade (*xie*)
(3,000 men)

Regiment (*biao*)

Battalion (*ying*)
(500 men)

Company (*dui*)

Platoon (*pai*)

Squad (*peng*)
(14 men)

SOURCE: Wen Gong-zhi, 1:42-43. The Bureau for the Supervision of Training (*Dulian chu*, also called *Dulian gongsuo*) replaced the Department of Military Administration in 1904 as Yuan's head office for administering the Beiyang Army.

TABLE 3. *Organizational Chart of the Huai and Xiang Armies*

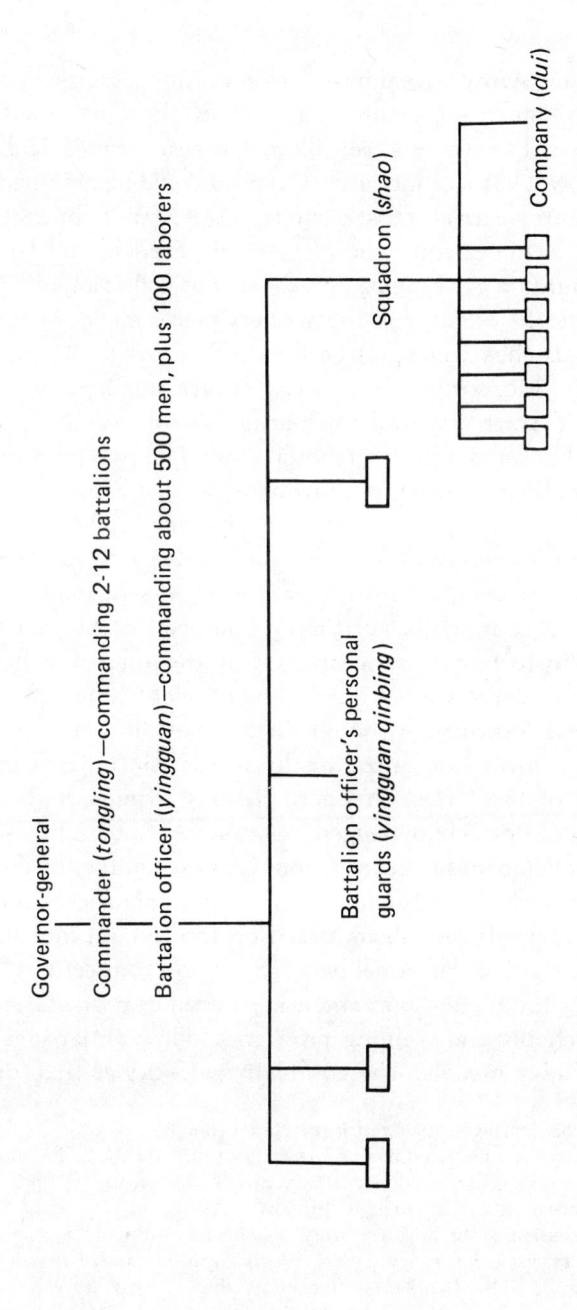

Governor-general
Commander (*tongling*)—commanding 2-12 battalions
Battalion officer (*yingguan*)—commanding about 500 men, plus 100 laborers

Battalion officer's personal guards (*yingguan qinbing*)

Squadron (*shao*)

Company (*dui*)

SOURCE: Wang Er-min, pp. 77, 108-110.

The Beiyang Army's weakness was munitions. Here the situation was not much different from that of the Huai and Xiang Armies. Since the Taiping rebellion, Chinese armies had been equipped with whatever modern weaponry could be obtained. The Beiyang infantry carried mostly model 1888 Mauser or 1898 Japanese rifles. Artillery consisted of German, French, and Japanese field and mountain guns, and a heterogeneous collection of 57-mm. guns. The weight of some of the artillery pieces made them virtually useless, as they could not be transported over north China's muddy roads. Moreover, there was a severe shortage of reliable ammunition for artillery and small arms. There were not enough funds available for purchases from abroad. The two principal domestic arsenals, at Wuchang and Shanghai (Jiangnan), produced ammunition of rather poor quality and were unable to fill even half of the orders they received. As a result, the only significant advance made by the Beiyang Army in weaponry was in maintenance, which was indeed much better than it had been in the past.[33]

Despite shortcomings in weaponry, at the time, the Beiyang Army was considered a great improvement over Chinese armies of the nineteenth century. Although in a sense the Beiyang Army represented a return organizationally to the centralized military bureaucracy of the Green Standard (*Lüying*) Armies of the early Qing, this was not acknowledged. Yuan's conscious models were foreign, mainly Japanese, and not from Chinese military tradition.[34] For example, in the recruitment and promotion of officers and men Yuan stressed professionalism, based on the foreign model, over combat experience or personal background and connections. What seemed most innovative was the army's organizational structure and many schools and training programs following Japanese and Western military models. The cumulative effect was that, despite

33. FO 17/1655, Intelligence Diary for the period ending April 12, 1904; 17/1688, Intelligence Diary for the period ending March 28, 1905; 371/31, G. Pereira, no. 4, Jan. 14, 1904; 371/39, enclosure no. 15 in Carnegie no. 332 of Aug. 6, 1906; Powell, p. 238. More discussion of arsenals will follow.

34. For a discussion of the Japanese army in the context of its European models, see Ernst L. Presseisen, *Before Aggression: Europeans Prepare the Japanese Army* (Tucson, 1965), esp. chap. 5. The dominant influence on the Japanese army had been a German military scholar, General Jakob Meckel, whose tactical thinking was peculiar and old-fashioned but fit rather well the *bushido* military tradition of his Japanese students. Indirectly, Presseisen's careful study offers a picture of the tactics, training techniques, and organization that Yuan was trying to instill into the Beiyang Army.

the fact that the army was never tested in combat against a foreign foe, the British minister in Beijing was sufficiently impressed by 1905 to warn against another armed expedition by the Powers like the one sent in 1900.[35] Ralph Powell has summarized the positive impressions on foreign observers made by the Beiyang Army at large-scale maneuvers held near Hejian, Zhili in October 1905:

> The enlisted men were a better type than the old-style soldiers. They were excellent physical specimens, tough, well-fed, and healthy. The discipline was outstanding and, despite some desertions, the morale of the men appeared to be high. Within the units, there were signs of developing *esprit de corps* and attempts were being made to stimulate patriotism. From a political and social standpoint, the maneuvers had the result of presenting to the common people, a disciplined army far different from the hordes of uniformed bandits with whom they were familiar. In the presence of these well-behaved troops, the local populace soon lost their fear and became curious about the neat and orderly soldiers. The people were finally being shown that the military profession could be respectable.[36]

Beijing's Financial and Administrative Control of the Beiyang Army

Yuan Shi-kai's achievements in training, discipline, and organization of the Beiyang Army were as much the result of Beijing's interest in the army as of Yuan's zeal as a military reformer. This was expressed in the fact that the central government retained ultimate financial and administrative control over the army.

The financing of the Beiyang Army is a complex and controversial subject. Fortunately because Beijing carefully monitored the army's growth, detailed reports on its financing exist in the Grand Council archives now in Taiwan. These reports reveal Yuan in constant search for funds, often appealing to the Court for permission to make last-minute shifts from one source to another in order to make ends meet. The consent of the Empress Dowager and the Board (later Ministry) of Revenue was required because, acting as a conduit, Beijing controlled most of the army's revenue sources. To demonstrate the extent of Beijing's control, I have

---

35. FO 17/1673, Satow, Nov. 2, 1905; see also *Morrison Correspondence*, pp. 384-85.
36. Powell, p. 208.

pulled together data from Yuan's myriad financial reports to the throne into a series of tables. Table 4 is Yuan's projection of revenues needed in 1904 for the expansion of the Beiyang Army. Table 5 shows actual revenue sources for the entire army in 1904. Table 6 gives revenue sources of the army in 1906 when it reached its full strength of 60,000 men. Table 7 breaks down funding sources for the army by division.

TABLE 4. *1904 Plan for Financing of Two New Beiyang Divisions*
(million taels)

Direct from Board of Revenue	0.450 to 0.460
Funds retained by or diverted to Zhili by order of Board of Revenue	1.710
(1) Grain tribute from Jiangsu, and tea, sugar, wine, and tobacco taxes from Anhui (1,070,000 taels)	
(2) 20% surcharge on foreign and native customs at Tianjin (540,000 taels)	
Directly raised by Yuan Shi-kai in Zhili	1.000
Total	3.160

SOURCE: YSKZZ, p. 1290.

TABLE 5. *Actual Beiyang Army Revenues for 1904*
(million taels)

Board of Revenue (including retained and diverted funds)	3.600
Revenue assistance as savings on disbandment of troops	1.000
From Zhili direct: (half in special tax revenues and half loans)	2.063
Total	6.663

SOURCE: YSKZZ, pp. 1321-22, 1668, 1679, 1732, 1838, 2187-88, 2285-86.

TABLE 6. *Revenues of Beiyang Army in 1906*
(million taels)

Board of Revenue (Army Reorganization Fund)	3.500
Revenue assistance in savings from disbandment of troops	1.000
Self-strengthening army subsidy (Hubei)	0.223
Profits from Beijing-Shenyang Railway	0.706
Shandong revenues (including revenue assistance)	0.987
Retained Shandong tax revenues and Yongping (Zhili) salt revenues	1.160
Zhili salt, wine, and tobacco surtax	0.625
Profits from Changlu salt (Zhili)	0.120
Zhili Maritime Defense Fund	0.062
Meltage and grain price differentials	0.261
Total	8.844

SOURCE: *Duzhi bu junxiang si zouan huibian* (Beijing, 1908), *juan* 1:58-60. Both Guping and Xiangping taels appear in this financial report, although mostly the former. The Guping was worth slightly less than the Xiangping tael, but for the purpose of analyzing the figures in general terms, the difference is not important.

TABLE 7. *Beiyang Army Divisions:
Their Major Funding Sources, 1904-06*
(Each division was allotted
about 1.5 million taels per annum)

First Division	Manchu Banner Revenues (Beijing controlled)
Second Division	Board of Revenue
Third Division	Board of Revenue
Fourth Division	Retained Shandong tax revenues, Yongping salt and Board of Revenue
Fifth Division	Shandong Revenues and Revenue Assistance
Sixth Division	Self-strengthening Army subsidy, Retained Shandong tax revenues, and Yongping salt

SOURCE: YSKZZ, pp. 1668, 1934, 1935-36, 2319, 2379; FO 17/1654, Intelligence Diary for period ending February 2, 1904; and 17/1655, Intelligence Diary for period ending February 16, 1904.

Without the Empress Dowager's decision to provide financial support, the expansion of the Beiyang Army in 1904 would have been impossible. Maintenance of a single division required 1.25 to 1.5 million taels annually, while recruiting, equipping, and training of a new division cost even more, over 2 million taels in the first year.[37] The expense of weapons, ammunition, and other supplies ordered from abroad (chiefly from Germany and Japan) likewise ran into millions of taels.[38] As indicated in Chapter 2, Yuan's control of Zhili revenues was limited. Not surprisingly then, as Table 5 demonstrates, in 1904 Yuan succeeded in raising only about 2 million taels directly from Zhili sources (half in loans) out of a total budget for the Beiyang Army that year of over 6 million taels.

In January, 1904, when Yuan memorialized an urgent request for the addition of thirty thousand troops to the Beiyang Army, the plan, as reflected in Table 4, called for the Board of Revenue to match Zhili funds on a 2:1 basis. Beijing was to make available two million taels in the form of direct grants, revenues diverted to Zhili from other provinces, and certain Tianjin tax revenues which otherwise would have been forwarded to Beijing (such as a percentage of customs revenues or contributions to the Beijing Fund). Yuan Shi-kai was to raise 1 million taels directly from Zhili sources—800,000 taels from new wine and tobacco taxes and the rest in savings by reducing official peculation and over-staffing in his administration.[39] Soon Beijing found it was unable to provide Yuan with funds from the sources as indicated. For example, the 20 percent surcharge on Tianjin customs revenues which Yuan was permitted to retain for the army had been spent. So Yuan requested and was granted use of an alternative source—500,000 taels in profits from the Beijing-Shenyang Railway.[40] Sometimes Yuan would have to scramble to find last-minute revenues from local sources such as the provincial salt administration or commercial loans.[41] But the

37. YSKZZ, p. 2157; FO 17/1655, Intelligence Diary for the period ending Feb. 16, 1904; Ch'en, *Yuan Shih-k'ai* (1972), p. 63; DFZZ 1.5 (1904): *caizheng* 138; ibid., 1.11 (1904):284-86.

38. YSKZZ, pp. 1239-41, 1814; FO 17/1654, Intelligence Diary for the period ending Feb. 2, 1904; 17/1657, Intelligence Diary for the period ending Nov. 8, 1904.

39. YSKZZ, pp. 1205-09, 1338, 1473-75; DFZZ 1.1 (1904): *caizheng* 21-22, and 1.7:192; Luo Yu-dong, "Guangxu chao. . . ," p. 249.

40. YSKZZ, p. 1732.

41. YSKZZ, pp. 1290, 1679, 1838, 2285-86; FO 17/1657, Intelligence Diary for the period ending Nov. 8, 1904.

overall financial picture did not change. Table 5 shows that by the end of 1904 Beijing was responsible for about two-thirds of the financing of the Beiyang Army, which was in line with the original projection for financing the expansion of the army in Table 4.

By 1906 the Beiyang Army budget had grown but, as Table 6 demonstrates, the ratio between Beijing controlled revenues and funds raised directly by Yuan Shi-kai in the Zhili-Shandong region had not significantly changed. In Table 7 I have broken down the data by division. Again one finds the financing of four divisions (First through Fourth) dominated by Beijing with the Zhili-Shandong region providing major funding for the remaining two (Fifth and Sixth) divisions. Certainly Yuan tried as hard as possible to raise funds regionally. The training and equipping of an army of the size and sophistication of the Beiyang Army was just too expensive. Thus tables 4 to 7 show that from the beginning Beijing's help was crucial to the development of the Beiyang Army, responsible on the average for about two-thirds of its annual funding. Doubtless without this help and relying solely on the resources of the Zhili-Shandong region, the Beiyang Army would have been a much more modest force, along the lines of Zhang Zhi-dong's units at Wuchang or Cen Chun-xuan's motley army at Guangzhou (see p. 109).

The central government agencies which handled the transfer or diversion of funds from Beijing to Tianjin for the Beiyang Army were the Board of Revenue, the Board of War, and the Army Reorganization Bureau. Their cooperation was assured by the fact that these three agencies were led by Yuan's allies and protégés.

The leaders of both the Boards of War and Revenue were intimates of Yuan. Early in 1904, Zhang-geng, who had been on good terms with Yuan for years, became president of the Board of War, while Yuan's erstwhile ally, Tie-liang, and associate Xu Shi-chang became board vice-presidents. In 1905 Tie-liang succeeded Zhang-geng as board president. Until its abolition late in 1906, the board consistently approved Yuan's plans for the Beiyang Army and his ideas for military reform throughout the Empire. Yuan and the Beiyang Army were supported on the Board of Revenue by Lu Chuan-lin, president of the board from 1902 through most of 1904, and by Tie-liang, who became a board vice-president in 1903 (and board president late in 1905). From 1903 to its abolition in 1906, the Board of Revenue forwarded millions of taels to Yuan in Tianjin for support of the Beiyang Army.[42]

Most important in rendering financial and administrative assistance to Yuan and the Beiyang Army was the Army Reorganization Bureau. It will be recalled that this bureau was established in December, 1903, as a high-level adjunct of the Grand Council which reported directly to the Empress Dowager about military reform. Its members were Yuan and allies Prince Qing, Xu Shichang, and Tie-liang. In Chapter 3 we saw how much of the bureau's organizational structure and personnel was borrowed from Yuan's military administration in Zhili. Indeed the bureau was so identified with Yuan's interests in Zhili that to the British military attaché in Beijing it seemed overshadowed by Yuan's command center in Zhili, the Bureau for the Supervision of Training, successor to the Department of Military Administration.

> The *'Lien-ping ch'u'* [Army Reorganization Bureau] in Peking corresponds to the War Office. . . . Its functions are more nominal than real. . . . The *'Tu-lien ch'u'* [Bureau for the Supervision of Training] at Tientsin is nominally a sub-war office and occupies a building in the same compound as Viceroy Yuan's yamen. It has the real working of the affairs of the *Lu-chun*.[43]

The Army Reorganization Bureau, however, was more significant than the above quotation suggests.

Through the Army Reorganization Bureau, Yuan controlled military reform throughout the Empire and channeled funds from other provinces to the Beiyang Army. This was particularly evidenced by the bureau's order early in 1904 that modern Regular Army units be raised in every province in preparation for a national *Lujun* system. Only Yuan as governor-general of Zhili received the bureau's assistance in financing additional new divisions. In other parts of the Empire, new Regular Army units were rarely raised; the name was simply given to existing units. In Shandong the Vanguard Army became Shandong's "Regular Army."[44] The governor of Shaanxi in 1904, Sheng-yun, memorialized that not enough

---

42. QS, 4:2830-32; and Powell, pp. 166-67, 205. On Chang-geng, see Fei Xingjian, *Jindai mingren xiaochuan*, pp. 236-37.

43. FO 371/31, G. Pereira, no. 4, Jan. 14, 1904.

44. Zhou Fu, *Zhou Que shengong quanji, zougao, juan* 2:15-17; FO 17/1654, Intelligence Diary for the period ending Feb. 2, 1904.

money existed for new troops, but that he was converting selected existing units into a "Regular Army."[45] In Henan to meet the Army Reorganization Bureau's requirements, four battalions of old-style troops and three battalions of more recently trained troops were merged and renamed "Regular Army." These troops, however, were never reconstituted and proved hopelessly corrupt, so that they were later disbanded.[46] In 1904 in the Liangjiang and Fujian areas, existing units were selected, rearmed with more modern weapons, and renamed. By 1906 the same areas had made little more progress toward creating new divisions for the *Lujun* system. Local governors and governors-general complained that they lacked sufficient resources.[47] At Wuchang by 1905, governor-general Zhang Zhi-dong had combined old regulars with new recruits into two new brigades of *Lujun* troops, totaling about 11,500 men. But limited to only the available financial resources of Hunan and Hubei, Zhang could do no more.[48] Elsewhere in the Empire, even less was done of a concrete nature about "Regular Armies" for the *Lujun* between 1904 and 1907. In the Guangdong-Guangxi region, for example, Cen Chun-xuan made a haphazard attempt, raising a small force that was subsequently disbanded because of its low standards.[49]

The Army Reorganization Bureau's order to establish "Regular Army" units throughout the Empire was a pretext for the channeling of men and especially money from other provinces to Zhili. In order to collect funds nationally for use in Zhili, the Army Reorganization Bureau established provincial quotas for a special assessment to be sent annually to Beijing for the Army Reorganization Fund (*lianbing xuxiang*). The quotas were to be met through additional taxes on wine, tobacco, opium, tea, and salt, as well as through new land and real estate registration (*tianfang*) taxes, custom revenues, and profits from minting. Were these sources to

---

45. FO 17/1655, Intelligence Diary for the period ending Feb. 16, 1904.

46. Chen Kui-long, *Yongji shangshu zouyi*, juan 4:1-2, 14-15, 18; DFZZ 3.4 (1906): *zazu* 26; FO 17/1655, Intelligence Diary for the period ending March 1, 1904; 371/41, enclosure no. 3 in Jordan no. 420 of Oct. 15, 1906.

47. *Guang-xu memorials*, 19:874-77; Zhou Fu, *zougao, juan* 3:29-32, 4:14-17; FO 17/1655, Intelligence Diary for the period ending March 1, 1904; and Powell, pp. 231-32.

48. Zhang Zhi-dong, *zougao, juan* 38:16-23, 40:14b; FO 17/1657, Intelligence Diary for the period ending Nov. 3, 1904; 17/1671, Satow, no. 92, March 14, 1905; and Powell, pp. 147, 220.

49. Rhoads, pp. 77-79.

prove inadequate, the provinces were expected to meet the quotas by transferring to the central government a part of their share of land taxes.[50] These new annual exactions from the provinces by the Army Reorganization Bureau were in addition to the annual revenue assistance (*xiexiang*) through which southern provinces supported remaining "Huai" army units in the north, including those in Zhili.[51] Although provinces did not always meet their quotas, Table 8 indicates that by 1905, 6.53 million taels or most of the amount required was being sent annually to the Board of Revenue and Army Reorganization Bureau in Beijing. Of this amount more than two-thirds was from provinces other than Zhili and Shandong.

Initially, southern governors and governors-general protested the sending of large sums to Beijing for the Beiyang Army. The London *Times* reported that the governors-general at Nanjing, Wuchang, and Fuzhou complained in a joint memorial to the throne that Prince Qing's and Yuan Shi-kai's military reorganization schemes were bleeding the provinces.[52] The Chinese original of this memorial has not been found, but, as we shall see, the governors-general did individually memorialize that they could not meet the quotas and may have expressed privately the strong sentiments noted in the *Times* despatch. The Army Reorganization Bureau responded to the protests by applying pressure. Tie-liang, then vice-president of the Board of Revenue and associate director of the Army Reorganization Bureau, toured the southern Yangzi provinces during the fall of 1904 and met with high provincial officials. Evidently as a result of the trip, Wei Guang-dao, governor-general at Nanjing, was transferred because of his lack of cooperation with Beijing in financial and military matters.[53]

By the end of 1904, southern governors and governors-general had yielded to pressure and were forwarding funds to Beijing for the Army Reorganization Fund. For example, Duan-fang, governor

50. DFZZ 1.1 (1904): *caizheng* 3-18; Luo Yu-dong, "Guangxu chao . . . ," pp. 251-52.
51. YSKZZ, pp. 421-22, 2187-88; Duan-fang, *Duan Zhongmin gong zougao* (1918), *juan* 3:20; Feng-gang [pseud.], ed., *Sanshui Liang Yan-sun xiansheng nianpu* (1939), p. 44.
52. *Times* (London), Sept. 5, 1904, p. 6; FO 405/154 (conf. print), January-March 1905, no. 71, "Review of military affairs in China during the year 1904 by Lieutenant-Colonel C.M. Ducat."
53. Wei also opposed Yuan and his allies at Court on the future of the Jiangnan arsenal; see Thomas Kennedy, "The Kiangnan Arsenal, 1895-1911: The Decentralized Bureaucracy Responds to Imperialism," *Ch'ing-shih wen-t'i* 2.1 (October 1969):29-31.

TABLE 8. *Army Reorganization Fund:*
Quotas and Amounts Actually Delivered to Beijing,
1904-06
(unit = million taels)

	Quotas 1904-05	Amounts delivered in 1905	Quotas for 1906
Zhili	1.10	1.50	1.100
Fengdian	0.80	0.00?	—
Jiangsu	0.85	1.61	1.611
Guangdong	0.85	0.15	0.850
Sichuan	0.80	0.30	0.800
Shaanxi	0.50	0.20	0.500
Jiangxi	0.50	0.20	0.500
Shandong	0.55	0.29	0.550
Hubei	0.50	0.53	1.030
Zhejiang	0.50	0.90	0.901
Fujian	0.40	0.02?	0.400
Henan	0.30	0.20	0.400
Anhui	0.25	0.10	0.350
Hunan	0.30	0.40	0.40
Guangxi	0.20	0.00?	—
Yunnan	0.20	0.12?	0.120
Gansu	0.06	0.10	0.100
Xinjiang	0.06	?	—
Guizhou		0.01	0.010
Totals	8.82	6.53	9.93

SOURCE: DHXL, *juan* 184:3b-4; DFZZ 2.10 (1905): *caizheng* 240-43; 3.2 (1906):22-25. These figures, and a Board of Revenue memorial in DHXL, *juan* 192:6-7, suggest that for 1904 probably less than the 6.53 total for 1905 was collected, but that the 1904 total still approached 6 million taels. Manchuria and Xinjiang had no quotas.

of Hubei, earlier in the year had memorialized that he found it impossible to raise the Hubei quota of 500,000 taels, but that he had sent 100,000 taels borrowed from native bankers.[54] Later, under pressure of Tie-liang's visit, Duan-fang's superior, the governor-general at Wuchang, Zhang Zhi-dong, who had also memorialized on the infeasibility of meeting the Beiyang Army quotas, produced the required additional 400,000 taels.[55] Before being re-

54. FO 17/1655, Intelligence Diary for the period ending May 10, 1904.
55. Zhang Zhi-dong, *zougao, juan* 38:12b-16, and *diangao, juan* 65:14b-15; FO 17/1671, Satow, no. 92, March 14, 1905.

moved as governor-general at Nanjing, Wei Guang-dao was having difficulty collecting the required amount, possibly because he feared that new taxes to raise funds would cause widespread insurrection against the government.[56] Wei's successor, Zhou Fu, however, succeeded in delivering *more* than the Liangjiang quota.[57] Interestingly, when earlier serving as governor of Shandong, Zhou Fu had met only half of the required quota for 1904.[58] In Henan, the newly appointed governor, Chen Kui-long, Rong-lu's former aide and an old ally of Yuan Shi-kai, memorialized that he could send the Army Reorganization Bureau only 100,000 taels for 1904, but for 1905, he promised 220,000 taels and actually delivered around 200,000 taels.[59] Similarly the amounts other provinces sent the Beiyang Army via Beijing and the Army Reorganization Bureau steadily increased. Sichuan's annual contribution to the Army Reorganization Fund, for example, rose from 300,000 taels in 1905 to 500,000 taels in 1906.[60]

The way in which Yuan's administration dealt with the Beiyang Army's production and procurement of arms illustrates again how Yuan relied on Beijing's support of the Beiyang Army at the expense of military needs in other parts of the Empire. After 1902, when the Powers lifted their ban on the importation of arms, Yuan made heavy purchases of munitions abroad—especially from the Japanese and Germans.[61] Since 1900, when the Tianjin arsenal, the most important in north China, had been razed by foreign troops, domestic production of weaponry and ammunition centered in the south, at the Hanyang and Jiangnan arsenals in Hankou and Shanghai respectively. Yuan mainly dealt with the Hanyang arsenal, where he was on good terms with Duan-fang, governor of Hubei and administrator of the arsenal. But production at both arsenals never satisfied demand. In 1904, for example, Hanyang filled only half of Yuan's orders.[62] The inadequacy of domestic munitions

56. *Guang-xu memorials*, 19:890-93; FO 17/1655, Intelligence Diary for the period ending March 1, 1904.
57. *Shilu, juan* 533:19a. For Liangjiang quotas, see Table 4, above.
58. Zhou Fu, *zougao, juan* 2:28-30.
59. Chen Kui-long, *Yongji shangshu zouyi, juan* 3:29-30, 6:1-2; FO 17/1657, Intelligence Diary for the period ending Sept. 13, 1904.
60. S. A. M. Adshead, "Viceregal Government in Szechwan," p. 48.
61. YSKZZ, pp. 1739-41; FO 17/1654, Intelligence Diary for the period ending Jan. 19, 1904; 17/1688, Intelligence Diary for the period ending March 28, 1905.
62. FO 17/1655, Intelligence Diaries for the periods ending Feb. 16 and March 1, 1904.

production necessitated the placement of large orders with foreign firms.⁶³ This dependency upon foreigners and southern arsenals disturbed Yuan and his advisors.

Beginning early in 1903 Yuan worked closely with Zhou Fu, governor of Shandong, to construct and purchase equipment for a major new arsenal at Dezhou on the Zhili-Shandong border. The arsenal was directed by one of Yuan's trusted officers, Zhang Xi-fan, and equipped with German machinery, which, arriving late, delayed full operation until 1905.⁶⁴

Yuan also maneuvered for control of the Jiangnan arsenal. After the death of Liu Kun-yi in 1902, considerable controversy arose over the future of the Jiangnan arsenal because of its revenues and importance as a munitions center. The contending provincial governors, governors-general, and central government officials agreed only about relocating the Shanghai arsenal inland because of its vulnerability to foreign interference or destruction (as happened to the Tianjin arsenal in 1900). New locations in Anhui, Hunan, Hubei, and Jiangxi were proposed, each serving the interests of a particular governor or governor-general. Finally, late in 1904, after an inspection tour and recommendations on the subject from Yuan's long-time collaborator, Zhou Fu, to the Liangjiang governor-generalship, Yuan's views prevailed. A memorial of the Army Reorganization Bureau and the Government Affairs Bureau supported Yuan's ideas and recommended that the Jiangnan arsenal be phased out and that most of its annual revenues be diverted to the development of Yuan's new arsenal at Dezhou.⁶⁵

The financing and munitions procurement of the Beiyang Army therefore depended ultimately upon the support of the Empress Dowager and officials in Beijing. In other words, Beijing financially controlled the development of the Beiyang Army, and with financial control went administrative control as well.

Until late in 1906 there was no conflict between Yuan and the central government in the exercise of administrative control over the Beiyang Army. Then rather suddenly, during the winter of 1906-07, a struggle for control developed which highlighted Yuan's

63. YSKZZ, p. 1814. Powell, pp. 108-09, 133, 239, 301-02, quotes existing figures.
64. Wang Er-min, *Qingji binggongye de xingqi* (Taibei, 1963), pp. 87-88; FO 17/1656, Intelligence Diary for the period ending June 7, 1904; 17/1688, Intelligence Diary for the period ending March 28, 1905.
65. Kennedy, pp. 28-32.

and the Beiyang Army's dependence upon Beijing for administrative as well as financial support.

Discussed in some detail in Chapter 3 were the attacks at Court upon Yuan and Prince Qing made by Grand Councillor Qu Hong-ji during the winter of 1906-07. Simultaneous with these attacks were heated debates at Court about how to reorganize government so as to increase centralization and to facilitate introduction of a constitutional form of government. Although in the past Yuan had been a supporter and beneficiary of centralization policies, he now collided with his erstwhile ally, Tie-liang, who in the name of centralization led a group of Manchu officials in the advocacy of the abolition of provincial governors and governors-general and the reassertion of Manchu control over central government at the expense of the power of Chinese officials. As will be recalled, earlier Tie-liang had been instrumental in helping Yuan to exercise control over Beijing's military policies. The first sign of trouble were sporadic incidents of fighting between Tie-liang's Manchu First Beiyang Division and Duan Qi-rui's Chinese Third Beiyang Division which occurred during the summer of 1906. Probably a combination of factors, including personal ambitions, the new Manchu drive for centralization and control of Chinese officialdom, and recent disagreements with Yuan over the establishment of a cabinet and abolition of provincial governors-general, brought Tie-liang to break openly with Yuan late in November, 1906. Although at the time Qu Hong-ji's attacks on Yuan and Prince Qing made Yuan more vulnerable at Court, there is no concrete evidence of a conspiratorial connection between Tie-liang and Qu.[66]

The immediate consequences of the rift between Tie-liang and Yuan are well known. The Army Reorganization Bureau was abolished and its functions absorbed by a new Ministry of War (*Lujun bu*), of which Tie-liang became president. Administrative jurisdiction over four (the First, Third, Fifth and Sixth) of the six Beiyang divisions shifted to Tie-liang's Ministry of War, with these divisions placed under the command of Feng-shan, a Manchu who was Tie-liang's right-hand man. Moreover, Tie-liang ordered that the two divisions (the Second and Fourth) that remained under Yuan in

---

66. Merebeth Cameron, *Reform and Revolution*, pp. 91-92; Li Chien-nung, *Political History*, p. 93; FO 371/41, enclosure no. 1 in Jordan no. 420 of Oct. 15, 1906; Powell, p. 210.

Zhili be supported financially by Yuan's Zhili administration and not by the central government.[67]

During the winter of 1906-07, Yuan was not alone in the Beiyang Army in feeling genuinely threatened by administrative changes in Beijing. Morale was low because of rumors of interference in the payment of the Beiyang troops' wages.[68] Commanders of the Third and Fifth Divisions, Duan Qi-rui and Zhang Huai-zhi, resigned rather than serve under Feng-shan.[69]

Tie-liang's victory, however, proved short-lived. In May, 1907, as we know, Yuan and Prince Qing regained favor with the Empress Dowager and undid their chief opponents at Court, Qu Hong-ji and Cen Chun-xuan. As a result Yuan recovered most of his influence over military affairs. In May, Prince Qing was appointed controller (*guanli lujun bu shiwu*) of the Ministry of War, a new post which was senior to that of ministry president, Tie-liang.[70] In July, Feng Guo-zhang, who had been associated with Yuan in military affairs since 1896, was named superintendent (*zhengshi*) of the Ministry of War's General Staff Council (*Junzi chu*), which was the chief administrative agency within the ministry.[71] At about the same time, Wang Ying-kai, a long-time associate of Yuan's and formerly commander of the Second Division of the Beiyang Army, became temporarily a vice-president of the Ministry of War and then chief deputy to Feng-shan.[72]

Yuan used his renewed influence with the Empress Dowager and within the Ministry of War to recover control over half of the Beiyang units lost a few months earlier to Tie-liang and Feng-shan. In April, 1907, Xu Shi-chang and three other of Yuan's old associates—Tang Shao-yi, Duan Zhi-gui, and Zhu Jia-bao—were appointed to lead a reform administration in Manchuria, which was to be divided into three new provinces (Fengtian, Heilongjiang, and Jilin). In order to defend Manchuria, Xu Shi-chang as governor-general requested the stationing in Manchuria of the Third Bei-

67. Powell, pp. 216-17, 251, 253. Revenue sources for the Fourth and Sixth divisions were exchanged. Yuan was already financing from Zhili sources the equivalent of about two divisions; see Table 7, above, and YSKZZ, p. 2379.
68. *Times* (London), Feb. 7 and 9, both p. 7; NCH, Jan. 4, 1907; Cameron, p. 93.
69. Powell, p. 218; FO 371/434, enclosure in Jordan no. 407 of Sept. 12, 1908.
70. *Shilu, juan* 572:13a.   71. *Shilu, juan* 572:20a; 575:8b-9a.
72. *Shilu, juan* 573:7b; and Jerome Ch'en, "A Footnote on the Chinese Army in 1911-12," *Toung-pao* 48.4-5 (1960):428.

yang Division and two mixed brigades, which were to be made up of units from Yuan's Second and Fourth Divisions and Feng-shan's Fifth and Sixth Divisions of the Beiyang Army respectively.[73] During the summer of 1907, the Third Division and the mixed brigades were transferred to Manchuria; thus, these units under Xu's command returned to Yuan's sphere of influence. Moreover, financial responsibility for the transferred units, including the Second and Fourth Divisions' mixed brigade, lay once again with the Ministry of War and not with Xu's or Yuan's provincial administration.[74] Therefore, in terms of troop strength, Tie-liang and Feng-shan retained control of only two (the Manchu First Division and one-half of the Fifth and Sixth Divisions) of the four full divisions of the Beiyang Army over which they had assumed command during the winter of 1906-07.[75]

By July, 1907, Yuan could boast about the return of most of the Beiyang Army to his control.[76] Tie-liang, meanwhile, was being accused of maladministration. In August, Yuan evidently had enough power to stop Tie-liang from cutting the wages of the officers and men in the Beiyang Army.[77] Tie-liang's attempt to wrest control of the Beiyang Army had been thwarted.

Although brief, Tie-liang's success in curbing Yuan's military power nevertheless demonstrated the crucial importance of a favorable balance of power at Court and within the Ministry of War to control of the Beiyang Army. Ultimate control of the Beiyang Army lay in Beijing with the central government, from which the army received essential administrative as well as financial support. Yuan's personal control over the army, in turn, depended primarily upon his influence in Beijing.[78]

73. *Shilu,* juan 571:10.
74. YSYZY, *juan* 43:2b-4; FO 371/434, enclosure in Jordan no. 407 of Sept. 12, 1908; 371/435, enclosure in Jordan no. 506 of Nov. 8, 1908.
75. Tie-liang had commanded the First Manchu Division since 1903, so in real terms by the summer of 1907 he had gained effective control over only one-half of the Fifth and Sixth divisions. Hatano Yoshihiro has made a similar argument in "Hokuyō gumbatsu no seiretsu katei," pp. 244-45.
76. FO 371/231, handwritten comments on cover of Jordan no. 332 of July 10, 1907.
77. YSYZY, *juan* 44:6b-9; and Ch'en, *Yuan Shih-k'ai* (1972), p. 60.
78. For a parallel view, see Chen Xu-lu and Lao Shao-hua, "Qingmo di xinjun yu xinhai geming," *Xinhai geming wushi zhounian jinian lunwenji* 1:157. For a recent statement of the contrary view, which attacks my argument directly and is based on many of the same sources, see Odoric Y. K. Wou's paper, "Financing the New Army: Yuan Shih-k'ai and the Peiyang Army, 1895-1907," read at the annual meeting of the Association of Asian Studies, Chicago, April 1, 1978.

Beiyang Officers and the Problem of Personal Loyalties

Despite the fact that Yuan ultimately owed financial and administrative control of the Beiyang Army to influence in Beijing, might it still be considered to be his personal army because of strong ties of officers and men to Yuan?

The Beiyang Army was organizationally structured so as to centralize authority in Yuan's hands and to minimize loyalties between officers and men. As discussed earlier (see Tables 2 and 3), compared to the Xiang and Huai Armies of Zeng Guo-fan and Li Hong-zhang, the Beiyang Army's chain of command was much less personalized. By means of a complicated, many-tiered command structure within which officers were frequently transferred, Yuan diluted ties between officers and men, and, to a lesser degree, between senior and junior officers. Thus the Beiyang officer was dependent upon Yuan as the man at the top of the structure and the arbitrator of available funds and promotions.

Were the Beiyang officers and men therefore primarily loyal to Yuan? As we shall see, in recruiting Beiyang officers Yuan emphasized professional qualifications over personal connections to him. The result was that the loyalties of Beiyang officers were very mixed. Those who had been associated with Yuan for a long time were his most loyal followers. Others, perhaps the majority, who recently had joined the Beiyang Army, were without personal ties to Yuan or to any of the Beiyang training centers where loyalty to Yuan may have been inculcated. It can be said of all Beiyang officers that they were loyal to Yuan only as long as he was in a position to further their careers.

The Beiyang Army required both literacy and a modern military education of its officers. The result was that officers were mostly the sons of rural gentry, rich peasant, and merchant families whose children were literate. The pay scale for officers was higher than it had been in the Huai and Xiang Armies (see Table 9). Added attractions were the positive popular image of the Beiyang Army as China's most modern military force and the promise of further military education under its auspices. There was also the promise of promotions in a rapidly expanding army based on further schooling and examination results.[79] Military service was again—perhaps

---

79. *Da Qing Guangxu xinfaling,* ce 14:1-5, 49b-50, 59; YSKZZ, p. 812; Cameron, p. 94; Hatano Yoshihiro, "The New Armies," in Mary C. Wright, ed., *China in Revolution,* pp. 273-75.

for the first time since the Ming—regarded by China's upper classes as a respectable profession.

Contrary to the rosy reports of foreign observers like those quoted earlier, the lot of the common soldier was not good enough to generate much feeling of personal loyalty to commanding officers, including Yuan Shi-kai. Forced conscription, poor living conditions, and severe discipline were the reasons. The pay of officers in the Beiyang Army was higher than previously, but the pay of the common soldier remained low. In 1906 there was an apparent near mutiny when Yuan seemed unable to come up with 4 million taels

TABLE 9. *Beiyang and Huai Army Pay Scales*
(Taels per Month)

Beiyang Army[a]		Huai Army[b]	
Division commander (*tongzhi guan*)	1,000.0		
Brigade officer (*tongling guan*)	500.0		
Regimental officer (*tongdai guan*)	400.0		
Battalion officer (*guandai guan*)	180.0 to 260.0	Battalion officer (*yingguan*)	150.0
Company officer (*duiguan*)	50.0 to 64.0	Squadron officer (*shaoguan*)	9.0
Sergeant (*zhengmu*)	5.1	Corporal (*shiqiang*)	4.8
Corporal (*fumu*)	4.8	Personal guards (*qinbing*)	4.5
Private 1st class (*zhengbing*)	4.5	Combat soldier (*zhengyong*)	4.2
Private 2nd class (*fubing*)	4.2	Soldier performing army services (*huobing*)	3.3
Laborers (cooks, stablemen, etc.) (*changfu*)	3.3	Laborers (*changfu*)	3.0

[a]*Da Qing Guang-xu xin faling*, ce 14:70-71.

[b]Wang Er-min, *Huaijun zhi*, p. 81; Wang indicated the daily salary, which, multiplying by 30, has been converted to a monthly salary scale. For a general estimate of Huai army salaries based on Western accounts, see Spector, p. 212.

of arrears in pay. Still, in contrast to Xiang and Huai armies, Beiyang troops were paid regularly, with probably less embezzlement of payrolls by officers than in the past.[80] A more serious problem was poor living conditions. Food and sanitation were especially bad.[81] Discipline was quite severe. After visiting the Fifth Division in 1908, a British officer noted (in racist terms) that:

> on the average about 100 men in the camp are beaten every month, namely over 90 percent with the stick (chun-kun-tzu) and the rest whipped across the shoulders, a barbarous punishment in the hands of the Chinese. . . . No antiseptics were applied to the wounds, which were allowed to mortify. Fortunately for the Chinese race what would kill a European or maim him for life, is often not so serious to a Chinese. 1 or 2 men have had their arms pierced for stealing a revolver. There are no opium-smokers among the men, the punishment for which would certainly be beheading.[82]

Moreover, regulations to the contrary, forced conscription was generally practiced in Zhili, Shandong, and northern Henan, where most of the Beiyang Army was recruited.[83] At least once, in Tongzhou in March, 1906, there was another significant local protest against forced conscription besides the incident which touched off the Jing Ting-bin uprising in southern Zhili in 1902.[84]

Thus the loyalty of the Beiyang soldier to his officers and to Yuan Shi-kai was not deep. In 1906, censor Li Zhou-hua charged that the oppressive treatment of the common soldier in the Beiyang Army was causing large-scale desertions.[85] Considering his forced conscription, his poor living conditions, and the severe discipline, it is not surprising that the Beiyang soldier was less loyal to the army, deserting much more often, than his soldier of fortune counterpart in the Huai and Xiang armies.[86] Moreover, if general

80. FO 371/41, enclosure no. 1 in Jordan no. 420 of Oct. 15, 1906; 371/217, enclosure in Jordan no. 504 of Dec. 1906.
81. Feng Yu-xiang, *Wodi shenghuo* (Shanghai, 1947), pp. 98-99, 108; FO 371/39, Carnegie, no. 332, Aug. 6, 1906.
82. FO 371/434, enclosure in Jordan no. 407 of Sept. 12, 1908.
83. FO 371/31, G. Pereira, no. 4, Jan. 14, 1906; 371/39, enclosure no. 15 in Carnegie no. 332 of Aug. 6, 1906; 371/41, enclosures nos. 1 and 4 in Jordan no. 420 of Oct. 15, 1906; 371/434, Jordan no. 407, Sept. 12, 1908.
84. FO 228/2482, Satow, no. 140, March 29, 1906.
85. DFZZ 3.6 (1906): *junshi* 99-101. For Yuan's response, see YSKZZ, pp. 2154-55.
86. FO 17/1656, Intelligence Diary for the period ending Aug. 11, 1906; 371/31, G. Pereira, no. 4, Jan. 14, 1906; 371/41, enclosure no. 10 in Jordan no. 420 of Oct. 15,

loyalty of the common soldier to the Bieyang Army was weak, it is likely that his personal loyalty to Yuan was even weaker.[87]

The personal loyalties of the Beiyang officer are the key to the question of whether or not the Beiyang was Yuan's personal army. The Beiyang officer was a new breed of Chinese military man. Typically he was from the literate classes and thus unusually well-educated for a soldier. Many, like Feng Guo-zhang and Wu Pei-fu, could boast a solid classical education. But more important were their professional qualifications. Although a few of the senior officers, like Zhang Xun and Jiang Gui-ti, were hold-overs from old-style armies, such as the Huai and Xiang, most had been through training in military academies in China or abroad and were unprecedentedly well qualified technically for their commands.

The senior leadership of the Beiyang Army was typified by Duan Qi-rui, Feng Guo-zhang, and Wang Shi-zhen. These three men, known at the time as the "three outstanding Beiyang men" (*Beiyang sanjie*), probably wielded the greatest influence in Yuan's military administration in Zhili.[88] All three were expert administrators, technicians of modern warfare, and from gentry backgrounds.

Duan Qi-rui (1865-1936) came from a prominent Anhui military family. As one of the best students in the first class at Li Hong-zhang's military academy (*Wubei xuetang*) in Tianjin, Duan was sent in 1888 to Germany where he studied artillery for two years. Before and during the Sino-Japanese War, Duan taught artillery classes at Weihaiwei. In 1896 at the suggestion of Yin-chang, a Manchu who was director of studies at the Tianjin academy, Yuan Shi-kai brought Duan to Xiaozhan as head of the Newly Created Army's artillery units and as an instructor at the Xiaozhan officers' academy. Duan performed similar duties for Yuan in Shandong

---

1906. Hatano Yoshihiro, in "The New Armies," pp. 365-82, has argued that the development of new armies during the last decade of the Qing dynasty siphoned off potentially explosive peasant discontent and channeled it into the revolutionary nationalist movements of the upper classes. For the Beiyang Army, there is little evidence that ordinary soldiers became politically conscious or identified themselves with the causes of their officers. They seemed more conscious of their bondage to an oppressive system which included their officers. When they could—or dared—they deserted.

87. As an indication of the personal loyalty of the Beiyang troops to Yuan, the fact that a portrait of Yuan hung in the barracks of the men is frequently cited; Powell, p. 227, and Hatano Yoshihiro, "The New Armies," p. 372.

88. Tao Ju-yin, *Beiyang junfa tongzhi shiqi shihua*, vol. 1, pp. 5-11; Chen Xi-zhang, p. 255; Xu Dao-lin, *Xu Shu-zheng xiansheng wenji nianpu* (Taibei, 1962), p. 200.

between 1899 and 1901. In November, 1901, when Yuan was appointed Zhili governor-general, he requested Duan's transfer to Zhili. As mentioned earlier, Duan was instrumental in the suppression of the Jing Ting-bin rebellion during the spring of 1902. In appreciation, the Empress Dowager promoted Duan to expectant *daotai* and awarded him the privilege of wearing a peacock feather.[89]

Feng Guo-zhang (1858-1919), a native of Zhili, began as an orderly in the Huai Army. He was chosen to attend Li Hong-zhang's Tianjin academy, where he specialized in infantry. On leave from the Tianjin academy in 1888, he won a civil *shengyuan* degree by passing a prefectural examination. Feng then returned to the Tianjin academy and, after graduation, joined the staff of Nie Shi-cheng's army (*Wuyi jun*) in 1891. In 1895 Nie sent Feng to Japan to study military affairs for a year. The following year Nie and Yin-chang recommended Feng to Yuan, who put him in charge of training troops and of teaching infantry tactics at Xiaozhan. Feng accompanied Yuan to Shandong and then back to Zhili in 1901.[90]

Wang Shi-zhen (1863-1932) was from Zhili and also a graduate of Li Hong-zhang's Tianjin military academy. Yuan Shi-kai first met Wang in 1894-95 when both were stationed near the Yalu River. In 1896, on the basis of Yin-chang's recommendation, Yuan put Wang in charge of officer training and planning at Xiaozhan and later in Shandong. Wang also commanded the Newly Created Army's engineering corps. Then in 1901 Wang accompanied Yuan to Zhili.[91]

As indicated earlier, Yuan's first step in the creation of a unified Beiyang Army was the establishment of a coordinating administrative body, the Department of Military Affairs, in June, 1902. Duan Qi-rui and Feng Guo-zhang, respectively, served as general directors (*zongban*) of the department's sub-bureaus of planning and training.[92] Wang Shi-zhen was in charge of the actual training of new troops at Baoding and acted as their commanding officer.[93] During the army's expansion from 1903 to 1907, the "three out-

89. Wu Ting-xie, *juan* 1:1-6; Liu Feng-han, *Xinjian lujun*, p. 113; and Shen Yun-long, "Duan Qi-rui zhi yisheng," *Xin Zhongguo pinglun* 33.6 (June 1967):13-17.
90. Chen Xi-zhang, *Beiyang cangsang shihua*, pp. 254-55; Liu Feng-han, *Xinjian lujun*, pp. 114-15; Xu Dao-lin, pp. 200-01; and Howard Boorman, *Biographical Dictionary*, vol. 2, pp. 24-28.
91. Chen Xi-zhang, p. 274; Liu Feng-han, *Xinjian lujun*, p. 117.
92. YSKZZ, pp. 566-68.
93. FO 405/128 (conf. print), December 1902, no. 25.

standing Beiyang men" held concurrent posts in Beijing and Tianjin, while also commanding troops in the field.

Duan Qi-rui held the most posts of the three. In 1903 he was in Beijing assisting Yuan in the establishment of the Army Reorganization Bureau, within which he became a department head. Between 1903 and 1904 he was also commander of what became the Beiyang Fourth Division (formerly the Newly Created Army and initially called the Third Division). In 1905 Duan commanded the Fourth Division until he was transferred in September to command the new Sixth Division. Moreover, in October Duan acted as general director of the large-scale maneuvers at Hejian, Zhili. In 1906 Duan became commander of the Third Division while concurrently supervising the Beiyang military academy and serving as general director of the staff college at Baoding. Finally in 1907 Duan retired briefly before becoming general director of the entire Qing military education system.[94]

From 1903 to 1907 Feng Guo-zhang also had a variety of assignments. In 1903 and 1904, during the most important stages of the expansion of the Beiyang Army, Feng, like Duan Qi-rui, served in Beijing as a department head on the Army Reorganization Bureau and in Tianjin as a bureau head of the Department of Military Affairs, both of which were the key military planning and coordinating agencies of the central government and of Yuan's provincial government respectively. In 1905 Feng became general director of the (Manchu) Military School for Princes and Nobles (*Guizhou xuetang*) and, briefly, commander of the Third Beiyang Division. Toward the end of the year, he went to Japan as an official observer at maneuvers of the Japanese army. In 1906 Feng continued as head of the military school for Manchu noblemen and late in the year assumed command of the Beiyang Sixth Division. In 1907 he became head of the new Ministry of War's General Staff Council.[95]

Wang Shi-zhen served as head of Yuan's military staff in Tianjin in 1903 and then in 1904-1905 as Yuan's liaison man in Beijing with the Army Reorganization Bureau. In 1906 Wang commanded the Sixth Division of the Beiyang Army until the fall, when he oversaw the *Lujun* maneuvers held at Zhangde, Henan province. In 1907

---

94. Wu Ting-xie, *juan* 1:7.
95. Liu Feng-han, *Xinjian lujun*, pp. 114-15; Chen Xi-zhang, pp. 254-55; Ch'en, "Footnote on the Chinese Army," pp. 426-34; YSKZZ, pp. 2156-57.

Wang became commander-in-chief of the Jiangbei military district in Jiangsu province, where he was to raise and train a new modern-style division.[96]

The frequent transferring of Duan, Feng, and Wang from post to post was not an unusual practice within the Beiyang Army. It is generally recognized that Yuan regularly transferred senior officers to insure his continued control over the Beiyang military organization.[97] This policy prevented the Beiyang divisions from becoming private armies, each loyal primarily to its division commander. As shown in Table 10, between 1903 and 1907 four out of six Beiyang divisions had a new commander every year or two.

TABLE 10. *Division Commanders of the Beiyang Army, 1903-1907*

1st (Manchu) Division		2nd Division	
1903-06:	Tie-liang and Yuan Shi-kai	1903:	Wang Shi-zhen
		1904-06:	Wang Ying-kai
1907:	Feng-shan	1907:	Ma Long-biao

3rd Division		4th Division	
1905:	Duan Zhi-qui, Feng Guo-zhang	1903-04:	Duan Qi-rui
		1905:	Duan Qi-rui, Wu Feng-ling
1906:	Duan Qi-rui		
1907:	Feng-shan, Cao Kun	1906–:	Wu Feng-ling

5th Division		6th Division	
1903-04:	Xia Xin-you	1905:	Duan Qi-rui
1905-06:	Zhang Huai-zhi	1906:	Wang Shi-zhen
1907:	Feng-shan (half division)		Feng Guo-zhang
		1907:	Feng-shan (half division)

SOURCE: Jerome Ch'en, "Footnote on the Chinese Army in 1911-12," pp. 426-34; *Rongan dizi ji, juan* 3:16b, 18a, 4:3a; Wu Ting-xie, *juan* 1:7; FO 17/1655, Intelligence Diaries for the periods from February 16 to May 10, 1904; 371/39, Enclosure no. 15 in Carnegie no. 332 of August 6, 1906; 371/41, Enclosure no. 1 in Jordan no. 420 of October 15, 1906.

96. Chen Xi-zhang, p. 274; FO 371/31, G. Pereira, no. 4, Jan. 14, 1906; 371/39, enclosure no. 15 in Carnegie no. 332 of Aug. 6, 1906; 371/41, enclosure no. 1 in Jordan no. 420 of Oct. 15, 1906.

97. Tao Ju-yin, *Beiyang junfa* . . . , vol. 1, p. 16; Ch'en, "Footnote on the Chinese Army," p. 426.

Yuan tried to recruit junior officers locally in Zhili in order to insure the development of personal ties to his military organization. However, he wanted to prevent the development of close ties between an officer and a particular unit. Therefore, as we shall see, junior officers, like senior officers, were frequently transferred. Probably close to Yuan's ideal for junior officers were Wu Pei-fu and Feng Yu-xiang, about whom a great deal is known because of their subsequent importance as warlords in the 1920s.

Wu Pei-fu (1874-1939) was the son of a shopkeeper in Shandong. When Wu was fourteen, his father made him join the Shandong navy as a common seaman. We nonetheless found time to study the classics and to pass a *shengyuan* examination in 1897. Winning this civil degree proved to be a turning point in his military career. In 1898 he was recruited for service with Nie Shi-cheng's troops at Tianjin. In 1900 he enrolled in a new military academy established at Kaiping in Zhili. Because of the Boxer affair, the academy closed and Wu fled to Tianjin where he remained idle for a year. When Yuan Shi-kai opened a new academy for the training of officers at Baoding in 1902, Wu enrolled. Specializing in cartography and surveying, Wu graduated in 1903, was commissioned a second lieutenant (*zhongwei*) and selected to do espionage work for Yuan in cooperation with the Japanese. Under the supervision of a Japanese officer, Wu spent 1904 in Shandong, Korea, and Manchuria spying on the Russians. Evidently a good spy, during the year Wu was recalled to Tianjin, commended, promoted to first lieutenant (*shangwei*) and sent back to Manchuria. There the Russians caught Wu and took him to Mukden where they sentenced him to death. He managed to escape, however, and after his return to Tianjin, received a medal from the Meiji Emperor. In 1906, he joined the Third Division of the Beiyang Army, at the time under the command of Duan Qi-rui and stationed at Baoding. Soon he became an infantry battalion officer and stayed with the Third Division through 1907. During this period, command of the division shifted to the Manchu Feng-shan and then back to one of Yuan's close associates, Cao Kun, under whom the division was transferred to Manchuria. Wu became a top assistant of Cao Kun and, early in 1908, commander of an artillery battalion.[98]

98. *Wu Pei-fu xiansheng ji* (Taibei, 1960), pp. 201-08, 306-09; Tao Ju-yin, *Wu Pei-fu jiangjun zhuan* (Shanghai, 1941), pp. 5-9; Odoric Y.K. Wou, *Militarism in Modern China: The Career of Wu P'ei-fu, 1916-39* (Canberra, 1978), pp. 9-17; Okano Masujiro, ed., *Go Hai-fu* (1939), pp. 3-4.

Feng Yu-xiang (1882-1948) had to struggle hard to become a battalion officer. Feng's father was a platoon officer (*paijiang*) in Li Hong-zhang's Huai Army stationed at Baoding. Feng joined his father's battalion in 1896 at the age of fourteen. In April, 1902, Feng left what he considered to be an outmoded and corrupt Huai Army to join Yuan Shi-kai's Newly Created Army as a common soldier. Feng's talents evidently were appreciated immediately because he was one of four men chosen from his company to study at the divisional school at Tianjin. But promotion depended on performing well on written examinations. Therefore Feng and a friend hired a tutor, with whom they studied the classics. Promotions followed. In 1905 Feng was transferred with a portion of his division (by then called the Fourth) to Nanyuan, south of Beijing, to serve in the new Sixth Division of the Beiyang Army. He first was appointed an infantry platoon officer, and then, because of good examination scores, he was promoted to company officer in another Sixth Division battalion. He also attracted the attention of Lu Jian-zhang, his brigade officer. In 1907 Feng married the niece of Lu's wife and was transferred to Xinmin, Manchuria as commander of an infantry company in a new mixed brigade led by Lu. Later in 1907, Feng was promoted to battalion officer, but not of the same battalion with which he had been associated as company officer.[99]

As battalion officers, both Wu Pei-fu and Feng Yu-xiang moved from battalion to battalion. Feng had also been moved at least twice as a company officer. Although general statistics on the change of the Beiyang Army's battalion and company officers between 1903 and 1907 are not available, the experience of Wu Pei-fu and Feng Yu-xiang suggests a pattern of frequent transfers which we have already found to be true for division commanders. That this was the general pattern is further demonstrated by Tables 11 and 12 on the makeup of the command of the Beiyang Second Division in 1904 and 1908. The fact that there was absolutely no continuity in command suggests that there was a system for the rotation of officers within and between divisions.

What has just been said about the frequent transferring of officers and about the careers of individual senior and junior officers suggests that the Beiyang Army officer's situation resembled that

99. Feng Yu-xiang, *Wodi shenghuo*, pp. 1-105, and *Wodi dushu*, pp. 80-138; and Sheridan, pp. 31-48.

TABLE 11. *Beiyang Second Division in 1904*
(stationed around Yongping *fu* in northeast Zhili)

	Background and career after 1904
Commander	
Wang Ying-kai	With Yuan since Xiaozhan; an educator with a civilian degree; in 1907 becomes General Feng-shan's chief deputy and vice-president of the Ministry of War.
Regiment officers	
Zhang Huai-zhi	Native of Shandong; Tianjin academy graduate; with Yuan since Xiaozhan; from 1905 to 1907 commander of the Beiyang 5th Division.
Liu Cao-bei	?
Wu Feng-ling	Tientsin academy graduate; with Yuan since Xiaozhan; a relative of Yuan's (?); after 1905 commander of the Beiyang Fourth Division.
Tian Zhong-you	Native of Zhili; Tianjin academy graduate; with Yuan since Xiaozhan; by 1907 holding high posts within Xu Shi-chang's chief-of-staff in Manchuria.
Battalion officers	
Li Chang-tai	Zhili native; Tianjin academy graduate; with Yuan since Xiaozhan.
Nan Cao-yuan	?

SOURCE: FO 17/1655, Intelligence Diary for the period ending April 12, 1904, and 17/1657, Intelligence Diary for the period ending Sept. 13, 1904. Biographical information from Liu Feng-han, *Xinjian lujun*, pp. 103, 107, 109-10, 119-20, 122, 151, 153, 173, 175, 336; *Wuwei jun*, pp. 527, 529, 492; Ch'en, "A Footnote on the Chinese Army in 1911-12," pp. 428, 430; FO 371/642, Willoughby no. 8 of Nov. 10, 1909.

TABLE 12. *Beiyang Second Division in 1908*
(split between Yongping *fu* and Baoding)

Commander	
Ma Long-biao	Age 55; Shandong Moslem; Huai army origins (?); with Yuan since Xiaozhan; became commander of the 2nd division in 1907.
Brigade officers	
Wang Zhan-yuan	Native of Shandong; in Song Qing's *Yijun;* Tianjin academy graduate; with Yuan since Xiaozhan; age 48.
Bao Gui-qing	Age 42; native of Fengdian; Tianjin academy graduate; with Yuan since Xiaozhan.
Chief-of-staff (zong canmou guan)	
Jia De-yao	Age 29; educated in Japan.
Regiment officers	
Wang Jin-jing	Age 42; native of Shandong; Tianjin academy graduate; with Yuan since Xiaozhan.
Wang Mao-shang	Age 38; ?
Zhu Ting-can	Educated in Japan.
Wang Tong-yu	?
Gao Weng-qui	Age 46; ?
Regiment's second-in-command (jiao lian guan)	
Kang Zong-yan	Age 26; educated in Japan
Liu Fu-hong	Age 33; Tianjin German school graduate.

SOURCE: FO 371/435, G. Pereira no. 88 of November 2, 1908, "The 2nd Division of Lu Chun." Biographical information from Liu Feng-han, *Xinjian lujun*, pp. 120-23; *Wuwei jun*, pp. 240, 493, 523-24; and Chen Xi-zhang, pp. 428-29.

of a traditional Chinese bureaucrat. The Beiyang Army was—in theory at least—a meritocracy. Recruitment and advancement of officers was supposed to be, and to a surprising degree actually was, based on education and examination performance.[100] The chain of command was an elaborate hierarchy in which decision-making power remained at the top, in the hands of Yuan and the division commanders. As was traditional Chinese bureaucratic practice, Yuan frequently transferred officers to check the growth of local vested interests within units and to develop primary loyalty only to himself. But was Yuan successful? Available evidence indicates that, between 1903 and 1908, Yuan achieved at least the former objective.[101] Since "loyalty" is less easy to measure, we can only offer some observations on the nature of the bonds between Yuan and his officers.

This is not to say that Yuan himself did not develop close personal ties with his senior commanders. Yuan's relationship with his top officers, such as Duan Qi-rui, Wang Shi-zhen, and Feng Guo-zhang, was based on close personal associations which antedated Yuan's governor-generalship of Zhili. But was Yuan always able to control men like Duan, Wang, and Feng? Inasmuch as the Beiyang Army was more directly under imperial government structure than was Li Hong-zhang's Huai Army, Beiyang officers had more ties with Beijing than the Huai Army commanders ever had. It was significant that after 1903 Duan, Wang, and Feng were promoted to such posts as provincial commanders-in-chief and to staff positions on the Army Reorganization Bureau and later in the Ministry of War. The Empress Dowager, not Yuan, also rewarded these and other senior Beiyang officers with traditional Green Standard and

---

100. *Da Qing Guangxu xinfaling,* ce 14:1-5, 49b-50, 59; YSKZZ, pp. 812-13; Cameron, p. 94; and Hatano Yoshihiro, "The New Armies," pp. 273-75.

101. Historians have assumed that splits within the Beiyang officer corps already had developed during the Qing period into cleavages—such as between Zhili and Anhui cliques—which after Yuan's death in 1916 defined much of "warlord" politics: see Tao Ju-yin, *Beiyang junfa* . . . , vol. 1, p. 13, and vol. 2, pp. 80-81; Jerome Ch'en, "Defining Chinese Warlords and Their Factions," *Bulletin of the School of Oriental and African Studies* 31.3 (October 1967):581-84; and Hatano Yoshihiro, "Hokuyō gumbatsu . . . ," p. 238. I have found no documentary support for such a hypothesis. Of course there were occasional disputes between officers, but there is no evidence of permanent cleavages developing which relate to post-Yuan warlord politics. On disputes between senior officers, for example, there were some at the large-scale maneuvers of the Beiyang Army in 1905 and 1906; FO 371/41, G. Pereira, "Report on Chinese Army Manoeuvres."

Banner forces' ranks and titles as well as absentee appointments as commanders-in-chief and brigade commanders in provinces other than Zhili.[102] Therefore, more than Li Hong-zhang's commanders, Yuan's generals developed their own independent status in the central government's military bureaucracy and in their relationships with officials in Beijing. As long as Yuan remained in power and enjoyed the Court's favor, leading Beiyang officers like Duan, Wang, and Feng would follow his leadership and work with him as members of a military clique. But it seems clear that by 1907-08 the loyalties of these men to Yuan were more professional and political than strictly personal—and thus were subject to change.

Besides these senior commanders, other Beiyang Army officers had less reason to be personally loyal to Yuan. There were old Huai Army commanders like Jiang Gui-ti and Zhang Xun, who served under Yuan in the Beiyang Army but who, the evidence suggests, felt more loyalty to the dynasty than to Yuan.

Jiang Gui-ti (1838-1922), a native of Anhui, began his career in the Huai Army under Li Hong-zhang. Later he served with Zuo Zong-tang on his campaigns against Moslem rebels in the northwest during the 1870s and 1880s. No more is heard about Jiang until the Sino-Japanese War of 1894-95, when Jiang emerged as a brigade commander (*zongbing*). After his troops suffered defeat at Port Arthur (Dalian), Jiang fled to Fuzhou where he joined the *Yijun* led by Song Qing. Then, in 1896, Yuan appointed Jiang to the highest post in his Newly Created Army as senior brigadier (*zuo yichang*). Jiang stayed with Yuan at Xiaozhan and in 1899 accompanied him to Shandong. Early in 1902, at the Empress Dowager's command, Yuan assigned Jiang permanently to Beijing with a thousand men to serve as her personal imperial guard. His troops were made up of semimodern units transferred from the *Yijun*. More under the Empress Dowager than Yuan, Jiang remained in Beijing until 1908 as commander of an imperial guard which grew to about 3,000 men.[103]

Zhang Xun (1854-1923), who was from a Jiangxi gentry family but orphaned during the Taiping war, rose from the rank of a

102. Powell, pp. 211-12. Liu Feng-han, in *Wuwei jun*, pp. 515-72, has documented at great length the rewarding and promoting of Yuan's subordinates by Beijing.
103. YSKZZ, p. 1206; FO 17/1655, Intelligence Diary for the period ending April 12, 1904; 371/39, enclosure no. 15 in Carnegie no. 332 of Aug. 6, 1906; 405/128 (conf. print), December 1902, no. 25; Liu Feng-han, *Xinjian lujun*, p. 117; *Wuwei jun*, pp. 461-62, 798; Chen Xi-zhang, p. 220; see also Chapter 2, above.

common soldier to the command of a cavalry unit in Guangxi province. Then in 1884 Zhang joined Li Hong-zhang's Huai Army, serving under Su Yuan-chun and rising to the rank of brigade general. In 1894 Zhang commanded cavalry units in Song Qing's *Yijun*. In 1895 Zhang met Yuan Shi-kai in Tianjin and soon thereafter joined Yuan's Newly Created Army as commander of an engineering company and battalion drill instructor. Zhang followed Yuan to Shandong and then to Zhili in 1901. Zhang led the cavalry units that met the Empress Dowager at the Zhili-Henan border in December, 1901, when she was returning to Beijing. For the next year and a half, Zhang served the Empress Dowager in Beijing on special duty, leading units which guarded her on trips to the Eastern and Western tombs in the spring of 1902 and 1903. In mid-1903 Zhang was transferred to Manchuria where as Tartar General of Kirin he vigorously suppressed banditry and tried to protect Chinese sovereignty against Russian incursions. In 1906 the Empress Dowager sent Zhang to Mukden where Tartar General Zhao Er-sun wanted him to lead an army against local bandits in the northern Shengjing district. In 1907 the new governor-general of a unified Manchurian administration, Xu Shi-chang, put Zhang in charge of reorganizing local Defense Corps (*Xunfang dui*) and carrying out further bandit suppression. The troops which Zhang commanded and used against bandits in Manchuria between 1903 and 1907 were of the old-style, Huai Army type.[104]

It is likely that Jiang Gui-ti and Zhang Xun felt more loyalty for the dynasty and the Empress Dowager than for Yuan Shi-kai and the Beiyang Army. Both served in positions which, although under Yuan's command, were outside of the mainstream of the activities of the Beiyang Army. Jiang and Zhang commanded units guarding the Empress Dowager and the imperial family. Zhang also engaged in bandit suppression activities in Manchuria. Moreover, the units which Zhang and Jiang commanded were only semimodern, organizationally structured like the Huai army, and therefore not usually identified with the newly raised and trained Beiyang Army units. Hence, the ties of Jiang and Zhang and their troops to Yuan and his new Beiyang Army were not so intimate. Between 1901

104. Liu Feng-han, *Xinjian lujun*, pp. 116-117; *Wuwei jun*, pp. 648, 756, 798; Wang Er-min, *Huaijun zhi*, p. 139; Reginald F. Johnston, *Twilight in the Forbidden City* (New York, 1934), pp. 146-60; Chen Xi-zhang, p. 247; FO 17/1654, Intelligence Diary for the period ending Feb. 2, 1904. On Zhang Xun's bandit suppression activities, see BYGD, *juan* 4:47b-50, and Xu Shi-chang, *Duigeng tang zhengshu* (1919), *juan* 21:8b-11.

and 1907 there was no evidence of developing hostility between Yuan and these men; in fact the record suggests that Yuan treated both with a great deal of courtesy.[105] However, it was not surprising that in 1911-12 Jiang, Zhang, and their troops more strongly supported the dynasty than other Beiyang units; and that later, in 1916, Zhang Xun was the leader of a Manchu restoration attempt.[106]

Yuan's most serious loyalty problem was with the junior officers. Yuan had tried to train as many of his junior officers as possible in the new academies that he established in Zhili with a view not only to assuring the technical competence of his officers but also to cultivating their loyalty to him. Wu Pei-fu and Feng Yu-xiang represented this type of junior officer. But, despite its rapid expansion, the capacity of Yuan's military educational system to produce competent officers was limited. Each new division required about 700 commissioned officers.[107] In 1904 and 1905, when three new divisions were created, Yuan needed about 2100 new officers. Yet figures on enrollment and numbers of graduates for those years (see Table 13 below) suggest that at most there were available about a thousand qualified men who were also products of the Beiyang educational system.

Both because Yuan insisted upon officers meeting definite professional standards and because he also sought the best professionally qualified candidates, Yuan was forced to recruit Beiyang officers from outside his own military academies and outside his political sphere of influence. Most of these new recruits were Chinese cadets trained in Japan. Between 1903 and 1907 there were probably from two to three thousand Chinese receiving some kind of military education in Japan. In 1908, 254 Chinese graduated from Japanese military academies.[108] By 1910 there were 620 Chinese graduates of the prestigious and rigorous Japanese Army Officers' Academy (Nihon rikugun shikan gakko).[109] However, statisti-

---

105. Liu Feng-han, Xinjian lujun, p. 117; Wuwei jun, p. 799; Johnston, pp. 148-55.
106. Powell, pp. 313-14, 327-28; and Johnston, pp. 131-59.
107. Wen Gong-zhi, vol. 1, p. 41.
108. Sanetō Keishū, Chūgokujin Nihon ryūgaku shi (Tokyo, 1960), pp. 138, 528-32, and graph on p. 544. It is estimated that in 1905-06 the number of Chinese students in Japan reached a peak of 8,000. Statistics about Chinese graduates from Japanese schools during the 1903-07 period suggest that from one-fourth to one-third of the students were receiving some sort of military education.
109. Ernest Young, "Yuan Shi-kai's Rise to the Presidency," p. 246, cites Shina Kenkyukai, ed., Saishin Shina kanshin roku (1918), vol. 2, pp. 292-405.

TABLE 13. *Estimates of Enrollment and Graduates from Beiyang Military Schools, 1903-1907*

	Enrollment				Annual Graduates		
	1904	1905	1906	1907	1905	1906	1907
Staff college	110	110	110	110	110	110	110
New model staff college			150-60	150-60			150-60
Primary schools		?	600	800			200?
Beiyang military academy	100	100	100	100	50	50	50
Accelerated training center	5-600?	5-600?	5-600?	1400	150	150-200	300+
Veterinary			170	170			170
Ordnance				81			
Medical (2)			350?	350			
Topography	200?	200?	200?	200	100?	100?	100?
Divisional schools	?	500	500	750?	300?	300?	500?
Rough Totals	400				6-700	6-700	1,000

SOURCE: The estimates in the table are liberally calculated from available sources. Figures with a question mark (?) are based on incomplete data. Sources are FO 371/79, Enclosure no. 15 in Carnegie no. 332 of Aug. 6, 1906; 371/41, enclosures 1, 2, 4 in Jordan no. 420 of Oct. 15, 1906; 371/435, enclosure in Jordan no. 506 of Nov. 8, 1908. The first class from Baoding graduated late in 1904; but its graduates, none of whom was from Zhili, were obliged to return to their native provinces (*Shilu, juan* 519:9b).

cal information on who and how many of these returning students joined the Beiyang Army is scarce. We do know that during the spring of 1904, Yuan recruited sixty young officers from the south, who had been trained at Zhang Zhi-dong's academy at Wuchang and/or in Japan.[110] In November, 1904, thirty students returned to Zhili from military studies in Japan to be immediately pressed into service with Yuan's Beiyang Army divisions.[111] Between 1905 and 1907, British military attachés who visited the Beiyang divisions and reported on their condition noticed varying but significant numbers of Japan-trained junior officers in each division.[112]

Although the loyalties of the Japan-trained officers in the Beiyang Army are difficult to document precisely, as a group they seemed restless under the authority and command of Yuan Shi-kai and his senior officers. We know that many were becoming increasingly anti-Manchu in their politics.[113] Paradoxically, during the brief period in 1906-07 when the anti-Yuan Manchu Tie-liang, who himself had studied in Japan, gained control over much of the army, he actively recruited and promoted youths from the southern Yangzi provinces who had studied in Japan. In the Beiyang Second Division, for example, recent graduates of Japanese military schools rose to the level of regiment commander and chief-of-staff by 1908 (see Table 8). This promotion and recruitment of young Japan-trained officers has been interpreted by contemporaries and historians alike as part of the attempt by Tie-liang—probably acting on the advice of a young Manchu, Liang-bi, who himself had just returned from military training in Japan—to loosen Yuan's grip on the Beiyang divisions. Certainly it suggests that Japan-trained officers were considered to be less than loyal to Yuan Shi-kai.[114]

Among the most radical of the Japan-trained officers were Lan

110. FO 17/1665, Intelligence Diary for the period ending March 1, 1904; Powell, p. 202.
111. FO 17/1657, Intelligence Diary for the period ending Sept. 17, 1904; 17/1686, Intelligence Diary for the period ending Nov. 22, 1904.
112. FO 371/31, G. Pereira, no. 4, Jan. 14, 1906; 371/39 enclosure no. 15 in Carnegie no. 332 of Aug. 6, 1906; 371/434, enclosure in Jordan no. 407 of Sept. 12, 1908; 371/435, G. Pereira, no. 88, Nov. 2, 1908.
113. This was noticed by contemporary Chinese and foreigners alike; see FO 228/1594, Hopkins, no. 62, Dec. 19, 1905; 371/434, enclosure in Jordan no. 407 of Sept. 12, 1908; Tao Ju-yin, *Beiyang junfa* . . . , vol. 1, pp. 13-14, 24.
114. Hatano Yoshihiro, "Hokuyō gumbatsu . . . ," pp. 245-53; Tao Ju-yin, *Beiyang junfa* . . . , vol. 1, p. 24; Li Chien-nung, pp. 214-16.

Tian-wei, Zhang Shao-zeng, and Wu Lu-zhen, who later led the famous Lanzhou mutiny of the Beiyang Sixth Division in 1911.[115] Lan Tian-wei and Wu Lu-zhen were natives of Hubei; Zhang Shao-zeng was from Zhili. Wu had a *xiucai* degree and had been a personal protégé of Zhang Zhi-dong in the late 1890s. In 1899 Zhang Zhi-dong sent Wu to the Japanese Army Officers' Academy in Tokyo. In 1900, without Zhang's knowledge, Wu stole briefly back to China in order to participate in the abortive Datong uprising in Anhui. At Zhang Zhi-dong's recommendation Zhang Shao-zeng and Lan Tian-wei were also sent to the Japanese Army Officers' Academy, from which Wu and Zhang graduated in 1903 and Lan, in 1904. In 1903 the three of them had organized a Tokyo branch of the student brigade for the defense of Chinese sovereignty in Manchuria against Russian aggression.[116] Returning to China after graduation, Zhang Shao-zeng was assigned to the Fifth Division of the Beiyang Army in Shandong. Feng Yu-xiang in his memoirs recalled bitter disputes between Zhang and Zhang Huai-zhi, commander of the Fifth Division and an associate of Yuan since 1896.[117] Zhang Shao-zeng soon was transferred, joining Lan Tian-wei and the Sixth Beiyang Division at Nanyuan, near Beijing, where they probably served as battalion officers.[118] From 1903 to 1904 Wu Lu-zhen taught in Zhang Zhi-dong's officer training school at Wuzhang and helped Zhang generally with training troops. By 1905 Wu was in Beijing on the staff of the Army Reorganization Bureau. Wu angered Board of War president Tie-liang, however, so that by 1906 he was in temporary retirement and *persona non grata* in Beijing's official circles. In 1907 Xu Shi-chang brought Wu to Manchuria as a member of his military staff and thereafter Wu rose rapidly, becoming commander of the Beiyang Sixth Division by late 1910. In the meantime Zhang Shao-zeng and Lan Tian-wei also

---

115. Except for that separately footnoted, basic biographical data on Lan, Zhang, and Wu is from Chen Xi-zhang, pp. 376-77, 380-81, 378-79, and Zhu Yan-jia, "Wu Lu-zhen yu Zhongguo geming," in Wu Xiang-xiang, ed., *Zhongguo xiandai shi zongkan* (Taibei, 1964), vol. 6, pp. 161-232. See also Daniel Bays, *China Enters the Twentieth Century*, pp. 143-48, 157, 161-62, 215. A good account in English of the Lanzhou mutiny is in Sheridan, pp. 43-48.

116. On the student brigades, see Mary B. Rankin, "The Manchurian Crisis and Radical Student Nationalism, 1903," *Ch'ing-shih wen-t'i* 2.1 (October 1969):87-101.

117. Feng Yu-xiang, *Wodi shenghuo*, pp. 93-94.

118. FO 371/39, enclosure no. 15 in Carnegie no. 332 of Aug. 6, 1906. In 1906, Zhang Shao-zeng also was on the staff which supervised the *Lujun* maneuvers at Zhangde.

came to Manchuria as officers in Xu's new Second Mixed Brigade, of which Lan eventually became brigade commander. As early as the spring of 1907, Wu, Lan, and Zhang were conspiring together again for radical political change, in conjunction with exiled revolutionary and reform groups in Japan. Unlike Wu Pei-fu and Feng Yu-xiang, Wu Lu-zhen, Lan Tian-wei, and Zhang Shao-zeng owed little to Yuan Shi-kai, his senior officers, or Yuan's military educational system. Their previous associations in Japan and their preoccupation with nationalist causes made them potentially subversive to the ruling Qing dynasty and unreliable from the point of view of Yuan's military organization.

To summarize, the Beiyang Army depended for its very existence upon the financial and administrative support of the central government in Beijing. Unlike the Xiang and Huai Armies, the Beiyang Army did not originate from a local response to an internal crisis of the sort created by the Taiping rebellion. Instead, external threats to national and dynastic security, the most important of which was the Russo-Japanese War over Manchuria in 1904-05, caused the Empress Dowager to allocate large sums, much of which came from the southern Yangzi provinces, for the buildup of the Beiyang Army in northeast China. As with funding, administrative control of the Beiyang Army also depended upon the balance of power at Court and its commander-in-chief's influence with the Empress Dowager. Yuan controlled the development of the Beiyang Army through his influence with the Empress Dowager and chief grand councillor Prince Qing and through the positions he, his protégés, and his allies had on two key administrative agencies in Beijing—the Army Reorganization Bureau and the Board (after 1906, Ministry) of War. Thus, late in 1906 and early in 1907, when Yuan came under attack at Court and his influence with the Empress Dowager was at its nadir, the Manchu president of the new Ministry of War, Tie-liang, challenged Yuan and was able, temporarily, to take administrative control over four out of the six Beiyang divisions away from Yuan.

Internally, the Beiyang Army was organized and functioned more along professional bureaucratic lines than its Huai and Xiang Army predecessors. Its organization had been deliberately thought out and modeled after Japan's modern armies. Criteria for qualification as an officer or soldier in the Beiyang Army emphasized education and professional military training over personal and regional connections. Available evidence also suggests that officers in the Beiyang Army at all levels of command were transferred frequently. This militated against the development of primary loyalties between a body of troops and their commander and no doubt increased the dependence of the officers and men upon their commander-in-chief, Yuan Shi-kai (the exceptions were the small semimodern units on the periphery which were commanded by older officers with Huai Army experience). But the personal loyalties of the Beiyang officers to Yuan varied a great deal because of Yuan's emphasis on education and professional military training in the recruiting of officers. Just discussed were three factions within the Beiyang Army from which different degrees of loyalty to Yuan were to be expected: loyal senior and junior officers like Duan Qi-rui and Wu Pei-fu, less loyal ex-Huai Army officers like Jiang Gui-ti and Zhang Xun, and the large group of Japan-trained junior officers whose ties to Yuan were minimal. The commitment of all three types of Beiyang officers to Yuan depended on his fulfilling their career and political goals, which in turn depended upon Yuan's influence in Beijing.

CHAPTER V

Reform and the Exercise of Power in Zhili, 1901-1907

So far we have been analyzing Yuan Shi-kai's political power in terms of two nodes at the central and regional government levels of the Qing state. After rising to high office through influence in Beijing (Chapter 1), Yuan found that there were political limits to what he could accomplish simply as a regional figure (Chapter 2). Yuan therefore turned to Beijing to consolidate his position and build up a power base at Court and within Beijing's new reform bureaucracy (Chapter 3). The essential dependence on Beijing of Yuan's growing military power in Zhili and north China is clear from examining the growth, financing, and organization of the Beiyang Army in detail (Chapter 4). It is time now to look at the other major expanding node of political power during the late Qing—the informal power of local elites at the *xian* level—and Yuan Shi-kai's relationship to it.

The expansion of local elite influence during the suppression of the Taiping Rebellion up to the 1911 Revolution is widely accepted by most scholars. The debate, as pointed out in the Introduction, is over the extent of elite independence from formal political power structure at the local level. Here regional differences played an important part, with different answers for different localities. In this chapter, by concentrating on officially-inspired reform in rural Zhili, we shall see how Yuan satisfied local elite desires, co-opted their leadership and, in the process, increased his own power and expanded administrative authority within the *xian*.

During Yuan Shi-kai's tenure as governor-general of Zhili, the subjects of greatest concern to local elites were reforms in education, police, and economics. These were also Yuan's greatest reform successes, particularly in the countryside. As available statistics show (see Table 14), in a six-year period a quasi-modern school system with over 160,000 students was established; the Empire's largest modern police force patrolled the province; and an ambitious plan for commercial and industrial development commenced. Yuan's pioneer efforts in judicial reform, opium control, modernization of communications, postal, and transport systems, and self-government are better known because of recent studies, but were more superficial and limited in effect to Zhili's big cities, Tianjin and Baoding.[1]

Educational Reform

Before coming to Zhili, Yuan had established a national reputation as an educational reformer. The Empress Dowager's edict of November 25, 1901, stated that the models for new schools in the Empire were the schools at various levels which Yuan had pioneered in Shandong.[2] Moreover, Yuan was a leader in the campaign to abolish the traditional examination system. As early as April, 1901, he had called for the gradual replacement of the traditional examinations by new "practical examinations" (*shike*).[3] The Empress Dowager passed over Yuan's suggestion; instead, she adopted Liu Kun-yi's and Zhang Zhi-dong's proposal for the establishment of a new comprehensive school system while gradually phasing out the old examination system. Not surprisingly, there was resistance in Beijing to the drastic changes in the school and examination system which Yuan, Zhang Zhi-dong, and Liu Kun-yi proposed. Sensing the strength of the opposition, Yuan advised a more cautious

---

1. On judicial reform, see M. J. Meijer, *The Introduction of Modern Criminal Law in China* (Batavia, 1949). On opium control, see Merebeth Cameron, *Reform and Revolution*. On the Tianjin self-government experiment, see Jerome Ch'en, *Yuan Shih-k'ai* (1972), p. 73; Philip Kuhn, "Local Self-Government Under the Republic: Problems of Control, Autonomy, and Mobilization," in Wakeman and Grant, eds., *Conflict and Control in Late Imperial China*, pp. 276-78; and John Fincher, "The Chinese Self-Government Movement, 1900-1912" (Ph.D. dissertation, University of Washington, 1969). On modernization of communications, see Imperial Maritime Customs, *Tientsin Decennial Report*, 1892-1901, pp. 551-63, 589; FO 228/1594, Intelligence Report for December quarter, 1904; and 371/634, "Progress of Tientsin on Western lines," enclosure in Jordan no. 25 of Jan. 17, 1909. Abundant source material on these subjects exists in collections of Yuan's memorials and yamen papers in BYGD and DFZZ.

2. *Shilu, juan* 488:8.   3. YSYZY, *juan* 9:4-5.

TABLE 14. Education, Police, and Economic Reform Activity in Zhili, Circa 1907

Number of students/police		Number of students/police	
I. *Shuntian fu*		*Zhuozhou	919
		Liangxiang	401
		*Fangshan	891
		(Beilu ting)	
(Donglu ting)		*Chang-ping zhou	1171
†*Tongzhou	1575	Shunyi	422
Sanhe	251	*Miyun	451
Wuqing	342	Huairou	142
Baodi	440	†*Pinggu	129
*Jizhou	575		
Xianghe	1200/200		
	(350 in 1904)	II. *Baoding fu*	
Ninghe	519		
(Nanlu ting)		*Qingyuan	1458
Bazhou	826	*Mancheng	1233/247
Baoding (Xinzhen)	167	Ansu (Xushui)	554
Wenan	1008	*Dingxing	435
*Dacheng	1545	†*Xincheng	492
Guan	616	Tang	749
Yongqing	448	*Boye	979
†*Dongan (Anci)	355	Wangdu	834/243
(Xilu ting)		Rongcheng	442
Daxing	46	Wan	38
Wanping	84		

TABLE 14. (continued)

Number of students/police		Number of students/police	
Li	3378	IV. *Yongping fu*	
*Xiong	340	† Lulong	564/260
*Qizhou (Anguo)	3794	† Qianan	1436
*Shulu	4681	*Funing	750
Anzhou (Anxin)	498	*Changli	1243
†*Gaoyang	890	*Luanzhou	1257
		*Leting	1224
III. *Zhengding fu*		*Linyu	413
Zhengding	1449/523		
Huolu	484/314	V. *Hejian fu*	
Jingxing	367/152	Hejian	842/395
Fuping	247	Xian	607/368
Luancheng	150/224	Fucheng	1055/152
Xingtang	1278/21	Suning	1132/124
Lingshou	1056/218	*Renqiu	1367/374
*Pingshan	883/52	Jiaohe	271/194
*Yuanshi	745/189	*Ningjin	1345/220
*Zanhuang	476/82	*Jingzhou	1206/600+
Jinzhou	977/269	*Wuqiao	2593/400+
Wuji	925/314	Dongguan	1485/290
*Gaocheng	1767	*Gucheng	774/460
*Xinle	527/242		

Number of students/police			Number of students/police		
VI.	*Tianjin fu*		VIII.	*Shunde fu*	
	Tianjin	3855		†*Xingtai	693/87
	*Qing	443		Shahe	589/505
	†*Jinghai	335		*Nanhe	660/236
	*Nanpi	117/140 (in 1909)		*Pingxiang	375/227
				*Guangzong	385/147
	*Yanshan	687		†*Julu	196/341 (260 in 1906)
	†*Cangzhou	589			
	*Qingyun	818		† Tangshan (Yaoshan)	689/196
				*Neiqiu	1449/123
VII.	*Daming fu*			*Ren	1321/310 (267 in 1906)
	† Daming	967/240			
	Yuancheng	676	IX.	*Guangping fu*	
	*Nanle	662		*Yongnian	262/137
	*Qingfeng	251		Quzhou (xian)	1754
	Dongming	924		*Feixiang	1138
	Kaizhou (Buyang)	3296		Jize	547
	*Changyuan	1256		Guangping	633
				*Handan	1862/800+

TABLE 14. *(concluded)*

Number of students/police		Number of students/police	
† Chengan	1373	*Yuzhou	834
Wei	1604	Xining (Yangyuan)	454
*Qinghe	573	Huaian	318
*Cizhou	3054/40	† Yanqing zhou	1120
		Baoan zhou (Zhuolu)	970
X. *Chengde fu*		XIII. *Koubei siting*	
Luanping	240		
*Pingquan zhou	545	*Zhanjia kou	275
Fengning	79	Dushikou	
Longhua		*Duolunnoer	151
		Weichang	218
XI. *Chaoyang fu*		XIV. *Chifeng*	
Fuxin		Chifeng	176
*Jianchang (Lingyuan)	236	Kailu	
Jianping	99	Suidong	
		Linxi	
XII. *Xuanhua fu*		XV. *Zunhua*	
*Xuanhua	542		
*Chicheng	260	Zunhua	905
Wanquan	526	Fengrun	2008
Longmen (Longguan)	489	*Yutian	795/240 (in 1906)
Huailai	1147		

	Number of students/police		Number of students/police
XVI. *Jizhou*		Wuqiang	292
*Jizhou	2875/434	*Raoyang	2494
	(in 1909)	Anping	2872/302
*Nangong	3206	XIX. *Dingzhou*	
Xinhe	894		
Zaoqiang	3892	Dingzhou	1716/650
*Wuyi	2347	Quyang	1229/262
*Hengshui	1939	*Shenze	1385/353
XVII. *Zhaozhou*		XX. *Yizhou*	
*Zhaozhou	63/297	Yizhou	130/153
*Baixiang	111/280	*Laishui	147/135
*Longping	912/441	Guangchang (Laiyuan)	710/165
	(418 in 1906)	Gaoyi	899/108
XVIII. *Shenzhou*		†*Lincheng	1588/65
Shenzhou	5881	*Ningjin	1515/758

† Agricultural association or experimental station
* Industrial Bureau (model textile factory)
SOURCE: See notes 11, 66, and 101 to this chapter for sources of education, police, and economic reform statistics respectively.

approach. The Empress Dowager agreed, and in late 1901 she decreed the establishment of two parallel routes to official status and office: one via a new school system and the other through the traditional examination process. However, this was a frustrating compromise because it left the traditional examination system intact with no promise of extinction. To supplement this reform she decided in the spring of 1902 to accept Yuan's idea of requiring present officials to be reeducated by attending new institutions of higher learning and traveling abroad whenever possible. At Yuan's suggestion, the Empress Dowager set an example for the provinces by establishing a college for officials (the *Renxue yuan*) in Beijing.[4]

In February, 1903, Yuan and Zhang Zhi-dong tried again, proposing in a joint memorial the gradual replacement of old exams with new exams which were tied to the new school system. Conservatives at Court denounced the memorial and brought impeachment charges against Zhang and Yuan. The memorial was shelved until later in 1903 when the death of Rong-lu and Yuan's new alliance with Prince Qing paradoxically improved the political climate in Beijing. In January, 1904, the Empress Dowager approved substantially the same sort of gradual abolition of the traditional examination system that had been proposed a year earlier by Zhang and Yuan.[5] Finally, in August, 1905, after the crises associated with the Russo-Japanese War had further demonstrated the dynasty's desperate need for officials with modern training, Yuan as chief memorialist led Zhang and other senior provincial officials in calling for the immediate abolition of the new examination system. The Empress Dowager endorsed the memorial, and the battle was won.[6]

Considering Yuan's record in Shandong and his role in this epoch-making national reform, it was no surprise that upon assuming office in Zhili, Yuan initiated a series of measures which virtually transformed education in the province. For advice, Yuan relied on Dr. C.D. Tenney, former aide to Li Hong-zhang and later an important American diplomat in China.[7] As his key adminis-

4. YSYZY, *juan* 14:13-15 and 9:2b-3.
5. Wolfgang Franke, *The Reform and Abolition of the Traditional Chinese Examination System* (Cambridge, Mass., 1960), pp. 57-59, 89.
6. William Ayers, *Chang Chih-tung and Educational Reform in China* (Cambridge, Mass., 1971), pp. 242-43.
7. YSKZZ, pp. 559-61; PTT, March 1 (supp.), April 5 (supp.) and 9 (supp.), May 17 (supp.), July 5, Sept. 20, and Oct. 11, 1902.

trator he chose Yan Xiu, a progressive Tianjin *jinshi* and protégé of Wu Ru-lun.⁸ Yuan began in the spring of 1902 by establishing at Baoding a Department of Schools (*Xuexiao si*) with three sub-bureaus (*chu*): technical education (*zhuanmen jiaoyu*), general education (*putong jiaoyu*), and translation and publication (*bianyi*).⁹ Then, during the summer of 1902, he announced the establishment of two normal colleges to train teachers, one in Baoding and the other in Tianjin, and plans for an elementary school system which would extend to every *xian* in the province. The curricula in the new school system would be a mixture of modern language, science, and history with study of the traditional Chinese classics.¹⁰

The growth of the Zhili school system was phenomenal. By 1907 there were 164,172 students enrolled in 8,723 new schools.¹¹ Only a small percentage were converted *shuyuan* or local academies.¹² Of these the bulk were newly established lower primary (*chudeng*) schools (five-year course for boys six years and older). The number of students attending lower primary schools in Zhili was the following:¹³

School Year	Attending
1902-03	1,000
1903-04	6,000
1904-05	36,344
1905-06	68,000
1906-07	109,000
1907-08	148,399

8. *Shin-matsu Minsho Chūgoku kanshin jimmeiroku* (Beijing, 1918), p. 782; YSKZZ, pp. 1280, 1330; Franke, p. 46; Zhang Yi-lin, *Xin taiping shiji* (1947), juan 7:1, 11; 8:34-36; *Rongan dizi ji*, juan 3:16, 4:10b-11a.

9. YSKZZ, p. 644. During the winter of 1904-05, the Department of Education moved from Baoding to spacious quarters in Tianjin, where it took on new personnel and reorganized into seven subbureaus: accounting, special schools, general education, supervision, vocational, map drawing, and overseas students. Having begun in 1902 with eight senior officials, by 1908 the Zhili Department of Education (renamed *Xuewu ju*) employed fifty-two senior officials—twenty-three of whom either had traveled and studied abroad or were graduates of one of the new normal schools or academies in Beijing; Harry E. King, *The Educational System of China as Recently Reconstructed* (Washington, D.C., 1911), pp. 41, 46; and YSKZZ, p. 2243.

10. YSKZZ, pp. 559-61; PTT, Oct. 11, 1902.

11. Xuebu zongwusi, *Guangxu sanshisan nianfen, Diyici jiaoyu tongji tubiao* (Beijing, 1910), pp. 63-137.

12. Richard Orb, "Chihli's Academies and Other Schools in the Late Ch'ing: an Institutional Survey," in Cohen and Schrecker, eds., *Reform in Nineteenth-Century China*, pp. 231-34.

13. King, p. 56.

How did Zhili's school system compare with other provinces? It was second only to larger and more prosperous Sichuan.[14]

What was also impressive about Zhili's new school system was the remarkably even distribution of primary schools throughout the province. Other provincial officials, like Zhang Zhi-dong in Liangjiang and Cen Chun-xuan in Guangdong, had great difficulty in establishing primary schools outside major towns and cities.[15] In 1906 Yuan reported that in every *xian* or administrative unit in Zhili there were roughly twenty primary schools, each with about thirty students on the average.[16] Available evidence from other sources (see Table 14) confirms Yuan's figures. For example, in the remote and poor southeastern *xian* of Guangzong which had been ravaged by the Jing Ting-bin rebellion of 1902, in 1904 there were only five lower primary schools and an academy or *shuyuan* converted into a higher primary (*gaodeng*) school (four year course for boys up to age fifteen). By 1907 there were nineteen primary schools, rising to over fifty by 1909—a remarkable growth rate for so remote and poor a district.[17] Most active was the old provincial capital area of Baoding *fu*, which had a strong literati elite who during the nineteenth century had been promoting education in their districts and throughout Zhili by expansion of the academy or *shuyuan* system. Led by Shulu *xian* with 201, Baoding *fu*'s fifteen *xian* averaged sixty-two lower primary schools in 1907.[18]

The curriculum in the new schools varied a great deal, although not by design. The standard course of study for the lower primary schools was supposed to be as shown in chart on facing page.[19]

A similar course of study was drawn up for the higher primary schools. Moreover, an energetic effort was made by Zhili's Education Bureau to publish and distribute new texts, teacher's manuals, and a periodical, *Xuebao*, which carried translations of foreign works on science, politics, history, and economics, as well as reports on educational reform throughout the Empire.[20] In practice,

14. See *Diyici jiaoyu tongji tubiao* for comparisons between provinces; for a general summary, see Orb, p. 239, table 1.
15. Ayers, pp. 234-35. See also *Diyici jiaoyu tongji tubiao*; and Rhoads, pp. 72-77.
16. YSKZZ, pp. 2243-46.
17. *Guangzong xianzhi, juan* 8:5; and *Diyici jiaoyu tongji tubiao*, p. 79.
18. Orb, p. 233; and *Diyici jiaoyu tongji tubiao*, pp. 65, 75-76.
19. King, p. 51.
20. See *Beiyang Xuebao* for years 1905-06 (at the Hoover Library, Stanford University). Another journal, *Beiyang Baihua Bao*, was designed for adults who were learning

teaching and course content varied considerably from one *xian* to another. The more remote the location of the school, the more traditional the teaching methods and course content were likely to be.[21]

	Hours per week
Ethics	2
Chinese classics	12
Chinese literature & writing	4
Mathematics	6
History (Chinese)	1
Geography (Asian)	1
Science (elementary zoology, botany, & mineralogy)	1
Military drill	3
	30 Total

Built into Zhili's new school system was a strong sex and class bias. Essentially the system served the well-to-do male child. Probably about 95 percent of school-age children in the province went without formal education. Yet, in the context of the times, any formal education for women and the poor was a step forward and in this respect Zhili was ahead of all other provinces. More was done for the upper-class woman than for the poor, male or female. By 1907, 121 schools for women had been established in Zhili with 2,523 students attending.[22] They were of all kinds, including medical, industrial arts, liberal arts colleges, middle schools, and primary schools. Although these schools tended to be concentrated in Tianjin and Baoding, primary schools for women were being opened in such outlying areas as Gaoyang, Bazhou, Poxiang, Shulu, Wujiao, Miyun, and Handan *xian*.[23] For the poor, 122 "half-day" or night schools (*Banri xuetang*) and 135 lecture halls (*Xuanjiang suo*) had been established by 1907. They were spread rather haphazardly

---

to read. In it reform subjects were discussed in simpler terms. A number of issues for 1905-06 are available in the East Asiatic Library, University of California, Berkeley.

21. King, pp. 50-55.
22. *Diyici jiaoyu tongji tubiao*, p. 63; and King, pp. 89-90.
23. Li You-ning and Zhang Yu-fa, eds., *Jindai zhongguo nüquan yundong shiliao* (Taibei, 1975), pp. 1052-85.

throughout the province, depending apparently on the initiative of a magistrate or the gentry in a given *xian*.[24]

Along with establishing new schools, the sending of students abroad for study, particularly to Japan, was also promoted actively by the central and provincial governments during the last decade of the Qing.[25] The peak of activity seemed to come in 1907-08 when there were probably about 15,000 Chinese studying in Japan. Precise figures are not available, but Zhili was the only northern province which sent students abroad on a scale similar to the richer southern provinces such as Guangdong, Jiangxi, Zhejiang, and Hunan.[26] Numerous reports in the press, and Yuan's own memorials, show that Zhili was sending many students to Japan on partial or full government scholarships.[27] Moreover, Yuan pioneered in encouraging local officials and prominent gentry to travel to Japan.[28] Examples are given below of prominent local figures from Jizhou, Cizhou, and Guangzong *xian* who led educational reforms in their home district after having visited Japan. No doubt this was the case in other *xian* as well.

The institutional heart of the new school system and of educational reform in the countryside was the education promotion office (*chuanxue suo*). These were established in every *xian* of the province. Acting like a school board, the education promotion office took responsibility for financing, construction, and supervision of a *xian* school system. It was usually headed by a well-known member of the local elite who was appointed directly by the magistrate. Three examples are Zhang Ting-xiang, Chen Ji-xu, and Zhang Ke-ming, all of whom had traveled to Japan. Zhang Ting-xiang of Jizhou *xian* was a *sui gongsheng* in his sixties who had been a student of Wu Ru-lun and active since the 1880s in the affairs of the local academy (*Xindu shuyuan*). Chen Ji-xu of Cizhou was younger (in his thirties), from a local gentry family, and had been instrumental in

24. *Diyici jiaoyu tongji tubiao*, pp. 63-64, 73-83; and King, pp. 47-48, 89-90.
25. Cameron, *Reform and Revolution*, and Y.C. Wang, *Chinese Intellectuals and the West, 1872-1949* (Chapel Hill, 1966), emphasize this point.
26. Sanetō Keishū, pp. 58-59, 544; Robert A. Scalapino, "Prelude to Marxism: The Chinese Student Movement in Japan, 1900-1910," in Albert Feuerwerker et al., eds., *Approaches to Modern Chinese History*, p. 192; Fang Chao-ying, *Qingmo Minchu yangxue xuesheng diming lu chuji* (Taibei, 1962); and King, pp. 92-94, 98; *Beiyang Xuebao* (1905), *kexue zonglu*, no. 4, *diaocha*, no. 11, pp. 19-20.
27. BYGD, *juan* 11:13-23; DFZZ 1.7 (1904): *jiaowu* 160; 1.9:216; 2.11 (1905):294; YSKZZ, p. 514.
28. BYGD, *juan* 11:14b-16, 18-19; DFZZ 2.8 (1905): *jiaowu* 201.

converting the local *shuyuan* into a higher primary school before going to Japan. After serving as head of the education promotion office, he attended law school in Tianjin. Guangzong's Zhang Keming was in his fifties, progressive-minded, and apparently of gentry background. Later he would also head the *xian* self-government bureau (*zizhi ju*).[29]

The key to the success of educational reform in Zhili was the support of urban and rural elites because it was not Yuan's administration, but they, along with local magistrates, who funded the new school system. Yuan's provincial government financed a few model secondary schools, technical schools (law, medicine, electrical, surveying, and foreign languages), one university, some agricultural and industrial schools and a few normal schools in Tianjin and Baoding.[30] But for the most part new schools were funded privately and/or by local governments. The public record is replete with instances in which Yuan awarded official titles and ranks to local gentry and merchants for cash contributions of usually about ten to twenty thousand taels toward the establishment of one or more primary schools in a given district or town. Big landlords often gave the annual rent (or a proportion thereof) from a certain amount of land in order to support a new school.[31] A 1907 survey of Zhili schools and their funding found that such "compulsory contributions" (*lejuan*) were a major source of revenue for *xian* school systems.[32]

Gazetteers document the energy with which *xian* magistrates also raised funds locally, often through increased taxation, to help finance the establishment of new lower and higher primary schools, normal schools, and an occasional middle school. For example, in Guangzong, Nangong, Ding *xian*, and Cizhou, land taxes were raised to finance new schools. In Ding *xian* where we have precise figures, land taxes doubled from 1906 to 1908. There was resistance. In March, 1908, a dispute over increased land taxes for

29. *Ji xianzhi* (1929), *juan* 19:30-1, 39; *Cixian xianzhi* (1941), *zhang* 17:14-15; *Guangzong xianzhi*, *juan* 8:5, 12:11b, 14:10b; Orb, pp. 234-35.

30. YSKZZ, pp. 2243-46; DFZZ 1.11 (1907): *jiaowu* 263-89; King, pp. 62, 72-73, 75-85; and *Diyici jiaoyu tongji tubiao*, p. 64.

31. YSKZZ, pp. 1212, 1455, 1675, 1739, 1740-41, 1759, 1802-03, 1825, 1832, 1890, 1966, 2012, 2082, 2153, 2186, 2208, 2210, 2215-16, 2327-28, 2331-32; DFZZ 1.5 (1904): *jiaowu* 120 and 1.6:142-44; 2.6 (1905):156-57, 2.8:199, and 2.11:288; 3.5 (1906):96, 3.6:135, 3.9:231-32, 3.10:276, 3.11:328, 3.12:369, 3.13:408-09; 4.2 (1907):21, 4.3:54-55, 4.4:121-22, 4.9:214-17, 4.11:292.

32. *Diyici jiaoyu tongji tubiao*, pp. 84-95.

new schools and police in Longping *xian* erupted into violence, killing nine people. In general, however, public protests about new taxes occurred less frequently in Zhili than elsewhere. Probably this was because of fear of the brutal suppression which a protest would meet, as happened in Longping and earlier in Julu and Guangzong *xian* over the Jing Ting-bin affair of 1902 when thousands were killed.[33] At any rate, there is no question that local magistrates and elites were together responsible for the astonishing expansion of Zhili's school system and that in the end the peasants paid for it. Outside of Tianjin and Baoding, the part played by Yuan's administration was largely indirect and advisory.

Still it was Yuan who initiated educational reform in Zhili and it was he who received the political credit for its success. From the Empress Dowager on down, Beijing was impressed. In 1904 she declared the Zhili school system to be a national model. A year later she established a Ministry of Education in which a number of Yuan's top education aides, including Yan Xiu, were given high posts.[34] Moreover, just as politically important in the long run was the fact that educational reform endeared Yuan to Zhili's gentry and merchant elites, and by reputation to similar elites throughout the Empire. Similarly Yuan's encouragement of overseas study and travel was enthusiastically received and supported by Zhili's gentry and merchant elites. It was, after all, their sons and daughters who were going abroad, with they themselves following suit in increasing numbers. In short, educational reform made Yuan popular and more powerful because it met the perceived needs of the majority of Zhili's elites.

It is clear that Yuan designed educational reform to serve the needs of urban and rural elites throughout Zhili. The support which gentry and merchants gave to Yuan's educational reforms demonstrates this. Local elites, not the provincial government, financed most of Zhili's new and rapidly expanding school system. In Zhili, educational reform had the effect of cementing ties between provincial government and local elites, more so than it evidently did in provinces such as Hunan and Hubei.[35] Through

33. *Guangzong xianzhi, juan* 7:16, 8:5; *Cixian xianzhi, zhang* 15:10-12; YSKZZ, p. 2082; *Ding xianzhi* (1934), *juan* 7:5b-7; Li Wen-zhi, ed., *Zhongguo jindai nungye shi ziliao*, pp. 306, 309-10, 320-21, 957; BYGD, *juan* 11:45-46; DFZZ 4.9 (1907): *jiaowu* 218-19.
34. Cameron, pp. 71-74; Qian Shi-fu, pp. 31, 38, 44, 70.
35. Esherick, pp. 40-46, 108, 111, 118-19, 146-48, 162.

educational reform, Yuan was also selecting and giving experience to his team of administrators, at both the provincial and *xian* level. It was these men who translated paper reforms into concrete results and stimulated support among local elites. In the process, Yuan was extending his influence and that of the provincial government below the *xian* level. This last point in particular is demonstrated by examining Yuan's introduction of modern police in Zhili.

Police Reform

Upon assuming office in Zhili in 1901, Yuan Shi-kai outlawed *lianzhuang hui* village associations, discouraged *tuanlian* militia units, and abolished the old *baojia* system for mutual security and surveillance. Like Zhang Zhi-dong, Yuan was suspicious of the informal networks of power which local elites had built up since the Taiping and Nian rebellions.[36] Yuan's intent was to establish tighter social and political control at the local level by the introduction of modern police responsible directly to the *xian* magistrate.

Traditionally, Zhili was policed through the *baojia* mutual protection and surveillance system, as well as by special yamen runners (usually known as *buban*). By the nineteenth century, the *baojia* system had become more or less defunct, and runner police were considered by officials and citizens alike as hopelessly corrupt and often little better than the thieves they were supposed to be apprehending.[37] Not until the reform atmosphere after the Sino-Japanese War of 1894-95 did ideas about replacing the *baojia* system and *buban* runners with Western-style police begin to gain currency. Initial, tentative attempts to establish modern police forces were made in Changsha in 1898 and in Beijing in 1901-02. But the first substantial, province-wide effort was made by Yuan Shi-kai in Zhili.[38]

36. Bays, *China Enters the Twentieth Century*, pp. 15-18, 216. On Yuan's treatment of the *lianzhuang hui*, see Chapter 1, above. A discussion of the abolition of the *baojia* follows. As governor of Shandong, Yuan began dissolving *tuanlian* units (YSKZZ, pp. 111, 159) and, judging from their absence from gazetteers of the period, succeeded in bringing about their dissolution in Zhili as well. (See note 72 below, for the few instances in which *tuanlian* were converted into police.)

37. On the *baojia* system, see Hsiao Kung-ch'uan, *Rural China: Imperial Control in the Nineteenth Century* (Seattle, 1960), pp. 25-83; and Philip Kuhn, *Rebellion and Its Enemies in Late Imperial China*, pp. 24-28, 94-97, 59-62, 100, 121-22. On runner police, see Ch'ü T'ung-tsu, *Local Government in China Under the Ch'ing* (Cambridge, Mass., 1962), p. 57 and chap. 4.

38. *Zhongyang jingguan xuexiao xiaoshi* (Taibei, 1967), pp. 5-8, 12; Frank Y.C. Yee, "Police in Modern China" (Ph.D. dissertation, University of California, Berkeley,

Yuan began by experimenting in Baoding (when Tianjin was still occupied by the Powers). In May, 1902, he reorganized and retrained five hundred former soldiers for police work. He also established a Head Office of Police Affairs (*Jingwu zongju*) and an Academy of Police Affairs (*Jingwu xuetang*). Three months later Yuan memorialized the throne about his experiment in Baoding and the general need for modern police. Modern police, he argued, should replace the *baojia* system: "although it [*baojia*] is incapable of preventing lawlessness, it has been more than sufficient in harassing the people." In other countries, policing is considered a vital function of government, for which top officials are made responsible. Moreover, a government needs police as its "responsible eyes and ears." In Zhili particularly, because of the Boxer rising, there is a need for restoration of order and reliable intelligence. "Without an imperial decree sanctioning the prompt establishment of a police system, [the existing machinery] will be inadequate to enforce the law and to ascertain the actual conditions of the people." Yuan then reported on how five hundred police successfully restored law and order to the Baoding area. He concluded by indicating his intention to establish police at the *xian* level throughout the province.[39]

When Tianjin was recovered from the Allies in September, 1902, Yuan moved his administration there from Baoding, taking with him most of Baoding's police force and the police academy as well. Tianjin's new police force consisted of about one thousand retrained ex-soldiers and about eight hundred constables who constituted the "native police" used by the Allied occupational government. And during the fall and winter of 1902-03, Yuan recruited in the Hejian area of southern Zhili about one thousand more men to be trained as additional police for Tianjin. Thus Yuan quickly made Tianjin the heart of his police reform program.[40]

Tianjin's police were divided administratively into two sections, north and south of the Beihe river, with most of the city falling within the jurisdiction of the southern section. Within the southern section there were five headquarters (*ju*) with four sections (*qu*)

1942), pp. 8-10; *Neizheng nianjian* (Shanghai, 1936), vol. 2, pp. 1-3; *Shilu*, juan 494:13; Zhang Zhi-dong, *juan* 53:13, 16a.

39. YSKZZ, pp. 643-44; Ho Ping-ti, *Studies in the Population of China, 1368-1953* (Cambridge, Mass., 1959), pp. 71-72.

40. YSKZZ, pp. 1656-59; FO 371/31, "New Police in Chihli," enclosure in Satow, March 10, 1906; 371/33, "Report on the Tientsin Constabulary," enclosure in Satow no. 90 of March 3, 1906; PTT, Aug. 23, 1902.

attached to each of the headquarters. Fifty constables (*xunbing*), five sergeants (*xunzheng*), and one inspector (*xunbian*) manned each section. The supervisory body at headquarters was the central office (*xunjing zongju*), and attached to it was a law court (*fashen chu*) where four magistrates (*fashen guan*) daily tried petty civil and criminal cases in the police law courts. They also administered prisons, dealt with legal problems created by foreigners, and served as buffers between the local population and Chinese troops stationed in the vicinity of the city.[41] Precisely how Tianjin's police were funded is not clear. However, there is evidence that many of the constables were ex-soldiers still on the Beiyang Army payroll, and that funds were being raised locally in Tianjin through new taxes on shops, vehicles, boats, and entertainment.[42]

Contemporary reporting by Chinese and foreigners testified to the success of Tianjin's new police in bringing law and order to the city. Much of the credit went to Zhao Bing-jun, who as head of the southern section was an equivalent of a police chief. Zhao was a fellow provincial of Yuan's from an upper-class family, who came to Yuan's attention because of his effectiveness in suppressing Boxers in and around Beijing. Yuan first recruited Zhao in 1902 to help in the formation of the Baoding police.[43] He moved quickly to clean up, improve, and expand the force. New, more military looking uniforms were issued to constables. Any charges of corruption within were promptly investigated and severe punishments meted out on a number of occasions. Local newspapers and foreign observers reported the dismissal of over one hundred constables during Zhao's initial months in office. Moreover, the police academy in Tianjin, which Zhao also oversaw, expanded its faculty and enrollment, becoming the training center of police personnel for all of north China.[44]

In October, 1905, at Yuan Shi-kai's urging, Empress Dowager Ci-xi established a Ministry of Police (*Xunjing bu*). Zhao Bing-jun was appointed vice-president of the new ministry—with one of Yuan's closest associates, Xu Shi-chang, as president.[45] But despite

41. BYGD, *juan* 8:1, 9:4b-6; FO 371/31, "New Police in Chihli"; 371/33, "Report on the Tientsin Constabulary."
42. FO 371/31, "New Police in Chihli." *Zhili qingli caizheng shuoming shu*, *bian* 6:17-23; *Da Gong Bao* (Tianjin), April 23, 1903.
43. YSKZZ, p. 2005; Chen Xi-zhang, pp. 95-96.
44. *Da Gong Bao*, April 29, May 1, 9, 17, 20, 28-31; June 3, 4, and July 11, 1903; FO 371/33, "Report on Tientsin Constabulary."
45. Yee, pp. 15-16; Brunnert and Hagelstrom, p. 114.

the fact that he was now administering police affairs on a national level in Beijing, Zhao continued as head of Tianjin's police. Zhao would decide major issues in Beijing and then make routine inspection tours to Tianjin, where everyday administration was entrusted to an able assistant, Duan Zhi-gui.[46] Until the dynasty fell in 1911-12, Zhao continued to monitor Tianjin's police from Beijing and use it as a national model.[47]

Success in prison reform and rehabilitation programs contributed to Tianjin's and Police Chief Zhao's progressive reputation. Reform began with a trip to Japan in 1903 by Tianjin Prefect Ling Fu-beng to study the Japanese penal system. Based on his investigations, Prefect Ling, Police Chief Zhao, and others drew up plans for the construction of a model prison just outside the city proper which would house over 500 inmates. Along with the erection of a modern physical plant, which for the first time in China included medical and recreational facilities, a new distinction was to be made between prisoners who committed petty crimes and those convicted of serious offenses. For those convicted of petty misdemeanors, a workhouse (*xiyi suo*) was attached to the prison so that a sentence could be worked off and a trade learned at the same time. Construction of the prison itself took three years but the workhouse opened almost immediately.[48] The workhouse idea caught on fast and was the most publicized of Yuan's prison reforms. Soon vagrant workhouses (*youmin xiyisuo*) were established in Tianjin for derelicts as well as for criminals.[49] By 1905, workhouses similar to those in Tianjin were being established in Baoding, and plans were developed for the establishment of workhouses elsewhere in the province.[50] The workhouse was part of an effort to deal constructively with Tianjin's lumpen proletariat—the beggars, petty thiefs, and derelicts—and get them off the streets. Other measures in-

46. FO 371/33, "Report on Tientsin Constabulary"; Chen Xi-zhang, pp. 69-70.
47. *Da Qing Guangxu xinfaling*, *ce* 9:2b-3b, 13b-14; *Guangxu zhengyao*, *juan* 33:25b-26; DFZZ 3.12 (1906): *neiwu* 274.
48. BYGD, *juan* 5:2b-24; DFZZ 1.1 (1904): *neiwu* 4, and 1.7:86. For a picture of the traditional prison system, see Derk Bodde, "Prison Life in Eighteenth-Century Peking," *Journal of the American Oriental Society* 89 (1969):311-33. In the spring of 1972 I had the good fortune to visit what remains of Yuan Shi-kai's model prison in Tianjin. A number of the original buildings are still standing, and interestingly, the prison retains its model status.
49. BYGD, *juan* 5:18b-20, 27-30.
50. YSKZZ, pp. 1792-93; BYGD, *juan* 5:31-39; Peng Ze-yi, ed., *Zhongguo jindai shougongye shi ziliao* (Beijing, 1957), vol. 2, p. 533.

cluded the establishment of free meal stations (*jiaoyang ju*) and poor houses (*pinmin yuan*).⁵¹

Efforts were also made to improve conditions in existing prisons. By 1905, the following improvements had been made in Baoding's three prisons: repair of prison walls, provision for better ventilation, and general improvement of drainage.⁵² Attempts were also being made to provide separate modern quarters for women.⁵³

With Tianjin and, to a lesser degree, Baoding established as showplaces of police and prison reform, Yuan and Zhao Bing-jun began to extend police reform to the province at large. Indeed, during the late Qing, there was no other province where police reform penetrated the countryside as it did in Zhili.⁵⁴ Crucial to this success, as we shall see, was the vigor with which local magistrates pursued police reform and the willingness of local gentry to support financially and to take part in the administration of police forces in their home *xian*.

The introduction of modern police in areas other than Tianjin and Baoding began in 1904 when Yuan instructed five *xian* (Yanshan, Jinghai, Jing, Nanpi, and Qingyun) to abolish existing *baojia* organizations and establish modern police.⁵⁵ In each *xian* the initial police force consisted of about one hundred constables. The *xian* were divided into section (*qu*) within which constables were stationed in strategic villages. Of the five pilot *xian*, at least Qingyun also established a small academy for training police.⁵⁶

What was expected of the rural policeman? Regulations developed under Zhao Bing-jun for the rural areas around Tianjin set standards for the entire province, both in recruitment policies and in the duties of the new police. According to these regulations, a *xian* should be divided for policing purposes into headquarters (*ju*), each supervising three or four sections. Each headquarters should be responsible for about 10,000 people; each section for 3,000 people. The village headmen and gentry should select candidates of upright character for training as police. These same gentry and headmen were also made responsible for raising from local sources the funds required to provide a monthly salary ranging from four to

51. DFZZ 1.1 (1904): *neiwu* 4.
52. BYGD, *juan* 5:1-2; DFZZ 2.10 (1905): *neiwu* 199.
53. DFZZ 2.10 (1905): *neiwu* 199, and 4.10 (1907):294.
54. *Da Qing Guangxu xinfaling, ce* 9:2b-3.   55. DFZZ 1.7 (1904): *neiwu* 86.
56. BYGD, *juan* 9:25-27; *Nanpi xianzhi* (1932), *juan* 5:44; *Jinghai xianzhi* (1934), *zhengshi bu*, p. 44.

nine taels, depending on qualifications of recruits and local resources. The suggested number of recruits was one per fifty households for wealthy areas, and one per one hundred households in poorer areas. After selection, recruits were to go through an intensive training course lasting two months. After graduation from this course, they were expected to attend further training classes once a week. Their salaries should in part be based on performance in these classes. Moreover, like his urban counterpart, the rural policeman's duties were extremely broad. Besides census and intelligence gathering, protection of property and people, apprehension and prosecution of petty criminals, and maintenance of public morality, police were even expected to double as firemen. In carrying out these myriad duties, the regulations emphasized, police should cooperate with local gentry and village headmen. Whenever possible, disputes should be settled though discussion and arbitration. Police should at all times be respectful and friendly in their relations with local gentry and never adopt attitudes of official arrogance. Police should carry arms only when necessary—as on night patrols, for example. Finally, the regulations stipulated limits to the power of local police. Police were expected to deal (through police courts) with petty crimes, leaving major robberies, family altercations, or land disputes to be settled by the *xian* magistrate.[57] So much for the regulations and models which were supposed to be followed. How did the introduction of modern police into the Zhili countryside work out in practice?

At the same time that police were being created in five pilot *xian* on an experimental basis, Yuan ordered all other departments (*zhou*) and *xian* in Zhili to send local representatives to Tianjin's police academy in preparation for establishing modern police forces in their home areas. Soon afterward Yuan established in Tianjin a provincial Police Bureau (*Jingwu chu*). This was supposed to coordinate and supervise the development of modern police throughout Zhili. The new bureau issued instructions to *zhou* and *xian* governments on such subjects as training, salary levels, investigation of corruption, and census work.[58] Most *xian* tried to meet the standards set by the Police Bureau, and by Zhao Bing-jun's model regulations for rural areas.[59] But, by its own admission, the Police Bureau failed to regulate effectively the size or quality of

57. BYGD, *juan* 9:4b-6.   58. BYGD, *juan* 7:16-19, 9:11-16.
59. BYGD, *juan* 9:20; DFZZ 3.11 (1906): *neiwu* 238.

police forces at the *xian* level.⁶⁰ In short, after initial sponsorship, Yuan and his administration's contribution to local police reform was indirect and technical, limited for the most part to setting standards and training leaders in central police academies.

Control, leadership, and financing of Zhili's new rural police were basically in the hands of local magistrates and gentry. The importance of local initiative is demonstrated by the variety in size, kind, and timing of the forces which sprang up. When and where police departments were established seemed to relate more to the interest of a local magistrate or gentry elite than it did to the size or importance of a particular *xian*. The head of the police was chosen by the *xian* magistrate or the local gentry themselves. Some *xian* established special training schools for new police and others did not. In fact, about all that was homogeneous about Zhili's rural police was terminology. All new police forces were directed by a Central Police Office (*xunjing zongju*) which oversaw its sections and branches (*fensuo*).

Comparing the development of the police in Daming *xian*, in a rural and remote part of south central Zhili, with Cizhou, a much more populous and less remote district because of its location on the Beijing-Hankou Railway, illustrates the importance of local initiative. Daming began to organize its police force in 1904. Initially it was limited to three sections within the walled city of Daming. By 1906, the *xian* had been divided into thirteen branches which were manned by about 240 constables. Through contributions by local gentry, Daming also was able to open a small police academy in 1906. The importance of gentry support of Daming's new police was shown by the fact that gentry members themselves selected the police director (*jingdong*).⁶¹ On the other hand, Cizhou did not begin organizing a police force until 1907. And then its police force was small, only forty constables, all of whom were stationed within the city walls. Yet Cizhou's police force, small as it was, was beset by serious financial difficulties and problems of inadequate uniforms and equipment.⁶²

Information is available about the police forces of Anping and Lulong, two small, rural *xian* in central and northeastern Zhili

60. BYGD, *juan* 9:14b-16.
61. *Daming xianzhi* (1934), *juan* 6:31b, *juan* 12:3b-6; DFZZ 3.13 (1906): *jiaowu* 48-49; BYGD, *juan* 9:16-20.
62. *Cixian xianzhi*, *zhang* 12:1, *zhang* 14:3; DFZZ, 4.12 (1907): *neiwu* 563-64.

respectively. Anping discarded its *baojia* system in favor of modern police during the fall of 1904, but progress at first was slow. By 1906 Anping had only fifty constables, all within its walled city. These men were poorly equipped, evidently quite corrupt, and irregularly paid (their salaries ranged from four to seven taels a month). But in 1907, due to the initiative of a new magistrate, Jin Yong, the Anping police force expanded and reorganized. The *xian* was divided into twelve sections and the force expanded to 302 constables. Twenty men were assigned to each of the outlying sections and seventy-two remained to police the *xian* capital. Attending special training classes at four locations was required of all police. Magistrate Jin appointed members of the local gentry whom he considered to be responsible to lead police at headquarters (as *juzhang*) and out in the sections (as *quzhang*). Salaries were regularly paid and rose on the average to nine taels a month for a policeman attached to headquarters and seven taels a month to men at the outlying sections. About 30,000 taels were needed to run Anping's police force for a year. A small portion of this was raised through a new sales tax in shops and a tax on horse-tail hair, a local product; but most of the money came from a new land tax surcharge (*ditan*) of fifty cash (*wen*) on every *mou* of arable land in the *xian*. So in the end it was the peasantry of Anping who paid for the new police.[63]

Like Anping, Lulong *xian* started police work slowly. In 1906 her police force amounted to only ten mounted constables. However, merchants and gentry in the walled city of Lulong were trying to raise funds through a special retail sales tax for the recruiting and training of eighteen more police to patrol the city. Then in 1907 an energetic new magistrate, Cao Lin, came to Lulong and suddenly the police force expanded to over 280 men, all of whom were uniformed and receiving training. This force was spread over four sections and a headquarters. Magistrate Cao described Lulong's police as "official-directed and gentry-operated" (*guandu shenban*). Indeed, local elite participation and support seemed the key to success in Lulong. Local elites selected from their own ranks the heads of the new police force, both at headquarters and out at the sections. But what was more crucial was the local elite willingness to raise the funds needed to support the police. The few mounted policemen were financed directly by the *xian* government, and the shop tax mentioned earlier continued to support police at the

63. BYGD, *juan* 9:24; DFZZ 3.1 (1906): *neiwu* 25 and 4.7; (1907):359-60.

capital seat. Most of the expansion, however, was financed through assessments at the village level, which were left to the village headmen and local elites to raise as they wished. So again, with the local elite doing the levying, the result was probably the same as in Anping *xian*. The peasants were made to shoulder most of the financial burden for Lulong's new police.[64]

Information on the local elites who participated actively in police reform is sketchy. Still, from biographical material in gazetteers of five *xian* (Jizhou, Miyun, Gaoyang, Ci, and Jingxing) a composite picture emerges. They were uniformly "lower" or "local" elite members, at best holders of the lowest *shengyuan* or *fusheng* degrees. Du Yuan-zhao, an activist in police reform in Jingxing *xian*, was simply wealthy (probably from mining) with no degree at all. Few had been educated abroad. Many were also active locally in other reforms besides police reform.[65]

For these few rural *xian*, police reforms and reformers are well documented. How pervasive were police reforms in the province as a whole? A survey by the Yuan administration in 1907 provides a partial answer. The results of the survey, along with the few other available figures, were given earlier in Table 14 on reform activity.[66] To summarize, the total number of police for 57 *xian* was 15,390—an impressive figure—which averages to 270 police per *xian*. But local figures varied tremendously. Handan, a small southern *xian* just north of Cizhou on the Beijing-Hankou Railway, had the largest force—over 800 constables—and remote Xingtang in west central Zhili had the smallest, with 21 police on duty. The size did not seem to relate to population or geopolitical importance. A small, remote *xian* like Ren in south central Zhili (population probably around 10,000) had 310 police in 1907, when a much larger, more important *xian* like Nanpi along the Grand Canal (with a population of over 150,000) had at most 140 police.[67] Police force size seemed to relate mostly to the vigor with which particular

64. BYGD, *juan* 9:33-35; DFZZ 4.4 (1907): *neiwu* 177.
65. *Ji xianzhi*, *juan* 19:30-31; *Miyun xianzhi* (1914), *juan* 6-4:6b; *Cixian xianzhi, chang* 17:14b-15; *Jingxing xianzhi* (1934), *bian* 11:16; *Gaoyang xianzhi* (1931), *juan* 5:10.
66. BYGD, *juan* 9:14b-16. Other sources: DFZZ 3.8 (1906): *neiwu* 184, and 3.11: 238; 4.4 (1907):177, 4.6:295, 4.7:359-60, 4.12:563-64; *Daming xianzhi* (1934), *juan* 12:3b-6; *Nanpi xianzhi*, *juan* 5:44; *Ji xianzhi*, *juan* 17:2b; *Baxian xianzhi* (1935), *juan* 3:4; *Xianghe xianzhi* (1936), *juan* 4:3b-4. In 1909, the British estimated that Zhili's police numbered over 20,000; FO 405/195, Jordan Annual Report for 1909, p. 45.
67. *Ren xianzhi* (1915), *juan* 3:22; *Nanpi xianzhi*, *juan* 5:44; Gilbert Rozman, *Urban Networks in Ch'ing China and Tokugawa Japan* (Princeton, 1973), pp. 174-177.

magistrates pursued police reform. The large police forces of Handan, Ren, Dingzhou, Miyun, and Xianghe, for example, were created by energetic magistrates who pushed police reforms in their *xian*.[68] Moreover, many but certainly not all of the leading *xian* in police reform (like Dingzhou or Jizhou) were also in the vanguard of reform generally in Zhili.[69] Probably in a few *xian* (like Julu, Xincheng, or Anping), the creation of relatively large police forces was also related to immediate problems of banditry and peasant unrest.[70] But generally this was not the case.

How representative the figures in Table 14 are for Zhili province as a whole is an open question. The fifty-seven for which we have figures represented about one-third of Zhili's *xian*. But Yuan's 1907 survey covered only four out of Zhili's nineteen supra-*xian* administrative units (*fu* or *zhou*—see table). A few of the figures were from gazetteers and other sources, so certainly one cannot assume that only *xian* named in the 1907 survey had modern police. Just how many more *xian* had forces and how many police manned them cannot be determined by the data so far available.

Nevertheless, by the end of Yuan Shi-kai's term as governor-general in 1907, the creation of modern police in Zhili had become a genuine, locally-rooted movement spreading throughout the province. By all appearances, it was remarkably successful, making Zhili the leading province in police reform. During the initial stage, 1902-1904, activity centered in Tianjin and Baoding, where Yuan and Zhao Bing-jun established large police forces, police academies, model prisons, and workhouses. After 1904, beyond offering political and administrative encouragement, Yuan left it to local initiative by *xian* magistrates and local elites to establish and finance modern police forces in their areas. The result was rapid proliferation, but also semiautonomous and irregular development.

The new police were intended, and functioned, as a replacement for the *baojia* security system and not as a defense corps. The task of suppressing peasant insurgencies and banditry was handled di-

---

68. *Ren xianzhi* (1915), *juan* 4:23; *Miyun xianzhi*, *juan* 5-2:1 and *juan* 6-3:8b; *Handan xianzhi* (1940), *juan* 1:14-15; *Xianghe xianzhi*, *juan* 4:3b-4.

69. *Ding xianzhi*; and Sidney D. Gamble, *Ting Hsien, a North China Rural Community* (New York, 1954). Jizhou in general had been unusually progressive since Wu Rulun was magistrate there from 1888-89; see *Ji xianzhi*.

70. The Jing Ting-bin uprising in 1902 in Julu was discussed in Chapter 2, above. On banditry problems in Xincheng and Anping *xian*, see BYGD, *juan* 4:42b-47. On Xincheng's police, see *Xincheng xianzhi* (1935), *juan* 5:16-17. See also note 71, below.

rectly by Beiyang Army and other government troops. To be sure, Yuan retrained some former soldiers as police. But the new police were created chiefly for intelligence gathering and law enforcement. They did not constitute a local paramilitary peace-keeping force like the militia or *tuanlian* which elites had organized under official sanction in the early and mid-nineteenth century.

Usually the new police were formed without reference to previous or still existing self-defense organizations, and often were not even armed.[71] Moreover, there is no evidence that the division of a *xian* administratively into police sections or *qu* was simply giving *fait accompli* recognition to powerful local interests previously organized around such units as *tuanlian*. In Zhili it appears that the *qu* was imposed by the magistrate with elite cooperation in order to control and limit geopolitical power clusters within a *xian*. Administratively, the *qu* seemed a fluid unit, subject to changes in number, size, and shape as *xian* magistrates changed. Thus, in Zhili at least, the emergence of *qu* in the 1920s and 1930s as semi-independent political fiefdoms seems a distinctly different phenomenon.[72] Socially then, the new police altered the *status quo* in the countryside. More clearly than their predecessors—*buban* runners, *baojia*, and *tuanlian*—the new police served the interests of the *xian* magistrate and his local elite allies to the detriment of others, especially peasants. Not surprisingly, after 1904, when "modern" police were being introduced widely throughout the Empire, protest riots by peasants broke out; but not in Zhili where the security provided by the new system was the tightest.[73]

Finally, the key to Yuan's success in using police reforms to extend the influence of formal government below the *xian* level lay in the appointment of compatible and able *xian* magistrates. Yuan's influence over the appointment of magistrates was indirect, through Beijing. As governor-general, Yuan could impeach but not appoint a *xian* magistrate. The latter prerogative was jealously guarded by the Board of Civil Appointments (*Libu*), which insisted that procedures for appointments, impeachments, and temporary appointments be meticulously followed, even during the heyday of

---

71. Three exceptions are Julu, Huaian, and Xincheng *xian*. In the cases of Julu and Xincheng at least, peasant unrest and banditry had just been suppressed with the help of *tuanlian* or militia forces, which were then organized into police forces; see *Xincheng xianzhi*, juan 12:18, *Huaian xianzhi* (1934), juan 2:68; and YSKZZ, p. 1803.
72. On the latter, see Kuhn, *Rebellion and Its Enemies*, pp. 218-20.
73. See Introduction, note 10, above.

Yuan's influence at Court. For example, in the fall of 1905, Yuan tried quietly to circumvent the Libu by taking advantage of the *liu* (retain) prerogative of governors-general to make temporary emergency appointments of *xian* magistrates. In a memorial recommending the impeachment of three *xian* magistrates, he simply invoked the phrase *kouliu waibu* to indicate that he would fill the resulting vacancies himself. He did not identify his choices. This memorial was otherwise innocuous and followed standard format so that it took three months for the Libu to discover what Yuan was up to and respond. It insisted firmly that Yuan follow the statutes, that he identify for its approval his choices to succeed the deposed magistrates, and that they be chosen from the Libu's list of approved candidates. Yuan quickly caved in and contritely followed instructions.[74] Nevertheless, by using his political influence at Court and within the Libu, Yuan did exercise more than the usual degree of control over the appointment and transfer of magistrates as well as over their on-the-job duties. This was in part because Yuan paid an enormous amount of attention to the subject—about one quarter of his collected memorials are devoted to the affairs of magistrates.[75] That it was worth the effort is signified by the comparative success of Yuan's reform program in the Zhili countryside; and by Zhang Zhi-dong's complaints that he was losing good men to Yuan Shi-kai and Beijing.[76]

Despite his tight, Beijing-centered control over *xian* magistrates, Yuan's involvement in police reform outside of Tianjin and Baoding was necessarily indirect. The initiator and direct beneficiary of police reform in rural Zhili was the *xian* magistrate. It was he whom the new police served as a much more effective and controllable instrument than the *baojia* or unruly runner police of the past. Financing and leadership of the new police forces were in the hands of *both* magistrates and local elites. But the latter, although cooperative, seemed on the whole less enthusiastic about police reform

---

74. YSKZZ, pp. 2004-05, 2158-59. On procedures for appointment and transfer of *xian* magistrates, see John Watt, *The District Magistrate in Late Imperial China* (New York, 1972), pp. 46-47, 74.

75. The reference here is to the YSKZZ collection.

76. Bays, *China Enters the Twentieth Century*, pp. 187-88, 259 (note 11). A recent study of neighboring Henan province suggests continuity of tight, Beijing-centered controls on *xian* magistrates into the early Republican period; see Odoric Y.K. Wou, "The District Magistrate Profession in the Early Republican Period: Occupational Recruitment, Training and Mobility," *Modern Asian Studies* 8.2 (April 1974):217-45.

than about educational reform, in which they were the direct beneficiaries.

Economic Reform

Economic reform was the other sphere in which Yuan's administration had some success in penetrating the Zhili countryside. Characteristically, as in education and police work, Yuan directed economic reform at Zhili's scholar-elite class and *xian* magistrates; again, it was from them that he wanted leadership. Urban and rural merchants, while being expected to cooperate, were left for the most part to their own devices.

In his approach to the economy and commercial development, Yuan was just as traditional and probably more bureaucratic or public-sector-minded than his predecessor, Li Hong-zhang, promoter of the *guandu shangban* approach to modern enterprise. Yuan often articulated the need to foster merchant initiative in developing Zhili's economy, but in practice he more often than not presumed to act for the merchant group. Clearly Yuan thought for the most part in terms of a government-managed economy. For example, Yuan had a number of men around him from comprador-merchant backgrounds—associates such as Tang Shao-yi, Wu Ting-fang, Zai Shao-ji, Liang Ru-hao, and Liang Dun-yan. But unlike Li Hong-zhang, Yuan preferred to use these men almost exclusively in foreign, legal, and customs-related matters. For advice and management responsibilities in economic matters, Yuan relied more upon men from traditional scholar-official backgrounds. In Beijing it was Yang Shi-qi, and in Zhili it was Zhou Xue-xi.

Zhou Xue-xi was from a prominent Anhui scholar-official and landlord family. His father was Zhou Fu, one of the Empire's most important officials, who after 1901 served as governor in Shandong, Henan, Hunan, and then Guangdong. Zhou Xue-xi first worked with Yuan Shi-kai in 1900 in Shandong, where he helped with educational reform. By 1902, Zhou was in Zhili where he and Yuan established (as discussed in Chapter 2) a highly profitable mint in Tianjin. In 1903, Yuan sent Zhou to Japan to study industrial progress there. Upon returning, Zhou was appointed head of a new provincial Bureau of Industries (*Gongyi ju*) and thereafter served Yuan as his economic czar in Zhili. It was Zhou Xue-xi, for instance, who led the well-known campaign to recover the Kaiping mines from the British and to establish a rival mining company at Luanzhou.[77]

The Bureau of Industries was intended to coordinate and promote industrial development throughout the province. With revenues from the new mint, the Bureau ran industrial exhibitions, researched markets and products, established technical schools and workshops, and started pilot factories in important industries, like textiles. Zhou and the Bureau of Industry accomplished a great deal in a short time. By 1907 Zhou could report that there were eleven new privately-owned modern factories and three new industrial schools in Tianjin, as well as over sixty new factories with modern machinery elsewhere in the province.[78] Available figures on capital investment also indicate that investment in the modern sector in Zhili was high compared to other provinces.[79] Present scholarly opinion considers Zhili to have the most impressive provincial program in the Empire for the promotion of modern industry.[80]

Zhou Xue-xi labored to create an atmosphere congenial to gentry and merchant investment by himself setting an example. He invested privately in a variety of modern enterprises, the largest being the Luanzhou Official Mining Company (*Beiyang Luanzhou Guankuang youxian gongsi*) and the Qi Xin Cement Company (*Qixin yanghui youxian gongsi*). Scholars seem to agree that within his enterprises and the Bureau of Industries, Zhou operated in quite a different manner than did Li Hong-zhang's economic czar, Sheng Xuan-huai. Although he certainly used his official position to the advantage of his private investments, Zhou was not corrupt and was a stickler about efficiency. He had a reputation for keeping down the size of administrative staffs, and encouraging austerity and frugality. Not surprisingly perhaps, most of the enterprises which he founded and personally managed lasted well into the 1920s, with the Qi Xin Cement Company the most profitable.[81]

77. Boorman, vol. 2, pp. 409-13; YSKZZ, pp. 771, 1134-36, 1419, 1429; *Zhou Zhi-an (Xue-xi) xiansheng biezhuan*, pp. 13-24; Watanabe Atsushi, "En Seigai seiken no keizaiteki . . . ," pp. 138-47. The scholarly literature on Zhou Xue-xi is becoming extensive: see Feuerwerker, "Industrial Enterprise in Twentieth-Century China: The Chee Hsin Cement Company," pp. 304-42; Wang Jin-yu, ed., *Zhongguo jindai gongye shi ziliao dierji* (Shanghai, 1957), vol. 2, pp. 931-34, 1021; Wellington Chan, *Merchants, Mandarins, and Modern Enterprise*; and Ellsworth Carlson, *The Kaiping Mines*.

78. *Zhou Zhi-an (Xue-xi) xiansheng biezhuan*, pp. 14-17.

79. Wang Jing-yu, p. 1017.

80. Watanabe Atsushi, "En Seigai seiken . . ."; see also Wellington Chan, pp. 109-18, 204-05, and *passim*.

81. Chan, pp. 109-18; Watanabe Atsushi, "En Seigai seiken . . ."; Carlson; and Feuerwerker, "Industrial Enterprise."

Merchant virtues and good business sense aside, Zhou Xue-xi eschewed merchants and recruited as associates friends from the scholar-elite upper class who shared his interest in modern industrial and commercial enterprises. Merchants were not treated on an equal footing by Zhou and the Bureau of Industries. None of Zhou's inner circle in the Bureau of Industries, or partners in private enterprise, were merchants. All were men from upper-gentry, administrative backgrounds. Prominent among them was Sun Duo-shen, son of grand councillor Sun Jia-nai; Li Shi-wei, from a prominent Tiangjin family of scholar-officials; and Yuan Ke-ding, Yuan Shi-kai's eldest son.[82]

Even when a concerted effort was made to attract merchant capital (mostly from Tianjin) for modern enterprises, Zhou and his associates were not willing to provide sufficient guarantees or share management with merchants. Instructive in this respect was the failure to develop modern banking facilities in Tianjin for the merchants of the province.

As discussed in Chapter 2, when Yuan took office Tianjin was in the throes of a business depression which stemmed from the Boxer troubles. Early in 1902 the Tianjin Official Bank (*Tianjin guanyin hao*) was established as the instrument through which Yuan could funnel provincial funds into various projects. Its services to the public were limited to issuing notes of deposit, exchange, and currency.[83] But Yuan and Zhou Xue-xi soon understood the need for a large Chinese bank which could lend money at reasonable rates to stimulate business and to modernize the economy generally, as well as to compete successfully with foreign banking interests in Tianjin. Yuan turned first to the central government and its Board of Revenue, proposing late in 1902 that an official bank of the Board (Hu Bu Yinhang) be established in Tianjin with Board funds. When this scheme failed, Yuan approached Tianjin's merchant community in the spring of 1903. He proposed the establishment of a new bank, Tianjin Yinhang, with seed capital of four million taels. Most of this was to be raised by the merchants themselves, with Yuan offering up to one million taels in official funds to help get the bank started. The leadership of Tianjin's merchant community, who themselves were just getting organized (see next paragraph), were willing only if Yuan's administration would guarantee the bank up

---

82. Wang Jin-yu, pp. 927-28; *Shin-matsu Minsho Chūgoku kanshin jimmeiroku*, pp. 133-34; Feuerwerker, "Industrial Enterprise," pp. 334-35.
83. *Zhili qingli caizheng shuoming shu*, bian 7:3.

to one and one-half million taels of unrecoverable loans. Yuan flatly refused and negotiations broke off.[84] The result was that for the remainder of Yuan's tenure as Zhili governor-general, Tianjin and the province did not have a locally-controlled modern banking and loan institution. Branches of foreign banks and, later, branches of the Ministry of Finance's Da Qing Bank were the modern institutions which, along with the much smaller traditional banks and pawnshops, dominated Tianjin's money market.[85]

To help cope with the deep depression and monetary confusion which beset Tianjin in the wake of the Boxer troubles and occupation by foreign powers, cloth and silk merchants on their own initiative began organizing in early 1903 a modern chamber of commerce (*shangwu gongsuo*). The intent was to go beyond guild organizations (*huiguan*) in coordinating and developing commerce. The new organization grew fast; by 1904 thirty-six different guilds were represented. Chosen as head was Bian Ying-guang, a senior silk merchant who was on good personal terms with Yuan's administration. In 1904 Bian retired as head because of illness and was succeeded by Wang Xian-bing, a salt merchant, who restructured and renamed the organization (*shangwu zonghui*) in accordance with new directives from Beijing's Ministry of Commerce.[86]

Despite the earlier disagreement over the Bank of Tianjin, by 1904 Yuan's relations with this leading body of Tianjin merchants were good enough to enable him to borrow money for the Beiyang Army on two occasions.[87] However, a crisis in their relationship occurred in the summer of 1905 when a boycott of American goods spread to Tianjin. In response to the Exclusion Act of 1905 and other racist legislation against Chinese in the United States, a boycott of American goods developed among merchants and students in Shanghai and Canton. To the relief of the Americans and with the applause of the British, Yuan took a public stand against the boycott. Understandably, the Tianjin Chamber of Commerce

84. BYGD, *juan* 20:21-26; 21:15b-16; YSKZZ, pp. 938-41.
85. *Zhongguo jindai huobi shi ziliao*, vol. 1, pp. 1008-10, 1021-22, 1058-60, 1098.
86. Chen Zhen, ed., *Jindai gongye shi ziliao* (Beijing, 1957), vol. 1, pp. 639-41; BYGD, *juan* 20:17b-28, 21:7-9, 14b-15, 20; DFZZ 3.2 (1906): *caizheng* 25; *Shin-matsu Minsho Chūgoku kanshin jimmeiroku*, pp. 22-23, 65.
87. YSKZZ, pp. 2286, 2319. The key liaison figure appears to have been the old Tianjin comprador-merchant, Wu Mao-ding, who had official relations with Yuan while serving on the Chamber of Commerce board; see Chen Zhen, pp. 639-41; BYGD, *juan* 21:16; Wang Jing-yu, pp. 970-71; DFZZ 2.4 (1905): *zazu* 46; and YSKZZ, pp. 938-41.

was reluctant to take action. But finally, under prodding from a popular merchant-owned local daily, *Da Gong Bao*, over two hundred of its members voted in favor of the boycott at a meeting on June 18, 1905. Yuan was outraged. The Chamber of Commerce quickly backed down from any commitment to the boycott, and the *Da Gong Bao* was forcibly closed by Tianjin police.[88] Thus Yuan and the Tianjin Chamber of Commerce learned to work together, but not as equals. Yuan made sure that ultimate authority and control over commerce rested with him.

By 1906, the major functions of the Tianjin Chamber of Commerce had become clear. Its activities were tame and reformist, reflecting the desire to avoid any jurisdictional conflict with Yuan's administration. The chamber: (1) published and distributed a newspaper, *Tianjin Shangbao*, as a means of exchanging news and views between guilds; (2) operated a school of commerce (*Shangye xuexiao*); (3) assisted bankrupt merchants by helping to find sources of capital; (4) established and operated an opium control board; (5) promoted new industry and circulation of goods by running an industrial fair once a month; and (6) operated a valuation office (*gongzhan qu*) for standardizing currency and thus helping to stabilize the currency market.[89]

Opium control was an area in which Yuan's administration and the Chamber of Commerce cooperated successfully. Yuan gave the Chamber of Commerce responsibility for organizing and directing a monopoly bureau to control the production and sale of opium in Tianjin. Opium would be controlled by regulating its source, at the same time making a profit for the merchants and the provincial government. Thus the Opium Control Monopoly Bureau (*Guangao zhuanmai chu*) when it opened in the spring of 1907 was run strictly as a business. Capital was put up by the chamber and the bureau's officers were chamber officials. Profits were divided three ways: 10 percent for the chamber, 40 percent for use by local government in educational and other reforms, and 50 percent for merchant shareholders.[90]

Promotion of industrial exhibitions and trade fairs was another area of merchant-government cooperation. Quite early, Yuan and Zhou Xue-xi felt that ignorance explained the reluctance of many

88. Peng Ze-yi, vol. 2, p. 498; Wang Jing-yu, pp. 732-37; Zhang Cun-wu, *Guangxu sanshiyi nian Zhong Mei gangyue fengchao* (Taibei, 1966), pp. 55-56, 67, 75, 200, 232, 247.
89. Chen Zhen, pp. 639-41.   90. BYGD, *juan* 25:19b-20.

merchants and gentry to invest in the modern sector of Zhili's economy. By putting on display advanced commercial and industrial products from Zhili and other provinces as well as foreign countries, they hoped to inform the public, and merchants in particular, about potential opportunities. The idea was an important part of Yuan's and Zhou's plan to stimulate and develop Zhili's economy.[91] The first such exhibition (*gao gongchang*) opened to the public in June, 1904.[92] It was quickly a success, with thousands of Chinese and foreign merchants and ordinary people attending.[93] In charge was Ning Shi-fu, vice-chairman of Tianjin's Chamber of Commerce.[94] Ning received permission for merchants at the next event not only to display but also to sell their products.[95]

Needless to say, the heavy taxes which Yuan levied on trade to help finance his administration were of major concern to Tianjin merchants. Imagine their excitement, therefore, when in 1906 the selling of Chinese goods tax-free at the next exhibition was negotiated. The success of this experiment prompted a proposal by the Tianjin Chamber of Commerce that separate tax-exempt bazaars or fairs be held for Chinese goods four times a year. Yuan's advisors feared that such tax-free bazaars would affect revenues too adversely, and that there would be serious problems in limiting tax-free sales to bazaars. Yuan and Zhou finally decided to approve a one-month bazaar in the spring of 1907. According to a Bureau of Industries report, it was a great success for both merchants and government. Increased sales actually produced more revenue, despite the twenty percent tax reduction. This is the only instance that I have found of Yuan ever giving Zhili merchants a substantial tax break.[96]

As in education and police reform, Yuan's administration placed heavy emphasis on creating models for economic development by establishing special schools, institutes, and model factories in Tianjin. The hope was that these institutions would serve as vocational training centers for the development of mechanized industry throughout the province. By 1907, three industrial schools (one for women), two agricultural, and one school of commerce were func-

91. YSKZZ, pp. 1134-36; BYGD, *juan* 16:1.
92. BYGD, *juan* 17:1-9; DFZZ 1.8 (1904): *shiye* 129.
93. YSKZZ, pp. 1770-72; DFZZ 1.11 (1904): *shangwu* 140.
94. Chen Zhen, pp. 639-41.   95. BYGD, *juan* 18:36b-37.
96. BYGD, *juan* 20:1-26; DFZZ 4.5 (1907): *shiye* 96-98; *Zhou Zhi-an (Xue-xi)* . . . , pp. 24-27.

tioning in Tianjin. Most advanced was the Tianjin Higher Industrial School, which offered its over two hundred students a wide variety of advanced courses, including English, Japanese, mechanical engineering, mathematics, and machine shop.[97] To provide a place where graduates from the new industrial schools could perfect newly acquired skills and pass them on to trainees from the countryside, Zhou Xue-xi established an Industrial Institute (*Shixi gongchang*) in 1904. Under the directorship of Zou Xue-xi's leading associate and coinvestor in numerous enterprises, Sun Duo-shen, the Industrial Institute became the provincial center for on-the-job training in modern techniques and technology in light industry, from textiles to candle and soapmaking.[98] The overwhelming majority of students at the industrial schools, including the Industrial Institute, were working in the textile fields of spinning, weaving, and dyeing. To further employ and train students and apprentices from the countryside in textiles, a model factory was established. The Weaving, Dyeing, and Stitching Company (*Zhiliang feng gongsi*) was a *guandu shangban* operation and its manager was the ubiquitous Ning Shi-fu, vice-chairman of the Tianjin Chamber of Commerce. The provincial government provided 15,000 taels in seed capital to be added to the 35,000 taels supplied by Ning Shi-fu and his merchant friends.[99] Moreover, to give apprentices more training in such basic metalworking skills as mold making, iron casting, boilermaking, and mechanics, Zhou Xue-xi established a model foundry (*tie gongchang*) in 1906, using the facilities and grounds of the Beiyang mint.[100]

Many, if not most, of the worker-students at these model factories and schools in Tianjin had been sent from the countryside to learn skills which they were expected to bring back and introduce to villagers in their home *xian* through industrial bureaus (*gongyi ju*) then being established in *xian* across Zhili. Nowhere else in the Empire was there a comparable program of economic modernization and outreach into rural areas. These industrial bureaus at the

97. *Zhou Zhi-an (Xue-xi)* . . . , pp. 18-22; *Diyici jiaoyu tongji tubiao*, p. 65; FO 228/1621, Hopkins no. 48 of May 31, 1906; BYGD, *juan* 18:7-11.
98. YSKZZ, pp. 1771-72; *Zhili qingli caizheng* . . . , bian 7:9; BYGD, *juan* 18:1-7; *Zhou Zhi-an (Xue-xi)* . . . , pp. 14-16. Regulations for the Industrial Institute in 1908, including names of directing officials, is in the University of California, Berkeley, East Asiatic Library (title: *Zhili shixi gongchang xuding zhangcheng*).
99. BYGD, *juan* 18:15-17; *Zhou Zhi-an (Xue-xi)* . . . , p. 15.
100. *Zhou Zhi-an (Xue-xi)* . . . , pp. 16-17.

xian level focused almost exclusively on modernization of the traditional textile industry by establishing small demonstration factories where mechanized looms and new techniques for spinning, weaving, and dyeing were introduced by returned trainees from Tianjin workshops. The hope was that local gentry and merchants, as well as enterprising peasants, would adopt these ideas and start their own small factories or "put out" the new techniques and machinery to cottage industry. In practice, industrial bureaus proliferated with remarkable velocity. By 1907 (the program began in 1904) about ninety of Zhili's *xian* had some sort of demonstration factory (variously called *shixi gongchang, gongyi ju, jiaoyang ju,* and *zhibu gongchang*). The greatest number were established in 1904 and 1906, quite possibly as a result of the stimulus created by major industrial exhibitions in Tianjin. Interestingly, the first places to establish model factories after Tianjin and Baoding were not necessarily the larger, more urban administrative and commercial centers like Tongzhou and Shunde (later known as Xingtai). In fact, by far the largest single operation was the factory founded in 1906 at Nangong in southeast Zhili (Ji *zhou*) with 126 worker-students. Those *xian* that we know did establish a model factory of some sort between 1904 and 1908 are noted in Table 14.[101]

Generally the new factory schools were concentrated in the agriculturally and commercially more developed parts of Zhili. There were relatively few north and northwest of Beijing and the Great Wall, in the poor mountainous districts along the Shanxi border, or in Daming prefecture, which comprised the poor panhandle area in Zhili's deep south. The more rural *xian* usually began on a shoestring budget with 5 to 10 worker-students. The larger, more commercialized *xian* like Shulu and Xincheng in Baoding *fu,* or Luanzhou, Cizhou, and Zhengding (a prefectural capital) averaged twenty to thirty worker-students in the beginning.[102] Although most of the more urban and commercialized *xian* did establish model factories, the size and success of these varied considerably. In Shunde, for example, an energetic magistrate established a model factory, a chamber of commerce, and an agricultural improvement society (*nonghui*), all in 1906.[103] Compared to police and educa-

101. Peng Ze-yi, vol. 2, pp. 502-76, provides a comprehensive survey of the subject. Shandong seemed to have the other successful provincial program. Specific figures on Zhili are on pages 528-32.
102. Peng Ze-yi, vol. 2, pp. 528-32.
103. DFZZ 3.11 (1906): *shangwu* 150-51; BYGD, *juan* 21:4b-7.

tional reform, the importance of official stimulus seemed pronounced in the establishment of model factories. Guangzong *xian* is another case in point. Since the Jing Ting-bin uprising in 1902, the Court had appointed strong, honest *xian* magistrates in an effort to rehabilitate Guangzong. Between 1904 and 1908, three small model factories were established there, more than in any other *xian* of its size and type.[104]

Thus again, as in police reform, initiatives by local magistrates—more than interest and investment on the part of local gentry and merchants—seem to be the key to the rather haphazard pattern in which model factories sprang up, particularly in the poorer, more rural *xian*. To further illustrate this point, let us look at what happened in one whole prefecture or *fu*. Zhengding *fu* was in west central Zhili, bordering Shanxi and straddling the Beijing-Hankou Railway. On the whole, Zhengding *fu* was only moderately active in the model factory movement, with seven of its fourteen *xian* participating. Out of ten poorer and less developed *xian*, only four had model factories: Yuanshi, Xinle, Pingshan, and Zanhuang. The last three were neither more nor less developed economically than neighboring *xian* that had no model factories, nor were they known for having active gentry reformers in police and educational work. It seems safe to conclude that the model factories in these three *xian* were the work of enterprising magistrates. Besides the *fu* capital, the most commercially developed and prosperous *xian* were Huolu, Jinzhou, and Gaocheng. In these places, merchant and gentry initiative might well have been important in getting factories started; only Jinzhou had no model factory by 1907-08.[105]

Funing, Xincheng, and Jianchang *xian* may or may not be typical, but they are among the few *xian* about whose model factories we have some detail. Funing *xian* in Yongping *fu*, along the Beijing-Shenyang Railway, had a population of over 280,000 by the end of the nineteenth century. This population, however, was not particularly urbanized or commercialized. The largest concentration of people was within the walls of the *xian* seat and numbered only about 10,000. Funing organized its first model factory in late December, 1904, with three worker-students engaged exclusively in

104. Peng Ze-yi, vol. 2, pp. 528-32.
105. Gilbert Rozman, *Urban Networks in Ch'ing China and Tokugawa Japan* (Princeton, 1973), pp. 168-71; Charles Gary Watson, "Economic Change," pp. 95-102; Peng Ze-yi, vol. 2, pp. 528-32.

weaving. Then in 1907 an energetic magistrate expanded the number of worker-students and added dyeing to weaving.[106]

Xincheng was to the south of Beijing in Baoding *fu*. Like Funing, it was heavily populated, with probably over 200,000 inhabitants by 1900. But Xincheng was more commercialized, having become a relatively sophisticated trading center for peanuts, peanut oil, wine, and cotton cloth. Xincheng was also active in police and educational reforms. Not surprisingly, the establishment of its model factory in 1907 attracted the attention and energies of the same elites and magistrates who were active in police and education work. A joint stock company was formed to raise 5,000 taels in capital and a site chosen in a temple near the northern gate of the walled *xian* seat. The model factory concentrated on weaving and dyeing and began with about twenty young workers (aged fifteen to twenty), all on scholarships, who were expected to finish their apprenticeship at the factory after eight months.[107]

Jianchang in Chaoyang *fu* was beyond the Great Wall in northeastern Zhili in the bandit-infested area also known as Jehol. During the early twentieth century, Jianchang and the neighboring prefectural capital of Chaoyang were growing fast in terms of population and economic development. Cash crops such as castor beans, hemp, cotton, tobacco, indigo, and opium were important. Crop and animal by-products were processed locally and sent south. 100,000 ounces of opium was being produced and exported annually by 1904. In 1907 an energetic magistrate, Tao Cao-hua, established a model factory in Jianchang for twenty worker-students in weaving and dyeing. To finance the operation, he solicited gentry and merchants to form a *guanshang* joint stock company, but succeeded in raising only 1,800 taels of the initial 5,000 which he needed. Presumably Magistrate Tao found the rest through an increase in taxes of some kind.[108]

Considering how unprecedented it was, the model textile factory program of Yuan and Zhou was remarkable for its penetration of rural areas in Zhili in such a short time. Since most model factories were initiated by local magistrates, we see that here again reform strengthened the influence of local and provincial government at the *xian* level. Moreover, just as with police and educational re-

106. Rozman, p. 179; Peng Ze-yi, vol. 2, p. 531; DFZZ 4.12 (1907): *shiye* 197.
107. *Zhili tuchan biao* (1904), p. 21, in *Beiyang Xuebao* (1905), *kexue zonglu* no. 4, *diaocha* no. 1; *Xincheng xianzhi*, *juan* 12:18; BYGD, *juan* 18:20-21; DFZZ 4.12 (1907): *shiye* 197.
108. *Zhili tuchan biao*, p. 32; Peng Ze-yi, vol. 2, p. 529; DFZZ 4.12 (1907): *shiye* 197.

forms, the model factory idea was welcomed—though not perhaps with equal enthusiasm—by local merchant and gentry elites.

On a much smaller scale, agricultural modernization was also pursued in Zhili through the establishment of schools, associations, and experimental stations. Afforestation and cotton production in particular were encouraged. Those *xian* which started an agricultural school, association, and/or experimental station between 1904 and 1908 are also noted in Table 14. In every case, agricultural reform coincided with the establishment of a model textile factory, and hence was very likely due to the initiative of *xian* magistrates. One example was Jinghai *xian* in Tianjin *fu* where local government cooperated with the provincial government in planting 9,000 mulberry trees in a nursery, from which over three million shoots were raised for distribution throughout the province.[109]

Soon after Yuan left Zhili as governor-general, his economic reform program seems to have collapsed.[110] One of the reasons was that initiative for reform lay chiefly with the provincial government and the local *xian* magistrate. Reform from the top down was shallow and politically fragile. The lack of strong local roots made the new institutions particularly vulnerable to disruption and destruction in the political turmoil of subsequent years. The glaring exceptions were Gaoyang *xian* in southeastern Baoding prefecture and Baodi *xian* in northeastern Shuntian *fu*, the metropolitan prefecture housing Beijing. In both places merchants took the initiative, led the modernization of the local textile industry, and brought to their *xian* prosperity which lasted well into the 1920s.

After 1900 Gaoyang became a center for production of quality

---

109. *Tientsin Decennial Report, 1902-11*, p. 214; DFZZ 5.4 (1908): *shiye* 59. See also BYGD, *juan* 23 and 24; Zhou Zhi-an (Xue-xi) . . . , p. 22; and YSKZZ, p. 632.

110. In 1909, just two years after Yuan left as governor-general, the Industrial Institute in Tianjin closed, dispersing hundreds of student apprentices and faculty; see H.D. Fong, *Rayon and Cotton Weaving in Tientsin* (Tianjin, 1930), p. 13. A reading of Ramon Myers' book, *The Chinese Peasant Economy*, suggests that in rural areas model weaving factories did not develop or continue much into the Republican period (possible exceptions were Ding and Xincheng *xian*, although they too never developed with the success of Gaoyang and Baodi *xian*). For example, Shunde, noted earlier as a large administrative and commercial center where reforms had been vigorously pursued in the 1900s, did not develop a modern textile industry. Although into the 1920s it retained its importance as a trading center for cotton, wool, and skins, Shunde weavers persisted in the use of traditional looms; "Shunteh, An Agricultural and Skin and Wool Trading Center in Hopei," *Chinese Economic Journal* 3 (December 1928):1059-68.

textiles. The key to its success was the merchant community's leadership in the introduction of machine-spun yarn and a new iron wheel handloom (*tielun ji*) from Japan. During the nineteenth century, Gaoyang had developed a sizeable merchant community around a traditional weaving and spinning industry. These merchants included men like Yang Xin-fu, a native of neighboring Anxin *xian*, who was first a moneychanger and then owner of a yarn and cloth shop. In 1905 Yang and his fellow merchants formed a chamber of commerce and an agricultural association, began sending student trainees to Tianjin's industrial institute, and pooling resources to purchase iron wheel looms. In 1908 the merchants formalized their activity around the Gaoyang Weaving Workshop (*Gaoyang zhibu gongchang*) which they founded with ten students and a budget of five hundred strings of cash. Conspicuous by their lack of involvement were Gaoyang's great gentry families, like that of Grand Councillor Li Hong-cao or *jinshi* and constitutionalist Yan Feng-ge. They appeared to have taken only a minimal interest in what the merchants were doing. Thus, despite (or because of?) the secondary roles played by gentry and magistrates, Gaoyang's merchants and peasant weavers quickly turned their *xian* into a comparatively sophisticated production and trade center for textiles. By 1914 Gaoyang was producing over 500,000 pieces of cloth annually. Its subsequent success in developing a national reputation and market is well known.[111]

Even more clearly than in Gaoyang, Baodi *xian* became an important textile center because of merchant initiative. By the turn of the century, a strong merchant community had developed in Baodi because of its geographic position as a conduit for trade into rapidly growing Jehol. Once in touch with the Industrial Institute in Tianjin, Baodi's merchants saw that the importation of yarn and new looms from Tianjin might enable them to capture Jehol's lucrative textile market. In 1906 merchant Ma Jin-hua raised 14,000 *yuan* (Chinese dollars) in capital for modern machinery and established the Bao Hua Weaving Factory. Baodi continued to developed quickly, so much so that in 1910 local merchants raised 140,000 *yuan* to

111. Li Feng, "Wushi nian lai shangye ziben zai Hebei xiangcun mianzhi shougongye zhong zhi fazhan jincheng," *Zhongguo nongcun* 1:3 (1934):307-22; Peng Ze-yi, vol. 2, pp. 253-56, 411-24, 529, 629-37, 692-92; DFZZ 4.9 (1907): *shangwu* 96; Wu Zhi, *Xiangcun zhibu gongye de yige yanjiu* (Shanghai, 1936); *Gaoyang xianzhi* (1931). See also Watson, "Economic Change"; and Linda Grove, "Creating a Northern Soviet," *Modern China* 1.3 (July 1975):243-70.

establish the Li Sheng Cotton Mill, one of the few such mills in Zhili outside of Tianjin and Beijing. Indicative of the lack of gentry or official involvement was the fact that Baodi never had a model factory or even a formal chamber of commerce. Nevertheless Baodi cornered the Jehol market and remained a major textile production center in north China through the 1920s.[112]

Certain patterns can be seen in Yuan's education, police, and economic reforms. More than any other provincial official of his generation, Yuan carried reform to the countryside and effected change, particularly in education. As with the Beiyang Army, Yuan emphasized professional training—the development of expertise through formal education. Under tutelage from the provincial government in Tianjin, *xian* magistrates and elites recruited local residents (presumably the offspring of the elite) to go to Tianjin and Baoding for training as technicians in education, economic, and police work, with the expectation that they would return to work to their home *xian*. To provide concrete examples of what to strive for, model school systems, police forces, and factories were established in Tianjin and Baoding.

Statistically, reform activity in the province as a whole was uneven. In the majority of *xian* either one or two, but rarely all three major types of reform—police, education, and economic— were carried out. The greatest reform activity occurred in the relatively wealthy southern part of the province, but within that area not necessarily in the most prosperous and populous *xian*. Interestingly, in Baoding *fu*, Jizhou, Dingzhou, and Shenzhou— areas where there was the most evidence of elite interest in reform —there was a great deal of educational and economic reform and little police reform. In Dingzhou and Shulu *xian*, reform seemed to focus exclusively on education. Jizhou itself, which was probably the busiest reform area in the province, was concerned much more with educational and economic reform than with police. More balanced reform, which included all three types, occurred in poorer, more remote areas like Zhaozhou and Guangping *fu*.

These statistics, and what has been said about reforms in particular places, suggest a number of conclusions about the impact of

112. Wang Jing-yu, pp. 892-95; DFZZ 4.6 (1907): *shiye* 150; Peng Ze-yi, vol. 2, pp. 414-15, 419-20, 669; Yan Zhong-ping, *Zhongguo mian fangzhi shigao* (Beijing, 1955), pp. 273-83; and H. D. Fong, "The Growth and Decline of Rural Industrial Enterprise in North China: A Case Study of the Handloom Weaving Industry in Paoti," *Nankai Social and Economic Quarterly* 8 (October 1935):692-772.

reforms on the Zhili countryside. First, energetic magistrates were generally responsible for instituting all three kinds of reform in any one *xian*. This explains the concurrence of reforms in *xian* like Handan or Renjiu, relatively remote areas which just happened to have energetic and capable magistrates. Second, long-term success in any field—education, economic, or police—depended upon the cooperation of local elites. In *xian* like Handan, where there was intense activity at the instigation of the local magistrate, reform did not continue into the Republican period—as it did in places like Dingzhou where the gentry were active. Likewise merchant initiative was the key to long-term success of Gaoyang's and Baodi's economic reforms. Local elites had particular interests which varied from *xian* to *xian*. They were interested and willing to work for certain reforms and not for others. Generally, it was in relatively prosperous and populous areas with strong local elites where a more successful but less even and orderly reform program was worked out with the local magistrate. Moreover, as reforms were carried out, evidence suggests that a select new group of local elites and merchants coalesced around the *xian* magistrate and wielded new power in the community (such as in the selection of students for higher primary or middle schools). In Laiyang *xian*, in neighboring Shandong province, resentment against this new power elite was great enough to cause a massive uprising in 1910.[113] Thus reform at the *xian* level in north China contributed to the creation of a new elite which was directly tied to the *xian* magistrate—not in opposition to him, as was apparently the case in Hunan-Hubei. As in Laiyang *xian*, this generally increased the potential for elite/magistrate exploitation and personal aggrandisement at the expense of the peasants, merchants, and others who were left out. Finally, some of the larger, more urban areas clearly outdid their counterparts elsewhere in Zhili. But this too seemed to depend on the quality of local officials. For example, Cizhou under reform administrator Li Diao-zhen was more active than a larger town, Tongzhou, which was under the old conservative general, Ma Yu-kun, and rife with corruption and maladministration. In Zhili reform did not lead to the kind of urban/rural splits, and emergence of an

---

113. See James C. Manwarren, "Rural-Urban Conflict in Shantung: the 1910 Laiyang Tax Uprising" (M.A. thesis, Arizona State University, 1976) and documents in *Shandong jindaishi ziliao* (Jinan, 1957-58), pp. 1-64.

independent new urban reformist elite, that Esherick argues was characteristic of contemporary Hunan-Hubei.[114]

As for Yuan Shi-kai, reform expanded his own authority in the province beyond that of any modern governor-general on record. Exercising control in the cities was relatively simple. Tianjin and Baoding had been devastated and occupied by foreign powers during the Boxer affair. Since Yuan enjoyed such good relations with most of the major powers, he could move quickly and decisively to reestablish order and reconstruct along Western and Japanese lines. In Tianjin and Baoding, thoroughfares were widened, trolley cars and street lights installed, modern police organized, schools from universities to kindergartens established, and modern industry actively encouraged.[115] In the countryside, the task was more difficult. His first actions were negative. He legislated the abolition of the *baojia* security system, outlawed the allied villagers protection systems, discouraged *tuanlian*, and dealt swiftly with even the slightest insurgency through the deployment of overwhelming military power (Beiyang or Huai army troops). Through local magistrates, he then instituted positive educational, police, and economic reforms. Guangzong *xian*, where the Jing Ting-bin rebellion of 1902 had occurred, is an example of a place in which all reforms were rigorously applied in rapid succession. Where successful, these

---

114. Clearly Li Diao-zhen was one of Yuan's model magistrates: see YSKZZ, pp. 610, 762; DFZZ 1.7 (1904): *jiaowu* 294; *Cixian xianzhi, zhang* 16:4. Yuan was able to keep Li in Zhili and have him promoted from Cizhou to Luanzhou; see Esherick on Hunan and Hubei.

115. The British consul summarized recent "progress" in Tianjin in this way: "All about Tientsin good carriage roads are to be found, and wherever possible the narrow native streets are being widened and improved. The native city is well policed and well lighted, and the roads are kept clean and in good repair. Electric tramways fly along the main thoroughfares, and every official yamen and every shop of importance is fitted with electric light and telephones. Numbers of the wealthy Chinese live in houses foreign or semi-foreign in design and drive in foreign carriages drawn by foreign horses, while still greater numbers make use of bicycles. It is now a common sight to see Chinese clerks and even workmen of the skilled class proceeding to and from their employment on bicycles. In the river, though here foreign interests and influences are mainly responsible, steam dredgers can be seen at work and steam traffic is on the increase, while the river is spanned by bridges capable of supporting heavy traffic and of being raised or opened to permit vessels to pass. Thus it may be seen that in such important matters as road-making, sanitation, dredging, and locomotion, the methods of Europe have become part of the everyday life of the Tientsin Chinese." FO 371/634, enclosure in Jordan no. 25 of Jan. 17, 1909.

reforms cemented ties between the magistrate, local elites, and Yuan's provincial government. In other *xian*, magistrates pushed reforms ahead on their own with less long-run success. Regardless, the immediate political effect was the same. Through its role as coordination and education center for all reforms and through the judicious use of authority over the local magistrates, Yuan's administration both increased its influence in the countryside and its popularity with local elites. Finally, the key to Yuan's successes was the quality of the *xian* magistrate himself—who was often selected by Yuan, appointed through the adroit use of Yuan's influence in Beijing, and hence amenable to control by Yuan.[116]

As for overall social impact, there is no question in my mind that, although cast in benevolent terms, Yuan's reforms were repressive. Blaming loose government for the conditions which led to the Boxer uprisings, Yuan was intent upon imposing tighter controls. Education, police, and economic reforms were his vehicles. Certainly, from the point of view of Zhili's short-term security and economic stability, Yuan succeeded.

Yuan was firm in handling merchants and peasants, although the former fared better than the latter. Basically his reform package was directed toward scholar-gentry elites; it was their cooperation which Yuan actively sought. In practice, merchants and peasants were managed and exploited in new and old ways. They paid for the new reforms, but benefitted little from them. In the long-run Yuan's attitude toward the merchant group in particular limited the effect of his economic reforms, even in Tianjin and Baoding. Only in Gaoyang and Baodi, where merchants seemed unusually well organized, did they take the initiative and achieve the kind of long-term economic growth that Yuan had sought for the province as a whole.

Yuan's handling of local elites was deft, to say the least. The reforms improved the *xian* magistrate's ability to govern, and thereby increased Yuan's influence as well, but not apparently at the expense of local elites. Through the reforms, Yuan and his *xian* magistrates took the initiative, legitimizing and co-opting elite leadership and projects at the local level. In the name of modernization, they disbanded or suppressed informal policing and militia organi-

116. For a parallel assessment, see Watanabe Atsushi, "Shin-matsu En Sei-gai to hokuyō shinsei, Hokuyōha no keisei o megutte," *Rekishi kyōiku* 16.1-2 (January and February 1968):135-48.

zations such as the *lianzhuanghui*, *baojia*, and *tuanlian*. These were replaced by "modern" police and the Beiyang Army. It was no accident that, except for some banditry in northeastern Zhili, popular unrest was minimal during Yuan's tenure as governor-general as compared to the situation elsewhere in the Empire. Local elites, who well remembered the Boxers, were pleased with the results, as well as with the new opportunities which Yuan was helping to provide for their sons (and a few daughters) to receive an up-to-date education. Thus, Yuan's brand of social control was endorsed by Zhili's local elites, and they helped to lead and find ways to pay for it.

In short, Yuan's reforms in Zhili were another manifestation of his political genius—wooing and winning local elite support without allowing them to interfere in real terms with the expansion of administration controls at the *xian* level. No doubt Yuan was fortunate in the sense that absent in Zhili, and to a lesser degree in Shandong, was the railway rights recovery issue that was so divisive in the south. Moreover, Yuan was later applauded in the north and south for his consistent stand in Beijing in support of a constitution, and for his pioneering experiment with self-government in Tianjin which included an election during his last few months in office. Indeed, through such journals as the progressive *Dongfang zazhi* of Shanghai, Yuan's reforms in Zhili were advertised throughout the Empire, thus laying a base for local elite support on a nation-wide scale during the 1911 revolution.

CHAPTER VI

Yuan Shi-kai as Grand Councillor and Foreign Minister in Beijing, 1907-1908

On September 4, 1907, after a special audience with the Empress Dowager Ci-xi, Yuan Shi-kai was transferred from the Zhili governor-generalship to the presidency of the Ministry of Foreign Affairs and a grand councillorship in Beijing. Simultaneously, the other Chinese official of comparable status, Hu-guang governor-general Zhang Zhi-dong, was given a grand councillorship and special responsibilities in education.[1] The diplomatic community, particularly the British, were delighted. Yuan was the only man, they thought, who could break the logjam of inaction and confusion in decision making which had gripped the capital since early in the year.[2] Yuan himself was not so sure. He tried to decline the appointments, and delayed for two weeks in handing over the seals of office to the next Zhili governor-general, his friend and associate Yang Shi-xiang. The rumors were that he feared that the move to Beijing would undermine his power.[3]

To be sure, the political atmosphere in Beijing was still unstable and ambiguous, despite the purge of Qu Hong-ji and Cen Chun-

1. *Shilu*, *juan* 576:21a; Guo Ding-yi, p. 1284.
2. FO 405/175 (conf. print), July-December 1907, no. 85. FO 405/178 (conf. print), Jordan Annual Report, 1907, p. 6.
3. FO 228/1661, Tianjin Consul-general Hopkins, no. 54, Sept. 28, 1907, and Hopkins' Intelligence Report for September quarter, 1907; 405/178 (conf. print), Jordan Annual Report, 1907, p. 6.

xuan in June, 1907. Yuan and Zhang Zhi-dong were severely enough criticized by censors in July for them both to request leaves of absence for alleged illness. There were rumors all summer that their transfer to Beijing or elsewhere was imminent. Moreover, for the first time Beijing was feeling pressure from provincial elites about constitutional reform and the establishment of provincial assemblies. As if to test sentiment at Court, in July Yuan Shi-kai joined others in memorializing in favor of speedier moves toward implementing a constitution. He also began experimenting with self-government in Tianjin. The Court was mute, not acting on this or much else.[4]

Speculation about the Empress Dowager's reasons for transferring Yuan to Beijing still continues. A background event of importance was the assassination by revolutionaries of the Manchu governor, En-ming, of Anhui province on July 6, 1907. It produced considerable alarm in Beijing and, in the view of contemporaries, impressed upon the Empress Dowager and her Manchu advisers the need for strong and loyal Chinese officials in Beijing to protect her and the dynasty from anti-Manchu revolutionaries.[5] Subsequently, Republican historians have argued that after the En-ming assassination a number of young Manchu officials, led by Tie-liang, persuaded the Empress Dowager to assert greater Manchu control over provincial governments by transferring the most powerful of the Chinese governors-general, namely Yuan and Zhang Zhi-dong, to grand councillorships in Beijing.[6] Available evidence, however, suggests strongly that by the end of August the Empress Dowager was motivated much more by her recognition of the need for decisive and stable leadership in Beijing, especially in the handling of stalled negotiations with various Powers over railway matters and the future status of Manchuria, but also in the matter of constitutional reforms. The consensus of recent scholarship is that "both Yuan and Chang [Zhang] were coming into a situation where they might hope to have a good deal of influence, rather than into a trap designed to reduce them to impotence."[7] Thus, in retrospect,

4. Daniel Bays, *China Enters the Twentieth Century*, pp. 190-91, 204; Guo Ding-yi, pp. 1281-82; *Zhengzhi Guanbao* 1.1 (Oct. 26, 1907):276-78; YSYZY, *juan* 44:10-12.

5. FO 371/231, Jordan no. 332, July 10, 1907.

6. Li Chien-nung, pp. 211-12.

7. Bays, *China Enters the Twentieth Century*, p. 191. See also Liu Hou-sheng, *Zhang Jian zhuanji*, pp. 153-57, and Esther Morrison, "The Modernization of the Confucian Bureaucracy," pp. 1033-34.

the Beijing appointments signaled that Yuan was back in favor again. The Empress Dowager was genuinely rewarding Yuan with the grand councillorship, which was traditionally the highest ambition of a Qing official. The presidency of the Ministry of Foreign Affairs was an additional honor, as it was the only presidency of a ministry that could be held concurrently with membership on the Grand Council after the reorganization of November, 1906.

No doubt, remaining enemies at court like Tie-liang hoped that by having Yuan in Beijing it would be easier to control and limit his power and it was this—and the ambiguous atmosphere in Beijing—that frightened Yuan. In fact, as he had at earlier crisis points in his career, Yuan would make the best of the situation, using the new posts to further recoup and indeed enhance his political power.

Yuan and the Powers

From August, 1907, to January, 1909, Yuan dominated foreign policy decision making more than any president of the Ministry of Foreign Affairs before him.[8] As chief architect of Qing foreign policy, Yuan both succeeded and failed, depending on one's point of view and level of analysis. In terms of agreements, treaties, diplomatic initiatives and the like, Yuan accomplished a great deal. But 1907-08 was the period when around the world the great Powers through a series of agreements tried to bury their differences and to agree to work in concert preserving the political status quo and strengthening their financial interests where possible in semicolonial countries like China. Thus when Yuan tried to contain the Japanese in Manchuria by inviting in the Americans, he failed; and the effect was to seriously isolate China diplomatically and make the dynasty, and Yuan Shi-kai, more vulnerable politically.

One of Yuan's first moves was to staff the Ministry of Foreign Affairs with men trained in the West and Japan. Since 1901 young

---

8. Yuan shared the presidency of the Ministry of Foreign Affairs with Na-tong, an able senior Manchu official who held concurrent appointments in finance, customs, and military areas. Thus preoccupied, Na-tong left the decision-making in foreign affairs to Yuan, acting only in an advisory capacity himself. The two seemed to get along well together. The British minister, Jordan, later wrote that Yuan and Na-tong "were probably the strongest combination the Chinese Foreign Office ever produced"; John Jordan, "Some Chinese I Have Known," *Nineteenth Century* 88 (December 1920):956. See also Qian Shi-fu, p. 80; and Michael H. Hunt, *Frontier Defense and the Open Door*, pp. 121, 191. Na-tong became much more important and active in foreign policy after Yuan's forced retirement in 1909. (Note Na-tong on the right in frontispiece photograph.)

protégés of Yuan—particularly Cantonese with a Western or Japanese education—had been seeping into the ministry. Yuan now saturated the ministry with these men, most important of whom was Liang Dun-yan, whom Yuan brought with him from Zhili (where he had been Tianjin customs *daotai*) as vice-president. The long-run impact was significant, as it was men such as Zhao Ru-lin, Alfred Sze, Wellington Koo, and W.W. Yen who in the service of various warlords and the Guomindang continued to represent China to the world until well into the 1940s.[9]

The speed with which Yuan and his new army of Cantonese diplomats went to work and achieved results astounded and pleased many. In November-December, 1907, Yang Shi-qi was despatched in two of the navy's finest war ships to tour Hong Kong, Manila, Saigon, Bangkok, Singapore, Batavia, Semarang, Bangka island off Sumatra, Penang and the Malay States. The purpose was to show the flag and to encourage overseas Chinese capital investment in modern enterprises such as railways and factories. In January and March, 1908, Yuan completed loan agreements for the construction of the Tianjin-Pukou and Shanghai-Hangzhou-Ningbo Railways—the former with the British and Germans, and the latter with the British. In March, Yuan also concluded with all the Powers an agreement for a ten-year moratorium on the importation of opium. In July, Tang Shao-yi left on a special mission to the United States to give thanks for remission of the American portion of the Boxer indemnity and to encourage large-scale American investment in Manchuria. In October, 1908, Yuan and the Ministry of Posts and Communications concluded an agreement for redemption of the Beijing-Hankou Railway from a French-Belgian syndicate. By April, 1908, the British minister in Beijing, Jordan, observed that Yuan was accomplishing more in one year as ministry president than anyone else "in any previous year within experience."[10]

Most of these developments were applauded by Chinese and foreigners alike. The recovery of the Beijing-Hankou Railway was hailed as a victory, despite the inflated price paid through more

9. Cao Ru-lin, *Yisheng zhi huiyi*, pp. 60-62; Hunt, pp. 122-24; Stephen Uhalley, Jr., "The Wai-wu, the Chinese Foreign Office from 1901 to 1911," *Journal* of the China Society, Taibei, 5 (1967):9-27; see also W.W. Yen, *East-West Kaleidoscope, 1877-1944: An Autobiography* (New York, 1974), and Alfred Sao-ke Sze, *Reminiscences of His Early Years* (Washington, 1962).

10. *Morrison Correspondence*, p. 448.

foreign loans, because of the railway's great economic and strategic importance as the only completed north-south artery (extending over 800 miles).[11] Similarly the opium agreements, and the special missions to Southeast Asia and the United States, were viewed as laudable efforts in pursuit of a "rights recovery" foreign policy.[12]

There was controversy, however, over the railway construction loan agreements, in particular over the Suzhou-Hangzhou-Ningbo line. Yuan was accused of conceding too much to his British friends. Yuan and the foreign community disagreed, pointing out that the terms of the loans were the best yet achieved.[13] But to many, the terms of the loan agreement *per se* was not the central issue. Since the beginning of negotiations for a loan to construct the Suzhou-Hangzhou-Ningbo Railway in 1898, there had been resistance by Jiangsu and Zhejiang gentry to the idea. They wanted to raise the necessary capital to build the railway themselves, including negotiation of a foreign loan if necessary, and they formed the Zhejiang Railway Company to do so. Until 1908 the Zhejiang Railway Company worked in concert with Beijing. Then as president of the Ministry of Foreign Affairs, Yuan stepped up negotiations with the British without the Company's participation. Yuan was convinced that Zhejiang and Jiangsu gentry and merchants would never raise sufficient capital on their own and that the railway must be built soon. Furthermore, railways were too valuable a national resource to entrust to elites or even to a provincial government. Railway development should be properly controlled and coordinated from Beijing. While Yuan completely ignored protests and petitions from Jiangsu and Zhejiang gentry and senior officials, Prince Qing and others were more sensitive and seemed reluctant to initial the final agreement. Therefore, to bring greater pressure to bear at Court for a fast settlement, Yuan asked the British minister, Jordan, to make a strong protest about elite interference.[14] The strategy worked. In March, 1908, due mainly it seems to pressure from

11. Stephen MacKinnon, "Liang Shih-i and the Communications Clique," pp. 585-87.

12. Michael R. Godley, "The Late Ch'ing Courtship of the Chinese in Southeast Asia," *Journal of Asian Studies* 34.2 (February 1975):361-85. On the opium agreements, see Merebeth Cameron, *Reform and Revolution*, pp. 144-46. On Tang Shao-yi's mission to the United States, see Michael Hunt's exhaustive study.

13. E-tu Zen Sun, *Chinese Railways and British Interests, 1898-1911* (New York, 1954), pp. 66-67, 130-36.

14. FO 371/409, Jordan no. 579, Dec. 11, 1907; also Zhang Yi-lin, *Xin taiping shiji*, *juan* 8:40b.

Yuan and the British, a loan agreement was signed which left out the Zhejiang and Jiangsu elites.[15]

The Suzhou-Hangzhou-Ningbo Railway agreement of 1908 reveals once again the growing intimacy of Yuan's relationship with the British, particularly with Minister Jordan in Beijing, and Yuan's willingness to conspire with him to influence the Court when it seemed to serve the interests of both. In this case the British reciprocated by not pressing Yuan on the Kaiping-Luanzhou mine matter.[16] Throughout it all, Yuan remained confident that his tacit alliance with the British was the best way for both to achieve results for China and to insure Great Power support for his own position in Chinese politics.

Much has been written about late Qing foreign policy under Yuan Shi-kai. Not surprisingly, Chinese of all political stripes have increasingly criticized Yuan for his cozy relationship with the Powers. But at the time there were many of his class who felt what he was doing was necessary and enlightened. As Yuan argued through Tang Shao-yi and others, railways needed to be built if China was to be strong. One had to make the best of China's semicolonial predicament. It was futile at this point to try to drive the Powers away or to ignore them. Why not use their capital and expertise to best advantage, if by playing one off against another one does not further compromise Chinese sovereignty?[17] Yet, as is still true for many semicolonial Third World countries today, the danger inherent in playing such games with great powers is that at any time one may lose the ability or the threat of playing one off against the other, resulting in isolation and further erosion of sovereignty. This was precisely what happened to Yuan Shi-kai in 1907-08

---

15. The literature on the Suzhou-Hangzhou-Ningbo railway problem is considerable. A thorough recent study which treats both gentry and central government sides is Li En-han, "The Chekiang Gentry-merchants vs. The Peking Court Officials: China's Struggle for Recovery of the British Soochow-Hangzhou-Ningpo Railway Concession, 1905-1911," *Jindai shi yanjiusuo jikan* 3.1 (July 1972):223-68. For a British view, see FO 405/178 (conf. print), Jordan Annual Report, 1907, pp. 14-17.

16. FO 405/182 (conf. print), January-June 1908, nos. 18 and 145.

17. See Louis T. Sigel, "Tang Shao-yi," pp. 170-73; and *Sanshui Liang Yansun xiansheng nianpu* 1:71. This argument is developed in the most positive terms possible by John Schrecker in both *Imperialism and Chinese Nationalism* and "Late Ch'ing Responses to Imperialism," *Ch'ing-shih wen-t'i* 2.1 (October 1969):5-16. Schrecker concentrates on Shandong, where Yuan had limited success in using the British and Japanese against the Germans. I have reviewed Schrecker's book and the issues involved in *Bulletin of Concerned Asian Scholars* 9.1 (January-March 1977):71-73.

when he tried to use the Americans against the Japanese in Manchuria.

The sad story of Yuan's efforts to attract large scale American investment in Manchuria in order to offset deepening Japanese involvement there has been thoroughly examined in a recent book by Michael Hunt. Attraction of American capital and the possible forming of an alliance were the real reasons for sending Tang Shao-yi on a special mission to the United States in mid-1908. Although Washington never clearly understood his intent or took it very seriously, Yuan's biggest problem was the fact that in 1907-08 the Powers were trying to settle their differences around the world in a series of treaties and agreements. In China and elsewhere they decided not to compete, but instead to recognize spheres of influence, and to try where possible to profit in combination through loans by international banking consortiums. Particularly damaging to Yuan's effort in Manchuria was the Root-Takahira Agreement which the Americans signed in Tokyo while Tang Shao-yi was still in Washington. In it the Americans essentially conceded Manchuria to Japan as a sphere of influence. At about the same time, the British also renewed their alliance with Japan, which meant that they too were not willing to publicly support Yuan in Manchuria. In the end, Yuan's maneuvering in Manchuria achieved little, but increased enmity and pressure from the Japanese.[18]

Yuan's Continuing Domination of Politics and the Bureaucracy in Beijing and North China

Yuan Shi-kai's political position in Beijing and the Empire was strongest in the 1907-08 period. This was best evidenced by the Empress Dowager's unwavering support. Twice, in October, 1907, and October, 1908, Yuan and Prince Qing were subjected to impeachment attacks at Court. The charges of corruption and excesses of power resembled those lodged earlier against the two men by Qu Hong-ji and Wang Kang-nian. Choosing to ignore the attacks, the Empress Dowager this time did not even order an in-

---

18. Hunt, *passim*. Throughout his tenure as president of the Ministry of Foreign Affairs, Yuan also sparred with the Japanese on a series of jurisdictional disputes in Manchuria—without any long-run success. On Japanese anger with Yuan, Tang Shao-yi, and others, see Matsushima Shūe, *Shinchō matsuro hishi* (Tokyo, 1925), pp. 140-43.

vestigation of the charges.[19] Moreover, from April, 1908, until her death in November, the Empress Dowager was in poor health, which further increased her dependence upon Yuan and Prince Qing in such matters of state as foreign and railway policy. Yuan's remarkable two-day fiftieth birthday party in September, 1908, which nearly all of Beijing's officialdom attended to present congratulations and gifts, seemed to observers a spectacular demonstration of Yuan's influence at the time. The Empress Dowager's gifts were especially numerous and costly, arriving in a long line of yellow sedan chairs accompanied by a band and "deposited on tables covered with yellow drapery that had been arranged at the end of the large reception room [with] a long file of officials standing on either side." Yuan bowed to the presents twenty-seven times.[20]

Although Yuan and Prince Qing did not dominate the Grand Council as completely as they had earlier, they and Zhang Zhidong were its most dynamic and influential members. Yuan's personal relations with Zhang, which had been cordial in the past, remained distant and proper, but not hostile.[21] Politically, because Zhang was senior to Yuan by over twenty years, more issue-oriented, and much less interested in building a network of bureaucratic and political influence in Beijing and elsewhere, their relationship was noncompetitive. Since 1902 they had learned to work effectively together, as in the campaign to abolish the examination system, and continued to do so during the 1907-08 period. They agreed on most issues, differences being chiefly ones of nuance. For example, Yuan went further than Zhang in support of constitutional reform, and Zhang was more nationalistic than Yuan on the subject of foreign loans. Their alliance was further cemented by the Empress Dowager's apparent view that their cooperation (with one another) was essential to the stability and effectiveness of her government. One indication of this was her insistence on the betrothal of Zhang's daughter to Yuan's son in 1908.[22]

19. Zhao Bing-lin, "Xuantong da shiji," *juan* 1:2b; *Shilu, juan* 580:4b-5a. Yuan's attacker in October 1907, Liang Ding-fen, was retired from public office shortly thereafter; see *Shilu, juan* 585:8b.

20. *Morrison Correspondence*, pp. 462-63; for another account, see Bland and Backhouse, *China Under The Empress Dowager*, pp. 443-63.

21. Shen Yun-long, "Tan Yuan Shi-kai," *Xiandai zhengzhi renwu shuping* 1:65-67; Xiao Yi-shan, *Qingdai tongshi*, pp. 2462-66.

22. Bays, *China Enters the Twentieth Century*, esp. pp. 194-96.

The other grand councillors in 1908 were Lu Chuan-lin, Shi-xu, and Zai-feng. Lu we have met before. He was Zhang Zhi-dong's relative and alter ego who had been working smoothly with Yuan since his initial appointment to the Grand Council in 1900. Shi-xu was an innocuous figure who had supported Yuan during the Qu Hong-ji crisis of 1907.[23] Zai-feng (or Prince Chun) was the only man who represented a serious threat to the power of Yuan and Prince Qing.

Zai-feng (1883-1952) was the fifth son of the first Prince Chun, Yi-huan, and a brother of the Guang-xu emperor.[24] In 1901, at age 18, Zai-feng received his first substantive appointment as head of a mission to Germany to apologize for the slaying of the German ambassador to Beijing, Baron von Ketteler, by the Boxers in 1900. Later Zai-feng headed the high-level review commission which recommended the administrative and constitutional reforms that were adopted by the Empress Dowager in November, 1906. He was not involved in the ensuing struggle between Yuan and the group of young Manchus led by Tie-liang for control of the Beiyang Army.[25] Early in 1908 the Empress Dowager appointed Zai-feng to the Grand Council. Lacking background and seniority, he was a quiet and respectful member. However, his hatred for Yuan, whom he considered to have betrayed his brother, the emperor, in 1898 was no secret. At Yuan's fiftieth birthday celebration, for example, Zai-feng was conspicuously absent and sent no present.[26]

As a grand councillor, Yuan Shi-kai was in an even better position than earlier to dominate the Government Affairs Bureau, the important liaison body between the ministries and coordinator of reforms for the Grand Council. Yuan's only adversary on the bureau was Tie-liang. Of its eight members, half (Prince Qing, Xu Shi-chang, Sun Jia-nai, and Rong-qing) were close associates of Yuan. The other two members were Zhang Zhi-dong and Lu

23. On Shixu, see Chapter 3, note 53, above.

24. Arthur Hummel, *Eminent Chinese*, p. 385; see also the biographical sketch in Chen Xi-zhang, *Beiyang cangsang shihua*, pp. 179-80.

25. In fact, Zai-feng and Sun Jia-nai led the investigation which cleared Prince Qing and his son, Zai-zhen—and indirectly Yuan—of corruption charges; see *Shilu*, *juan* 571:14, 572:4. See also Chapter 3, above. It is not well understood that during the post-1906 period there were serious splits at Court between leading Manchu officials, young and old. There is no evidence, for example, that Tie-liang and Zai-feng were ever allies. Later, in 1910, Zai-feng would cashier Tie-liang altogether.

26. Bland and Backhouse, p. 451; FO 405/182 (conf. print), January-June 1908, no. 64; Matsushima Shūe, p. 140.

Chuan-lin, with whom Yuan had a good working relationship.[27]

On the Government Affairs Bureau and Grand Council, Yuan was an ardent proponent of a nine-year plan for the gradual implementation of constitutional government and of early convocation of provincial assemblies and other consultative elected bodies down to the *xian* level. No doubt it was Yuan who was most responsible politically for pushing through the promulgation of these reforms in 1908. Yuan tended to see constitutional reforms and provincial assemblies in terms of what he had achieved in Zhili: as a means by which the state could extend and centralize its authority, as well as improve its financial base. Perhaps there was also a political calculation: Yuan's support and the successful promulgation of these reforms enhanced his liberal credentials enormously with Chinese elites throughout the Empire and overseas. Others, like Zhang Zhi-dong, were more hesitant and fearful of the consequences. That these reforms, and the expectations they raised, eventually did lead to the overthrow of the dynasty, to the establishment of a republic, and to Yuan's emergence as its chief executive was not anticipated—at least not by Yuan. At best he saw the reforms as an aid in becoming premier or prime minister of a reconstituted Qing state.[28]

Influence over Beijing's new ministries was to be the most enduring feature of Yuan's power as a metropolitan official. On November 6, 1906, eleven ministries had been established to replace the traditional six boards and the four ministries added since 1901.[29] Having influence with the Empress Dowager as a grand councillor and having available a network of young, enterprising officials who were formerly under him in Zhili, Yuan was in a position to take advantage of the resulting infusion of new blood into Beijing's top administrative agencies. While he was governor-general of Zhili, Yuan had placed men in some of the new min-

27. Qian Shi-fu, p. 54.
28. In *Zhengzhi Guanbao* for 1907 and 1908 there is abundant documentation of activity, but little direct, documentary evidence pertaining to Yuan's support of constitutional reforms in 1908—or even of his opinions on the question—because as a grand councillor he no longer memorialized directly on the subject, and his yamen papers for these years were never made available. But circumstantial evidence abounds. For a sophisticated discussion of constitutional reforms, including Yuan Shi-kai's role, see Bays, *China Enters the Twentieth Century*, esp. pp. 204-05. On the reforms *per se* and their implementation, see the detailed studies by John Fincher and Esther Morrison. The latter is good on Yuan Shi-kai's role as well.
29. Merebeth Cameron, pp. 105-106.

istries. In 1907 and 1908, Yuan, his allies, and protégés assumed control of a majority of the new ministries in Beijing. At the same time, Yuan retained his influence over provincial administrations in north China generally.

Table 15 provides a crude gauge of the extent of Yuan's influence on the ministries at Beijing from September, 1907, to November, 1908. The table contains the names of top officials in each ministry during this period. Each ministry had one president (an exception was the Ministry of Foreign Affairs with two), two vice-presidents, two councillors, and two secretaries. The number of names per post vary because officials were transferred frequently. Marked with an asterisk are those men who are known to have been allies or protégés of Yuan. The table demonstrates that Yuan and his allies regularly held senior posts on at least five ministries: Foreign Affairs; Education; Justice; Agriculture, Industry, and Commerce; and Posts and Communications. Not so apparent from the table but well-known at the time for reasons discussed below, the Ministry of Civil Affairs was also under Yuan's influence.

While having friends and protégés in leadership positions over different ministries is not an absolute measure of influence or bureaucratic power, it still suggests the existence of a network of bureaucratic ties which were politically important. More substantial evidence of political influence lies in the internal bureaucratic history of individual ministries and their conduct politically vis-à-vis Yuan Shi-kai. This is especially important for the 1907-08 period because it was one in which top officials were frequently transferred, so that lower officials provided the necessary continuity for carrying out the business of the ministry and often wielded more real power. Understanding this, Yuan arranged the placement of allies and protégés in key posts within a ministry and supported their empire-building. A case in point was the Ministry of Posts and Communications.

The Ministry of Posts and Communications was established in November, 1906, to administer all modern means of communications, including railways, shipping, postal services, telegraph and telephone. Railways, however, were the chief concern of the ministry.[30] From the beginning, leadership of the ministry was in flux. Between 1906 and 1911, for example, the presidency changed

---

30. For full documentation and a discussion in greater detail of the following, see MacKinnon, "Liang Shih-i and the Communications Clique," pp. 581-602.

TABLE 15. *Leadership of Beijing's Ministries: September, 1907, to November, 1908*[a]

Ministries	President	Vice-presidents	Councillors (cheng)	Secretaries (canyi)
Foreign Affairs (*Waiwu bu*)	Yuan Shih-kai* Na-tong	Lian-fang Wang Da-xie Liang Dun-yan*	Zou Jia-lai Liang Dun-yan* Liang Ru-hao*	Yang Zhu Gao Er-jian Liang Ru-hao*
Civil Appoints (*Li bu*)	Lu Jun-hsiang	Tang Zing-zhong Zhang Ren-fu You Shi-mei	Zhang-yu Bao-ming Sun Shao-yang	Sun Shao-yang Yu-shan Wu Jing-xiu
Civil Affairs (*Min-cheng pu*)	(Na-tong) Shan-qi*	Yu-lang Yuan Shu-xun* Zhao Bing-jun*	Yu-hou Liu Peng-nian	Liu Peng-nian Yan-hong Wang Rong-bao
Finance (*Duzhi bu*)	Zai-ze	Shao-ying* Chen Bang-rui	Chen Zong-gui Fu Lan-dai	Zeng Xi-jing Liu Shi-heng
Rites (*Li bu*)	Pu-liang	Zhang Heng-jia* You Shi-mei Jing-hou Guo Zeng-zhe	Ying-mian Liu Guo	Liang-kui Cao Guang-quan

TABLE 15. (continued)

Ministries	President	Vice-presidents	Councillors (cheng)	Secretaries (canyi)
Education (Xue bu)	Rong-qing*	Yan Xiu* Da-shou* Bao-xi	Jiao Shu-nan Meng Qing-rong	Lin Hao-shen Liu Ting-chen
War (Lujun bu)	Tie-liang	Shou-xun* Yin-chang*	Yao Xi-guang Zhu Peng-shou	Xu Bing-qi Qing-fan
Justice (Fa bu)	Dai Hong-ci*	Shao-chang Shen Jia-ben*	Ding-zhen Zeng Jian Huang Jun-long	Huang Jun-long Wang Shi-qi
Agriculture, Industry, and Commerce (Nong-kong-shang-bu)	Pu-ding	Xi-zhan* Yang Shi-qi*	Qi-ling Shen Yun-bei	Zhu Ying-yuan Yuan Ke-ding*
Posts and Communications (You-chuan bu)	Chen Bi*	Wu Chong-xi* You Shi-mei Sheng Xuan-huai	Guo Zeng-zhe Na-jin Li Jing-zhu	Zhang Yuan-qi Cai Nai-huang Li Ji-xun Li Jing-zhu Hu Zu-yin

Colonies	Shou-qi	En-shun
(Li-fan bu)		Kun-xiu
		Da-shou*

Known ties of officials with asterisk (*) to Yuan:[b]

- Liang Dun-yan — formerly Tianjin Customs Daodai under Yuan.[c]
- Liang Ru-hao — former classmate of Tang Shao-yi in the United States who had been associated with the Beijing-Mukden Railway administration and had been Customs Daodai at Shanhaiguan.[d]
- Zhang Yin-tang — protégé of Tang Shao-yi, accompanied him to India in 1904-05.[e]
- Yuan Shu-xun — ally of Prince Qing, later governor of Shantung.
- Zhao Bing-jun — formerly Yuan's police commissioner in Zhili.
- Shao-ying — later member of Yuan's November, 1911 cabinet.[f]
- Zhang Heng-jia — educator and a relative of Yuan.[g]
- Rung-qing — former grand councillor and ally at court of Yuan and Prince Qing.
- Yan Xiu — earlier Yuan's chief education administrator in Zhili and recommended to this post by Yuan.
- Da-shou — later member of Yuan's November, 1911 cabinet.[h]
- Yin-Chang — ally and friend of Yuan since 1890s.
- Dai Hong-ci — allied to Yuan through Tang Shao-yi.[i]
- Shen Jia-ben — Yuan was a consistent supporter of Shen's legal reforms and Shen later was a member of Yuan's 1911 cabinet.[j]
- Xi-zhan — later a member of Yuan's November, 1911 cabinet.[k]
- Yang Shi-qi — one of Yuan's closest associates.

TABLE 15. (concluded)

Ministries	President	Vice-presidents	Councillors (cheng)	Secretaries (canyi)
Yuan Ke-ding	— Yuan's eldest son.			
Chen Bi	— had worked closely with Yuan in Zhili.[l]			
Wu Chong-xi	— formerly Yuan's judicial commissioner in Zhili and an old friend since his youth in Henan.[m]			
Shan-qi	— rose to office through the patronage of Yuan and Prince Qing.[n]			

[a] Guo Ding-yi, biao, pp. 13-16; Qian Shi-fu, pp. 32-33, 39-40, 45-56.
[b] Notes are given for those officials not mentioned elsewhere in the body of the text.
[c] YSKZZ, pp. 1606, 1764, 1982, 2021, 2221.
[d] YSKZZ, pp. 742, 1709-11, 1862-64; YSYZY, juan 42:5b-6a.
[e] Sanshui Liang Yensun xiansheng nianpu, I, pp. 45-46.
[f] Guo Ding-yi, biao, p. 17.
[g] QS, p. 4923.
[h] Quo Ding-yi, biao, p. 17.
[i] QS, pp. 4915-17.
[j] Boorman, 3:95-99; YSYZY, juan 14:6-8; 42:3b-5; 44:1.
[k] Guo Ding-yi, biao, p. 17.
[l] DHXL, juan 182:3b-4b; see also MacKinnon, "Liang Shih-i and the Communications Clique," p. 591.
[m] Rongan dizi ji, juan 1:3b; 3:10a.
[n] Morrison Correspondence, p. 558.

hands ten times; the senior and junior vice-presidencies, eight times. This situation provided Liang Shi-yi, who was a protégé of Yuan and Tang Shao-yi, with the opportunity to develop extraordinary influence within the ministry.

Liang Shi-yi's (1869-1933) initial ties to Yuan Shi-kai were through Tang Shao-yi. Like Tang, Liang was Cantonese. A scholar-official in the traditional mold, Liang won a *jinshi* degree in 1894. He was recruited by Tang in 1903 to join Yuan's entourage in Zhili. Liang accompanied Tang to India in 1904-05 and in December, 1905, helped Tang and Yuan negotiate the Sino-Japanese agreement over the status of Manchuria in the aftermath of the Russo-Japanese War. Late in 1906, using his influence in Beijing, Yuan secured for Tang the senior vice-presidency of the new Ministry of Posts and Communications. Liang followed Tang to the Ministry of Posts and Communications and within a year had become head of the General Railway Office (*Tielu zongju*), which was the ministry's chief agency administering railways.

In 1907-08 when Yuan was in Beijing, Liang became quite powerful in the Ministry of Posts and Communications through a personal network of well-placed subordinate officials. Liang's position as head of the General Railway Office and the cooperation of the then ministry president, Chen Bi, who was an ally of Yuan, enabled Liang to keep men loyal to him in key posts, both within the bureaucracy of the ministry in Beijing and those of the railways themselves. Most important of these men were Ye Gong-chuo, Guan Geng-lin, Guan Mian-jun, and Zhao Qing-hua, who became pillars of a bureaucratic clique led by Liang and known during the Republican period as the "Communications Clique" (*Jiaotong xi*). All four were appointed to the Ministry of Posts and Communications in 1906 and 1907 through the patronage of Yuan or his allies. But once in the ministry they owed their advancement more to Liang Shi-yi. Ye Gong-chuo, a Cantonese, who served as a liaison between Liang and the ministry president's office, soon became Liang's most important aide in the General Railway Office. Guan Geng-lin, also a Cantonese, held a variety of appointments within the General Railway Office, Council of the Ministry (*Chengzheng ting*), and its Secretariat (*Canyi ting*). Guan Mian-jun, a native of Guangxi province, was an old schoolmate of Liang's. He became deputy managing director (*huiban*) of the Beijing-Zhangjiakou Railway. Zhao Qing-hua was from Zhejiang province.

He and Liang had once shared offices as Tang Shao-yi's secretaries. Zhao served under Liang in the General Railway Office and later became managing director of the Canton-Kowloon Railway.

Proof of the strength of the grip Liang and his clique of bureaucrats held on the Ministry of Posts and Communications came in February, 1909, after Yuan's forced retirement, when ministry president Chen Bi and some subordinates were impeached for corruption. Although Chen Bi was the principal target of attack, Liang, Ye, the two Guans, and Zhao were also accused of corruption. Yet Liang and his cohorts survived the purge, evidently because they had become so indispensable to effective management of the ministry's railways and revenues. When Yuan returned to Beijing in 1911, Liang became Minister of Posts and Communications and, later, Yuan's alter ego under the Republic.

In other new ministries—the Ministries of Agriculture, Industry, and Commerce; Civil Affairs; and Education—Yuan's former protégés also were building bureaucratic empires like that of Liang Shi-yi in the Ministry of Posts and Communications. In 1907 and 1908 Vice-President Yang Shi-qi and Secretary (*canyi*) Yuan Ke-ding were the controlling forces in the Ministry of Agriculture, Industry, and Commerce. The ministry's predecessor had been the Ministry of Commerce, which was established in 1903 with Prince Qing's son, Zai-zhen, as its president until 1906. Since 1903, Yang Shi-qi, who has been frequently mentioned as one of Yuan's closest associates, held leading posts in both ministries, and in 1907 he was joined by Yuan's eldest son, Yuan Ke-ding.[31] From his position as vice-president, Zhao Bing-jun dominated the Ministry of Civil Affairs, which was mainly concerned with police problems. This ministry succeeded the Ministry of Police (*Xunjing bu*), which was established in 1905 by Xu Shi-chang and Zhao Bing-jun, Yuan's former police commissioner in Zhili. Not surprisingly, most of the reforms coming from the Ministry of Civil Affairs were modeled after what Zhao had done earlier in Zhili.[32] Finally, although Zhang Zhi-dong had supervisory authority over the Ministry of Education, he made little effort to staff the ministry with his protégés. Beneath Zhang, the pivotal figure in the ministry was its vice-president, Yan Xiu, who had been Yuan Shi-kai's top education officer in Zhili. In concert with Zhang, Yan is generally given credit for the progress

---

31. Watanabe Atsushi, "En Seigai seiken . . . ," p. 152; Wang Xi, pp. 114-15; Wellington Chan, p. 116.

made in educational reform by the ministry during the 1907-08 period. Within the ministry Yan gathered around him a number of able associates from Zhili like Fu Zeng-xiang whose influence in educational circles would be felt well into the Republican period.[33]

Yuan's pervasive influence in the central government bureaucracy was matched by influence in the provincial governments of north and northeast China. It will be recalled that since 1901 Shandong's governors had worked closely and well with Yuan. In 1907 and 1908 Shandong, under governor Yuan Shu-xun, who was an ally of Yuan and Prince Qing, remained within Yuan's sphere of influence.[34] As noted in Chapters 3 and 4, Xu Shi-chang, one of Yuan's closest associates, became governor-general of the three new provinces created in Manchuria during the spring of 1907. Under Xu, as governors of Fengtian, Jilin, and Heilongjiang provinces respectively, were Tang Shao-yi, Zhu Jia-bao, and Zheng De-quan—all allies or protégés of Yuan.[35] Table 16 summarizes Yuan's persisting influence over governorships in north China for the 1902-11 period.

Most important was Yuan's continuing influence on Zhili's provincial government. Yang Shi-xiang succeeded Yuan as governor-general of Zhili. It was he and his brother, Yang Shi-qi, who had served as liaisons between Yuan and Prince Qing when they forged their alliance in 1903. As might have been expected, when Yang Shi-xiang was governor-general, there were no striking reversals of Yuan's policies in Zhili.[36] There was also considerable continuity in high-level administrative personnel between Yuan's and Yang's administrations. For example, Zhou Xue-xi continued to manage the Luanzhou mines for Yang as he had for Yuan; and Lu Jia-gu, formerly Zhili Salt Commissioner and adviser to Yuan on economic and financial problems, served under Yang as judicial commissioner.[37] New appointees were usually men connected to

32. Xu Shi-chang, *zuoyi*, *juan* 3, 4, 7, 8; Chen, *Yuan Shih-kai* (1961), pp. 80-110.
33. Chen Gong-lu, *Zhongguo jindai shi* (Shanghai, 1934), p. 582; Bays, *China Enters the Twentieth Century*, pp. 197-99; Boorman, vol. 2, pp. 46-47.
34. Chen Xi-zhang, p. 186; David Buck, *Urban Change in China*, chap. 3, esp. pp. 43-44.
35. On Zheng De-quan, see Chen Xi-zhang, pp. 26-28. On Zhu Jia-bao, see YSKZZ, pp. 416, 2027. On the activities of these reform governors in relation to Yuan in Beijing, see Hunt.
36. Abundant documentation of this point is to be found in BYGD, and its continuation, *xubian*, in three more volumes compiled in 1910.
37. YSKZZ, p. 1481; *Zhou Zhi-an (Xue-xi)* . . . , p. 38; Watanabe Atsushi, "En Seigai seiken . . . ," p. 144. Lu eventually retired because of illness; *Shilu*, *juan* 587:12b.

TABLE 16. *North China Governors, 1902-1911*

	Henan	Shanxi	Shandong	Fengtian	Jilin	Heilongjiang
1902	Song-shou Xi-liang Zhang Ren-jun*	Cen Jun-xuan Ding Zhen-tuo* Yu Lian-san	Zhang Ren-jun* Zhou Fu*			
1903	Zhang Ren-jun* Chen Kui-long*	Yu Lian-san Zhang Zeng-yang*	Zhou Fu*			
1904	Chen Kui-long*	Zhang Zeng-yang*	Zhou Fu* Yang Shi-xiang*			
1905	Chen Kui-long*	Zhang Zeng-yang Zhang Ren-jun*	Yang-Shi-xiang*			
1906	Chen Kui-long* Zhang Ren-jun*	Zhang Ren-jun* En-shou	Yang Shi-xiang*			
1907	Zhang Ren-jun* Lin Shao-nian	En-shou Zhang Zeng-yang* Bao-fen*	Yang Shi-xiang* Wu Ding-bin	Tang Shao-yi*	Zhu Jia-bao*	Cheng De-quan*

	Henan	Shanxi	Shandong	Fengtian	Jilin	Heilongliang
1908	Wu Zhong-xi*	Bao-fen*	Yuan Shu-xun*	Tang Shao-yi*	Zhu Jia-bao*	Cheng De-quan*
					Chen Shao-zhang*	Zhou Shu-mou*
1909	Wu Zhong-xi*	Bao-fen*	Yuan Shu-xun*	Cheng De-quan*	Chen Shao-zhang*	Zhou Shu-mou*
		Ding Bao-quan	Sun Bao-qi*			
1910	Wu Zhong-xi*	Ding Bao-quan	Sun Bao-qi*	Cheng De-quan*	Chen Shao-zhang*	Zhou Shu-mou*
	Bao-fen*					
1911	Bao-fen*	Ding Bao-quan	Sun Bao-qi*	Cheng De-quan*	Chen Shao-zhang*	Zhou Shu-mou*

* indicates political ties to Yuan Shi-kai.

Ties to Yuan Shi-kai that are not mentioned in the text:
Zhang Ren-jun, by blood.
Zhang Zeng-yang, Ding Zhen-tuo, and Bao-fen, recommended for appointment by.
Chen Shao-zhang, through Ministry of Posts and Communications (Communications Clique).
Zhou Shu-mou, through Xu Shi-chang.
Sun Bao-qi, through Prince Qing.

SOURCES: Qian Shi-fu, *Qingli zhongyao zhiguan nianbiao* (Beijing, 1959), pp. 213-222; Des Forges, pp. 37, 88, 89; Liu Feng-han, *Wuwei jun*, pp. 252, 546, 570, 572; Chen Xi-zhang, pp. 82, 150.

Yuan; the new Salt Commissioner, for instance, was Zhang Zhen-fang, Yuan's cousin.[38] As for Zhili's military establishment, as we shall see, it too remained in friendly hands.

Yuan's Continuing Influence in Military Affairs and His Relationship to the Beiyang Army

Especially indicative of Yuan's continuing strength during the 1907-08 period was his influence in military affairs. Yuan improved his position in Beijing through the appointment of former top Beiyang officers to the Ministry of War and to its General Staff Council. Yuan's control of the Beiyang Army seemed unchanged, although it probably was made more remote by the loss of personal contact with all divisions of the army. However, through the appointment of former subordinates, Yuan gained influence over two new forces of division size, one in Zhili and the other in northern Jiangsu province.

As president of the Ministry of War in 1907-08, Tie-liang remained a problem for Yuan and his allies. Tie-liang, however, was now surrounded by pro-Yuan officials. Prince Qing was controller of the ministry and—nominally at least—Tie-liang's superior. The two vice-presidents of the ministry were Shou-xun and Yin-chang, both of whom were allies of Yuan and Prince Qing. Yin-chang in particular was an influential and active figure in military affairs. He had been director of studies at Li Hong-zhang's military academy at Tianjin in the late 1880s and early 1890s. It was he who recommended Duan Qi-rui, Feng Guo-zhang, and Wang Shi-zhen to Yuan in 1896. Yin-chang was also the most knowledgeable of Manchu officials about Germany. He had studied there and his wife was German. In 1900 he assisted Yuan in his dealings with the Germans in Shandong and then from 1901 to 1905 he was the Qing ambassador to Germany. In 1907-08 as vice-president of the Ministry of War, Yin-chang traveled throughout the Empire to oversee troop training.[39]

Attached to the Ministry of War, the General Staff Council (mentioned in Chapter 4) advised divisions of the new national *Lujun* on tactics and training. The General Staff Council appointed

38. YSKZZ, pp. 1339, 1676, 2234; FO 228/1694, half-year intelligence report of Tianjin Consul-general Hopkins, June 1908; Chen Xi-zhang, p. 128.

39. Chen Xi-zhang, p. 259; Cao Ru-lin, p. 88; Schrecker, *Imperialism and Chinese Nationalism*, p. 121. For Yin-chang's 1908 activities, see *Shilu, juan* 588:7b; 591:13a; 595:12b.

General Staff officers (*canmou guan*) to serve in each division as chief deputy to the division commander, and as a liaison between him and Beijing. Throughout the 1907-08 period, Feng Guo-zhang, one of "the three outstanding Beiyang men," headed the General Staff Council. Feng's appointees as General Staff officers were young, well-trained (frequently in Japan), and—as often as not—thought to be among the most dynamic and influential members of a division's command.[40]

Through former protégés who were division commanders, Yuan's influence over the Beiyang Army itself probably remained about the same as before his transfer to Beijing. Two of Yuan's closest associates, Xu Shi-chang and Yang Shi-xiang, as governors-general of Manchuria and Zhili respectively, each supervised two Beiyang divisions. These divisions were, moreover, commanded by Yuan's former subordinates. Ma Long-biao, who commanded the Second Beiyang Division under Yang in Zhili, had risen up from the ranks of Yuan's Newly Created Army.[41] Wu Feng-ling, who commanded the Fourth Beiyang Division also in Zhili, was a graduate of the Tianjin academy and allegedly a relative of Yuan.[42] The Third Beiyang Division in Manchuria was commanded by Cao Kun, a Tianjin academy graduate and a subordinate of Yuan since Xiaozhan.[43] Also in Manchuria were the First and Second mixed brigades formed from units of the Second and Fourth Beiyang divisions and the Fifth and Sixth Beiyang divisions respectively. The brigade commanders were Wang Ro-xian and Wang Hua-dong, both of whom had been officers under Yuan in the Beiyang Army from the beginning.[44] Still, Yuan himself no longer had direct supervisory control over a single Beiyang division and this weakness was exploited by Feng-shan, Tie-liang's protégé and commander of the First Division.

Since late in 1906, Feng-shan commanded the First Beiyang Division and the portions of the Fifth and Sixth Beiyang divisions

---

40. Brunnert and Hagelstrom, *Present-Day Political Organization in China*, pp. 61-64; Qian Shi-fu, p. 60; FO 371/434, enclosure in Jordan no. 407 of Sept. 12, 1908; 371/435, G. Pereira report, no. 88, Nov. 2, 1908; 371/642, Willoughby, no. 8, Nov. 10, 1909.

41. Liu Feng-han, *Xinjian lujun*, pp. 123-24.

42. Wen Gong-zhi, vol. 1, p. 3; and Liu Feng-han, *Xinjian lujun*, pp. 107, 109, 153, 336.

43. Liu Feng-han, *Xinjian lujun*, pp. 115-16.

44. Feng Yu-hsiang, *Wodi shenghuo*, pp. 82, 97-124; Liu Feng-han, *Xinjian lujun*, p. 124.

which were not stationed in Manchuria. Feng-shan was more powerful than the ordinary division commander because as chief-of-staff of the Metropolitan Circuit (*dulian jinji yidai gezhen dachen*), he was independent of the provincial governors-general and answerable only to the Empress Dowager.[45] Feng's First Beiyang Division and his units of the Sixth Division were stationed in the Metropolitan Circuit area around Beijing. There seems to be little question that Feng-shan's control over units of the Fifth Beiyang Division in Shandong was complete and considered a threat by Yuan and his allies. It was reported that the personal relations between Feng-shan and the Shandong governor, Yuan Shu-xun, who was in Yuan's camp, were very bad.[46] Late in 1907, Yuan and Prince Qing failed in a maneuver to strip Feng-shan of his commands and to transfer him to an innocuous post in Shaanxi.[47] After that, Yuan's only possible means of restraining Feng-shan was through the influence of Feng's Court-appointed deputy, Wang Ying-kai. Wang was a long-time associate of Yuan who at one time commanded the Beiyang Sixth Division.[48]

While Yuan made little headway in offsetting Feng-shan's power, he succeeded in using his influence with the Empress Dowager and the Ministry of War to place new forces under his sphere of influence. Yuan had a great deal to do with the raising and training of the new Seventh Divsion of the *Lujun* in Jiangbei (northern Jiangsu). The division began in 1906 when Liu Yong-qing, one of Yuan's top Beiyang officers, came to northern Jiangsu as Jiangbei commander-in-chief with a nucleus of 2,000-3,000 Beiyang troops. Liu died in 1907 and was replaced by Wang Shi-zhen, former commander of the Sixth Beiyang Division and one of "the three outstanding Beiyang men." Working independently of Jiangsu's governor and with direct support from Beijing (which allocated new funds), Wang brought the Seventh Division up to full strength.[49] No doubt without Yuan's backing in Beijing, Wang's appointment

45. Brunnert and Hagelstrom, p. 303; Tao Ju-yin, *Beiyang junfa* . . ., vol. 1, p. 17.
46. FO 371/434, enclosure in Jordan no. 407 of Sept. 12, 1908.
47. *Shilu, juan* 581:6, 16a; FO 405/178 (conf. print), Jordan 1907 Annual Report, p. 25.
48. *Shilu, juan* 581:6b; 594:7b-8a; see references to Wang in Chapter 4, above. An indication of Wang's importance was the fact that in 1907-08 he was promoted and given additional responsibilities.
49. Ralph Powell, pp. 210-11; *Shilu, juan* 588:17b; Jerome Ch'en "A Footnote on the Chinese Army," pp. 433-34. Chen Kui-long's collected memorials indicate that as governor of Jiangsu in 1906-07 he was not directly involved in the development of the Seventh *lujun* Division. Wang Shi-zhen seemed to be in full control of the

and subsequent success in Jiangbei would have been impossible. Therefore the Seventh *Lujun* Division can be legitimately considered as an extension of Yuan's military influence into the lower Yangzi region.

In addition to the Seventh *Lujun* Division, in the fall of 1908 Yuan finally gained control of Ma Yu-kun's *Yijun*. It will be recalled that since 1901 the semi-modern *Yijun* of about 8,000 men had rivaled the Beiyang Army and, earlier, the Newly Created Army, for influence in Zhili and north China generally. In September, 1908, Ma Yu-kun, who was both Zhili commander-in-chief and commander of the *Yijun*, died. Ma's replacement in both positions was Jiang Gui-ti, an ally of Yuan since 1896.[50] With the *Yijun* now under Jiang, all other forces in north China except those under the Manchu Feng-shan were commanded by Yuan's allies and former protégés.

Further indications of Yuan's influence in military affairs were the promotions and new responsibilities given by the Empress Dowager to Yuan's former top ranking Beiyang officers. While Yuan was in Beijing from 1907 to 1908, the Empress Dowager promoted Duan Qi-rui, Wang Ying-kai, and Zhang Xun in rank. Zhang Xun, Xia Xin-you, Jiang Gui-ti, and Wang Shi-zhen became provincial commanders-in-chief (of Gansu, Yunnan, Zhili, and Jiangbei respectively) and Feng Guo-zhang became head of the General Staff Council.[51] The honors and new posts presumably reflected the increased power of these men and Yuan's support of them.

In 1907 and 1908, as a metropolitan official, Yuan thus preserved his military influence and, with the addition of the *Yijun* and the new Seventh Division of the *Lujun*, even expanded it. But having to work through Beijing also eroded Yuan's ability to command the personal loyalties of younger Beiyang officers below the division commander level. Available evidence suggests that during the 1907-08 period when Yuan was in Beijing, Japan-trained officers whose careers owed little to Yuan were being recruited and promoted into the Beiyang Army in large numbers.[52]

In conclusion, the maintenance and growth of Yuan's civil and

---

division, reporting directly to Beijing. See, in addition to the above, *Shilu, juan* 581:14a; 583:2a; 587:18b; 596:3.

50. *Shilu, juan* 595:9b. On Jiang Gui-ti, see Chapter 4, note 117, above.
51. *Shilu, juan* 579:10b; 581:6b; 586:5; 588:14a; 595:9b, 11b.
52. Hatano Yoshihiro, "Hokuyō gumbatsu no seiritsu katei," pp. 248-49; FO

military power after his transfer to Beijing was not surprising inasmuch as Yuan's power as Zhili governor-general was already structured around influence in Beijing. Even more than before, Yuan's power became focused on the capital, bureaucratic in nature, and dependent on his relationship to the British and on success in foreign affairs. In many ways, Yuan's political power reached new heights. Clear evidence of this was the way in which Yuan was able to push through railway loan agreements and constitutional reforms at a pace not seen since the 1890s.

Critical, as always, was the support of the ailing Empress Dowager, whose long illness and resulting dependence on Yuan strengthened his position still further. When she died in November, 1908, Yuan's web of influence dominated not only foreign affairs, key metropolitan ministries and agencies, and top provincial posts in north China, but also most of the Beiyang Army, including its new beachhead in Jiangsu to the south.

371/434, enclosure in Jordan no. 407 of Sept. 12, 1908; 371/435, G. Pereira report, no. 88, Nov. 2, 1908; 371/642, Willoughby, no. 8, Nov. 10, 1909.

CHAPTER VII

Epilogue: Yuan Shi-kai's Fall from Power

By fall, 1908, it was clear that the Guang-xu emperor was dying and that the Empress Dowager Ci-xi, although still wielding power as confidently as ever, was herself aging and ailing. For at least a year, the central issue in Court politics had been the Empress Dowager's choice of a successor to the throne. It is thought that as early as October, 1907, Yuan had urged the Empress Dowager to choose Zai-zhen, Prince Qing's son, and was flatly refused. By October, 1908, Yuan and Prince Qing had regrouped and were vigorously supporting Pu-lun, the senior great-grandson of the Dao-guang emperor, whom they were confident of controlling. Although the Empress Dowager kept her own counsel, most observers seemed to think that indeed she would choose Pu-lun. Imagine the shock of her announcement on November 13, 1908, the day before the Guang-xu emperor died, that the new emperor would be Pu-yi, the infant son of Zai-feng, who would rule as prince regent. Her decision was apparently not the result of a campaign at Court against Yuan, Prince Qing, and Pu-lun. She decided in favor of Pu-yi chiefly because she expected to live and rule as before through the new child-emperor and his father, Zai-feng, who was younger and seemingly more docile than Pu-lun.[1]

1. FO 405/182 (conf. print), January-June 1908, no. 64; FO 405/183 (conf. print), June-December 1908, no. 127; Aisin-Gioro Pu-yi, *Wodi qianbansheng* (Beijing, 1964), vol. 1, p. 19; *Times* (London), Oct. 30, 1908; Bland and Backhouse, pp. 458-59; Jerome Ch'en, *Yuan Shi-k'ai* (1972), p. 75. If Bland and Backhouse are to be believed, even Zai-feng had seemed to support the candidacy of Pu-lun.

A second shock occurred two days later. The Empress Dowager died suddenly on November 15, 1908. On her deathbed she decreed that in a crisis the Prince Regent Zai-feng should consult the widow of the Guang-xu emperor, Long-yu, who was her niece and clanswoman. The intent of course was to insure continued influence of her clan (Yehonala) at Court.[2] But aside from this important restriction, Zai-feng was suddenly on his own as regent for his three-year-old son. Yuan Shi-kai must have been stunned and extremely apprehensive. The prince regent was the younger brother of the just-deceased Guang-xu emperor and rumor had it that he intended to settle a score with Yuan for betraying his brother in 1898 at the time of the Empress Dowager's *coup d'état*. It was even said that the prince regent was planning to have Yuan tried and executed for treason. Such talk was probably fueled by Yuan's Manchu enemies at Court such as the Minister of War, Tie-liang, and the prince regent's brother and Minister of Finance, Zai-ze. Besides Prince Qing, a major moderating influence at Court was said to have been Zhang Zhi-dong, grand councillor and senior Chinese official, who was upset by the arbitrary manner in which Yuan was being treated and steadfastly opposed to replacing Yuan with Kang You-wei and Liang Qi-chao, a reported wish of the prince regent. It is alleged by some that more severe action against Yuan was also precluded by the possibility of military insurrection by the Beiyang Army. But no concrete evidence (of mutinous activity or restlessness among Beiyang officers or men) exists to support the allegation.[3]

Yuan Shi-kai watched and waited, hoping for an opportunity to somehow forge a bond with the young prince regent. He was given responsibility for the funerals of the Guang-xu emperor and the Empress Dowager, for which he received a promotion to senior guardian of the infant emperor.[4] His position at Court, however, remained precarious. By mid-December, censors were submitting formal impeachment charges against Yuan, and rumors of assassi-

2. *Shilu, Xuan-tong, juan* 1:5-6, and Bland and Backhouse, pp. 464-65.
3. Guo Ding-yi, pp. 1319-22; Pu-yi, pp. 21-22; Xiao Yi-shan, *Qingdai tangshi*, pp. 2492-94; Liu Hou-sheng, pp. 165-68; Tao Ju-yin, *Beiyang junfa* . . . , vol. 1, p. 3b; Shen Yun-long, "Tan Yuan Shi-kai," p. 67; Cao Ru-lin, p. 80; Bays, *China Enters the Twentieth Century*, pp. 195-96, 211-12. On Yuan's initial reaction to the news of Zai-feng's regency, see Jordan, p. 956.
4. See FO 228/2243, entirely devoted to the funerals; Lau Kit-ching, "Sir John Jordan and the Affairs of China," p. 75; Guo Ding-yi, p. 1321.

nation plots were rife.[5] The news in late November of the signing of the Root-Takahira agreement in Tokyo, which signaled the failure of Yuan's major effort to ally with the Americans against the Japanese in Manchuria, did not help Yuan's position. In anger, the Japanese were conspiring in Beijing against Yuan, encouraging his ouster.[6] On January 2, 1909, as a compromise solution suggested by Zhang Zhi-dong, Yuan was allowed to resign, the pretense being an infected foot. Two days later Yuan and his family left Beijing by train for Tianjin, where he sought and received British protection.[7]

Suddenly Yuan Shi-kai was out of office and a near fugitive. Except for the Japanese, who remained silent, foreign reaction was immediate and negative. The British communicated their outrage to the prince regent. With Yuan living under British protection in Tianjin, the British minister, John Jordan, also insisted upon and received the prince regent's guarantee of safe passage for Yuan back to Henan. Foreign pressure, mainly British, was the decisive factor which deterred the prince regent from dealing with Yuan more severely.[8] Yuan's replacement as president of the Ministry of Foreign Affairs was his protégé, Liang Dun-yan, who was well liked in the foreign community. But compared to Yuan, Liang was

5. Zhao Bing-lin, *zoushi, juan* 5:11-18. Censor Zhao Bing-lin led the campaign not only to impeach Yuan but to bring back constitutional monarchists Kang You-wei and Liang Qi-chao, exiled in Japan since the *coup* against the Guang-xu emperor in 1898. Zhao was stopped by Zhang Zhi-dong, Prince Qing, and others. See Esther Morrison, pp. 1106-07; Li Chien-nung, *Political History*, p. 230; Bays, *China Enters the Twentieth Century*, pp. 211-12; Xiao Yi-shan, pp. 2501-04; and Zhao's works, "Xuantong da shiji." Tao Ju-yin, *Beiyang junfa* . . . , vol. 1, pp. 36-37, exaggerated the situation by saying that before his dismissal Yuan fled to Tianjin and took refuge under the British consul's protection. Wu Xiang-xiang, *Minguo renhe shi*, p. 46, has asserted that Yuan fled to Tianjin for a few days after the Empress Dowager's death. British Foreign Office documents indicate that this happened only after Yuan's dismissal; see note 8 below.

6. Hunt, pp. 176-77; Li Chien-nung, p. 229; Lancelot F. Lawton and H. Hobden, "The Fall of Yuan Shih-k'ai," *Fortnightly Review* (March 1910):431-34; Wu Xiang-xiang, "Sanhan fuxie suojian Yuan Shi-kai guanxi shiliao," in *Zhongguo xian shi zongkan* 4:446-48. For documentary evidence on the Japanese side of complicity in the ouster of Yuan, see Ernest P. Young, *The Presidency of Yuan Shih-k'ai*, p. 271.

7. Guo Ding-yi, p. 1322; *Rongan dizi ji, juan* 4:30b; Lau Kit-ching, "Jordan and Affairs of China," p. 75; Jordan, p. 956.

8. *Times* (London), Jan. 4, 1909; Hunt, p. 178 (on the American protest); Lau Kit-ching, "Jordan and Affairs of China," pp. 75-80; FO 405/190 (conf. print), January-June 1909, nos. 7, 8, 20, 24, 26, 28-31, 58, 60, 75, 100, 150, 174; see also FO 228/2637, devoted to the problem of Yuan Shi-kai's dismissal; Jordan, p. 956; Tao Ju-yin, *Beiyang junfa* . . . , vol. 1, pp. 36-37.

powerless. Railway negotiations stalled, opium reform dragged, and a large international consortium loan for naval construction bogged down. Jordan, singularly unhappy about Yuan's departure, increasingly thereafter seemed to withhold support from the regency.[9]

Yuan Shi-kai withdrew to the small railway junction of Danshang, near Zhangde, on the Beijing-Hankou Railway. There he bought a large estate and, on the surface at least, lived the life of a retired official—collecting his papers, writing poetry, and supervising the affairs of his huge family.[10] Yuan's large secretariat dissolved.[11] Only two associates, Yang Shi-qi and Yang Du, remained with him at Danshang. But Yuan was in daily contact by courier with his son, Yuan Ke-ding, still a high official in the Ministry of Agriculture, Industry, and Commerce in Beijing, and received at Danshang a parade of important visitors traveling from Beijing and elsewhere on the railway.[12] In this way Yuan kept in touch with his old network of associates and protégés, most of whom were still in office. Still, Yuan was under a kind of house arrest. All contact with foreigners virtually ceased. His estate at Danshang was under constant surveillance, with a careful record kept of visitors as they arrived and left.[13]

Regardless, the rumor persisted in Beijing that Yuan was about to return, because, despite being stripped of office and isolated physically from the levers of power, Yuan's influence was still pervasive.[14] Basically this influence was the result of a stalemate in the power struggle at Court among three factions: one led by the

9. *Times* (London), Sept. 7, 1909; *Morrison Correspondence*, pp. 511-12, 587; FO 405/191, July-December 1909, no. 33; FO 405/195 (conf. print), Annual Report for 1909, p. 5; 405/196 (conf. print), Memoranda, 1909, on Waiwu bu, p. 2; 405/200 (conf. print), July-December 1910, no. 47. This led to Britain's studied "neutrality" during the 1911 Revolution and her leadership of the other Powers in that direction; see Lau Kit-ching, "British Policy of Neutrality During the 1911 Revolution in China," *Journal of Oriental Studies* 8.2 (1970):357-79.

10. *Rongan dizi ji, juan* 4:31; Yuan Ke-wen, comp., *Dansheng sicheng*.

11. Zhang Yi-lin, *juan* 8:40; Boorman, vol. 1, pp. 72-73. I have avoided the term *mufu* because Yuan's secretariat was a much more amorphous and unstructured body than the famous *mufu* organizations of the nineteenth century. The best description of Yuan's secretariat is by Zhang Yi-lin, *juan* 8.

12. Ch'en, *Yuan Shih-k'ai* (1972), p. 85; Tao Ju-yin, *Beiyang junfa* . . . , vol. 1, pp. 74-75.

13. FO 228/2637, Ker telegram of Feb. 24, 1909.

14. *Times* (London), Oct. 11, 1909; FO 405/191, 200 (conf. prints), July-December 1909 and 1910, nos. 75, 20, and 33; Lawton and Hobden, p. 434; Lau Kit-ching, "Jordan and Affairs of China," p. 83.

Dowager Long-yu, another by Prince Regent Zai-feng, and the last by the senior Manchu grand councillor, Prince Qing. In terms of everyday policy and administration, the prince regent's group of young Manchu noblemen were particularly at odds with Prince Qing, Na-tong, and the coterie of senior Chinese officials around them like Xu Shi-chang, Zhang Zhi-dong (who died in October, 1909), and Tang Shao-yi. The Dowager Long-yu's faction seemed in the middle, swinging its support back and forth between these two opposing factions.[15] The young Manchu noblemen were interested in centralizing and expanding Beijing's military, railway, and financial organizations. Their plans were ambitious: a modern budget; a new navy and army; and an expanded, centralized railway network. Financing for all this was to come from foreign loans. In work style, the young noblemen were cliquish and overtly pro-Manchu. They had only one able administrator among them, the prince regent's brother and Minister of Finance, Zai-ze.[16] Leading the vested bureaucratic interests, meaning most of Yuan's old associates, was Prince Qing, who did his best to thwart the young Manchus. His chief tactic was delaying action by absenteeism.[17] Working with grand councillor Xu Shi-chang and Yin-chang, the high Manchu military official with close ties to Yuan, Prince Qing managed to keep units of the Beiyang Army in the hands of Yuan's protégés like Feng Guo-zhang and Duan Qi-rui. In 1910 they also succeeded in unseating the Minister of War, Tie-liang, who since 1906 had led the opposition to Yuan and Prince Qing.[18] A year earlier, in 1909, Xu Shi-chang, Tang Shao-yi, and other Yuan Shi-kai associates lost their posts in Manchuria. But most of them

15. Matsushima Shūe, pp. 182-83; Pu-yi, pp. 17-23; *Morrison Correspondence*, pp. 557-58.
16. Esther Morrison, pp. 1108, 1125-1202; Ch'en, *Yuan Shih-k'ai* (1972), pp. 82-83; Xiao Yi-shan, pp. 2506-07.
17. FO 405/191 (conf. print), July-December 1909, no. 33; 405/199 (conf. print), January-June 1910, no. 128; 405/200 (conf. print), July-December 1910, no. 47; 405/304 (conf. print), January-July 1911, no. 9; *Morrison Correspondence*, p. 587; *NCH*, May 20, 24, and 27, 1911; Shen Yun-long, "Zhangwo wanqing zhengbing zhi Yi-kuang," p. 80.
18. Hatano Yoshihiro, "Hokuyō gumbatsu no seiritsu katei," pp. 248-49; Jerome Ch'en, "A Footnote on the Chinese Army," pp. 425-46; Guo Ding-yi, p. 1352; Powell, pp. 265-66, 272. Tie-liang was disliked by both Prince Qing and the young noblemen around the prince regent. At about this time another able Manchu official, Duan-fang, was also dismissed. Moreover, Yuan and Prince Qing temporarily recovered influence over the Beiyang Fifth Division in Shandong in 1910 with the appointment of Zhang Huai-zhi, Yuan's old associate, as commander.

returned to Beijing to take up other important positions. Xu and Tang, for example, became a grand councillor and president of the Ministry of Posts and Communications respectively. In late 1910, the rumors that Yuan himself would be returning were reaching a crescendo, an indication again of his latent influence in Beijing.[19]

The situation, however, rapidly reversed itself during the spring of 1911. The hold of Yuan's old network of associates on Beijing's bureaucracy was clearly broken. The Ministry of Posts and Communications, for example, fell to Yuan's old rival, Sheng Xuan-huai. Sheng immediately purged Liang Shi-yi and hundreds of other railway officials who had been associated with him and Yuan.[20] Control over the Beiyang Army and the Ministry of War was likewise lost. Both Feng Guo-zhang and Duan Qi-rui were removed from high positions in the Ministry of War. A young and headstrong Japan-trained officer, Wu Lu-zhen, was appointed division commander of the Beiyang Sixth Division; and Zhang Huai-zhi, Yuan's old associate, was replaced as head of the Beiyang Fifth Division in Shandong. As a result, the Beiyang divisions over whose commanders Yuan had some influence were whittled down to four (the First through Fourth divisions). Moreover, young Japan-trained officers, who had little or no connection to Yuan and his associates, were being appointed to positions below commander throughout the Beiyang Army, thus further undermining Yuan's influence.[21] Finally, when, as a first step toward constitutional government, a long promised cabinet was formed in April, 1911, it was predominantly Manchu. Prince Qing was given only nominal authority as premier (the ministries remaining more or less autonomous).[22]

Fortunately for Yuan, this series of setbacks disassociated him and his associates from the central government at a time when provincial unrest against the dynasty was reaching a breaking point during the spring and summer of 1911.

The events of the 1911-12 revolution are well known.[23] By

19. *Morrison Correspondence*, p. 546; *Times* (London), Sept. 6 and 10, 1910; FO 405/200 (conf. print), July-December 1910, no. 75; 405/204 (conf. print), January-July 1911, no. 9.
20. MacKinnon, "Liang Shih-i and the Communications Clique," p. 595.
21. Hatano Yoshihiro, "Hokuyō gumbatsu no seiratsu katei," pp. 248-49, 252-53.
22. Xiao Yi-shan, pp. 2512-16.
23. The best single scholarly book on the subject is still the collection of articles edited by Mary C. Wright, *China in Revolution*.

summer, 1911, the prince regent Zai-feng and his coterie of young Manchu noblemen were floundering badly. The Qing dynasty was in serious trouble. Inexperience, corruption, and heavy-handed favoritism toward Manchus crippled their administration. Particularly serious was the mismanagement of enormous sums in the attempt to rebuild the imperial navy. By 1911 the dynasty was bankrupt and desperately trying to negotiate a large blanket loan with a consortium of foreign bankers at the further expense of China's fiscal autonomy vis-à-vis salt monopoly, railways, and other revenues. This attempt and the push to centralize control over all tax revenues and railways seriously alienated provincial elite leadership, who since 1909 had been meeting in provincial assemblies to organize and voice their grievances. Beginning in May, 1911, there was a series of violent confrontations in Sichuan between elite assemblymen and the provincial government over the railway nationalization issue. Moreover, tensions were already high because of assassination, putsches, and secret society activities by revolutionaries against the Manchus and their dynasty. For the first time in centuries, racial feelings—of the Han against the Manchu—were running high among China's upper classes. Finally the top blew off in October, 1911, when a successful putsch at Wuchang forced provincial elites and local Chinese officials to take a stand and secede province by province from the Empire.

Unable to cope militarily with the crises of October, 1911, the prince regent and the Dowager Long-yu turned in desperation to Yuan Shi-kai. In general, they hoped that his reappointment to office would restore elite and foreign confidence in the central government. More concretely, they needed Yuan to lead the Beiyang Army against the rebels in the south and to help in securing massive foreign loans. After some bargaining, Yuan returned to Beijing in November, 1911, as premier, a post which he had coveted since a cabinet and constitutional form of government was first proposed in 1906. Yuan played his hand brilliantly, functioning as a power broker between the frightened and hapless Manchu Court, the new elite-dominated provincial governments, the young revolutionary insurgents, Beijing's bureaucracy, the Beiyang Army, and, of course, the foreign powers. By February, 1912, after much negotiating and maneuvering but little fighting, Yuan had the dynasty pensioned off and himself declared president of the new Republic of China.

Clearly Yuan's ability to exercise control effectively from Beijing, especially in the crucial areas of military and foreign affairs, returned him to power in 1911-12.[24] Later, when his ability to control military and foreign affairs broke down in 1915-16, Yuan's fall from power was quick and complete. More precisely, his failure to deal adequately with the Japanese threat during the Twenty-one Demands crisis of 1915 and the subsequent defection of Beiyang generals Duan Qi-rui and Feng Guo-zhang in 1916 finished him. During the spring of 1916, Yuan spent his last days in Beijing, surrounded by Liang Shi-yi, the Communications Clique, and other remnants of the late Qing reform bureaucracy.[25] He spoke wistfully of those golden years of accomplishment as a high Qing official in Tianjin and Beijing.[26]

24. See Ernest P. Young's "Yuan Shih-k'ai's Rise to the Presidency." The rest of the paragraph derives from another work by Young, *The Presidency of Yuan Shih-k'ai*.

25. *Sanshui Liang Yan-sun xiansheng nianpu*, vol. 1, pp. 319-21, 332, 339-40, 344; Ch'en, *Yuan Shih-k'ai* (1972), p. 192.

26. Jordan, p. 955.

Conclusion

The strengths and weaknesses of Yuan Shi-kai's political position which brought him down in 1909, back in 1911-12, and down again in 1915-16 were shaped by the structure of his power as a Qing official during the post-Boxer decade. Political power in the late Qing hinged on influence in Beijing with the Powers and with the Empress Dowager and her Court. Where they stood in Beijing was what Yuan and Zhang Zhi-dong, the other great Chinese official of the period, worried about the most.[1] While there may have been a drift away from Beijing before 1900, in the post-Boxer period the flow of power was reversed by the dynamism of the central government's *xinzheng* reforms and the increased influence of the foreign powers, who preferred to exert pressure through Beijing. In becoming the dynasty's most powerful official, Yuan Shi-kai capitalized on both trends. He based his power on the domination of civil and military reform, and on the foreign relations of the period. After reforms in Beijing and Tianjin, Yuan's influence dominated the state's new civil and military bureaucracies, the most important of which, politically, was the Ministry of War's Beiyang Army. By effectively managing foreign affairs without another violent confrontation or undue loss of territorial sovereignty to the Powers, Yuan became indispensable to the Empress Dowager while at the same time deftly building up political support among the Powers themselves, especially the British. Moreover, Yuan's politics were the politics of Imperial China's traditionally strong upper elite or scholar-gentry class. Except for a group of Cantonese with expertise in foreign affairs, Yuan surrounded himself with men from wealthy gentry families who had *juren* or *jinshi* degrees. It was their support which gave Yuan's power legitimacy and put him squarely in the tradition of the great scholar-official reformers before him like Li Hong-zhang and Zeng Guo-fan.

1. Bays, *China Enters the Twentieth Century*, esp. chap. 9 and conclusion.

As governor-general of Zhili in Tianjin and a high official in Beijing from 1901 to 1907, Yuan was able to operate effectively and simultaneously at *xian*, provincial, and central government levels. This was crucial to his success in the use of reform as a source of political power. Zhili became the testing ground of ideas and personnel in the development of a new reform bureaucracy which by 1906 dominated Beijing and was spreading throughout the Empire. In Zhili, Yuan operated less as a regional boss and more as an able, reform-minded administrator who, in education, police, and economic reforms, seemed particularly sensitive to the interests of local elites at the *xian* level. More than in other provinces, local elites in Zhili responded by working with magistrates in directing and financing Yuan's reform program (especially in education) in the countryside. But Yuan's ability to reform effectively in Zhili was always derived from influence in Beijing, which he used, for example, to control *xian* magistrates and revenues. As Yuan ferried back and forth between Beijing and Tianjin, he exchanged experiences and personnel. Protégés like Yang Shi-qi, Tang Shao-yi, Liang Shi-yi, and Zhao Bing-jun applied what they had learned in Zhili to new ministries in Beijing.

Yuan's most important reform, the creation of the Beiyang Army, illustrates the symbiotic relationship between what Yuan did in Zhili and what he did in Beijing. The Boxer Rebellion and the armed intervention of the Powers had left the central government's military forces in a shambles, and Beijing defenseless against another foreign invasion. In 1903 and 1904 with the approach of the Russo-Japanese War over Chinese territory in the northeast (Manchuria), the situation reached crisis proportions. Because of the very real possibility of being drawn into the conflict, the Empress Dowager and her advisors, including Yuan Shi-kai, decided that as soon as possible they had to raise a large force, modernized and powerful enough to deter—or at least slow down—a foreign invasion. The obvious choice to lead and organize this new Imperial army was Yuan Shi-kai because earlier in Zhili, he had raised the Newly Created Army, hitherto the country's most modern army. To finance the new army, Yuan raised what he could in Zhili and Shandong, but the lion's share came through Beijing, with large amounts extracted by special decree from the richer southern provinces. By 1906 this new national army, or Beiyang Army as it was called, consisted of six divisions or 60,000 men who were armed, organized, and strictly trained in accordance with Japanese models. About one-half to two-thirds of the army was stationed in Zhili, with the other units in Manchuria and Shandong. In short order, the Beiyang Army achieved Beijing's aims. By 1905-06 Western military experts were conceding that China could no longer be easily invaded by an expeditionary force like that which sacked Beijing and Tianjin in 1900.

Command of the Beiyang Army enhanced Yuan's power in Beijing and Tianjin but it did not turn him into a proto-warlord, as is often alleged. Just as the army was not financed or controlled at the regional or provincial level, neither was it Yuan's personal army in terms of loyalties of officers and men. Structurally, the Beiyang Army was much less reliant on personal ties than the mid-nineteenth century Xiang and Huai armies of Zeng Guo-fan and Li Hong-zhang. In the Beiyang Army the emphasis was on professionalism and on impersonal command structure. Its senior officers were as closely tied to Beijing as they were to Yuan Shi-kai. Other Beiyang Army officers had less reason to be personally loyal to Yuan. There were old Huai Army commanders like Jiang Gui-ti and Zhang Xun, whom Yuan retained as senior officers in the Newly Created and Beiyang Armies, but who proved in the 1911-12 period and afterwards to be more loyal to the dynasty than to Yuan. The most serious loyalty problem, however, was the junior officers. Yuan had tried to train as many junior officers as possible in the new academies that he established in Zhili with a view not only to assuring the technical competence of his officers but also to cultivating their loyalty to him. But the capacity of Yuan's military educational system to produce competent officers was limited. The result was that probably about half of the army's commissioned officers were trained outside of Yuan's academies. Most were Chinese cadets trained in Japan; a few were graduates of modern military academies in south China. Their allegiance to Yuan was questionable (especially the officers trained in Japan), which was why they were recruited and promoted in such numbers by Prince Regent Zai-feng after Yuan's eclipse in 1909. In short, the personal loyalties of Beiyang Army officers to Yuan varied a great deal, depending upon the backgrounds and career interest of different factions and individuals, but overall their loyalties to Yuan were not strong enough to justify a description of the Beiyang as Yuan's personal army. Organizationally, the Beiyang Army was more analogous to the centrally controlled and standardized Green Standard forces of the early Qing than to the warlord armies of the 1920s.

In raising the Beiyang Army, just as in bringing stability and elite pleasing reforms to Zhili, the key to Yuan Shi-kai's success lay in Beijing. Thus there was no separatist regional quality to Yuan's military or political power. In the last analysis, the power which Yuan derived from reform, civil and military, was bureaucratic and fundamentally Beijing-centered.

Yuan Shi-kai's position in Beijing depended on the trust of the Empress Dowager, a favorable personal balance in court politics, and good relations with a majority of the foreign powers. Compared to the 1890s, an underlying consensus existed at Court about the major issues of the day, such as support for constitutional government, foreign railway loans, and abolition of the examination system. This made the power struggle at Court much less ideological and issue-oriented than it had been earlier. Thus, after the death of Rong-lu in 1903, Yuan easily forged an alliance on foreign policy and other issues with his former critic at Court, Prince Qing. Thereafter, with Prince Qing's support, the Empress Dowager's dependency upon Yuan grew. The only serious direct challenge to his position was made by Qu Hong-ji and Cen Chun-xuan in 1906-07, by which time Yuan was too well entrenched to be dislodged. Only after the death of the Empress Dowager herself was Yuan toppled, and even then his influence in Beijing continued while he was retired in Henan. The outlines of Yuan's changing position in court politics are relatively clear. What is more complicated and more controversial is the chief basis on which Yuan became indispensable to the Empress Dowager, i.e., his handling of foreign relations.

The Empress Dowager Ci-xi first became dependent politically and personally on Yuan because of his effectiveness in managing foreigners, the bane of her existence. After the Boxer debacle, she expected Yuan and associates like Tang Shao-yi to handle such major affairs as the lifting of the foreign occupation of Tianjin, the commercial treaties of 1903, negotiations over the status of Tibet in 1904-06, the Beijing Convention of 1905 with the Japanese following the Russo-Japanese War, and countless railway and loan agreements. Yuan proved trustworthy, from her point of view, because on the one hand he consistently defended the dynasty's sovereign rights from direct imperialist encroachment, and on the other hand he was able to mollify the Powers sufficiently to prevent disastrous confrontations.

Yuan Shi-kai's relationship with the foreign powers was complex. Yuan was consistently the favorite of the diplomatic community in Beijing. They respected him as a progressive, tough-minded man who was capable of fighting fiercely direct attacks on Chinese sovereignty as in the matter of the Kaiping mines, tariff autonomy, or questions of suzerainty in Manchuria. But they also considered Yuan a realist, a man who understood the weakness of China's international position and the financial straits of his government. They were pleased when Yuan granted concessions which indirectly compromised Chinese sovereignty, particularly economic concessions in the form of voluntarily opening new treaty ports and agreeing to new railway loans. Clear evidence of the latter was the fact that more loan negotiations were completed in the year and a half while Yuan was president of the Ministry of Foreign Affairs than during the rest of the 1901-1911 decade combined. Not surprisingly, the Powers preferred to negotiate with Yuan and they let the Court know it. Indeed, as we have seen, Yuan owed high office in part to intervention on his behalf by the Powers, especially the British.

Beginning in 1901, Yuan carefully cultivated a special relationship with the British, the Power with the largest interests in China and the most influence over the other Powers. Their relationship developed into a tacit alliance through a series of trade-offs. Yuan facilitated amicable settlement of a Beijing-Shenyang Railway agreement in 1902 and a number of commercial treaties in 1903, and then followed British advice on the Russo-Japanese War by adopting a position of studied neutrality while in reality helping Japan, Britain's ally. In return, the British intervened on Yuan's behalf at Court, first in 1902 when he was attacked over the Beijing-Shenyang Railway settlement and then again in 1903 when it seemed that Yuan was about to be removed from north China and possibly high office altogether. Moreover, the British carefully monitored the Empress Dowager's appointments to high provincial and central government posts. She was no doubt aware of their satisfaction when a Yuan Shi-kai associate or protégé was appointed, as in the case of Xu Shi-chang's reform administration in Manchuria.[2] After 1906, when Yuan befriended the new British

2. Hunt, pp. 133, 136; FO 405/174 (conf. print), April-June 1907, nos. 20 and 26;

minister in Beijing, Sir John Jordan, the Yuan-British relationship became intimate. Thereafter, Jordan expressed deep concern over attacks upon Yuan at Court, showed delight when Yuan was made foreign minister and grand councillor in 1907, and then protested and protected Yuan after his dismissal in 1909. Yuan reciprocated by insuring the completion of the Suzhou-Hangzhou-Ningbo and Tianjin-Pukou Railway agreements. All the while, Jordan's and Yuan's friend, G. E. Morrison of the influential London *Times*, championed Yuan's accomplishments to the outside world. Finally, there is no question that British support facilitated Yuan's political comeback in 1911-12.³

Except in his dealings with the British, Yuan also adopted a tactic still prevalent in the Third World today of trying to play one power off against another. Initially this was a successful tactic in offsetting the Russians in Manchuria and the Germans in Shandong. But it backfired badly when Yuan tried to play the Americans off against the Japanese in Manchuria in 1907-08. The consequences were serious. China became more diplomatically isolated and vulnerable to incursions by the Japanese, who encouraged Yuan's dismissal in 1909 and thereafter consistently conspired against him until his death in 1916.

Finally, there was a major contradiction inherent in the direction of late Qing foreign policy under Yuan Shi-kai. The chief aim of Yuan and the Empress Dowager was short-term: the stabilization of the dynasty's relations with the foreign powers. But to achieve this, it was necessary to make concessions—like railway loans and the piecemeal loss of sovereignty in Manchuria to the Japanese. These produced elite-inspired nationalist unrest which toppled the dynasty in 1911-12 and caught up with Yuan Shi-kai in 1915-16 and a number of his associates in 1919.

In political style, Yuan Shi-kai identified with China's traditional scholar-official elite and derived legitimacy from them. Yuan himself was from one of the most important scholar-official and landlord families in Henan province. Although Yuan had no civil service examination degree, he was surrounded by formidable scholars who did. Yuan's secretariat and inner circle of associates

---

405/175 (conf. print), July-December 1907, no. 39.
3. Lau Kit-ching, "British Policy of Neutrality during the 1911 Revolution," pp. 363-68.

was saturated with pragmatic Confucian scholars from upper-class backgrounds. A number of them, like Xu Shi-chang, Yan Xiu, and Zhang Yi-lin, were disciples of Wu Ru-lun (1840-1904), master in the 1890s of the Lianzhi academy in Baoding and leader of the important Tongcheng school of Confucian scholarship which rivaled the Gongyang school of Liang Qi-chao and Kang You-wei.[4] Thus, although hardly a scholar himself, Yuan had substantial intellectual backing—a fact that is often forgotten in preoccupation with his military career. Yuan's link with the scholar-official class is best symbolized by his close friendship with Zhang Jian, probably the most admired scholar-reformer of the period, who neither served in Beijing nor in any way could be considered part of Yuan's network of power.[5]

Yuan's associates and protégés also included Western-trained individuals from comprador-merchant backgrounds, like Tang Shao-yi, Liang Dun-yan, and Liang Ru-hao. But, as pointed out in Chapter 5, these men were used almost exclusively in areas relating to foreign affairs. In economics, where they also had expertise, Yuan relied instead upon classically educated scholar-officials from famous families, like Zhou Xue-xi, Sun Duo-shen, and Yang Shi-qi. For top officers in the Beiyang Army, Yuan preferred those with a mixture of traditional and modern professional training, such as Feng Guo-zhang, Duan Qi-rui, and Wu Pei-fu.

In the exercise of power in Zhili, we also saw in Chapter 5 how Yuan naturally favored reform directed primarily toward urban and rural elites. Conversely, these elites' embrace of educational reform accounts for its dramatic, long-term success in Zhili. Theoretically, the benefits of Yuan's reform programs were supposed to trickle down to the peasantry. In reality of course the Zhili peasant suffered under Yuan Shi-kai. His reforms made the males vulnerable to forced conscription into the Beiyang Army and the nightmare of its "modern" discipline. Furthermore, it was the peasantry who, through extra taxes and higher rents, paid for most of the education, police, and economic reform programs that were enacted in the countryside.

4. Ye Long, *Tongcheng pai wenxue shi* (Taibei, 1975), pp. 268-312. See also Guo Li-zhi, ed., *Tongcheng Wu xiansheng (Ru-lun) nianpu* (1943), and Hummel, pp. 870-72. Wu Ru-lun's son, Wu Kai-sheng, was active in Yuan's secretariat and later was one of the authorized biographers who compiled the *Rongan dizi ji* in 1913.
5. Their relationship is explored in detail in Liu Hou-sheng, *Zhang Jian zhuanji*.

Rhetoric to the contrary, commercial development and merchant-run modern enterprises were inhibited as much as they were helped by Yuan's administration. Yuan's treatment of the Tianjin Chamber of Commerce illustrated his unwillingness to go very far in permitting merchant initiatives. Moreover, with the important exception of the merchants of Gaoyang and Baoti and a few Tianjin merchants like Ning Shi-fu, modern enterprise in Zhili was dominated by bureaucratic capitalists like Zhou Xue-xi, Li Shi-wei, and Sun Duo-shen. Indeed, probably even more than Li Hong-zhang, Yuan Shi-kai adopted the bureaucratic capitalist approach to economic development in Zhili, and it was applied on a much larger scale in Beijing by protégés like Yang Shi-qi and Liang Shi-yi.[6] Merchants tended to be forgotten in the process.

All this suggests that Yuan Shi-kai's power represented the interests of China's traditional elites—upper and lower—and especially the interests of the great landlord families with ties to the government at provincial and national levels. Although Yuan was often instrumental in introducing drastic reform, such as the abolition of the traditional examination system, he was careful to do so in coalition with the mainstream of Chinese officialdom at that time. Yuan's strong class sense was reflected too in his tolerance for associates with a wide spectrum of political and ideological beliefs—when they were from the same class as he. His coterie of followers included a number of radicals like the socialist Jiang Kang-hu and the constitutional monarchist—later communist— Yang Du, as well as commanders of Beiyang Army units who were obvious Tong Meng Hui (Sun Yat-sen's revolutionary party) members, like Wu Lu-zhen, Zhang Shao-zeng, and Lan Tian-wei.[7] When

---

6. On bureaucratic capitalism in Beijing, see MacKinnon, "Liang Shih-i and the Communications Clique."

7. On Jiang Kang-hu, who worked in Yuan's secretariat mainly on such publications as the *Xuebao* and *Beiyang Guanbao*, see Frederick Wakeman, Jr., *History and Will* (Berkeley and Los Angeles, 1973), pp. 207-10. Yang Du was one of the most remarkable men of his generation and deserves a monograph. He was a radical constitutional monarchist with ties to revolutionary groups when he returned from Japan in 1903 and received the top mark on the central government's special economic examination (*jingji teke*) held that year. He was arrested briefly, then became active in women's education, and, after 1906, worked on various constitutional commissions in Beijing as well as the railway recovery movement in his native Hunan. In the process he somehow befriended Yuan Shi-kai, with whom he became particularly close after Yuan's retirement in 1909. Today Yang Du is best known as the leading polemicist of the Zhouanhui, which propelled him into the leadership of Yuan's monarchical movement in 1915-16. In the 1920s Yang Du

persecuting political dissenters, Yuan cracked down chiefly on constitutional monarchists of the Kang-Liang school against whom he had a personal grudge running back to 1898.[8] His attitude changed when dealing with those from other classes; Yuan did not tolerate boycotting merchants who dared to challenge his authority—nor, of course, any political activity on the part of the peasantry. Along with ability, what seemed to matter most to Yuan was the class background of the men around him. About this he was consistent, preferring men, with some professional training, who were from landed scholar-official families, the traditional powerholders in Chinese society. Thus Yuan's choice of associates fits the overall thrust of his power as a late Qing official, bureaucratic and semi-colonial in nature and Beijing-centered to the core.

As for what motivated Yuan Shi-kai's lifelong quest for power, this remains today an elusive subject. Yuan was secretive by nature and careful to leave very little in the way of personal papers. This difficulty is compounded by the fact that Yuan has always been a controversial figure. Unfortunately for him, the result has been that, without documentary evidence to the contrary, volumes of gossip have built a solid image of Yuan as a legendary villain in Chinese history.[9] From his actions, the studies of others, and a close reading of Yuan's public statements and what seems to have been most reliably reported about him privately, I conclude that Yuan saw the salvation of the Chinese nation in the creation of a strong, centralized state which then would be in a position to stand up to and throw out the foreigners. To achieve this end, Yuan was willing to take the quickest and most effective means possible, even if it led at times to humiliating compromises with foreign powers.

---

joined the fledgling Chinese Communist Party, working with Zhou En-lai and almost saving the life of party theoretician Li Da-zhao. Yang Du died quietly in Shanghai in 1932. See *Guomin riri bao* (1903), pp. 38, 39, 55; *Xuebao, kexue zonglu*, no. 2, *diaocha* no. 5, pp. 30-31; Zhang Yi-lin, *juan* 8:40; Xiao Yi-shan, pp. 2502-03; Morrison, 1123-24; Tao Ju-yin, *Beiyang junfa* . . . , vol. 1, pp. 50, 75; Bays, *China Enters the Twentieth Century*, pp. 121-22; 171; Joseph Esherick, *Reform and Revolution*, pp. 78-79, 92, 151; *Renmin ribao*, July 30, 1978.

8. Besides the Wang Kang-nian and *Jingbao* affair discussed in Chapter 3, above, Yuan was behind the closing of the *Jinghua Bao* in August 1906, and the banishment of its constitutional monarchist publisher, Peng Yi-sun, for publishing an attack upon his military secretariat; Ke Gong-zhen, *Zhonggo baoxue shi*, p. 174. On the other hand, Yuan rarely seemed to participate in central government campaigns against more revolutionary groups like the Tong Meng Hui. The only instance that I have found was a tame memorial in 1907; *Shilu, juan* 568:19a.

9. Probably the most influential single work is Tao Ju-yin's *Beiyang junfa*. . . .

Yuan saw himself as the powerbroker who was indispensable to the creation of a strong, centralized state—either as its premier during the Qing, president during the Republic of China, or emperor in his own Hongxian dynasty. Thus, although he shared a class perspective with major reform ideologues of the period such as Zhang Zhi-dong and Zhang Jian, Yuan contrasted sharply with them.[10] He probably understood the realities of political power in China and the world better than they, especially the need for military strength and the role of foreign influence. In memorials to the throne, Yuan kept historical allusions to the minimum, more frequently citing Western and Japanese models. For this he was applauded as being "progressive" and "modern" by Western observers. But in other ways Yuan was fundamentally more shortsighted than the two Zhangs. Like Zhang Zhi-dong, Yuan was a bureaucratic nationalist, but much less principled and consistent. Like Zhang Jian, Yuan supported constitutional and self-government, but only as a means to winning acceptance and financing for greater centralization and strengthening of the state, and not as positive ends in themselves. Thus Yuan's nonideological stance was itself an ideological position. He was seriously inhibited by his own brand of pragmatism: the single-minded pursuit of stability and the maximization of his own power, both prerequisites in his mind for the creation of a strong, centralized state.

It is often said that Chinese politics from the Taiping Rebellion to the Revolution of 1911 is best understood in terms of patterns peculiar to Chinese history and the downturn of the dynastic cycle. Military weakness in the face of foreign invasion; peasant uprisings on the scale of the Taiping and Nian; growing regional concentration of political and military power in the hands of certain governors-general; and, most importantly, the growing intellectual ferment, militancy, independence, and co-optation of local government functions in rural areas by local elites, all fit the classic symptoms of dynastic decline—or so the argument goes.[11] In the enormous body of popular literature on Yuan Shi-kai, a favorite comparison is with the infamous Cao-cao, the colorful warlord who

10. On Zhang Zhi-dong, see Bays, *China Enters the Twentieth Century*. On Zhang Jian, see Marianne Bastid, *Aspects de la reforme de l'enseignement en Chine au début du 20e siecle, d'après des écrits de Zhang Jian* (Paris, 1971); Zhang Yu-fa, *Qingji de lixian tuanti*; and Samuel C. Chu, *Reformer in Modern China: Chang Chien, 1853-1926* (New York, 1965).

11. See, for example, Ichiko Chūzō, "The Role of the Gentry: An Hypothesis"; and Roger Des Forges, *Hsi-liang and the Chinese National Revolution*, pp. 196-98.

was partly responsible for the downfall of the Han dynasty in the third century A.D.[12] It follows that the next step is to view the 1911-49 period as a dynastic interregnum of almost fifty years and the politics of the People's Republic of China itself in dynastic terms; and indeed this is a point of view which is popular today in Taiwan, Hong Kong, and among a number of distinguished Western and Japanese scholars.

No doubt, traditional cyclical factors were present in late nineteenth and early twentieth century Chinese politics, for example, the corruption of late Qing bureaucracy.[13] But, as this study attempts to demonstrate, secular trends were more pronounced. The power politics of the last decade of the Qing simply do not fit the calculus of dynastic decline. Instead of crumbling, the central government of Empress Dowager Ci-xi was not only becoming stronger but beginning through reforms to assert its centralizing influence below the *xian* level to a degree unheard of for centuries. The fact that the Chinese state was propped up heavily by foreign powers *in the short run* added to its strength domestically rather than weakened it. This is the conclusion one draws from an examination of the power of Yuan Shi-kai, the Chinese figure who most dominated the decade politically. A similar conclusion about growing strength at the center was reached recently by Daniel Bays in his study of the career of the other major Chinese political figure of the time, Zhang Zhi-dong.[14] Although regional concentrations of power, as well as widespread peasant unrest, persisted until 1911, there is little evidence that either threatened the dynasty. The primary political connections and allegiances of the major regional figures of the period, such as Yuan Shi-kai and Zhang Zhi-dong, were in Beijing. Likewise, Beijing's new armies and Western arms were more than sufficient to deal with peasant insurgencies, which never once showed signs of getting out of hand. Finally, there is no question that the power of local elites continued to grow before 1911, but at least in north China not necessarily at the expense of central and regional nodes of power. We have seen how Yuan Shi-kai carefully placed himself at the intersection of the three power nodes discussed in the introduction, successfully deriving political

12. Ch'en, *Yuan Shih-k'ai* (1972), p. 195.
13. Kwang-ching Liu, "Nineteenth-Century China: The Disintegration of the Old Order and the Impact of the West," in Ho Ping-ti and Tsou Tang, eds., *China in Crisis*, vol. 1, pp. 93-120.
14. Bays, *China Enters the Twentieth Century*, conclusion.

influence from all of them. In Zhili, Yuan met local elites halfway, responding to their needs and legitimizing their role in local government while at the same time increasing the administrative reach of his representatives at the *xian* level, the magistrates.

Yuan Shi-kai's political power had two fundamental aspects. One, Yuan's recognition of the domestic influence of the foreign powers on Chinese politics and his use of it to achieve personal influence and security in Beijing, derived from his tacit alliance with the British. The second was the power Yuan accumulated by straddling three expanding nodes of power—the formal political power of state bureaucracies at the center in Beijing and at the regional level in Tianjin, as well as the more informal political influence of local elites in Zhili and elsewhere.

Yuan's political genius during the late Qing was expressed in his ability to derive power from all three power centers simultaneously. Logically the next step was to centralize power from these three nodes into a single system over which Yuan could exercise dictatorial control. Yuan tried to take this step as president of the Republic of China, after first shoring up his regime with massive foreign financial assistance. Yuan failed, both because World War I cut off vital foreign support and because of opposition at all levels of the power structure—not the least of which came from within the Beiyang army.[15] Thus, the political power structure of late Imperial China fell, in the north especially, with Yuan Shi-kai in 1916 and not with the dynasty in 1911-12.

15. The definitive work on the subject is Ernest Young's *Presidency of Yuan Shih-k'ai*.

Glossary

Characters are provided for terms and names of people used in the text. *Xian* and other place names available in such standard reference works as *Zhongguo diming dazidian* or *Hanyu Pinyin Zhongguo diming shouce* are not included.

Banri xuetang	半日學堂
Bao-fen	寶芬
Bao Gui-qing	鮑貴卿
baojia	保甲
Bao-ming	寶銘
Bao-xi	寶熙
Beiyang dachen	北洋大臣
Beiyang jiangbian xuetang	北洋將弁學堂
Beiyang jun	北洋軍
Beiyang Luanzhou guankuang youxian gongsi	北洋灤州官礦有限公司
Beiyang sanjie	北洋三傑
Beiyang tongyuan ju	北洋銅元局
Beiyang yiyuan	北洋醫院
bianxiu	編修
bianyi	編譯
Bian Ying-guang	卞煜光
biao	標
bingbei chu	兵備處
buban	捕班
Cai Nai-huang	蔡乃煌
Cai Shao-ji	蔡紹基
Caizheng chu	財政處
canmou chu	參謀處

canmou guan	參謀官
canyi	參議
canyi ting	參議廳
Cao Cao	曹操
Cao Guang-chuan	曹廣權
Cao Kun	曹錕
Cehui xuetang	測繪學堂
Cen Chun-xuan	岑春煊
Changbei jun	常備軍
changguan	常關
Chang-yu	常裕
Chen Bang-rui	陳邦瑞
Chen Bi	陳璧
Chen Ji-yu	陳繼虞
Chen Kui-long	陳夔龍
Chen Tian	陳田
Chen Zong-wei	陳宗嬀
Cheng	丞
Chengzheng ting	丞政廳
Cheng De-quan	程德全
Choukuan zongju	籌款總局
chudeng	初等
chuan xuesuo	勸學所
Ci-xi	慈禧
Dai Hong-ci	戴鴻慈
Da-shou	達壽
Dianbao zorgju	電報總局
diding	地丁
ditan	地攤
Ding-cheng	定成
Ding Zhen-tuo	丁振鐸
Dong Fu-xiang	董福祥
Duan-fang	端方
Duan Qi-rui	段祺瑞
Duan Zhi-gui	段芝貴
dui	隊
duiguan	隊官
Dulian chu	督練處

GLOSSARY

Dulian gongsuo	督練公所
dulian jinji yidai ge zhen dachen	督練近畿一帶各鎮大臣
Duzhi bu	度支部
En-ming	恩銘
En-shun	恩順
Fa bu	法部
Feng Guo-zhang	馮國璋
Feng-shan	鳳山
Feng Yu-xiang	馮玉祥
Fenjian xuetang	分建學堂
fu	府
Fu Lan-tai	傅蘭泰
Fu Zeng-xiang	傅增湘
fubing	副兵
fumu	副目
Gang-yi	剛毅
gaodeng	高等
Gao Er-qian	高而謙
gao gongchang	高工廠
Gaoyang zhibu gongchang	高陽織布工廠
gongyi	工藝
gongyi ju	工藝局
gongzhan ju	公佔局
guandai guan	管帶官
guandu shangban	官督商辦
Guan Geng-lin	關賡麟
Guan Mian-jun	關冕鈞
Guang-xu	光緒
guanli lujun bu shiwu	管理陸軍部事務
guan yingye	官營業
Guangao zhuanmai ju	官膏專賣局
Guizhou xuetang	貴冑學堂
Huaijun	淮軍
Huai Ta-bu	懷塔布
Huang Jun-long	黃均隆

Hu bu	戶部
Hubu yinhang	戶部銀行
huiban	會辦
huiban dachen	會辦大臣
huiguan	會舘
Hu Jing-gui	胡景桂
Hu Lin-yi	胡林翼
Hu Yu-fen	胡燏棻
Hu Zu-yin	胡祖蔭
huobing	伙兵
Jia De-yao	賈德耀
Jiangbian xuetang	將弁學堂
Jiang Gui-ti	姜桂題
jiangjun	將軍
Jiang Kang-hu	江亢虎
jiangwu tang	講武堂
Jiaolian chu	教練處
jiaolian guan	教練官
Jiaotong xi	交通系
jiaoyang ju	教養局
jin	斤
jinshi	進士
Jingbao	京報
Jing-hou	景厚
jingli	經理
Jing Ting-bin	景廷賓
Jingwu xuetang	警務學堂
Jingwu zongju	警務總局
Jingxiang	京餉
Junguan xuetang	軍官學堂
junwu chu	軍務處
Junxue	軍學
Junzheng si	軍政司
Junzi chu	軍諮處
Junyi xuetang	軍醫學堂
juren	舉人
Kang You-wei	康有爲

GLOSSARY

Kim Yun-sik	金允植
kouliu waipu	扣留外補
Kun-xiu	堃岫
Lan Tian-wei	藍天尉
lejuan	勒捐
Li Chang-tai	李長泰
Li Han-zhang	李瀚章
Li Hong-cao	李鴻藻
Li Hong-zhang	李鴻章
Li Jing-chu	李經楚
Li Ji-xun	李稷勳
Li Lian-ying	李蓮英
Li Shi-wei	李士偉
Li Zhao-zhen	李兆珍
Li Zhuo-hua	李灼華
Li bu	吏部
Lianbing chu	練兵處
Lianbing xuxiang	練兵需餉
Lian-fang	聯芳
lianzhuang hui	聯莊會
Liang-bi	良弼
Liang Dun-yan	梁敦彥
Liang-gui	良揆
Liang Qi-chao	梁啟超
Liang Ru-hao	梁如浩
Liang Shi-yi	梁士詒
Lin Hao-shen	林灝深
Lin Shao-nian	林紹年
Lin Xu	林旭
Liu Bing-zhang	劉秉璋
Liu Guang-di	劉光第
Liu Guang-jing	劉廣京
Liu Guo	劉果
Liu Kun-yi	劉坤一
Liu Ming-chuan	劉銘傳
Liu Peng-nian	劉彭年
Liu Shi-heng	劉士珩
Liu Ting-shen	劉廷琛

Liu Yong-qing	劉永慶
Lu Ben-yuan	呂本元
Lu Chuan-lin	鹿傳霖
Lu Jia-gu	陸嘉穀
Lu Jian-zhang	陸建章
Lu Run-xiang	陸潤庠
luanmin	亂民
Lujun	陸軍
Lujun bu	陸軍部
Lunchuan zhaoshangju	輪船招商局
Ma Long-biao	馬龍標
Ma Ting-liang	馬廷亮
Ma Yu-kun	馬玉崑
maiguo zei	賣國賊
Mao Qing-fan	毛慶蕃
Mayi xuetang	馬醫學堂
Mei Dong-yi	梅東益
Meng Qing-rong	孟慶榮
Minzheng bu	民政部
mou	畝
mufu	幕府
Na-jin	那晉
Na-tong	那桐
Nie Shi-cheng	聶士成
Nihon rikugun shikan gakko	日本陸軍士官學校
Ning Shi-fu	寧世福
Nonggongshang bu	農工商部
nonghui	農會
Nongwu ju	農務局
pai	排
paizhang	排長
Pan Ding-xin	潘鼎新
peng	棚
Pu-liang	溥艮
Pu-lun	溥倫
Pu-ting	溥颋

GLOSSARY

Pu-yi 溥儀
putong jiaoyu 普通教育

Qi-ling 耆齡
Qiang Xuehui 強學會
Qiao Shu-nan 喬樹枬
qinbing 親兵
Qing-fan 慶蕃
qingliu pai 清流派
qingyi 清議
Qixin yanghui youxian gongsi 啟新洋灰有限公司
qu 區
Qu Hong-ji 瞿鴻禨

Renxue yuan 仁學院
Rong-hong 容閎
Rong-lu 榮祿
Rong-qing 榮慶

sao-Qing mieyang 掃清滅洋
Shan-qi 善耆
Shang bu 商部
shangwei 上尉
shangwu gongsuo 商務公所
Shangwu ju 商務局
Shangwu zonghui 商務總會
Shangye xuexiao 商務學校
shao 哨
shaoguan 哨官
Shao Xun-zheng 邵循正
Shao-chang 紹昌
Shao-ying 紹英
Shen Gui-fen 沈桂芬
Shen Jia-ben 沈家本
Shen Yun-pei 沈雲沛
Sheng Xuan-huai 盛宣懷
shengyuan 生員
Shi Zhao-ji 施肇基
Shi-xu 世續

shidu xueshi 侍讀學士
Shixi gongchang 實習工廠
shizhang 什長
Shou-qi 壽耆
Shou-xun 壽勳
Shuiwu chu 稅務處
shuyuan 書院
Song Qing 宋慶
Song-shou 松壽
Su Yuan-chun 蘇元春
Sucheng xuetang 速成學堂
Suiying xuetang 隨營學堂
Sun Bao-qi 孫寶琦
Sun Duo-sen 孫多森
Sun Jia-nai 孫家鼐
Sun Shao-yang 孫紹陽
Sun Wan-lin 孫萬林

Taizi shaobao 太子少保
tankuan 攤款
Tan Si-tong 譚嗣同
Tang Jing-chong 唐景崇
Tang Mao-zhi 唐茂枝
Tang Shao-yi 唐紹儀
Tang Ting-shu (Tang Jing-xing,
　Tong King-sing) 唐廷樞（唐景星）
Tao Cao-hua 陶藻華
Tian Zhong-yu 田中玉
tianfang 田房
Tianjin Shangbao 天津商報
Tianjin yinhao 天津銀號
tidu 提督
Tie-liang 鐵良
Tie gongchang 鐵工廠
Tielu zongju 鐵路總局
Tongcheng 桐城
tongdaiguan 統帶官
tongling 統領
tongling guan 統領官

tongzhi guan	統制官
tuanlian	團練
Waiwu bu	外務部
wang dachen	王大臣
Wang Da-xie	汪大燮
Wang Jin-jing	王金鏡
Wang Kang-nian	汪康年
Wang Nai-zheng	王乃徵
Wang Rong-bao	汪榮寶
Wang Rui-gao	王瑞高
Wang Shi-qi	王世琪
Wang Shi-zhen	王世珍
Wang Wen-shao	王文韶
Wang Ying-kai	王英楷
Wang Zhan-yuan	王占元
Wang Zhao	王照
Wei Guang-dao	魏光燾
Weng Tong-he (Shu-ping)	翁同龢（叔平）
Wu Chang-qing	吳長慶
Wu Feng-ling	吳鳳嶺
Wu Jing-xiu	吳敬修
Wu Lu-zhen	吳祿貞
Wu Mao-ding	吳懋鼎
Wu Pei-fu	吳佩孚
Wu Yong	吳永
Wu Zhong-xi	吳重熹
Wubei xuetang	武備學堂
wujuren	武舉人
Wuwei jun	武衛軍
Wuyi jun	武毅軍
Xi-liang	錫良
Xi-yan	熙彥
Xia Xin-yu	夏辛酉
Xiangjun	湘軍
xiangyong	鄉勇
Xiaoxue tang	小學堂
xie	協

xiexiang	協餉
xian	縣
Xianfeng dui	先鋒隊
Xinjian lujun	新建陸軍
Xinjun	新軍
Xu Bing-qi	許秉琦
Xu Ren-lu	徐仁錄
Xu Shi-chang	徐世昌
Xu Tong	徐桐
Xu Ying-kui	徐應騤
Xu Zhi-jing	徐致靖
Xuanjiang suo	宣講所
Xubei jun	續備軍
Xue bu	學部
Xuewu chu	學務處
Xuewu ju	學務局
Xuexiao si	學校司
Xuezheng	學政
Xunfang dui	巡防隊
Xunjing bu	巡警部
Yan Feng-ge	閻鳳閣
Yan Xiu	嚴修
Yan-hong	延鴻
Yang Chong-yi	楊崇伊
Yang Du	楊度
Yang Rui	楊銳
Yang Shi-qi	楊士琦
Yang Shi-xiang	楊士驤
Yang Shu	楊樞
Yang Zong-lian	楊宗濂
Yangwen zongban	洋文總辦
Yangwu chu	洋務處
Yao Xi-guang	姚錫光
Ye Gong-chuo	葉恭綽
Yi Hui	李熙
Yi-huan (Chun qinwang)	奕譞（醇親王）
Yi-kuang (Qing qinwang)	奕劻（慶親王）
Yi-xin (Gong qinwang)	奕訢（恭親王）

GLOSSARY

Yijun	毅軍
Yin-chang	蔭昌
ying	營
Ying-nian	英年
yingguan	營官
Yingwu chu	營務處
Yong-lin	永璘
yongying	勇營
Youchuan bu	郵傳部
Yu Shi-mei	于式枚
Yu-hou	裕厚
Yu-lang	毓朗
Yu-shan	毓善
Yu-xian	毓賢
Yuan Bao-heng	袁保恒
Yuan Bao-ling	袁保齡
Yuan Bao-qing	袁保慶
Yuan Bao-zhong	袁保中
Yuan Jia-san	袁甲三
Yuan Ke-ding	袁克定
Yuan Shi-kai	袁世凱
Yuan Shi-xun	袁世勳
Yuan Shu-xun	袁樹勛
Yun Yu-ding	惲毓鼎
Zai-feng (Prince Chun)	載灃
Zai-lan	載瀾
Zai-xun	載洵
Zai-yi	載漪
Zai-ze	載澤
Zai-zhen	載振
Zeng Guo-fan	曾國藩
Zeng Guo-quan	曾國荃
Zeng Jian	曾鑑
Zeng Xi-jing	曾習經
Zeng-qi	曾祺
Zhan Tian-you	詹天佑
Zhang Huai-zhi	張懷芝
Zhang Pei-lun	張佩綸

Zhang Jian	張謇
Zhang Ren-fu	張仁黼
Zhang Ren-jun	張人駿
Zhang Shao-zeng	張紹曾
Zhang Shu-sheng	張樹聲
Zhang Ting-xiang	張廷湘
Zhang Ke-ming	張鶴鳴
Zhang Xi-fan	張錫鑾
Zhang Xiang-jia	張享嘉
Zhang Xun	張勳
Zhang Yi (Zhang Yan-mou)	張翼（張燕謀）
Zhang Yin-tang	張蔭棠
Zhang Yuan-ji	張元濟
Zhang Zeng-yang	張曾敭
Zhang Zhen-fang	張鎮芳
Zhang Zhi-dong	張之洞
Zhang-geng	張庚
Zhao Bing-jun	趙秉鈞
Zhao Bing-lin	趙炳麟
Zhao Er-xun	趙爾巽
Zhao Qi-lin	趙啓霖
Zhao Qing-hua	趙慶華
Zhao Shu-qiao	趙舒翹
zhen	鎮
zhengbing	正兵
zhengmu	正目
zhengshi	正使
Zhengwu chu	政務處
Zhengyang men	正陽門
zhengyong	正勇
zhibu gongchang	織布工廠
Zhongguo tongshang yinhang	中國通商銀行
Zhongshu ke shongshu	中書科中書
zhongwei	中尉
Zhou Fu	周馥
Zhou Xue-xi	周學熙
Zhu Bao-kui	朱寶奎
Zhu Jia-bao	朱家寶
Zhu Peng-shou	朱彭壽

GLOSSARY

Zhu Ying-yuan	祝瀛元
zikai	自開
Ziqiang jun	自強軍
zizhi ju	自治局
zongban zongbing	總辦總兵
zong canmou guan	總參謀官
Zou Jia-lai	鄒嘉來
Zuo Yi-zhang	左翼長
Zuo Zong-tang	左宗棠
zuodu yushi	左都御史

Bibliography

Adshead, S. A. M. "Viceregal Government in Szechwan in the Kuang-hsu period (1875-1909)." *Papers on Far Eastern History* 4 (September 1971): 41-52.
Ayers, William. *Chang Chih-tung and Educational Reform in China.* Cambridge, Mass.: Harvard University Press, 1971.
Bastid, Marianne. *Aspects de la reforme de l'enseignement en Chine au début du 20e siècle, d'après des écrits de Zhang Jian.* Paris and The Hague: Mouton, 1971.
Baxian xianzhi [New Ba xian gazetteer]. 1935.
Bays, Daniel H. "The Nature of Provincial Political Authority in Late Ch'ing Times: Chang Chih-tung in Canton, 1884-1889." *Modern Asian Studies* 4.4 (October 1970):325-47.
―――. *China Enters the Twentieth Century: Chang Chih-tung and the Issues of a New Age, 1895-1909.* Ann Arbor: University of Michigan Press, 1978.
Beiyang gondu leizuan [A classified collection of public documents of the Commissioner of Trade for the Northern Ports]. Comp. by Gan Hou-pi. 25 *juan.* 1907. *xubian* (continuation). 24 *juan.* 1910. (Abbreviated in notes as BYGD.)
Beiyang baihua bao [Beiyang colloquial journal]. 1905-06.
Beiyang xuebao [Beiyang educational journal]. 1905-06.
Bell, H. T., and H. G. W. Woodhead, eds. *China Yearbook, 1912.* London: G. Routledge, 1912.
Bland, J. O. P., and Sir Edmund Backhouse. *China Under the Empress Dowager.* London: Heinemann, 1910.
Bodde, Derk. "Prison Life in Eighteenth-Century Peking." *Journal of the American Oriental Society* 89 (1969):311-33.
Boorman, Howard, ed. *Biographical Dictionary of Republican China.* 4 vols. New York: Columbia University Press, 1967-71.
British Parliamentary Papers, State Papers, vol. 91 (1901), China nos. 2 and 4.
Brown, Arthur J. *New Forces in Old China.* New York: F. H. Revell, 1904.
Brunnert, H. S., and V. V. Hagelstrom. *Present Day Political Organization in China.* Trans. A. Beltchenko and E. E. Moran. Shanghai: Kelly and Walsh, 1912.
Buck, David D. *Urban Change in China: Politics and Development in Tsinan, Shantung, 1890-1949.* Madison: University of Wisconsin Press, 1978.

———. "The Provincial Elite in Shantung During the Republican Period: Their Successes and Failures." *Modern China* 1 (October 1975):417-46.
Cameron, Merebeth. *Reform and Revolution in China, 1898-1912*. Stanford: Stanford University Press, 1931.
Cao Ru-lin. *Yisheng zhi huiyi* [Memoirs of a life]. Hong Kong, 1966.
Carlson, Ellsworth. *The Kaiping Mines, 1877-1912*. Harvard University, Chinese Economic and Political Studies, Special Series. Cambridge, Mass.: East Asian Research Center, 1957, revised 1971.
Cen Chun-xuan. *Lezhai manbi* [Autobiographical notes]. Taibei reprint, 1962.
Chan, Wellington. *Merchants, Mandarins, and Modern Enterprise in Late Ch'ing China*. Cambridge, Mass.: Harvard, East Asian Research Center, 1977.
Chang Chung-li. *The Chinese Gentry*. Seattle: University of Washington Press, 1955.
Chen Gong-lu. *Zhongguo jindai shi* [History of modern China]. Shanghai, 1934.
Ch'en, Jerome. *Yüan Shih-k'ai (1858-1916)*. Stanford: Stanford University Press, 1961. 2nd edition, 1972.
———. "A footnote on the Chinese Army in 1911-12." *Toung-pao* 48 (1960):425-46.
———. "Defining Chinese Warlords and Their Factions." *Bulletin of the School of Oriental and African Studies* 31 (October 1967):563-600.
Chen Kui-long. *Mengjiao ting zaji* [Miscellaneous memoirs]. 1925.
———. *Yongji shangshu zouyi* [Memorials of Board President Chen Kui-long]. N.p., n.d.
Chen Xi-zhang. *Beiyang cangsang shihua* [History of the disorders of the Beiyang period]. 2 vols. Tainan, 1967.
Chen Xu-lu and Lao Shao-hua. "Qingmo di xinjun yu xinhai geming" [The New Armies of the late Qing and the 1911 Revolution]. In *Xinhai geming wushi zhounian jinian lunwenji* 1:147-65.
Chen Zhen, ed. *Jindai gongye shi ziliao* [Source materials on the recent history of industry]. Beijing, 1957.
Chesneaux, Jean, ed. *Popular Movements and Secret Societies in China, 1840-1950*. Stanford: Stanford University Press, 1972.
———, and Marianne Bastid. *China from the Opium Wars to the 1911 Revolution*. New York: Pantheon, 1976.
Ch'i Hsi-sheng. *Warlord Politics in China, 1916-1928*. Stanford: Stanford University Press, 1976.
Chu, Samuel C. *Reformer in Modern China: Chang Chien, 1853-1926*. New York: Columbia University Press, 1965.
———. "The Grand Council in the T'ung-chih Kuang-hsu Periods (1860-1900): A Preliminary Study." *Jindai shi yanjiusuo jikan* [Bulletin of the Institute of Modern History] 4 (1974):825-42.
Chü T'ung-tsu. *Local Government in China Under the Ch'ing*. Cambridge, Mass.: Harvard University Press, 1962.
Cixian xianzhi [Ci xian gazetteer]. 1941.

BIBLIOGRAPHY

Cohen, Paul, and John Schrecker, eds. *Reform in Nineteenth-Century China.* Cambridge, Mass.: Harvard, East Asian Research Center, 1976.
Da Gong Bao. Tianjin daily, 1903-1904.
Dai Xuan-zhi. *Yihetuan yanjiu* [A study of the Boxers]. Taibei, 1963.
Daming xianzhi [Daming xian gazetteer]. 1934.
Da Qing Dezong jing (Guangxu) huangdi shilu [Veritable records of the Qing Guang-xu reign]. 601 *juan.* Tokyo, 1937. (Abbreviated in notes as *Shilu.*)
Da Qing Guangxu xinfaling [New laws and ordinances of the Guang-xu reign]. 20 *ce.* Shanghai, 1909.
Der Ling, Princess. *Two Years in the Forbidden City.* New York: Dodd, Mead, and Co., 1911.
Des Forges, Roger. *Hsi-liang and the Chinese National Revolution.* New Haven: Yale University Press, 1973.
Ding xianzhi [Ding xian gazetteer]. 1934.
Dongfang zazhi (Eastern miscellany). Shanghai monthly, 1904-1908 consulted. (Abbreviated in notes as DFZZ.)
Duan-fang. *Duan Zhongmin gong zougao* [Drafts of Duan-fang's memorials]. 1918.
Duan Qi-rui et al., eds. *Xunlian caofa yangxiang tushuo* [The detailed and illustrated book of training and drilling methods]. Xiaozhan, 1899.
Duzhi bu junxiang si zouan huibian [Compendium of Ministry of Finance memorials on military provisions]. Beijing, 1908.
Eastman, Lloyd E. *Throne and Mandarins.* Cambridge, Mass.: Harvard University Press, 1967.
Esherick, Joseph W. *Reform and Revolution in China: The 1911 Revolution in Hunan and Hubei.* Berkeley and Los Angeles: University of California Press, 1976.
Fang Chao-ying. *Qingmo Minchu yangxue xuesheng diming lu chuji* [A preliminary compilation of names of students studying abroad at the end of the Qing and beginning of the Republic]. Taibei, 1962.
Farjenel, Fernand. *A travers la révolution chinoise.* Paris, 1914.
Faure, David. "Land Tax Collection in Kiangsu Province in the Late Ch'ing Period." *Ch'ing-shih wen-t'i* 3 (December 1976):5-73.
Fawn, Sue. "The Image of the Empress Dowager Tz'u-hsi." In Paul Cohen and John Schrecker, eds., *Reform in Nineteenth-Century China.*
Fei Xing-jian. *Jindai mingren xiaochuan* [Short biographies of famous people in modern times]. Shanghai, 1920.
Feng-gang [pseud.], ed. *Sanshui Liang Yan-sun xiansheng nianpu* [Chronological biography of Liang Shi-yi]. n.p. 1939.
Feng Yu-xiang. *Wodi shenghuo* [My life]. Shanghai, 1947.
──────. *Wodi dushu shenghuo* [My life of study]. Shanghai, 1947.
Feuerwerker, Albert. *China's Early Industrialization: Sheng Hsuan-huai (1844-1916) and Mandarin Enterprise.* Cambridge, Mass.: Harvard University Press, 1958.
──────. *The Chinese Economy, ca. 1870-1911.* Ann Arbor: University of Michigan, Center for Chinese Studies, 1969.

———. *The Foreign Establishment in China in the Early Twentieth Century.* Ann Arbor: University of Michigan, Center for Chinese Studies, 1976.

———. "Industrial Enterprise in Twentieth Century China: The Chee Hsin Cement Company." In *Approaches to Modern Chinese History.*

——— et al., eds. *Approaches to Modern Chinese History.* Berkeley and Los Angeles: University of California Press, 1967.

Fincher, John. "The Chinese Self-Government Movement, 1900-1912." Ph.D. dissertation, University of Washington, 1969.

Folsom, Kenneth. *Friends, Guests and Colleagues: the Mu-fu System in the Late Ch'ing Period.* Berkeley and Los Angeles: University of California Press, 1968.

Fong, H.D. *Rayon and Cotton Weaving in Tientsin.* Tianjin, 1930.

———. "The Growth and Decline of Rural Industrial Enterprise in North China: A Case Study of the Handloom Weaving Industry in Paoti." *Nankai Social and Economic Quarterly* 8 (1935):691-772.

Frank, Andre G. *Capitalism and Underdevelopment in Latin America.* New York: Monthly Review Press, 1967.

Franke, Wolfgang. *The Reform and Abolition of the Traditional Chinese Examination System.* Cambridge, Mass.: Harvard, East Asian Research Center, 1960.

Friedman, Edward. *Backward Toward Revolution: The Chinese Revolutionary Party.* Berkeley and Los Angeles: University of California Press, 1974.

Gamble, Sidney D. *Ting Hsien, a North China Rural Community.* New York: Institute of Pacific Relations, 1954.

Gaoyang xianzhi [Gaoyang xian gazetteer]. 1931.

Godley, Michael R. "The Late Ch'ing Courtship of the Chinese in Southeast Asia." *Journal of Asian Studies* 34 (1975):361-85.

Gongzhongdang Guangxu chao zouzhe [Secret palace memorials of the Guang-xu period]. 26 vols. Taibei: Guoli gugong bowuyuan [Palace Museum], 1973-75. (Abbreviated in notes as Guang-xu memorials.)

Great Britain, Foreign Office, Archives, Public Record Office. London. (Abbreviated in notes as FO.)

Grove, Linda. "Creating a Northern Soviet." *Modern China* 1 (1975):243-70.

Guangxu chao donghua xulu [Continuation of the Donghua records, Guang-xu reign]. Comp. by Zhu Shou-peng. Shanghai, 1909. (Abbreviated in notes as DHXL.)

Guangxu zhengyao [Important political (documents) of the Guang-xu reign]. Comp. by Shen Dong-sheng, Dong Yuan, and Dong Run. 30 *ce*. Shanghai, 1909.

Guangzong xianzhi [Guangzong xian gazetteer]. 1933.

Guo Li-zhi, ed. *Tongcheng Wu xiansheng (Ru-lun) nianpu* [Chronological biography of Wu Ru-lun]. 1943.

Guo Ding-yi. *Jindai Zhongguo shizhi erzhi* [A daily chronology of events in modern Chinese history]. 2 vols. Taibei, 1963.

Hall, Ray O. *Chapters and Documents on Chinese National Banking.* Shanghai: Commercial Press, 1920.

Handan xianzhi [Handan xian gazetteer]. 1940.
Hao Yen-p'ing. *The Comprador in Nineteenth Century China: Bridge Between East and West.* Cambridge, Mass.: Harvard University Press, 1970.
Hatano Yoshihiro. "Hokuyō gumbatsu no seiritsu katei" [Development of the Beiyang warlords]. In *Nagoya daigaku bungakubu kenkyu ronshu* [Collected studies from the faculty of letters of Nagoya University] 6:211-62 (1953). This article has been reprinted with Prof. Hatano Yoshihiro's other major articles in *Chūgoku kindai gumbatsu no kenkyu* [Studies on the warlords of Republican China]. Tokyo: Kawade Shobo Shinsha, 1973.
———. "The New Armies." In Mary C. Wright, ed., *China in Revolution.*
Ho Ping-ti. *Studies in the Population of China, 1368-1953.* Cambridge, Mass.: Harvard University Press, 1959.
———. *The Ladder of Success in Imperial China: Aspects of Social Mobility, 1368-1911.* New York: Columbia University Press, 1962.
——— and Tang Tsou, eds. *China in Crisis.* Vol. 1, book 1: *China's Heritage and the Communist Political System.* Chicago: University of Chicago Press, 1968.
Hou Chi-ming. *Foreign Investments and Economic Development in China, 1840-1937.* Cambridge, Mass.: Harvard University Press, 1965.
Hsiao Kung-ch'uan. *Rural China: Imperial Control in the Nineteenth Century.* Seattle: University of Washington Press, 1960.
Hsu Shu-hsi. *China and Her Political Entity.* London: Oxford University Press, 1926.
Huaian xianzhi [Huaian xian gazetteer]. 1934.
Hummel, Arthur W., ed. *Eminent Chinese of the Ch'ing Period, 1644-1912.* 2 vols. Washington: Government Printing Office, 1943-1944.
Hunt, Michael H. *Frontier Defense and the Open Door: Manchuria in Chinese-American Relations, 1895-1911.* New Haven: Yale University Press, 1973.
Hu Sheng. *Diguozhuyi yu Zhongguo zhengzhi.* Hong Kong, 1948. Translated as *Imperialism and Chinese Politics.* Beijing, 1955.
Ichiko Chūzō. "The Role of the Gentry: An Hypothesis." In Mary C. Wright, ed., *China in Revolution.*
Imperial Maritime Customs. *Tientsin Decennial Report, 1892-1901.* Tianjin, 1905. *1902-1911.* 1912.
"Imperialism in China." *Bulletin of Concerned Asian Scholars* 4 (December 1972):2-16.
Irick, Robert L. "The Chinchow-Aigun Railroad and the Knox Neutralization Plan in Ch'ing Diplomacy." *Papers on China* 14 (1960):80-112.
Iriye, Akira. "Public Opinion and Foreign Policy: The Case of Late Ch'ing China." In Albert Feuerwerker et al., eds., *Approaches to Modern Chinese History.*
Ji xianzhi [Ji xian gazetteer]. 1929.
Jian Bo-zan et al., eds. *Yihetuan* [The Boxers]. 4 vols. Shanghai, 1951.
Jiaotong Bu. *Jiaotong shi* [History of communications]. 37 vols. Nanjing, 1930.

Jin Liang. *Jinshi renwu zhi* [A gazetteer of modern personages]. Tianjin, 1934.

———. *Guang Xuan xiaoji* [A few memories from the Guang-xu and Xuan-tong reigns]. 1934.

Jinghai xianzhi [Jinghai *xian* gazetteer]. 1934.

Jing Su and Luo Lun, *Qingdai Shandong jingying dizhu di shehui xingzhi* [The social character of entrepreneurial landlords in Shandong during the Qing]. Jinan, 1959.

Jingxing xianzhi [Jingxing *xian* gazetteer]. 1934.

Johnston, Reginard F. *Twilight in the Forbidden City*. London: Appleton-Century, 1934.

Jordan, John. "Some Chinese I Have Known." *Nineteenth Century* 88 (1920): 947-56.

Kennedy, Thomas. "The Kiangnan Arsenal, 1895-1911: The Decentralized Bureaucracy Responds to Imperialism." *Ch'ing-shih wen-t'i* 2 (October 1969):17-38.

King, Harry E. *The Educational System of China as Recently Reconstructed*. Washington: Government Printing Office, 1911.

Kosaka Masataka. "Ch'ing Policy Over Manchuria (1900-1903)." *Papers on China* 16 (1962):126-53.

Krieger, Leonard. "Power and Responsibility: The Historical Assumptions." In his *The Responsibility of Power*, edited with Fritz Stern. New York: Doubleday, 1967.

Kuhn, Philip. "Comments." In Ho Ping-ti and Tang Tsou, eds., *China in Crisis*, vol. I, book 1.

———. *Rebellion and Its Enemies in Late Imperial China: Militarization and Social Structure, 1796-1864*. Cambridge, Mass.: Harvard University Press, 1970.

———. "Local Self-Government Under the Republic: Problems of Control, Autonomy, and Mobilization." In Frederick Wakeman, Jr., and Carolyn Grant, eds., *Conflict and Control in Late Imperial China*.

Lary, Diana. *Region and Nation: The Kwangsi Clique in Chinese Politics, 1925-1937*. London: Cambridge University Press, 1974.

Lasswell, Harold D., and Abraham Kaplan. *Power and Society: A Framework for Political Inquiry*. New Haven: Yale University Press, 1950.

Lau Kit-ching. "Sir John Jordan and Affairs of China, 1906-1916, with Special Reference to the 1911 Revolution and Yüan Shih-k'ai." Ph.D. dissertation, University of London, 1968.

———. "British Policy of Neutrality during the 1911 Revolution in China." *Journal of Oriental Studies* 8 (1970):357-79.

Lawton, Lancelot F., and H. Hobden. "The Fall of Yuan Shih-k'ai." *Fortnightly Review* (March 1910):420-34.

Li Chien-nung. *The Political History of China, 1840-1928*. Trans. by Teng Ssu-yü and Jeremy Ingalls. Princeton: Van Nostrand, 1956.

Li En-han. *Wan Qing di shouhui kuangquan yundong* [The late Qing movement for the recovery of mining rights]. Taibei, 1963.

———. "The Chekiang Gentry-merchants vs. the Peking Court Officials:

China's Struggle for Recovery of the British Soochow-Hangzhou-Ningpo Railway Concession, 1905-1911." *Jindai shi yanjiusuo jikan* [Bulletin of the Institute of Modern History] 3 (July 1972):223-68.

———. "Tang Shao-yi yu wan Qing waijiao." [Tang Shao-yi and late Qing foreign policy]. *Jindai shi yanjiusuo jikan* 4 (May 1973):54-126.

Li Feng. "Wushi nian lai shangye ziben zai Hebei xiangcun mianzhi shougongye zhong zhi fazhan jincheng" [The development of commercial capital in the handicraft cotton textile industry in the rural areas of Hebei in the last fifty years]. *Zhongguo nongcun* [Chinese village (journal)] 1 (1934):307-22.

Li Guo-qi. "Tongzhi zhongxing shiqi Liu Kun-yi zai Jiangxi xunfu rennei di biaoxian" [The performance of Liu Kun-yi as governor of Jiangxi during the Tongzhi restoration period]. *Guoli Taiwan shifan daxue lishi xuebao* [History journal of Taiwan National Normal University] 1 (1973):241-70.

Li Hong-zhang. *Li Wenzhonggong quanji* [Complete papers of Li Hong-zhang]. Ed. by Wu Ru-lun. 100 *ce*. Nanjing, 1905.

Li Wen-zhi, ed. *Zhongguo jindai nungye shi ziliao* [Source materials on the history of agriculture in modern China]. Beijing, 1957.

Li You-ning and Zhang Yu-fa, eds. *Jindai zhongguo nüquan yundong shiliao* [Source materials on the women's rights movement in modern China]. Taibei, 1975.

Lin Ming-de. *Yuan Shi-kai yu Chaoxian* [Yuan Shi-kai and Korea]. Taibei, 1970.

Ling Hong-xun. *Zhan Tian-you xiansheng nianpu* [Chronological biography of Zhan Tian-you]. Taibei, 1961.

Lippit, Victor. "The Development of Underdevelopment in China." *Modern China* 4 (1978):251-328.

Liu Feng-han. *Xinjian lujun* [The Newly Created Army]. Taibei, 1967.

———. *Yuan Shi-kai yu Wuxu zhengbian* [Yuan Shi-kai and the *coup d'état* of 1898]. Taibei, 1964.

———. *Wuwei jun* [The Wuwei Army]. Taibei, 1978.

Liu Hou-sheng. *Zhang Jian zhuanji* [Biography of Zhang Jian]. Shanghai, 1958.

Liu Kwang-ching. "Li Hung-chang in Chihli: The Emergence of a Policy, 1870-1875." In Albert Feuerwerker et al., *Approaches to Modern Chinese History*.

———. "Nineteenth-Century China: The Disintegration of the Old Order and the Impact of the West." In Ho Ping-ti and Tang Tsou, eds., *China in Crisis*, vol. I, book 1.

———. "The Confucian as Patriot and Pragmatist: The Formative Years of Li Hung-chang, 1823-1866." *Harvard Journal of Asiatic Studies* 30 (1970):5-45.

———. "The Limits of Regional Power in the Late Ch'ing Period." *Tsing Hua Journal of Chinese Studies*. New Series 10, no. 2 (July, 1974):176-233.

———. "Politics, Intellectual Outlook, and Reform: The T'ung-wen kuan Controversy of 1867." In Paul Cohen and John Schrecker, eds., *Reform in Nineteenth-Century China*.
———. "The Ch'ing Restoration." In John K. Fairbank, ed., *The Cambridge History of China: vol. 10, Late Ch'ing, 1800-1911, Part I.* Cambridge: Cambridge University Press, 1978.
Lo Hui-min, ed. *The Correspondence of G. E. Morrison, 1895-1912.* Cambridge: Cambridge University Press, 1976. (Cited in notes as *Morrison Correspondence*.)
Lung Chang. *La Chine à l'aube de XXe siècle.* Paris, 1962.
Luo Dun-yong. "Gengzi guobian ji" [The national disaster of 1900]. In Zuo Shun-sheng, comp., *Zhongguo jinbai nian shi ziliao* [Material for Chinese history of the last hundred years]. Shanghai, 1926.
Luo Er-gang. "Qingji bingwei jiangyou di qiyuan" [The origin of personal armies in the late Qing period.] *Zhongguo shehui jingji shi jikan* [Journal of Chinese social and economic history] 5.2 (1937):235-50.
———. *Xiangjun xinzhi* [A new treatise on the Hunan Army]. Changsha, 1939.
Luo Yu-dong. "Guangxu chao bujiu caizheng zhi fangce" [The governmental policies for meeting the financial crisis during the Guangxu period]. *Zhongguo jindai jingji shi yanjiu jikan* [Studies in modern economic history of China] 1.2 (May 1933):189-270
———. *Zhongguo lijin shi* [History of likin]. Shanghai, 1936.
MacKinnon, Stephen R. "Liang Shih-i and the Communications Clique." *Journal of Asian Studies* 29 (1970):581-602.
———. Review of John Schrecker, *Imperialism and Chinese Nationalism*, in *Bulletin of Concerned Asian Scholars* 9 (January-March 1977):71-73.
Malezemoff, Andrew. *Russian Far Eastern Policy, 1881-1904.* Berkeley and Los Angeles: University of California Press, 1958.
Manwarren, James C. "Rural-Urban Conflict in Shantung: The 1910 Laiyang Tax Uprising." M.A. thesis, Arizona State University, 1976.
Matsushima Shūe. *Shinchō matsuro hishi* [Secret history of the late Qing dynasty]. Tokyo, 1925.
Meijer, M.J. *The Introduction of Modern Criminal Law in China.* Batavia, 1949.
Michael, Franz. "Regionalism in Nineteenth-Century China." Introduction to Stanley Spector, *Li Hung-chang and the Huai Army: A Study in Nineteenth-Century Regionalism.* Seattle: University of Washington Press, 1964.
Miyun xianzhi [Miyun xian gazetteer]. 1914.
Morrison, Esther. "The Modernization of the Confucian Bureaucracy: An Historical Study of Public Administration." Ph.D. dissertation, Radcliffe College, 1959.
Morse, Hosea B. *The Trade and Administrations of the Chinese Empire.* London: Longmans, Green, 1908.
———. *The International Relations of the Chinese Empire.* 3 vols. London: Longmans, Green, 1910-1918.

Muramatsu, Yuji. "A Documentary Study of Chinese Landlordism in Late Ch'ing and Early Republican Kiangnan." *Bulletin of the School of Oriental and African Studies* 29 (1966):566-99.

Murphy, Rhoads. *The Treaty Ports and China's Modernization: What Went Wrong?* Ann Arbor: University of Michigan, Center for Chinese Studies, 1970.

———. *The Outsiders: The Western Experience in India and China.* Ann Arbor: University of Michigan Press, 1977.

Myers, Ramon. *The Chinese Peasant Economy: Agricultural Development in Hopei and Shantung.* Cambridge, Mass.: Harvard University Press, 1970.

Nacquin, Susan. *Millenarian Rebellion in China: Eight Trigrams Uprisings in 1813.* New Haven: Yale University Press, 1976.

Nanpi xianzhi [Nanpi xian gazetteer]. 1932.

Nathan, Andrew J. *Peking Politics, 1918-1923: Factionalism and the Failure of Constitutionalism.* Berkeley and Los Angeles: University of California Press, 1976.

North China Herald and Supreme Court and Consular Gazette. Shanghai weekly. 1901-1908 consulted. (Cited in notes as NCH.)

Okano Masujiro. *Go Hai-fu* [Wu Pei-fu]. 1939.

Orb, Richard A. "Chihli's Academies and Other Schools in the Late Ch'ing: an Institutional Survey." In Paul Cohen and John Schrecker, eds., *Reform in Nineteenth-Century China.*

Papers Relating to the Foreign Relations of the United States, 1902. Washington: Government Printing Office, 1903. (Cited as FRUS.)

Peking and Tientsin Times. Tientsin weekly. Available years, 1901 and 1902. (Cited in notes as PTT.)

Peng Yu-xin. "Qingmo zhongyang yu gesheng caizheng guanxi" [The financial relations between central and local government during the late Qing period]. *Shehui kexue zazhi* [Quarterly review of the social sciences] 9 (June 1947):83-110.

Peng Ze-yi, ed. *Zhongguo jindai shougongye shi ziliao* [Source materials on the history of the handicraft industry in modern China (1840-1949)]. Beijing, 1957.

Polachek, James. "Gentry Hegemony: Soochow in the T'ung-chih Restoration." In Frederick Wakeman and Carolyn Grant, eds., *Conflict and Control in Late Imperial China.* pp. 211-56.

Pong, David. "The Income and Military Expenditures of Kiangsi Province in the Last Years (1860-1864) of the Taiping Rebellion." *Journal of Asian Studies* 26 (November 1966):49-66.

Powell, Ralph. *The Rise of Chinese Military Power, 1895-1912.* Princeton: Princeton University Press, 1955.

Presseisen, Ernst L. *Before Aggression: Europeans Prepare the Japanese Army.* Tucson: University of Arizona Press, 1965.

Pu-yi, Aisin-Gioro. *Wodi qianbansheng* [The first half of my life]. Beijing, 1964.

Qian Shi-fu, comp. *Qingli xinshe zhiguan nianbiao* [Chronological tables of

newly established official posts and incumbents during the late Qing period]. Beijing, 1961.
Qingshi. [History of the Qing dynasty]. Comp. by Zhang Qi-yun, Xiao Yi-shan, et al. 8 vols. Taibei, 1961. (Cited as QS.)
Quested, Rosemary. *The Russo-Chinese Bank.* Birmingham, Slavonic Monographs no. 2, University of Birmingham, 1977.
Rankin, Mary B. "The Manchurian Crisis and Radical Student Nationalism, 1903." *Ch'ing-shih wen-t'i* 2 (October 1969):87-101.
──────. "Provincial Initiative and Elite Politics: The Chekiang and Kiangsu Railway Controversies, 1906-1911." Unpublished paper.
──────. "Local Reform Currents in Chekiang Before 1900." In Paul Cohen and John Schrecker, eds., *Reform in Nineteenth-Century China.*
Ren xianzhi. [Ren xian gazetteer]. 1915.
Rhoads, Edward J.M. *China's Republican Revolution: The Case of Kwangtung, 1895-1913.* Cambridge, Mass.: Harvard University Press, 1975.
Riskin, Carl. "The Symposium Papers: Discussion and Comments." *Modern China* 4 (July 1978):359-69.
Romanov, B.A. *Russia in Manchuria, 1892-1906.* Trans. by Susan W. Jones. Ann Arbor: University of Michigan Press, 1952.
Rong Meng-yuan. "Beiyang junfa di laili" [Origins of the Beiyang warlords]. In *Jin ershi nian zhongguo shixue lunzhu huibian* [Collection of essay studies over the last twenty years about Chinese history], Hong Kong, 1 (1971):336-38. (Originally appeared in *Lishi jiaoxue,* April 1956.)
Rongan dizi ji. [Biography of Yuan Shi-kai]. Comp. by Shen Zu-xian and Wu Kai-sheng. 1913.
Rosenbaum, Arthur. "Imperialism and Chinese Railway Policy: The Peking-Mukden Railway, 1895-1911." *Ch'ing-shih wen-t'i* 2 (October 1969):38-70.
Rozman, Gilbert. *Urban Networks in Ch'ing China and Tokugawa Japan.* Princeton: Princeton University Press, 1973.
Sanetō Keishū. *Chūgokujin Nihon ryūgaku shi* [A history of Chinese students in Japan]. Tokyo, 1960.
Scalapino, Robert A. "Prelude to Marxism: The Chinese Student Movement in Japan, 1900-1910." In Albert Feuerwerker et al., eds., *Approaches to Modern Chinese History.*
Schrecker, John. "Late Ch'ing Responses to Imperialism, Discussant Remarks." *Ch'ing-shih wen-t'i* 2 (October 1969):5-16.
──────. *Imperialism and Chinese Nationalism: Germany in Shantung.* Cambridge, Mass.: Harvard University Press, 1971.
──────. "The Reform Movement of 1898 and the Ch'ing-i: Reform as Opposition." In Paul Cohen and John Schrecker, ed., *Reform in Nineteenth-Century China.*
Shandong jindaishi ziliao [Source material on the modern history of Shandong province]. Jinan, 1957-58.
Shao Xun-zheng. "Xinhai geming qian wushi nian waiguo qinlue zhe he zhongguo maibanhua junfa guanliao shili di guanxi" [The relation-

ship between foreign aggressors and the power of those warlord-bureaucrats who sold out the country during the fifty years before the revolution of 1911]. *Lishi yanjiu* [Historical research] 4 (August 1954):53-64.
Shek, Richard. "The Politicization of a Millenarian Sect: The Tsai-li Sect in Jehol (1891)." Unpublished paper.
Shen Yun-long. "Zhangwo wanqing zhangbing zhi Yi-kuang" [Prince Qing, the late Qing power holder]. In his *Xiandai zhengzhi renwu shuping* [Notes on modern political personalities], 2:70-80. Taibei, 1966.
———. "Liang Qi-chao yu Wang Kang-nian" [Liang Qi-chao and Wang Kang-nian]. In *Xiandai zhengzhi renwu shuping*, 1:11-22.
———. "Qingmo minchu zhi Cen Chun-xuan" [Cen Chun-xuan in the late Qing and early Republican periods]. In *Xiandai zhengzhi renwu shuping*, 1:120-65.
———. "Tan Yuan Shi-kai" [Discussion of Yuan Shi-kai]. In *Xiandai zhengzhi renwu shuping*, 1:39-76.
———. "Duan Qi-rui zhi yisheng" [The life of Duan Qi-rui]. *Xin Zhongguo pinglun* [New China review] 33 (June 1967):13-17.
———. "Xu Shi-chang pingzhuan (1-3)" [Biography of Xu Shi-chang, parts 1-3]. *Zhuanji wenxue* [Biographical literature] 13 (July, August, September 1968):6-11, 25-29, 32-38.
Sheng Xuan-huai. *Yuzhai cungao* [Collected drafts of Sheng Xuan-huai], 101 *juan*. Wujin, 1939.
Sheridan, James E. *Chinese Warlord: The Career of Feng Yu-hsiang*. Stanford: Stanford University Press, 1966.
Shin-matsu Minsho Chūgoku kanshin jimmeiroku. [A directory of Chinese officials and gentry at the end of the Qing and the beginning of the Republic]. Beijing, 1918.
"Shunteh, An Agricultural and Skin and Wool Trading Center in Hopei." *Chinese Economic Journal* 3 (1928): 1059-68.
Sigel, Louis T. "T'ang Shao-yi (1860-1938): The Diplomacy of Chinese Nationalism." Ph.D. dissertation, Harvard University, 1972.
Spector, Stanley. *Li Hung-chang and the Huai Army: A Study in Nineteenth-Century Regionalism*. Seattle: University of Washington Press, 1964.
Subao. Shanghai, 1903.
Sun, E-tu Zen. *Chinese Railways and British Interests, 1898-1911*. New York: Columbia University Press, 1954.
Tan, Chester C. *The Boxer Catastrophe*. New York: Columbia University Press, 1955.
Tang Xiang-long. "Minguo yiqian guanshui danbao zhi waizhai" [The foreign loans secured on the customs revenue before 1911]. *Zhongguo jindai jingji shi yanjiu jikan* 3.1 (1935):1-49.
Tao Ju-yin. *Wu Pei-fu jiangjun zhuan* [Biography of Marshal Wu Pei-fu]. Shanghai, 1941.
———. *Beiyang junfa tongzhi shiqi shihua* [Historical tales about the period of rule by the Beiyang warlords]. 6 vols. Beijing, 1957-58.
Times. London, 1901-09.

Uhalley, Stephen, Jr. "The Wai-wu pu, the Chinese Foreign Office from 1901 to 1911." *Journal* of the China Society, Taibei, 5 (1967):9-27.
Wakeman, Frederick, Jr. *History and Will.* Berkeley and Los Angeles: University of California Press, 1973.
_____. and Carolyn Grant, eds. *Conflict and Control in Late Imperial China.* Berkeley and Los Angeles: University of California Press, 1975.
Wang Er-min. *Qingji binggongye di xingqi* [The emergence of armament industries during the late Qing period]. Taibei, 1963.
_____. *Huaijun zhi* [Treatise on the Huai Army]. Taibei, 1967.
Wang Jin-yu, ed. *Zhongguo jindai gongye shi ziliao dierji* [Source materials on the history of modern industry in China, second collection, 1895-1914]. 2 vols. Shanghai, 1957.
Wang Rang-qing (Kang-nian) xiansheng zhuanji [Biography of Wang Kang-nian]. Ed. by Wang Yi-nian. 1937.
Wang Xi. *Zhong Ying Kaiping Kuangquan jiaoshe* [Sino-British negotiations over rights to the Kaiping mines]. Taibei, 1962.
Wang, Y.C. *Chinese Intellectuals and the West, 1872-1949.* Chapel Hill: University of North Carolina Press, 1966.
Wang Yeh-chien. *Land Taxation in Imperial China.* Cambridge, Mass.: Harvard University Press, 1973.
Wang Yan-wei and Wang Liang, eds. *Xixun da shiji* [Journal of the western inspection trip]. 12 *ce.* Beijing, 1933.
_____. *Qingji waijiao shiliao* [Historical materials concerning foreign relations in the late Qing period, 1875-1911]. Beijing, 1933.
Wang Yu-quan. "Qingmo dianfu yu nongmin" [Land taxation and farmers during the late Qing period]. In Bao Cun-peng, Wu Xiang-xiang, and Li Ding-yi, comps., *Zhongguo jindaishi luncong* [Collection of essays on modern Chinese history], vol. 2, no. 5, pp. 63-84. Taibei, 1958.
Watanabe Atsushi. "En Seigai seiken no keizaiteki kiban-hokuyō-ha no kigyō katsudō" [The economic basis of the Yuan Shi-kai regime: the industrial activity of the Beiyang clique]. In *Chūgoku kindaika no shakai kōzō: shingai kakumei no shiteki ichi* [The social framework of Chinese modernization: the place of the 1911 revolution], pp. 135-71. Tokyo, 1960.
_____. "Shin-matsu En Sei-gai to hokuyō shinsei, Hokuyōha no keisei o megutte" [Yuan Shi-kai and Beiyang reform policy during the late Qing period, on the formation of the Beiyang clique]. *Rekishi kyōiku* [Studies in history] 16.1-2:135-48 (January and February 1968).
Watson, Charles Gary. "Economic Change and Development in Chihli: Preconditions and Early Growth of Handicraft Weaving in the Kaoyang Area, 1870-1914." M.A. thesis, Arizona State University, 1976.
Watt, John. *The District Magistrate in Late Imperial China.* New York: Columbia University Press, 1972.
Wehrle, Edmund S. *Britain, China, and the Anti-missionary Riots, 1891-1900.* Minneapolis: University of Minnesota Press, 1966.

Weiss, Robert. "Archival Material for the Study of Provincial Government: The Case of Hunan in the Nineteenth Century." Unpublished paper.
Wen Gong-zhi. *Zuijin sanshinian Zhongguo junshi shi* [History of Chinese military affairs for the past thirty years]. 2 vols. Shanghai, 1932.
White, John A. *The Diplomacy of the Russo-Japanese War.* Princeton: Princeton University Press, 1964.
Whitson, William, with Huang Chen-hsia. *The Chinese High Command: A History of Communist Military Politics, 1927-1971.* New York: Praeger, 1973.
Wilbur, C. Martin. "Military Separatism and the Process of Reunification Under the Nationalist Regime." In Ho Ping-ti and Tang Tsou, eds., *China in Crisis,* vol. 1, book 1.
Wilbur, Charles K., ed. *Political Economy of Development and Underdevelopment.* New York: Random House, 1973.
Wou, Odoric Y.K. "The District Magistrate Profession in the Early Republican Period: Occupational Recruitment, Training and Mobility." *Modern Asian Studies* 8 (April 1974):217-45.
──────. *Militarism in Modern China: The Career of Wu P'ei-fu, 1916-39.* Canberra: Australian National University Press, 1978.
──────. "Financing the New Army: Yuan Shi-k'ai and the Peiyang Army, 1895-1907." Unpublished paper.
Wright, Mary C. "Introduction: The Rising Tide of Change," in Mary C. Wright, ed., *China in Revolution: The First Phase, 1900-1913.* New Haven: Yale University Press, 1968.
──────. *The Last Stand of Chinese Conservatism: The T'ung-chih Restoration, 1862-1874.* Stanford: Stanford University Press, 1957.
Wu Pei-fu xiansheng ji [(Materials) by and about Wu Pei-fu]. Taibei, 1960.
Wu Ting-xie. *Hefei zhizheng nianpu* [Chronicle biography of (Provisional Chief) Executive Duan Qi-rui]. 1938.
Wu Yong. *The Flight of an Empress.* Chinese title: *Gengxi xishou congtan* (1918). Trans. by Ida Pruitt. London: Faber and Faber, 1937.
Wu Xiang-xiang. *Wan Qing gongding shiji* [History of the Late Qing court]. Taibei, 1952.
──────. "Sanhan fuxie suojian Yuan Shi-kai guanxi shiliao" [Source materials on Korean and Japanese perceptions and relations with Yuan Shi-kai]. In his *Zhongguo xiandai shi zongkan* [Selected articles on the contemporary history of China], vol. 4 (1962), pp. 423-49.
──────. *Minguo renheshi* [People and events in the Republican period]. Taibei, 1971.
Wu Yong. *The Flight of an Empress.* Chinese title: Gengxi xishou congtan (1918). Trans. by Ida Pruitt. London: Faber and Faber, 1937.
Wu Zhi. *Xiangcun zhibu gongye de yige yanjiu* [A study of the textile industry at the *xiang* and village level]. Shanghai, 1936.
Xianghe xianzhi [Xianghe *xian* gazetteer]. 1936.
Xiao Yi-shan. *Qingdai tongshi* [General history of the Qing dynasty]. 5 vols. Taibei, 1951-53.

Xincheng xianzhi [Xincheng xian gazetteer]. 1935.
Xinhai geming wushi zhounian jinian lunwenji [Essays commemorating the fiftieth anniversary of the 1911 revolution]. Compiled by Zhongguo lishi xuanhui [Chinese Historical Association]. 2 vols. Beijing, 1962.
Xu Dao-lin. *Xu Shu-zheng xiansheng wenji nianpu* [Chronological biography and writings of Xu Shu-zheng]. Taibei, 1962.
Xu Qi-heng and Li Xi-mi, eds. *Zhan Tian-you he Zhongguo tielu* [Zhan Tian-you and Chinese Railways]. Shanghai, 1957.
Xu Shi-chang. *Duigeng tang zhengshu* [Collected public papers of Xu Shi-chang]. 1919.
Xu Yi-shi. "Rong-lu yu Yuan Shi-kai" [Rong-lu and Yuan Shi-kai]. In Xu's *Yishi danhui* [Collected articles], pp. 103-11. 1945.
———. "Qu Hong-ji yu Zhang Bai-xi" [Qu Hong-ji and Zhang Bai-xi]. In *Yishi danhui*, pp. 112-27.
———. "Qing Guangxu dingwei zhengchao zhi zhongyao shiliao" [Important historical material relating to the political unrest of 1907]. *Guowen zhoubao* [Guowen weekly, illustrated] 14 (January 1937): 71-76, and (February 1937):73-76.
Xu Ying, Li Xi-mi, and Xu Qi-heng, eds. *Zhan Tian-you* [Zhan Tian-you]. Beijing, 1956.
Xuebu zongwusi [Ministry of Education, Department of General Affairs]. *Guangxu sanshisan nianfen, Diyici jiaoyu tongji tubiao* [The first statistical survey of education, 1907]. Beijing, 1910. Reprinted in Taibei.
Xunbing yaoyan [Important sayings for training troops]. Comp. by the Beiyang lujun bianyi ju [Translation and compilation office of the Beiyang Army]. 1908.
Yan Zhong-ping. *Zhongguo mian fangzhi shigao* [A draft history of Chinese cotton-spinning and weaving]. Beijing, 1955.
Ye Long. *Tongcheng pai wenxue shi* [Literary history of the Tongcheng school]. Taibei, 1975.
Yee, Frank Y.C. "Police in Modern China," Ph.D. dissertation, University of California, Berkeley, 1942.
Yen, W.W. *East-West Kaleidoscope, 1877-1944: An Autobiography.* New York, 1974.
Yihetuan dangan shiliao [Archival historical materials relating to the Boxers]. Comp. by Guojia dangan ju, Ming Qing dangan guan [National Archive Office, Ming Qing archives branch]. Beijing, 1959.
Yihetuan yundong shi luncong [Collected essays on the history of the Boxer movement]. Comp. by Shexue shuangzhoukan she ["Historical biweekly" Society]. Beijing, 1956.
Young, Ernest P. *The Presidency of Yuan Shih-k'ai: Liberalism and Dictatorship in Early Republican China.* Ann Arbor: University of Michigan Press, 1976.
———. "Yuan Shih-k'ai's Rise to the Presidency." In Mary C. Wright, ed., *China in Revolution.*
Young, L.K. *British Policy in China, 1895-1902.* London: Oxford University Press, 1970.

Yu Rong-ling. *Qinggong suoji* [Fragmentary notes on the Qing palace]. Beijing, 1957.
Yuan Ke-wen, comp. *Danshang sicheng* [Personal record from Danshang village]. n.p., n.d. Taibei reprint, 1966.
Yuan Shi-kai. *Yangshouyuan zouyi jiyao* [Selected memorials of Yuan Shi-kai]. Comp. by Shen Zu-xian. 44 *juan*. 1937. (Abbreviated in notes as YSYZY.)
──── . *Xinjian lujun binglue luzun* [Record of the military plans of the Newly Created Army]. 8 *juan*. Xiaozhan, 1898.
──── . *Yangzhou yuan diangao* [Drafts of Yuan Shi-kai's telegrams, 1886-1898]. Taiwan reprint, 1966.
──── . *Yuan Shi-kai zuozhe zhuanji* [The memorials of Yuan Shi-kai]. Comp. by Guoli gugong bowuyuan [National Palace Museum]. 8 vols. Taibei, 1971. (Abbreviated in notes as YSKZZ.)
Yuzhe huicun [Reprints from Beijing Gazette]. Edicts and memorials, daily, 1899-1901.
Zhang Cun-wu. *Guangxu sanshiyi nian Zhong Mei gongyue fengchao* [The controversy surrounding the Sino-American labor treaty in 1905]. Taibei, 1966.
Zhang Jian. *Zhang Jian jizi jiulu* [Nine records of Zhang Jian]. Shanghai, 1930.
Zhang Yu-fa. *Qingji di lixian tuanti* [Constitutionalists of the late Qing period]. Taibei, 1971.
Zhang Yi-lin. *Xin taiping shiji* [Collection of studies with a clear conscience]. 1947.
Zhang Zhi-dong. *Zhang Wenxianggong quanji* [The complete works of Zhang Zhi-dong]. 228 *juan*. Shucheng, 1928.
Zhao Bing-lin. *Zhao Bo-yan ji* [Collected works of Zhao Bing-lin]. 15 *ce*. Quanzhou, 1922-24.
Zhengzhi guanbao. Official daily, Beijing, 1907-1908.
Zhili qingli caizheng shuoming shu [Descriptive report of the Financial Reorganization Bureau of Zhili]. Comp. by the Bureau. 4 *ce*. 1911.
Zhili shixi gongchang xuding zhangcheng [Supplemental regulations for the Zhili industrial institute]. 1908.
Zhongguo jindai huobi shi ziliao [Materials on the history of currency in modern China], vol. I. Beijing, 1964.
Zhongyang jingguan xuexiao xiaoshi [A brief history of the central policy academy]. Taibei, 1967.
Zhou Fu. *Zhou Queshengong quanji* [Complete works of Zhou Fu]. 1922.
Zhou Zhi-an *(Xue-xi) xiansheng biezhuan* [Biography of Mr. Zhou Xue-xi]. Comp. by Zhou Shu-zhen. Beijing, 1948.
Zhu Yan-jia. "Wu Lu-zhen yu Zhongguo geming" [Wu Lu-zhen and the Republican revolution]. In Wu Xiang-xiang, ed., *Zhongguo xiandai shi zongkan*, vol. 6. Taibei, 1964.

Index

Agricultural modernization, 173
Americans: investment in Manchuria sought by Yuan, 185-186; local trade boycott against, 166-167; and Yuan's appointment to Zhili governorship, 23-24, 25
Anping, police reform in, 157-158
Army Reorganization Bureau: Beiyang Army financing and, 107, 108-112, 113, 122, 135; elimination of, 114
Army Reorganization Fund (*lianbing xuxiang*), 109-112

Bank of Tianjin, 60
Banks in Zhili, 57, 60, 165-166
Bao, Lieutenant, 46-47
Baodi, economic reform in, 173, 174-175
Baojia security system, 151-152, 155, 160, 161, 162
Bays, Daniel, 223
Beijing Fund, 55, 56
Beijing-Hankou Railway, 71, 72, 73, 74, 183-184
Beijing-Shenyang Railway: Yuan as head of, 72, 73, 74; Yuan's negotiations with British to take over, 39, 41-45, 67, 71, 217
Beiyang Army (*Beiyang jun*), 5, 73, 90-136, 200-203, 210; development of, 91-96; discipline in, 98-99, 103, 118, 119; forced conscription into, 119; as meritocratic, 125, 128, 135-136; munitions and, 102, 106, 112-113; organizational structure of, 99, 100 table, 102-103, 117, 128, 135-136; pay scale in, 98, 118-119; poor living conditions in, 119; recruitment into, 98, 102; relations of officers and common soldiers in, 98-99, 118, 119-120; training in, 96-98, 106, 132 table; Yuan's power base and, 213, 214-216
—central government control of, 103-116, 135, 215; through administration, 113-116, 135; through arms production and procurement, 112-113; through financing, 103-112, 135; officer loyalty and, 128-131
—officers in: division commanders, 99, 123 table, 128-131, 201-202; frequent transfers of, 123, 124, 125, 126-127 tables, 128, 136; Japanese-trained, 131, 133-135, 136, 203, 210, 215; pay scale for, 117, 118 table; personal loyalty of, to Yuan, 91, 117, 120-136, 215; promotion of, 98, 102, 117, 128; recruitment of, 117, 124, 128, 131-133, 135-136; relations of, with common soldiers, 98-99, 118, 119-120; training of, 93-94, 117, 120, 131, 132 table, 133, 135-136
Beiyang Officers Academy, 93-94, 132 table
Belgians, 25
Bian Ying-guang, 166
Board of Civil Appointments (*Libu*), 161-162
Board of Revenue, and Beiyang Army financing, 103, 104-105 tables, 107-108, 110
Board of War, 107
Boxer uprising, 3-4, 22, 23; Yuan and, 22, 24
British: appointment of Yuan to Zhili supported by, 23-24, 25-26, 35; Beijing-Shenyang Railway interest of, 41-45, 217; court politics and, 69, 88-89; economic penetration of China by, 3; internal Zhili affairs and, 44; Manchuria and, 68-69, 70-71; as Yuan's ally, 43, 44, 69, 70-72, 180, 184-185, 186, 207, 208, 217-218, 224; and Yuan's negotiation for troop withdrawal from Tianjin, 39-41, 43, 44
Buban runner police, 151, 161, 162
Bureau for the Supervision of Training, 108
Bureau of Industries (*Gongyi ju*), 163, 164, 165

Cao Kun, 124, 201
Cao Lin, 158
Cen Chun-xuan, 35, 44, 69, 107, 109, 180-181, 216; Yuan and Prince Qing attacked by, 83-89
Central government: and control of Beiyang Army, 103-116, 135, 215; Yuan's influence in, in 1907-1908, 186-197; and Yuan's power base, 10-11, 213, 216, 223, 224
Chamber of Commerce in Tianjin, 166-167, 168, 220
Chen Bi, 85, 195, 196
Chen Ji-xu, 148-149
Chen Kui-long, 18, 112
Chen Tian, 82
Chiang Kai-shek, 90
China Merchants' Steam Navigation Company, 73-74
Chu, Samuel C., 77n
Cizhou, police reform in, 157
Communications Clique, 195-196, 212
Court politics, 62-89, 186-200, 216-217; and control of Beiyang Army, 114-116; Foreign Powers' influence on, 23-26, 31, 63, 65-66, 69, 80-81, 87-89, 216; nonideological character of, 63, 65-66, 80-81, 87-89, 216; after resignation of Yuan from Foreign Ministry, 208-210; and succession to throne, 205, 207; Yuan—Prince Qing alliance attacked by Qu Hong-ji and Cen Chun-xuan, 76, 79-89. *See also* Empress Dowager Ci-xi; Prince Qing (Yi-kuang); Yuan Shi-kai
Currency, 57, 59-60
Customs revenues, 54-55, 56, 57

Daming, police reform in, 157
Department of Military Administration (*Junzheng si*), 91, 93, 108
Department of Military Affairs, 121, 122
Der Ling, Princess, 64
Dong Fu-xiang, 26, 27, 29
Duan-fang, 35, 85, 110-111, 112
Duan Qi-rui, 47-48, 49, 51, 73, 115, 120-122, 124, 128-129, 136, 203, 210, 212, 219
Duan Zhi-gui, 83, 154
Ducat, Lieutenant-Colonel, 92
Du Yuan-zhao, 159

Economic reform in Zhili, 138, 139-143 table, 163-179
Educational reform in Zhili, 138, 139-143 table, 144-151, 168-171, 175-179, 214, 219

Education Bureau (*Xuewu chu*), 77, 79
Education Promotion Office (*chuanxue suo*), 148-149
Elites, local gentry, 7-10; and economic reform in Zhili, 163, 169, 171, 172-173, 174, 175, 176, 214; and educational reform in Zhili, 148-151, 176, 214, 219; and Jing Ting-bin rebellion, 47; and police reform in Zhili, 155-156, 157-163, 176, 214; and railway construction loans, 184-185; and Yuan's power base, 10, 176-179, 223-224
Empress Dowager Ci-xi, 16; and appointment of Yuan to Zhili governorship, 23-24, 26, 30-38; and Beiyang Army financing, 103, 106, 113; and Beiyang Army formation, 94, 95-96; on cabinet reform, 81; *coup d'état* of, supported by Yuan, 21; and court politics, 30-38; and Ma Yu-kun, 49, 50-51; political skills of, 34-35, 87; Prince Qing and, 63, 66, 186-187; reasons for appointment of Yuan to Foreign Ministry, 180, 181-182; return to Beijing of, 36, 37-39, 46; Rong-lu and, 17n, 62-63; and successor to throne, 205-206; Yuan and, 21-22, 44, 63-65, 66, 67, 186-187, 216; on Zhili educational reform, 150
En-ming, 181
Esherick, Joseph, 7, 177
Examination system, 138, 144, 220

Fawn, Sue, 34-35
Feng Guo-zhang, 115, 120, 121-122, 128-129, 201, 203, 210, 212, 219
Feng-shan, 114, 115, 124, 201-202, 203
Feng Yu-xiang, 124, 125, 131, 134, 135
Finance Bureau (*Caizheng chu*), 77, 79
Foreign Powers: court politics influenced by, 23-26, 31, 63, 65-66, 69, 80-81, 87-89, 216-218; central government indebtedness to, 55, 56, 57, 58; and negotiations with Yuan for troop withdrawal from Tianjin, 39-45; Yuan's relations with, 23-26, 35, 66-72, 182-186, 213, 216-218, 223, 224. *See also* British; Japanese
French, 25
Funing *xian*, 171-172
Fu Zeng-xiang, 197

Gang-yi, 30
Gaoyang, economic reform in, 173-174
General Staff Council, 200-201
Germans, 23-24, 25, 26, 35

INDEX

Government Affairs Bureau (*Zhengwu chu*), 72, 76, 77; Yuan and Prince Qing dominant in, 79, 80, 188-189
Grand Council, 77-89, 180-182, 187-189
Grand Secretariat, 80-81, 87
Green Standard Army, 102
Guan Geng-lin, 195, 196
Guang-xu emperor, 14, 21, 188, 205
Guangzong, rebellion in, 46-49
Guan Mian-jun, 195, 196

Hart, Robert, 65, 68
Higher primary schools, 146-147
Hsiang Army, 99
Huai Army, 6, 15; compared to Beiyang Army, 90, 91, 93, 98, 99, 101 table, 102, 117, 118 table, 119, 128
Hu Jing-gui, 18
Hu Lin-yi, 48
Hunt, Michael, 186
Hu Yu-fen, 29, 41-42, 43

Ichiko Chūzó, 7
Imperialism as domestic force, 1-5, 10. *See also* Foreign Powers
Imperial Telegraph Administration, 72, 73-74
Industrial bureaus, 169-170
Industrial exhibitions, 167-168
Industrial Institute (*shixi gongchang*), 169
Industrial schools, 168-169. *See also* Model factories

Japanese: Beiyang Army influenced by, 97-98, 99, 102, 135; Chinese students and, 148, 150; and economic penetration of China, 3; and Manchuria, 68-69, 70-71, 186; and training of Beiyang Army officers, 131, 133-135, 136, 203, 210, 215; Yuan and, 25, 68-69, 70, 185-186, 207
Jianchang *xian*, 171, 172
Jiang Gui-ti, 27, 29, 120, 129, 130-131, 136, 203
Jiang Kang-hu, 220
Jing Ting-bin, rebellion led by, 46-47, 48-49, 56, 92
Jin Yong, 158
Jordan, John, 88, 182n, 183, 184, 185, 207, 208, 218
Julu *xian*, rebellion in, 46-49

Kaiping mines, 67, 71-72, 163-164
Kang You-wei, 21, 32, 86, 87
Kim Yun-sik, 16
Koo, Wellington, 183
Korea, Yuan's service in, 15-17
Kuhn, Philip, 6-7, 10

Land taxes, 55-56, 57; to finance schools, 149-150
Lan Tian-wei, 133-135, 220
Liang-bi, 133
Liang Dun-yan, 183, 207-208, 219
Liang Qi-chao, 21, 32, 86, 87
Liang Ru-hao, 68, 219
Liang Shi-yi, 68, 195, 210, 212, 214, 220
Liang Tun-yan, 68
Li Diao-zhen, 176
Li Hong-cao, 17, 18n, 32
Li Hong-zhang, 6, 11, 13n, 14, 22, 23, 163, 213; appointment of Yuan as Zhili governor opposed by, 33-34; death of, 36; discredited in Sino-Japanese War, 17-18, 20; and Kaiping mines, 71; as patron of Yuan, 16, 17; Yuan's distancing from, 13-14, 17, 18, 19-20; and Zhili military situation in 1901, 27, 28-29
Likin, 54, 55, 56, 57
Li Lian-ying, 31n
Ling Fu-beng, 154
Lin Shao-nian, 81, 85
Liquor tax, 57, 59
Li Shi-wei, 165, 220
Liu Kun-yi, 22, 34, 35, 92, 113, 138
Liu Kwang-ching, 7-8, 10
Liu Yong-qing, 73, 202
Liu Zhi-xiang, 19
Li Zhou-hua, 119
Long-yu, 206, 209, 211
Lower primary schools, 145-148
Luanzhou mines, 71-72, 164
Lu Ben-yuan, 27, 29, 93
Lu Chuan-lin, 31-32, 43, 78, 81, 107-108; in Grand Council, 188-189
Lu Jia-gu, 57, 197
Lu Jian-zhang, 125
Lulong, police reform in, 157-159
Luo Er-gang, 5-6, 7, 10

Ma Jin-hua, 174
Ma Long-biao, 201
Manchuria: American investment in, sought by Yuan, 185-186; as foreign policy issue, 65, 66-67, 68-72; Japan and, 68-69, 70-71, 186, 207
Mao Qing-fan, 60
Ma Yu-kun, 27-29, 37, 38, 39, 69, 176, 203; Empress Dowager and, 49, 50-51; as military rival to Yuan, 45, 49-51, 92, 93, 95
Mei Dong-yi, 27, 44, 93
Merchants: and economic reform in Zhili, 163, 164, 165-168, 170, 172-173, 174-175, 176, 220; Yuan and, 165-168, 178, 220

Military Guards Army (*Wuwei jun*), 21, 26-27, 94
Military Reorganization bureau (*Lianbing chu*), 72, 73, 76, 77, 79
Ministry of Civil Affairs, 191 table
Ministry of Civil Appoints, 191 table
Ministry of Education, 192 table, 196-197
Ministry of Finance, 191 table
Ministry of Foreign Affairs, 180-186, 191 table
Ministry of Justice, 192 table
Ministry of Posts and Communication, 190, 192 table, 195-196
Ministry of Rites, 191 table
Ministry of War, 114-116, 135, 192 table, 200-201
Model factories, 169-173
Morrison, G. E., 43, 70, 86, 218
Murphey, Rhoads, 53

National army (*Lujun*), 96, 108-109
Native custom duties, 56-57
Na-tong, 43, 182n
New Army (*xinjun*), 91
Newly Created Army (*Xinjian lujun*), 18, 20, 21, 22, 28, 92, 94, 96, 122
Nian rebellion, 5, 6, 90
Nie Shi-cheng, 26, 121
Ning Shi-fu, 168, 169, 220

Opium control, 167

Peasants, 10; educational reform paid by, 149-150; insurgencies of, quelled by Yuan, 47-49, 51; police reform paid by, 158-159; uprisings of, 3, 4-5, 45-47; Yuan as exploiter of, 178, 219
Police Bureau (*Jingwu chu*), 156-157
Police reform in Zhili, 138, 139-143 table, 151-163, 175-179; new elites and, 176-178; rural, 155-159, 160; urban, 152-154, 160
Police sections (*qu*), 155, 161
Powell, Ralph, 103
Power structure in late Imperial China, 1n, 7-11, 213-224; central or regional basis of, 5-6, 10; formal governmental or informal elite basis of, 7-10; imperialism and, 2-4, 10; overlapping nodes in, 10-11, 222-224
Prince Qing (Yi-kuang), 30, 31; after Yuan's resignation, 209-210; and appointment of Yuan to Zhili governorship, 33, 34; in Army Reorganization Bureau, 108; challenged by Qu Hong-ji and Cen Chun-xuan, 76, 79-89; Empress Dowager and, 63, 66, 186-187; as Grand Councillor, 63, 77; in Ministry of War, 115; opposed to Beijing-Shenyang Railway deal, 43; Yuan's alliance with, 63, 65-66, 77-79, 89, 187, 188, 216
Prince Qing (Yong-lin), 33
Prison reform in Zhili, 154-155
Provincial government, 10, 150-151, 197-200, 214. *See also* Zhili
Provincialism, 9-10
Pruitt, Ida, 19
Pu-lun, 205
Pu-yi, 205, 206

Qingliu pai faction, 17, 18
Qu Hong-ji, 35, 43, 76, 78, 180-181; on appointment of Yuan to Zhili governorship, 31, 32; Prince Qing—Yuan alliance challenged by, 76, 79-89, 114, 216

Railway construction loan agreements, 183-185
Regular Army (*Changbei jun*), 91-93, 108-109
Revolution of 1911-12, 5, 7, 210-212
Rong-lu, 14, 26; and appointment of Yuan to Zhili governorship, 30, 31, 32, 33-34, 35; death of, 62-63; Foreign Powers' dislike of, 24; as rival of Prince Qing, 33; as Yuan's patron, 17-19, 21, 43
Rong-qing, 78, 81, 188
Root-Takahira Agreement, 186, 207
Russians: and Beijing-Shenyang Railway negotiations, 41, 42, 43, 50; and Manchuria, 65, 68-69; and Yuan, 25
Russo-Japanese War, 67, 69, 70, 94

Salt monopoly, 57-59
Satow, Ernest, 25, 40, 43, 69, 93
Schrecker, John, 15
Self-Strengthening Army (*Ziqiang jun*), 92
Shandong, 22-23, 94
Shanghai-Hangzhou-Ningbo Railway, 183
Shao Xun-zheng, 23-24
Sheng Xuan-huai, 60, 73, 164, 210
Shi-xu, 81, 188
Shi Zhao-ji, 68
Shou-xun, 200
Sino-Japanese War, 3, 17, 18, 20
Song Qing, 26, 27-28, 49
Stamp tax, 57, 59
Sugar tax, 59
Sun Duo-shen, 165, 169, 219, 220
Sun Jia-nai, 188
Sun Wan-lin, 93

INDEX

Suzhou-Hangzhou-Ningbo Railway, 184-185, 218
Sze, Alfred, 183

Taiping rebellion, 5, 6, 7, 90, 91
Tang Mao-zhi, 67
Tang Shao-yi, 40, 41-42, 53-54, 58, 60, 67-68, 70, 83, 183, 185, 186, 195, 197, 209, 210, 214, 219
Tang Ting-shu, 67
Tao Cao-hua, 172
Tax revenues, 7-9, 54-61
Tea tax, 59
Tenney, C.D., 144
Tianjin: Allied occupation of, 3, 22, 23, 37; police reform in, 152-154; withdrawal of foreign troops from, negotiated by Yuan, 39-45; and Zhili economy, 53-55. *See also* Chamber of Commerce in Tianjin
Tianjin Higher Industrial School, 169
Tianjin-Pukou Railway, 183, 218
Tie-liang, 78-79, 81, 89, 107, 188; in Army Reorganization Bureau, 108, 110, 111; and control of Beiyang Army, 135; and government reorganization, 114; and Japan-trained army officers, 133; as Minister of War, 114-115, 116, 200, 209; Yuan opposed by, 81-82
Tobacco tax, 57, 59
Tong-zhi restoration, 1
Trade fairs, 167-168

Vanguard Army, 94, 96
Vanguard Division, 28

Wang Er-min, 6
Wang Hua-dong, 201
Wang Kang-nian, 32, 81, 83
Wang Nai-zheng, 76
Wang Ro-xian, 201
Wang Rui-gao, 58, 65
Wang Shi-zhen, 73, 120, 121-123, 128-129, 202-203
Wang Wen-shao, 17, 21, 31, 32, 43, 78
Wang Xian-bing, 166
Wang Ying-kai, 115, 202, 203
Warlordism, 5-6, 90-91, 128n
Wei *xian*, rebellion in, 46-49
Wei Guang-dao, 110, 111-112
Weng Tong-he, 21
Western Tombs, 62, 64-65
Wright, Mary, 1
Wu Chang-qing, 15
Wu Feng-ling, 201
Wu Lu-zhen, 133-135, 210, 220
Wu Pei-fu, 120, 124, 131, 135, 136, 219

Wu Ru-lun, 75, 219
Wu Yong, 19-20

Xiang Army, 6; compared to Beiyang Army, 90, 91, 98, 99, 101 table, 102, 117, 119
Xian magistrates: appointment of, 161-162; and economic reform in Zhili, 163, 170-171, 172, 173, 174, 178; and educational reform in Zhili, 176, 178; and police reform in Zhili, 157-163, 176, 178; and Yuan's power base, 224
Xia Xin-you, 94, 203
Xi-liang, 24, 35
Xincheng *xian*, 171, 172
Xu Shi-chang, 70, 73, 74, 78, 81, 107, 108, 115-116, 134-135, 153, 188, 197, 201, 209, 210, 219
Xu Tong, 30

Yang Du, 208, 220, 220-221n
Yang Shi-qi, 42, 65-66, 73-75, 86, 163, 183, 196, 197, 208, 214, 219, 220
Yang Shi-xiang, 65-66, 74, 82, 180, 197, 201
Yang Xin-fu, 174
Yang Zong-lian, 57
Yan Xiu, 145, 150, 196-197, 219
Ye Gong-chuo, 195, 196
Yen, W.W., 183
Yi Hui, 16
Yi-kuang. *See* Prince Qing (Yi-kuang)
Yin-chang, 120, 121, 200, 209
Yong Wing, 67
Young, Ernest, 5, 9
Yuan Bao-heng, 14
Yuan Bao-ling, 14
Yuan Bao-qing, 14
Yuan Bao-zhong, 14
Yuan Jia-san, 14
Yuan Ke-ding, 94, 165, 196, 208
Yuan Shi-kai, 1, 5-6, 10-11; appointed to Zhili governorship, 23-26, 30-38; and appointment of *xian* magistrates, 161-162; and Beiyang Army's development and organization, 91-103; and Beiyang Army's financing, 103-112, 114-116; British support for, 43, 44, 69, 70-72, 180, 184-185, 186, 217-218, 224; as central government official, 72-76, 180-200; and communications system, 73-74; on constitutional reform, 80-81, 187, 189; continuing influence in Zhili of, 197, 200; continuing relation to Beiyang Army of, 200, 201-203; court politics and, 30-38, 63-89, 180-182, 186-200, 204-208; early career of, 14-23; economic reforms of, 163-

179; educational reforms of, 138, 144-151; Empress Dowager and, 34-36, 37-39, 63-65, 66, 67, 186-187, 204, 216; fall from power of, 205-212; financial difficulties in Zhili of, 51-61; as Foreign Minister, 180-207; and Foreign Powers, 4, 22, 23-26, 41, 66-72, 182-186; and foreign relations, 182-186, 216-218; Huai Army service of, 15-16; influence of, on new ministries, 189-197; influence of, on provincial governments, 197-200; Japanese and, 25, 68-69, 70, 185-186, 207; Korean service of, 15-17; Li Hong-zhang and, 13-14, 16-17, 18, 19-20; Manchu opposition to, 81-82; and Manchuria, 65, 66-67, 68-72, 185-186; merchants and, 165-168, 178, 220; military power of, in 1901, 26-29; military rivalry with Ma Yu-kun, 45, 49-51; not a proto-warlord, 215-216; officers of Beiyang Army and, 91, 117, 120, 128-136; peasants and, 5, 47-49, 51; personal appearance of, 16-17; police reforms of, 151-163; political base of, 10-11, 213-224; political skills of, 13-14, 15-17, 21, 23, 34-35, 178-179, 218-222; Prince Qing as ally of, 63, 65-66, 77-79, 89, 187, 188, 216; Qu Hong-ji as challenger to, 76, 79-89; and railway construction loan agreements, 183-185; resignation from Foreign Ministry, 207; return to power in 1911-12 crisis, 211-212; Rong-lu and, 17, 18-19; scholar-official elite links of, 218-219; as Shandong governor, 22-23, 24, 28; traditional elite allegiance of, 220-221, 222; and withdrawal of troops from Tianjin and Beijing-Shenyang Railway, 39-45; Zhang Zhi-dong and, 187
Yuan Shi-xun, 94
Yuan Shu-xun, 197, 202
Yun Yu-ding, 86
Yu-xian, 22

Zai-feng, 188, 205, 206, 209, 211
Zai-yi, 30, 31
Zai-ze, 209
Zai-zhen, 74, 83
Zeng Guo-fan, 6, 48, 213
Zeng-qi, 42
Zhang-geng, 107
Zhang Huai-zhi, 115, 134, 210
Zhang Jian, 15, 17, 81, 219, 222
Zhang Ke-ming, 148, 149
Zhang Shao-zeng, 133-135, 220
Zhang Ting-xiang, 148
Zhang Xi-fan, 113
Zhang Xun, 120, 129-131, 136, 203
Zhang Yi, 71
Zhang Yi-lin, 219
Zhang Zhen-fang, 200
Zhang Zhi-dong, 11, 22, 31, 32, 34, 35, 63n, 72, 80-81, 92, 95, 107, 109, 111, 134, 213, 222, 223; appointed Grand Councillor, 180, 181; and educational reform, 138, 144; foreign support for, 4; Yuan and, 187, 188-189
Zhan Tian-you, 64
Zhao Bing-jun, 153-154, 155, 156, 160, 196, 214
Zhao Er-sun, 70
Zhao Qi-lin, 83
Zhao Qing-hua, 195-196
Zhao Ru-lin, 183
Zhao Shu-qiao, 30
Zhejiang Railway Company, 184
Zheng De-quan, 197
Zhengding *fu*, 171
Zhili: economy of, 52-54; military situation in 1901 in, 26-29; revenue sources for government in, 54-61. *See also* Economic reform in Zhili; Educational reform in Zhili; Police reform in Zhili
Zhou Fu, 25, 35, 59, 94, 112, 113
Zhou Xue-xi, 59, 71, 163-165, 167-168, 169, 197, 219, 220
Zhu Bao-kui, 84
Zhu Jia-bao, 197

Designer: Dave Comstock
Compositor: In-house, Berkeley
Printer: Braun-Brumfield
Binder: Braun-Brumfield
Text: Comp/Set Andover
Display: VIP Aster
Cloth: Holliston Roxite C 57567 Linen
Paper: 50lb P&S Offset Vellum B-32